EYEWITNESS TRAVEL

# JERUSALEM
## & THE HOLYLAND

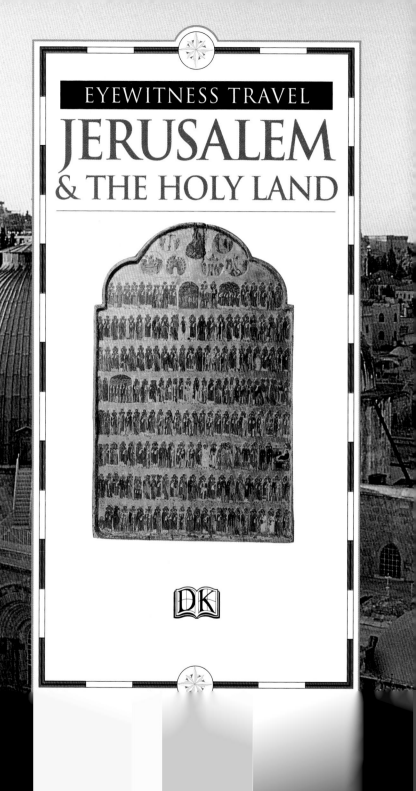

# EYEWITNESS TRAVEL

# JERUSALEM
# & THE HOLY LAND

DK

LONDON, NEW YORK,
MELBOURNE, MUNICH AND DELHI
www.dk.com

PROJECT EDITORS Nick Inman, Ferdie McDonald
ART EDITORS Jo Doran, Paul Jackson
COMMISSIONING EDITOR Giovanni Francesio
at Fabio Ratti Editoria S.r.l.
EDITORS Elizabeth Atherton, Cathy Day, Simon Hall,
Freddy Hamilton, Andrew Humphreys
DESIGNERS Chris Lee Jones, Anthony Limerick,
Sue Metcalfe-Megginson, Rebecca Milner, Johnny Pau
PICTURE RESEARCH Monica Allende, Katherine Mesquita
MAP CO-ORDINATOR Dave Pugh
DTP DESIGNER Maite Lantaron
RESEARCHER Karen Ben-Zoor

MAIN CONTRIBUTORS
Fabrizio Ardito, Cristina Gambaro, Massimo Acanfora Torrefranca

PHOTOGRAPHY
Eddie Gerald, Hanan Isachar, Richard Nowitz,
Magnus Rew, Visions of the Land

ILLUSTRATORS
Isidoro Gonzáles-Adalid Cabezas (Acanto Arquitectura y
Urbanismo S.L.), Stephen Conlin, Gary Cross, Chris Forsey,
Andrew MacDonald, Maltings Partnership, Jill Munford,
Chris Orr & Associates, Pat Thorne, John Woodcock

Reproduced by Colourscan, Singapore
Printed and bound by South China Printing Co. Ltd, China

First published in Great Britain in 2000
by Dorling Kindersley Limited, 80 Strand, London WC2R 0RL

**Reprinted with revisions 2002, 2007**
Copyright 2000, 2007 © Dorling Kindersley Limited, London
A Penguin Company

◁ **View over the rooftops of Jerusalem's Christian Quarter**

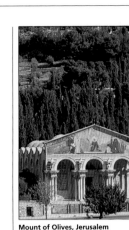

**Mount of Olives, Jerusalem**

# CONTENTS

HOW TO USE THIS
GUIDE **6**

## INTRODUCING
## JERUSALEM & THE
## HOLY LAND

DISCOVERING
JERUSALEM AND THE
HOLY LAND **10**

PUTTING THE HOLY
LAND ON THE MAP **12**

PUTTING JERUSALEM
ON THE MAP **14**

A PORTRAIT OF THE
HOLY LAND **16**

THE HOLY LAND
THROUGH THE YEAR **36**

**Old Jaffa's attractive waterfront**

Middle Eastern handicrafts

Window detail, Dome of the Rock

Bedouin camel, Western Jordan

Pomegranates

The remote St Catherine's Monastery in Sinai

# HOW TO USE THIS GUIDE

This guide helps you to get the most from your visit to Jerusalem and the Holy Land, by providing detailed practical information. *Introducing Jerusalem and the Holy Land* maps the region and sets it in its historical and cultural context. The Jerusalem section and the four regional chapters describe important sights, using maps, photographs and illustrations. Features cover topics from food to wildlife. Recommended hotels and restaurants are listed in *Travellers' Needs*, while the *Survival Guide* has tips on travel, money and other practical matters.

## JERUSALEM AREA BY AREA

The city is divided into five areas, each with its own chapter. A last chapter, *Further Afield*, covers peripheral sights. All sights are numbered and plotted on the chapter's area map. The detailed descriptions of the sights are easy to locate, as they follow the numerical order on the map.

**A locator map** shows where you are in relation to other areas of the city centre.

**Each area** of Jerusalem has its own colour-coded thumb tab, as shown inside the front cover.

**Sights at a Glance** lists the chapter's sights by category: Holy Places, Historic Districts, Museums and Archaeological Sites.

**1 Area Map**
*For easy reference, sights are numbered and located on a map. The central sights are also marked on the* Street Finder *maps on pages 156–59.*

**2 Street-by-Street Map**
*This gives a bird's-eye view of the key area in each chapter.*

**Stars** indicate the sights that no visitor should miss.

**Walking routes**, shown in red, suggest where to visit on foot.

**3 Detailed information**
*The main sights in the city are described individually. Addresses, telephone numbers and opening hours are given, as well as information on admission charges, guided tours, photography, wheelchair access and public transport.*

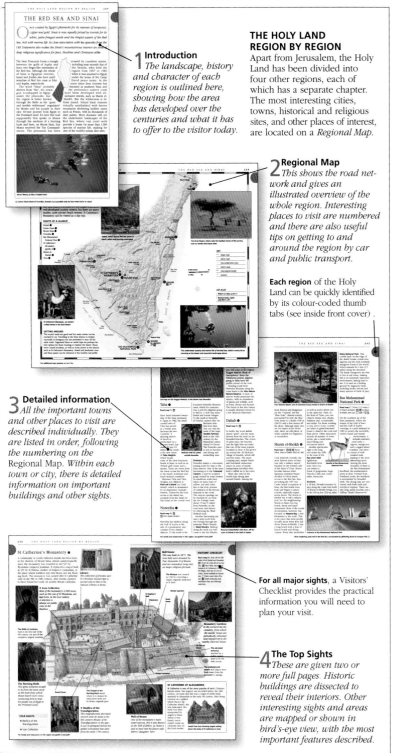

## THE HOLY LAND REGION BY REGION

Apart from Jerusalem, the Holy Land has been divided into four other regions, each of which has a separate chapter. The most interesting cities, towns, historical and religious sites, and other places of interest, are located on a *Regional Map*.

**1 Introduction**
*The landscape, history and character of each region is outlined here, showing how the area has developed over the centuries and what it has to offer to the visitor today.*

**2 Regional Map**
*This shows the road network and gives an illustrated overview of the whole region. Interesting places to visit are numbered and there are also useful tips on getting to and around the region by car and public transport.*

**Each region** of the Holy Land can be quickly identified by its colour-coded thumb tabs (see inside front cover).

**3 Detailed information**
*All the important towns and other places to visit are described individually. They are listed in order, following the numbering on the Regional Map. Within each town or city, there is detailed information on important buildings and other sights.*

**For all major sights**, a Visitors' Checklist provides the practical information you will need to plan your visit.

**4 The Top Sights**
*These are given two or more full pages. Historic buildings are dissected to reveal their interiors. Other interesting sights and areas are mapped or shown in bird's-eye view, with the most important features described.*

# INTRODUCING JERUSALEM & THE HOLY LAND

# DISCOVERING THE HOLY LAND

Mosaic in the Jewish Quarter

The "Holy Land" encompasses Israel and large regions of Jordan and Egypt. Rich in associations with three of the world's major faiths – Christianity, Judaism and Islam – it is a fascinating and diverse destination for pilgrims and holidaymakers alike. Religious highlights include the biblical sites of Jerusalem, Galilee and Mount Sinai, and an array of churches, monasteries and mosques. This is also an area of great natural beauty, from the desert landscapes of Jordan and Sinai to the lush greenery of northern Israel and the white sands of the Mediterranean and Red Sea coasts. These two pages are designed to help visitors pinpoint the highlights of this exciting region.

Jerusalem's Old City walls, built by Suleyman the Magnificent

## JERUSALEM

- **Biblical sites**
- **The Western Wall and Dome of the Rock**
- **Museum of the Holocaust**

It's hard to overstate the historical significance of Jerusalem. Any trip begins with an exploration of the tightly walled Old City, home to the cornerstones of three faiths. It has the **Western Wall** (see p85) of Judaism; the Christian sites of the **Via Dolorosa** (see pp30–31) and **Church of the Holy Sepulchre** (see pp92–5); and the third holiest site of Islam, the **Dome of the Rock** (see pp72–3). Beyond these are many more attractions of similar significance, including the Mount of Olives, with its marvellous views over the city, not to mention more churches, synagogues and mosques,

Roman and Byzantine remains, medieval walls and gates, and colourful markets and bazaars.

Visits to the **Mea Shearim** (see p125) quarter of the new city, the Holocaust museum of **Yad Vashem** (see p138), and an evening in the 19th-century neighbourhood of **Nakhalat Shiva** (see p123) bring the Jewish Jerusalem experience up-to-date.

## THE COAST AND GALILEE

- **Beach life in Tel Aviv**
- **The Crusader port of Akko**
- **The Sea of Galilee**

**Tel Aviv** (see pp168–73) is worlds apart from Jerusalem. Jerusalem is a millennia-old hill-top city, weighted with religious significance. Tel Aviv is a secular beachfront city that basks beneath a Mediterranean sun and is barely a century old. Visit Tel Aviv for the superb **Museum**

of the Jewish Diaspora (see p168) and the similarly impressive **Tel Aviv Museum of Art** (see p170), and for its unrivalled heritage of white-washed **Bauhaus architecture** (see p171). Also visit for the shopping, dining and nightlife, in which the city excels. Don't miss the neighbouring ancient port of **Jaffa** (see pp174–5) with its attractive harbour-side buildings, several of which house good seafood restaurants.

North along the coast, **Akko** (see pp178–9) is another old Arab port, although heavily shaped by the Crusaders, for whom this was one of their principal strongholds. It remains perhaps the most attractive old town in the entire Holy Land. Away from the coast, the **Sea of Galilee** (see pp182–3) is Israel's largest freshwater body. It has significant biblical links (it is where Jesus is said to have walked on the water), as well as a beautiful setting ringed by green hills.

The Mediterranean Sea laps at the beaches of central Tel Aviv

## THE DEAD SEA AND THE NEGEV DESERT

- Float on the Dead Sea
- Waterfalls and wildlife at Ein Gedi
- The legendary fortress of Masada

Bedouin guides lead their camels through Jordan's Wadi Rum

Floating on the highly saline waters of the **Dead Sea** *(see p197)*, reading a book, is the oddest of sensations, and one every visitor should experience for themselves. Most people choose to go to Ein Gedi, where there is a wide beach popular with bathers, and showers to remove the water's filmy residue. **Ein Gedi** is also home to a national park *(see p196)* with lush vegetation, twin gorges, waterfalls and abundant wildlife. Further south is **Masada** *(see pp200–201)*, a mountain-top fortress constructed by King Herod but famous for the Jewish defenders who killed themselves rather than be captured by the Romans.

The ancient mountain-top citadel of Masada in the Judaean desert

## WESTERN JORDAN

- Roman ruins at Jerash
- The rock-cut, secret city of Petra
- Wadi Rum's desert landscapes

Jordan's capital, **Amman** *(see pp212–14)*, boasts some Roman ruins of its own, but it also makes a good base for a day trip to the even more impressive ruins at **Jerash** *(see pp210–11)*. This is one of the best-preserved Roman cities in the Middle East, with an almost complete theatre that is still used during the annual Jerash Festival.

South of Amman, the town of **Madaba** *(see pp216–17)* is worth visiting for its unique Byzantine-era mosaic map. However, the real reason that most people visit Jordan lies farther south still: **Petra** *(see pp220–31)*. The legendary "Rose City" is one of the most spectacular of archaeological sites, and ranks alongside the likes of India's Taj Mahal and the Pyramids of Egypt as one of the world's must-see sights. It is possible to see the highlights in one day but there is so much to see that Petra rewards repeated visits. Make sure to allow time for **Wadi Rum** *(see pp232–4)*, with its wide landscapes of red sands and towering mountains of wind-eroded sandstone.

## THE RED SEA AND SINAI

- Dive among magnificent coral reefs
- Visit one of the world's oldest monasteries
- Watch the sun rise over the Sinai desert

The appeal for most visitors to the Sinai lies not on the land but in the dramatic underwater landscapes of the **Red Sea** *(see pp240–1)*. Here, vast coral reefs provide a home to a magical array of multi-hued marine life. This is one of the world's top diving locations, but a simple snorkel and flippers can be enough to experience this aquatic wonderland. Several resort towns provide beach-front accommodation and water-sport opportunities.

Another of Sinai's attractions is **St Catherine's Monastery** *(see pp246–8)*, where a community of Orthodox monks has lived in a walled compound since the sixth century. Visitors are allowed inside to visit parts of the holy retreat.

Behind St Catherine's rises **Mount Sinai** *(see p249)*, where, according to tradition, Moses encountered the "burning bush" and received the Ten Commandments. Modern-day pilgrims ascend the 3,700 steps to the summit to witness the sun rise over the peaks of the peninsula.

Scuba divers wading out from the beach on the Sinai coast

# Putting the Holy Land on the Map

The crossroads of three continents – Africa to the south, Asia to the east and Europe to the west – the Holy Land encompasses the whole of Israel and the Palestinian Autonomous Territories, and parts of Jordan and Egypt. Its boundaries could be said to stretch from the Mediterranean in the west, inland to the Jordanian deserts, and from Galilee in the north to the southern tip of the Sinai peninsula. At the core of the Holy Land is Jerusalem, an ancient walled city which stands on the Judaean hills, just to the west of the Dead Sea, the lowest point on earth.

**Infrared satellite image of Jerusalem**

*MEDITERRANEAN SEA*

Marsa Matruh

Alexandria     Baltim
Damanhur     Dumyat
Port Said
Nile Delta
Tanta

0 kilometres     100
0 miles     100

Suez Canal

Great Bitter Lake

Suez     Nakh

EGY
SIN

**EUROPE AND THE MEDITERRANEAN REGION**

SCOTLAND
IRELAND     ENGLAND
WALES
DENMARK
NETHERLANDS
BELGIUM     GERMANY
FRANCE     CZECH REPUBLIC
SWITZERLAND     AUSTRIA
SLOVENIA     HUNGARY
BOSNIA AND SERBIA
HERZEGOVINA
MONTENEGRO
ITALY     MACEDONIA
ALBANIA
PORTUGAL
SPAIN     GREECE     TURKEY
ESTONIA
LATVIA
LITHUANIA
RUSSIAN FEDERATION
BELARUS
POLAND
SLOVAKIA
UKRAINE
MOLDOVA
ROMANIA
BULGARIA
GEORGIA
ARMENIA
CYPRUS
LEBANON     SYRIA
ISRAEL     IRAQ
Jerusalem
JORDAN
IRAN
TUNISIA
MOROCCO
ALGERIA     LIBYA
EGYPT
SAUDI ARABIA
MALI     NIGER     CHAD     SUDAN

Gulf of Suez
El-T
Sha
S
Hur
Po
Saf
Nile

◁ **The Monastery at Petra** *(see p230)* in a 19th-century engraving by David Roberts

**KEY**

✈ International airport
🛪 Domestic airport
⚓ Major port
══ Motorway
▬▬ Major road
══ Minor road
── Rail line
┄┄ Wadi
─·─ International boundary
ˣˣˣ Boundary of disputed area

**TEL AVIV AND JERUSALEM**

# Putting Jerusalem on the Map

Jerusalem covers 125 sq km (48 sq miles). In terms
of geographical extent, this makes it Israel's largest
city. However, despite its surface area, it is less
populous than the Tel Aviv urban area. Only
700,000 people live here – 460,000 Jews, 225,000
Muslims and 15,000 Christians. At the core of
Jerusalem is the walled Old City, standing 800 m
(2,600 ft) above sea level. Dotted on the hilltops
around, and strung along the valley floors between,
are the ever-expanding modern suburbs. The city
limits extend almost to the Palestinian towns of
Ramallah in the north and Bethlehem to the south.

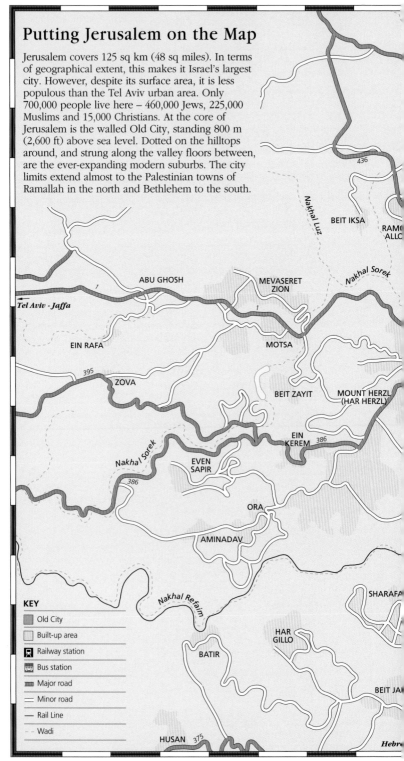

BEIT IKSA

436

*Nakhal Luz*

RAM(
ALLC

*Nakhal Sorek*

ABU GHOSH

MEVASERET
ZION

1

Tel Aviv - Jaffa

1

EIN RAFA

MOTSA

395

ZOVA

BEIT ZAYIT

MOUNT HERZL
(HAR HERZL)

EIN
KEREM

386

*Nakhal Sorek*

EVEN
SAPIR

386

ORA

AMINADAV

SHARAFA

HAR
GILLO

*Nakhal Refaim*

BATIR

BEIT JA

HUSAN

375

Hebr

**KEY**

| | |
|---|---|
| ▢ | Old City |
| ▢ | Built-up area |
| 🚇 | Railway station |
| 🚌 | Bus station |
| ▬ | Major road |
| = | Minor road |
| — | Rail Line |
| -- | Wadi |

# A PORTRAIT OF
# THE HOLY LAND

*A Jew growing up in New York, a Christian in Lisbon and a Muslim in Jakarta will have childhoods as different as can be imagined, but one thing they will share is a common set of reference points, which will include names such as Abraham and Moses, and, above all, Jerusalem and the Holy Land.*

For around 2,000 years this narrow corridor of land on the eastern shore of the Mediterranean has exercised an influence on world culture far out of proportion to its modest size. Events that are said to have taken place here in antiquity gave rise to the three great monotheistic religions. As these religions extended their influence throughout the world, so the Holy Land in general, and Jerusalem in particular, became overburdened with spiritual significance. Tradition has it that Jerusalem is where Solomon built his great temple, Christ was crucified, and the Prophet Muhammad visited on his Night Journey. It comes as a

**Mural at a Palestinian school in Jerusalem**

mild shock to some to discover that this spiritual world centre is no bigger than an average city neighbourhood. Those who come to Jerusalem expecting architectural grandeur to match the stature of these spiritual highlights will be disappointed. The city's churches don't begin to compare with the soaring Gothic cathedrals of Europe. The glorious Dome of the Rock aside, the buildings are quite humble. But the effect this has is to bestow on the city an altogether appropriate air of humility and authenticity, pleasingly at odds with the hyperbole and oversell of the new millennium.

**Bedouin encampment in the desert scenery of Wadi Rum, southern Jordan**

◁ **Greek Orthodox priest at the Church of the Holy Sepulchre, Jerusalem**

The Old City of Jerusalem, viewed from the Jewish cemetery on the Mount of Olives

While Jerusalem is a city rooted in ancient history, at the same time it lies at the heart of a region which possesses a distinctly youthful nature. Both Israel and Jordan, the two countries which, along with Egypt's Sinai peninsula, make up what we know as the Holy Land, are barely more than half a century old. It is a greatly over-used travel cliché, but here it is difficult to avoid commenting on the striking mix of the ancient and modern. In Jerusalem, ultra-Orthodox Jews wearing clothes that were fashionable in Eastern Europe

Young boy playing football at the Dome of the Rock

300 years ago mingle with Christian pilgrims armed with state-of-the-art digital cameras. In the wilderness of the Negev Desert, Bedouin tribesmen speak nonchalantly on mobile phones, while in Galilee Palestinian farmers lead oxen to fields that lie in the shadow of huge biotechnology plants.

Equally striking is the mix of peoples. The modern state of Israel has drawn its citizens from virtually every continent, embracing a worldwide roll call of Jewry, from Minnesota to Murmansk, Adelaide to Addis Ababa. Side by side with the Jews – and Arabs – are such minority peoples as the Druze, a mysterious offshoot sect of Islam, and the Samaritans, who speak Arabic but pray in Hebrew and number less than 600.

In this land of diversity, even the one common element shared by the majority of Israelis, the Jewish faith, is not the uniting factor it might be. The notion of what it is to be Jewish and, more pertinently, what form a Jewish state should take, are subjects of great contention. There are large, and increasingly influential, sections of society that believe Israel should adhere strictly to the laws prescribed in the Torah. The greater part of society, however, views the notion of a religious state with horror. The gulf between the two standpoints is best illustrated by the phenomenon of Dana International, the flamboyant transsexual singer who won the 1998 Eurovision Song Contest. It was a victory greeted with pride by a part of the nation, while to the religious sector it served only to confirm "the secular sickness of Israel".

An even more contentious issue is ownership of the land. Israel bases its right to exist on an ancient covenant with God, related in the Old Testament, in which this land was promised to the descendants of the Jewish patriarch Abraham. This is a covenant, needless to say, that is not recognized by the Palestinian Arabs, who have their own claims on the territory, based on centuries of occupancy. During the 20th century four major wars were fought between the Arabs and the Jews. The problem is still far from being resolved.

Conflict is no stranger to the region. Since the Hebrew tribes first emerged from the desert around the 12th century BC, this has been one of the world's most turbulent neighbourhoods. Every major Near Eastern empire fought here. This has resulted in a fantastic legacy of historical remains, including Roman cities, Byzantine churches and early Islamic palaces. Archaeologists are constantly at work to uncover what other riches this troubled land might yield. Often, their aims go far beyond the academic: some expeditions search for

Souk stall-holder in the town of Ramallah, a busy centre of Palestinian life and culture

**Divisive Dana International**

evidence to support territorial claims; others are seeking fabled artifacts such as the Holy Grail or the Ark of the Covenant, which they believe may hold the very key to human existence.

Amidst all this hullabaloo, one should not forget that the Holy Land is a marvellous region for the visitor. It is not necessary to have an advanced grasp of history to appreciate the magnificence of the region's ancient cities, isolated monasteries and hilltop fortresses, while the desert scenery of Wadi Rum is a setting in which to live out fantasies, and the diving in the Red Sea is reckoned by some to be unsurpassed anywhere in the world. Added to this, there is plenty of fine dining and comfortable accommodation. It is quite possible to visit the Holy Land and find that the only issue of concern is getting a decent spot on the beach.

Beach life at Tel Aviv, the vibrant cultural and commercial capital of Israel

# Old Testament Sites in the Holy Land

Many of the stories recounted in the Old
Testament are located within Egypt,
Sinai and the "Land of Canaan", which
corresponds roughly to present-day Israel.
The Bible gives plenty of precise geographical
references. Some places, such as Jerusalem
and Jericho, still exist and have yielded
archaeological evidence confirming some,
but by no means all, of the references to them
in the Old Testament. Other sites were only
attached to their biblical episodes much later.
Touring these sites, the visitor cannot but be
aware of the contrast between the importance
of the events and the often insignificant and
all-too-human scale of the places in which
they are said to have occurred.

**The Destruction of Sodom ①**
*When Sodom was destroyed by God
(see p202) only Lot and his family were
spared, but his wife looked back and
was turned into a pillar of salt.*

**The Sacrifice of Isaac ②**
*God asked Abraham to sacrifice his son,
Isaac. The patriarch was about to obey
when an angel stayed his hand and
instructed him to slaughter a ram
instead (Genesis 22). Tradition identifies
the place of sacrifice as Mount Moriah,
later a part of Jerusalem, and the site on
which Solomon's Temple is said to have
been subsequently built (see p41).*

**The Tombs of the Patriarchs ③**
*Acquired as a burial place for his
wife Sarah, the Machpelah cave was
the first plot in the Land of Canaan
purchased by Abraham (Genesis 23).
A mosque/synagogue now occupies
the traditional site of the tomb,
located in the present-day town of
Hebron (see p196).*

| 0 kilometres | 100 |
|---|---|
| 0 miles | 50 |

**Moses Receives the Ten Commandments ④**
*Since the 4th century, Mount Sinai (see pp246–7)
has been associated with the story of Moses and
the Ten Commandments (Exodus 20). The Bible
places Mount Sinai in a region called Horeb, but
the location of Horeb has never been identified.*

④
Mount Sinai

**The Death of Moses ⑤**
*Moses is said to have seen the Promised
Land from the summit of Mount Nebo and
died in the same place. Christian tradition
identifies Mount Nebo (see p215) as being
just southwest of modern-day Amman.
As the Bible states, the whereabouts of Moses'
tomb is unknown (Deuteronomy 34: 1-7).*

**Joshua Conquers Jericho** ⑥
*The Old Testament story tells how the walls of Jericho (see p190) fell to the blast of horns (Joshua 6). This ancient oasis was the first city conquered by the Israelites, led by Joshua, after they emerged from their 40 years in the wilderness.*

**The Ark of the Covenant** ⑦
*At Shiloh the Jews built the first temple and placed in it the Ark of the Covenant, the sacred container of the tablets of the Ten Commandments. The Ark is shown here in a 13th-century illumination being carried by two angels.*

**Samson and Delilah** ⑧
*The climax of this story, in which Samson pulls down the Philistines' temple, killing himself and his enemies, is described as taking place in Gaza (Judges 14–16).*

⑩ Mount Carmel
SEA OF GALILEE
Megiddo
Jordan River
GILEAD
Shiloh ⑦
Jerusalem ②
⑥ Jericho
⑨ Ha-Ela Valley
⑤ Mount Nebo
ron ③
DEAD SEA
eersheva
odom ①
M O A B

**David Defeats Goliath** ⑨
*As the champion of the Israelites during the reign of King Saul, David defeated Goliath and routed the Philistines (I Samuel 17). The site of the battle is given as the Ha-Ela Valley, northwest of Hebron.*

**Elijah and the Prophets of Baal** ⑩
*Elijah challenged the prophets of the Canaanite god Baal (left). An altar was set up and sacrifices prepared. Only Elijah's offering burst into flames, showing it had been acknowledged and proving who the true God was (I Kings 18). The traditional site of this event is Mount Carmel, at Haifa (see p177).*

## THE OLD TESTAMENT AS HISTORY

Unlike Mesopotamia or Egypt, where ancient texts have allowed the development of a detailed historical framework, the Holy Land has yielded few written archives. The only such resource is the Bible. The later books, which describe events not too far removed from the time they were written, may be relatively accurate. For example, events recounted in Kings I and II can be corroborated by contemporary Assyrian inscriptions. However, the historical basis of stories such as those relating to Abraham, Moses or Solomon, must be viewed with caution. The Old Testament as we know it was compiled from a variety of sources, no earlier than the 6th century BC. These narratives might well contain kernels of historical reality, but by the time they came to be set down they were essentially no more than folk tales.

**Assyrian obelisk (825 BC) showing Israelite King Jehu (I Kings 19)**

# Judaism

Jewishness is not just a matter of religion but of belonging to a people. Jews believe themselves to be descended from Abraham, to whom God promised a land "unto thee, and to thy seed after thee". Judaism traditionally passes through the female line or by conversion, different Jewish movements (Orthodox, Conservative, Reform) having different requirements. Practising Jews conduct their life by the *Torah*, which can be translated as "instruction" or "guidance". Its core is the Five Books of Moses, but the Torah also includes all the teachings and laws within the Hebrew Bible (Old Testament) and subsequent interpretations by rabbinic scholars. The creation of the State of Israel has presented the Jewish people with new political and religious challenges.

**The menorah**, *a seven-branched candlestick, derives from the candlestick that originally stood in Solomon's Temple.*

### THE WESTERN WALL

This is all that remains of the Jews' great Temple *(see pp44–5)*, built to hold the Ark of the Covenant *(see p21)*. It is the holiest of all Jewish sites and a major centre of pilgrimage *(see p85)*.

### THE SCROLLS OF THE TORAH

The Torah is traditionally inscribed on scrolls. During a synagogue service the scrolls are ceremonially raised to the congregation before being read. It is an honour to read them. A boy of 13 years of age or a girl of 12 (Reform Jews only) is *bar* or *bat mitzvah*, a "child of the command-ment", entitled to read from the scroll at a public service.

**The Scrolls**, *when not in use, are placed in the ark. They may be kept in an ornamental box* (right) *or else tied with a binder inside a decorated cover, adorned with a breast-plate, yad, bells or crown.*

**The yad** *("hand") is a pointer used to avoid touching the sacred text. It is also meant to direct the reader's attention to the precise word and to encourage clear and correct pronunciation.*

**Traditional Jewish life** *is measured by the regular weekly day of rest,* Shabbat *(from sundown Friday to sundown Saturday), and a great many festivals (see pp36–9). The blowing of the* shofar *(a ram's horn trumpet) marks* Rosh ha-Shanah, *the Jewish New Year.*

## DIVISIONS IN JUDAISM

As a result of their history of dispersion and exile, there are Jewish communities in most countries of the world. Over the centuries, different customs have developed in the various communities. The two main strands, with their own distinctive customs, are the Sephardim, descendants of Spanish Jews expelled from Spain in 1492, and the Ashkenazim, descendants of Eastern European Jews. In Western Europe and the US, some Jews adapted their faith to the conditions of modern life, by such steps as improving the status of women. This divided the faith into Reform (modernizers) and Orthodox (traditionalists), with Conservative Jews somewhere in between. Israeli Jews are frequently secular or maintain only some ritual practices. The ultra-Orthodox, or *haredim*, adhere to an uncompromising form of Judaism, living in separate communities.

**Yemenite Jewess in wedding dress**

**Ultra-Orthodox Jews in Jerusalem's Mea Shearim district in distinctive black garb**

## THE SYNAGOGUE

Synagogue architecture generally reflects the architecture of the host community, but with many standard elements. There must be an ark, symbolizing the Ark of the Covenant, usually placed against the wall facing Jerusalem. In front of the ark hangs an eternal light *(ner tamid)*. The liturgy is read from the lectern at the *bimah*, the platform in front of the ark. The congregation sits around the hall, although in some synagogues women are segregated. Traditionally, a full service cannot take place without a *minyan:* a group of 10 men.

Menorah

Eternal light, a symbol of the divine presence

Central platform for reading of the law

Lectern    Bimah    Ark

# Christianity

To his followers, Jesus of Nazareth was more than just a prophet, he was the Son of God and bringer of a new covenant replacing the one given by God to Abraham *(see p22)*. His Crucifixion in Jerusalem came to be seen as self-sacrifice for the salvation of humankind and inspired a new religious movement based on his teachings. At first this existed as a subsect of Judaism; Jesus came to be known as Christ *(Christos, the anointed one, in Greek)*, as he was held to be the Messiah of Jewish prophecies. However, the new religion spread far beyond Judaea. It saw persecution, then recognition by the Roman Empire, eventually becoming its dominant religion in the 4th century AD.

**The cross** *is a symbol of the Crucifixion of Christ. An empty cross shows that he has risen from the dead.*

## THE EUCHARIST (MASS)

Greek Orthodox priests celebrate the Eucharist, the taking of bread and wine, representing the body and blood of Christ. One of the central sacraments of Christianity, it was instituted by Jesus himself at the Last Supper *(see p117)*.

**The Christian Bible** *is in two parts: the Old Testament consists of Jewish sacred texts; the New Testament relates the life and teaching of Jesus and his Apostles. The latter was written from the mid-1st century. Most early texts were in Greek; a definitive Latin version by St Jerome (see p195) appeared in about AD 404. The Protestant Reformation inspired translations into many other languages, such as this English version, from the 16th century.*

**Icons** *play a major role in the Greek and Russian Orthodox churches. This example from St Catherine's Monastery (see pp246–9) shows* Christ in Majesty. *Usually painted on wood, they are used as aids to devotion, bringing the worshipper into the presence of the subject.*

**The Virgin and Child** *is a favourite Christian image. Depictions of the baby Jesus emphasize the human side of his nature, while the cult of his mother, the Virgin Mary, allows the faithful to identify with the joys and suffering of motherhood.*

**A Palm Sunday procession** *recreates Christ's entry into Jerusalem. This is a prelude to Holy Week, the most important Christian festival, commemorating the Crucifixion on Good Friday and Christ's Resurrection on Easter Sunday.*

## CHRISTIAN DENOMINATIONS

Almost all the major Christian churches are represented in Jerusalem. The Greek Orthodox *(see p100)* and Syrian churches were the first to be established in the city. Other ancient Christian communities include the Armenians *(see p107)*, Copts and Ethiopians. The Roman Catholic Church established its own Patriarchate here in the wake of the Crusades, and the most recent arrivals were the Protestants. The Greek Orthodox, Greek Catholic and Roman Catholic churches have large congregations, mostly of Palestinian Arabs, while priests and officials tend to be Greek and Italian.

**Syrian Orthodox Christmas in Bethlehem**

**Procession of Ethiopian priests in Jerusalem**

**Armenian priests in their black hooded copes**

## CHURCHES IN THE HOLY LAND

The first churches did not appear in the Holy Land until around AD 200 – the earliest Christians gathered together in each other's homes. Roman suspicion of unauthorized sects kept these churches underground. However, the conversion to Christianity of the Roman emperor Constantine signalled a rash of building on the sites connected with the life of Christ. The usual type of Byzantine church was the basilica, a longitudinal structure with a nave (central aisle) lit by windows in the walls of the side aisles. The apse area, containing the altar, was frequently concealed by an iconostasis, a three-panelled screen adorned with icons.

Nave
Drum
Side chapel
Apse
Pulpit
Altar
Iconostasis

# Islam

Islam was founded by Muhammad, a former merchant from Mecca in Arabia. Born around AD 570, at the age of 40 he began to receive revelations of the word of Allah. These continued for the rest of his life and were transcribed as the Quran. Muhammad's preachings were not well received in Mecca and in 622 he and his followers were forced to flee for Medina. This flight, or *hejira*, constitutes year zero in the Islamic calendar. Before Muhammad died in 632, he had returned to conquer Mecca. Within a further four years, the armies of Islam had swept out of the Arabian desert and conquered the Holy Land.

**The crescent moon**, *the symbol of Islam, has resonances of the lunar calendar, which orders Muslim religious life.*

### DOME OF THE ROCK
One of the oldest and most beautiful of all mosques, the richly decorated Dome *(see pp70–73)* is the third most holy site of Islam after the Prophet's cities of Mecca and Medina.

**The Quran**, *the holy book of Islam, is regarded as the exact word of Allah. Muslims believe that it can never be truly understood unless read in Arabic: translations into other languages can only ever paraphrase. The Quran is divided into 114 chapters, or* suras, *covering many topics, including matters relating to family, marriage, and legal and ethical concerns.*

### THE FIVE PILLARS OF FAITH
Islam rests on what are known as the "five pillars of faith". The first of these, known as the *Shahada*, is a simple declaration that "There is no god but Allah and Muhammad is his Prophet". The second pillar is the set daily prayers, performed in the direction of Mecca five times a day (though many Muslims don't completely observe this). The third pillar is the fasting during daylight hours that takes place for the whole of the holy month of Ramadan, and the fourth is the giving of alms. The fifth pillar is *Haj*: at least once in their lifetime all Muslims must, if they are able, make the pilgrimage to Mecca, birthplace of Muhammad.

**Muslim at prayer**

**House decorated with pilgrimage scenes, indicating the owner has made the *Haj***

**Muslim festivals** *are relatively infrequent, with just four major dates in the calendar (see p38). The most important of these are Eid el-Adha (which commemorates Abraham's covenant with God), marking the time of the pilgrimage, or Haj, and Eid el-Fitr, which marks the end of Ramadan. Celebrations tend to be communal.*

**The imam** *is an Islamic teacher, usually attached to a particular mosque. He delivers the khutba, or sermon, at the midday prayers on Friday. These prayers are always the best attended of the week.*

**The Night Journey** *was one of the defining episodes in the life of the Prophet Muhammad. He was carried during the night from Mecca to Jerusalem and from there made the Miraj, the ascent through the heavens to God's presence, returning to Mecca in the morning.*

## THE MOSQUE

Mosques come in many shapes and sizes but they all share some common characteristics. Chief of these is the mihrab, the niche that indicates the direction of Mecca. Most mosques also have a *minbar*, from which the imam delivers his Friday sermon. A dome usually covers the prayer hall. The minaret serves as a platform for the delivery of the call to prayer, once made by a *muezzin*, but these days more often a prerecorded cassette broadcast through a loudspeaker.

Minaret

Balcony, from where the call to prayer is traditionally made

Crescent-shaped finial

Dome

Prayer hall entrance, where footwear must be removed

Mihrab

Minbar

# Sites of the New Testament

The life of Jesus Christ, as narrated in the gospels, was played out in a relatively small geographical arena. He was born in Bethlehem; he grew up in Nazareth; his baptism took place at the Jordan River near Jericho; most of his public activity was carried out around the shores of the Sea of Galilee, where he preached, narrated parables and worked miracles; and his crucifixion, resurrection and ascension all occurred in Jerusalem. Unlike the sites of the Old Testament, those of the New Testament saw the rise of sanctuaries, churches and chapels built within two or three centuries of the death of Jesus. For this reason, a number of these sites have some claim to authenticity, although, as with so much in the Holy Land, nothing is beyond dispute.

**The Annunciation** ①
*At Nazareth Mary was visited by the angel Gabriel and told of her forthcoming child (Luke 1: 26–38). The episode is commemorated by the Basilica of the Annunciation (see p180).*

**The Birth of Jesus** ②
*In Bethlehem Jesus was born in a grotto and an angel appeared to shepherds in nearby fields, telling them of the birth (Luke 2: 1-20). A church was first built on the site in the 4th century (see pp194–5) and a star marks the alleged site of the Nativity.*

**The Wedding at Cana** ③
*Jesus performed his first miracle at this small village near Nazareth, at a wedding where he turned water into wine (John 2: 1–11).*

Joppa (Jaffa)•

**The Baptism of Christ** ④
*John the Baptist, a cousin of Jesus, baptized and preached the coming of the Messiah on the shores of the Jordan River. John recognized Jesus as the "Lamb of God" (Matthew 3). The site traditionally identified with the baptism is east of Jericho on the Jordanian border. It lies in a military zone and is only accessible to pilgrims for the Greek Orthodox Epiphany in January and on the third Thursday in October.*

```
0 kilometres          50
0 miles               30
```

**The Temptations** ⑤
*Following his baptism, Jesus went into the desert, where the Devil tried to tempt him from his 40-day fast (Matthew 4: 1–11). The Greek Orthodox Monastery of the Temptation on Mount Quarntal, just north of Jericho, marks the site of the supposed encounter (see p190).*

**The First Disciples** ⑥
*Christ's first Disciples were fishermen he
encountered on the banks of the Sea of
Galilee. He persuaded them to leave their
nets to become "fishers of men" (Matthew
5: 18–22). In the mid-1980s a fishing
boat was discovered in the mud of the
lake. It dates back to the 1st century AD,
roughly the time of Christ, and is on display
at Kibbutz Ginosar (see pp182–3).*

Tabkha ⑦⑧
⑥ Sea of Galilee
Cana ③
Nazareth ①
• Caesarea
GALILEE  • Beth Shean
DECAPOLIS
SHARON
SAMARIA
Jordan River
⑤ Mount Quarntal
④ River Jordan
• JERUSALEM
② Bethlehem
JUDAEA  DEAD SEA

**The Multiplication of the Loaves and Fishes** ⑦
*The gospels locate this famous miracle, more
colourfully known as the "feeding of the 5,000"
(Matthew 15: 32–39), on the shores of the Sea of
Galilee. The episode is commemorated in a church
at Tabkha on the lake shore (see p184), which has
a mosaic in front of the altar showing a basket of
bread flanked by fish.*

**The Sermon on the Mount** ⑧
*The longest and one of the key
sermons in the teachings of Jesus,
the Sermon on the Mount, begins
with the Beatitudes: "Blessed are
the meek for they shall inherit the
earth…" (Matthew 5–7). Tradition
has it delivered on a small rise
at Tabkha. It is celebrated by
the nearby, octagonal Church
of the Beatitudes (see p184).*

## JESUS IN JERUSALEM

In what was to be the last week of his life, Jesus made
a triumphal entrance into Jerusalem shortly before the
Jewish feast of Passover. He proceeded to the Temple
where he drove out the money changers (Matthew 21:
12–13). He gathered his Disciples to eat a Passover meal;
this was to be the Last Supper. After the meal they went
to the Garden of Gethsemane *(see p114)* where Jesus
was arrested (Matthew 26: 36–56). Condemned by the
Jewish authorities, he was put on trial before Pontius
Pilate, possibly in the Antonia Fortress or the Citadel
*(see p65)*. After being paraded through the city *(see
pp30–31)*, he was crucified and buried at Golgotha,
traditionally identified with the site of the Holy Sepulchre
church. Following his Resurrection, Jesus departed earth
with his Ascension from the Mount of Olives *(see p112).*

**The Last Supper (Matthew 26: 18–30),
traditionally associated with a room
on Mount Zion (see p117)**

# Via Dolorosa

**Via Dolorosa street sign**

The Via Dolorosa in Jerusalem traditionally traces the last steps of Jesus Christ *(see pp64–5)*, from where he was tried to Calvary, where he was crucified, and the tomb in the Church of the Holy Sepulchre, where he is said to have been buried. There is no historical basis for the route, which has changed over the centuries. However, the tradition is so strong that countless pilgrims walk the route, identifying with Jesus's suffering as they stop at the 14 Stations of the Cross, each connected with a particular event in the story.

THE CHRISTIAN QUARTER
THE MUSLIM QUARTER
THE JEWISH QUARTER

**LOCATOR MAP**

▢ Via Dolorosa

▬ Jerusalem City Walls

**Sixth Station**
*Veronica wipes away Jesus's blood and sweat, and her handkerchief reveals an impression of his face. The Chapel of St Veronica commemorates the story, which is not recorded in the gospels.*

**Seventh Station** Jesus falls for the second time. A large Roman column in a Franciscan chapel indicates this station.

**Eighth Station**
Jesus consoles the women of Jerusalem (Luke 23: 28). The spot is marked by a Latin cross on the wall of a Greek Orthodox Monastery.

**Fourteenth Station**
*The last Station of the Cross is the Holy Sepulchre itself. The tomb belonged to Joseph of Arimathea, who asked Pilate for Jesus's body.*

**Ninth Station**
Jesus falls for the third time. The place is marked by part of the shaft of a Roman column at the entrance to the Ethiopian Monastery *(see pp93–5)*.

**Steps to Ninth Station**

**Tenth to Thirteenth Stations**
*These four Stations (Jesus is stripped of his clothes; he is nailed to the cross; he dies; he is taken down from the cross) are all in the place identified as Golgotha (Calvary) within the Church of the Holy Sepulchre (see pp92–5).*

### First Station
*Jesus is condemned to death. The traditional site of the Roman fortress where this took place lies inside a Muslim college, the Madrasa el-Omariyya (see p68). Franciscan friars begin their walk along the Via Dolorosa here every Friday.*

**Second Station** Jesus takes up the cross, after being flogged, and crowned with thorns. This station is in front of the Franciscan Monastery of the Flagellation *(see p64).*

**Ecce Homo Arch** is where Pontius Pilate is said to have uttered the words "Behold the Man" *(see p64).*

| 0 metres | 50 |
| --- | --- |
| 0 yards | 50 |

### Fourth Station
*Jesus meets his mother Mary. This point is in front of the Armenian Church of Our Lady of the Spasm, which is built over an earlier Crusader church. This sculpture above the door shows the grief of Mary as she sees her son walking to his death.*

### Third Station
*Jesus falls beneath the weight of the cross for the first time. This is commemorated by a small chapel with a marble relief above the door.*

### Fifth Station
*Simon of Cyrene is ordered by the Roman soldiers to help Jesus carry the cross (Mark 15: 21). A Franciscan oratory marks this point on the Via Dolorosa, which is the start of the ascent to Calvary. This painting also shows St Veronica (see Sixth Station).*

# Celebrated Visitors

As a Spiritual or Utopian concept, Jerusalem has, over the centuries, been celebrated by poets and artists who have never been there, and who would perhaps hardly have known where it was on the map. However, the Holy City and the Holy Land have also been the subject of a no less impressive number of accounts, journals and paintings by a great many well-known travellers, writers and artists who did visit. From the early 19th century, the region also became a magnet for a steady flow of archaeologists and biblical scholars.

*Archaeologist Charles Warren*

## EARLY PILGRIMS AND TRAVELLERS

The establishment of Christianity as the religion of the Roman Empire in the 4th century AD triggered a wave of visitors, drawn by the region's biblical associations. One of the first pilgrims we know of is a nun named Egeria, who was perhaps Spanish, and visited the Holy Land from AD 380 to 415. An 11th-century manuscript found in Italy in 1884 contained a copy of her travel diary, which makes frequent mention of places such as Sinai and Jerusalem. Present-day writer William Dalrymple used a similar historical account (the journal of John Moschos, a 6th-century monk who wandered the Byzantine world)

as the basis for his own Holy Land travels recounted in *From the Holy Mountain* (1996).

Early travellers also visited the Holy Land for trade. The most famous of the merchants was Marco Polo who, in the course of his extensive travels, was entertained by the Crusaders in their halls at Akko.

The works of early Muslim travellers include some lively descriptions of the Holy City. The 10th-century historian El-Muqaddasi described Jerusalem as "a golden basin filled with scorpions". The Moroccan scholar Ibn Batuta

*Lady Hester Stanhope*

who, in the 14th century, travelled over 120,000 km (75,000 miles), also visited Palestine. His journals describe the Tombs of the Prophets in Hebron *(see p196)*, and Jerusalem's Dome of the Rock *(see pp72–3)*, of which he wrote, "It glows like a mass of light and flashes with the gleam of lightning."

## REDISCOVERING THE HOLY LAND

In the wake of Napoleon's invasion of Egypt (1798) and subsequent expedition into Palestine, and the interest it generated in the Orient, Europeans began to visit the Holy Land. First to arrive were the explorers and adventuring archaeologists, typified by Johann Ludwig Burckhardt *(see p222)*, who was one of the first Westerners ever to visit Jerash, and who discovered Petra in 1812. Lady Hester Stanhope was an eccentric British aristocrat who escaped from her high-society existence to live in Palestine. Although she did conduct some haphazard excavations in Ashkelon (north of Gaza) in 1814, she is more famous for wearing men's clothing in order to avoid wearing the veil.

In 1838, Edward Robinson, an American Protestant clergyman with an interest in biblical geography, was the first to make a proper critical study of supposed holy sites; his name is commemorated in Robinson's Arch south of the Western Wall *(see p91)*. In 1867–70, excavations south of the Haram esh-Sharif were carried out by Lieutenant Charles Warren of the Royal Engineers, a man who, some 20 years later, would lead the investigations into the infamous Jack the Ripper serial murders in

*Pilgrims in Jerusalem from the Book of Marvels on Marco Polo's travels*

**Jerusalem from the Mount of Olives (1859) by Edward Lear**

London. He is remembered in Jerusalem today through "Warren's Shaft", the popular name for the Jebusite well at the City of David archaeological site *(see p115)*.

## THE WRITERS

As the ground was broken by the early explorers, a steady stream of adventurous travellers followed in their wake, recording their experiences for eager audiences back in the West. François René de Chateaubriand's brief sojourn in Jaffa, Jerusalem, Bethlehem, Jericho and the Dead Sea area as related in his *Journey from Paris to Jerusalem* (1811) initiated the fashion for travel journals and descriptions of the Holy Land among 19th-century literati. The French poet Alphonse de Lamartine followed in his tracks in 1832, recording his experiences in *Remembrances of a Journey to the East*. In 1850 the creator of Madame Bovary, Gustave Flaubert, visited Palestine and Egypt, but found Jerusalem oppressive, writing in his diary, "It seems as if the Lord's curse hovers over the city." American authors Herman Melville and Mark Twain,

both visiting in the mid-19th century were hardly any more enamoured. Melville, author of *Moby Dick*, thought the Holy Sepulchre church "a sickening cheat". Twain was even more caustic, commenting in his 1895 book *The Innocents Abroad*, "There will be no Second Coming. Jesus has been to Jerusalem once and he will not come again." The tradition of scathing comment continued in the 20th century with George Bernard Shaw advising Zionists in the 1930s to erect notices at popular holy sites stating, "Do not bother to stop here, it isn't genuine." More recent writers have been kinder: Nobel laureate Saul Bellow produced a warm-hearted account of the city in *To Jerusalem and Back* (1976).

**Mark Twain**

## THE ARTISTS

With the writers came the artists, the best-known and most prolific of whom was David Roberts, a Scot who visited the Holy Land in 1839. He produced an enormous volume of very precise lithographs, collected and published in 1842, which ensured him fame in his own lifetime. His work remains ubiquitous today, adorning almost every book published on the Holy Land *(see pp8–9)*. Better known for his whimsical verse, artist, writer and traveller Edward Lear (1812–63) spent time in the Holy Land, painting a fine series of watercolours.

The English evangelical painter William Holman Hunt, who belonged to the Pre-Raphaelite movement, settled on Ha-Neviim Street in Jerusalem in 1854, where he painted several of his most famous works. This century, Russian-born Jewish artist Marc Chagall (1887–1985) has become closely identified with Jerusalem. His naïve-styled work, with its strong Jewish themes can be seen at the Israel Museum *(see pp132–7)*, in tapestry form at the Knesset *(see p131)*, and in stained-glass windows at the synagogue of the Hadassah Hospital *(see p139)*.

**The Finding of the Saviour in the Temple (1854–60) by William Holman Hunt**

# The Landscape and Wildlife of the Holy Land

Asian buttercup

From the life-giving Jordan River in the north to the scattered oases of the Negev and Sinai deserts in the south, water is precious in the Holy Land. In Israel it is rare to see water that is not used for irrigating land or creating fishponds. Away from the cultivated areas of Galilee and the coast, visitors will encounter a great variety of environments: mountains in the Golan Heights, green hills in Galilee, stony desert in the Negev and sandy desert in southern Jordan. Then there are the strange lifeless waters of the Dead Sea *(see p197)* and the astonishing abundance of life on the reefs of the Red Sea *(see pp240–41).*

**The Jordan River, which flows from the Golan Heights to the Dead Sea**

**Acacia trees growing in the Negev Desert**

## THE DESERT

Much of the Holy Land is desert. South of the Dead Sea, the landscape changes from scrubby steppe to rocky desert with spectacular craters such as Makhtesh Ramon *(see p203)*. The one common tree is the hardy acacia. Animals such as gazelles, ibexes and hyraxes are found at wadis and oases, but the predators that hunted them, the striped hyena and the wolf, are now extremely rare. A more common sight is that of a wheeling vulture or eagle.

**The fleet-footed Dorcas gazelle** *is found in the southern part of Israel and the Sinai peninsula, but in dwindling numbers.*

**Oases** *are rare in the deserts of this region. Those with plentiful water, like this one planted with date palms near the Dead Sea, are exploited to the full. Others act as magnets for the wildlife of the region.*

**A rock hyrax** *basks in the hot sun. Hyraxes are hard to spot as they remain hidden among the rocks if it is overcast or cold.*

**Ice plants** *are succulents that thrive in desert conditions, surviving drought by storing water in their fleshy leaves.*

**Wadis** *are riverbeds, dry for much of the year. After spring rains, they can fill rapidly with torrents of water, causing a brief explosion of flowers and grasses. Trees that manage to survive in these unpredictable conditions include the acacia and terebinth.*

## MOUNTAINS, HILLS AND CLIFFS

The highest mountains in the region are those on the Sinai peninsula and Mount Hermon in the Golan Heights. Trees on the lower slopes in the Golan include Aleppo pine and Syrian juniper. Vegetation in Sinai is very sparse as it is in the spectacular, rocky cliffs and gorges in the Judaean Hills and around the Dead Sea.

**Egyptian vultures** *are found in many of the wilder areas, such as the Negev and the mountains of northern Israel and northwestern Jordan.*

**The Golan Heights**

**Ibexes** *live high in the mountains, descending, in the cool of the morning and late afternoon, to wadis and oases to graze and drink.*

**The Madonna lily's** *beautiful white flowers symbolize purity. A number of Holy Land plants have names inspired by the Bible.*

**Prickly pears** *thrive in the hot dry climate. Introduced originally from the Americas, they are much appreciated for their sweet refreshing fruit.*

## CULTIVATED AREAS

Israel makes maximum use of the land available for agriculture, even using irrigation to create artificial oases in the desert. There are extensive plantations of oranges and other citrus fruits, avocados, bananas and dates. Jordan is less fortunate, its only fertile area being along the eastern side of the Jordan Valley. In Sinai there are only rare oases such as Feiran (see p249).

**Oranges** *are one of many fruits grown in the fertile areas; they constitute a major export for Israel.*

**The laughing dove,** *so called for its rising and falling, laughing cry, has spread dramatically since the 1930s in the cultivated regions of Israel and western Jordan.*

**Neatly cultivated fields at Migdal on the western shore of the Sea of Galilee**

## BIRDWATCHING IN THE HOLY LAND

Israel lies on one of the most important routes for migratory birds that winter in Africa then return to Europe and Asia to nest in the spring. Larger species

**Migrating stork**

include both black and white storks and many birds of prey. In terms of the number of species that can be seen, the area around Eilat (see p205) on the Gulf of Aqaba is reckoned the best place for watching migrating birds in the world. Another popular destination for birdwatchers is the Hula Reserve, an area of protected wetlands north of the Sea of Galilee.

**White pelicans taking off from a field near the Hula Reserve**

# THE HOLY LAND
# THROUGH THE YEAR

Shared as it is by Jews, Christians and Muslims, Jerusalem has an over-abundance of religious holidays. Add to these secular holidays, commemorations and cultural festivals, and rarely a week passes in which some significant event is not taking place. While visitors may want to time their visit to coincide with some of these events, they may equally want to avoid others. During religious holidays such

**Kaparot ritual, eve of Yom Kippur**

as Passover (and Ramadan in Israel's Arab areas and in Jordan) many shops, restaurants and museums close for the duration or open only for limited hours, and lodging is hard to find and inflated in price. The dates of religious and other holidays vary each year so visitors should check these when planning holidays. The Holy Land has year-round warm weather, but the heat in July and August can be extreme.

## SPRING

Spring in Jerusalem usually arrives in the latter part of March. This coincides with the Christian Easter and Jewish Passover celebrations, when the city is filled to bursting with pilgrims. The religious festivities are accompanied by cultural events, which increase in frequency as summer approaches. The weather is mild, and this is the best time for trips to Israel's many parks, even though around the Dead Sea the thermometer is already regularly above 30° C (86° F).

## MARCH

**International Book Fair**, Jerusalem. This annual event attracts visitors from more than 40 countries. The Jerusalem Prize is awarded.

**Easter** falls from late March to April for Catholics and Protestants; the Orthodox and Armenian churches celebrate a week later. Jerusalem's Easter week begins with a Palm Sunday procession from the Mount of Olives to St Anne's (see p67). The most striking ceremony is the Holy Fire (see p93), held on the Saturday of the Orthodox Easter.

## APRIL

**Passover**, or Pesach, falls from late March to the second half of April. It celebrates liberation from slavery under the pharaohs in Egypt. During the week-long festival, shops and restaurants are closed, and public transport limited.

**Palm Sunday procession in Jerusalem moving along the Via Dolorosa**

**Boombamela Festival** (1st week), Ashkelon, Israel. An alternative arts festival held on the beach.
**Armenian Holocaust Day** (24 Apr), Jerusalem. Marked with a procession, then a service at St James's Cathedral in memory of the Turkish massacres (see pp106–7).
**Mimouna** is celebrated the day after Passover ends by North African Jews, with festivities throughout Israel.
**Music Festival** (Passover), Jaffa (see pp174–5). This classical music festival takes place from May to July.
**Holocaust Day**. Periodically throughout the day sirens signal for two minutes' silence in remembrance of the victims of the Holocaust.
**Remembrance Day**. In the same fashion as Holocaust Day, this day honours the Israeli dead from past wars.

**Spring in Israel, the perfect time for exploring the countryside**

## AVERAGE DAILY HOURS OF SUNSHINE IN JERUSALEM

Hours: 15, 12, 9, 6, 3, 0

Jan Feb Mar Apr May Jun Jul Aug Sep Oct Nov Dec

**Sunshine Chart**
*Even during the winter, most days have some sunshine. The summer sun can be very fierce and adequate precautions against sunburn and sunstroke should be taken. Sun screen, a hat and sunglasses are recommended. Drinking plenty of water reduces the risk of dehydration.*

**Independence Day**. Israeli statehood is commemorated with parades and concerts.
**South Sinai Camel Festival** *(Apr/May)*, Sharm el-Sheikh, Egypt. The Bedouin tribes of Sinai bring their camels to this huge desert race meeting.

## MAY

**Festival of Israel** *(May/Jun)*. The most important cultural event in Israel: three weeks of music, dance and theatre in Tel Aviv, Jerusalem, Haifa and the Roman theatres at Caesarea *(see p176)* and Beth Shean *(see p185)*.

## SUMMER

With fewer religious festivals, the attention over summer shifts to the coast, where the soaring temperatures are tempered by sea breezes, and to the towns of Galilee, where the altitude partially counteracts the heat.

## JUNE

**Ascension** falls 40 days after Easter. It celebrates Christ's ascent to Heaven and in

Crowds watch an Independence Day air display on Tel Aviv's sea front

Jerusalem it is marked by prayers on the Mount of Olives *(see pp110–11)*.
**Beach Festival** *(all summer)*, Tel Aviv *(see pp168–73)*. The city-centre beaches are the venue for rock concerts and free open-air cinema.

## JULY

**Film Festival** *(early Jul)*, Jerusalem. Held at the Cinematheque *(see p122)*, this features the work of Israeli and foreign directors.
**Jaffa Nights** *(1st week)*, Tel Aviv. Two weeks of open-air concerts and shows in the setting of old Jaffa.
**Jazz Festival** *(Jul–Aug)*, Eilat. Held on the shores of the Red Sea, this festival draws international musicians.
**Jerash Festival** *(late Jul and Aug)*, Jerash. Jordan's most important festival is held in the spectacular setting of the Roman ruins *(see pp210–11)*. It includes folk dance, ballet, opera,

poetry competitions, theatre, classical music and displays of local handicrafts.

## AUGUST

**Puppet Festival**, Jerusalem. This is a festival aimed at the young, with shows in various venues, notably the Train Theatre in the Liberty Bell Gardens.
**Klezmer Festival**, Safed *(see p181)*. A festival devoted to traditional Eastern European Jewish music.

### JEWISH HOLIDAYS

The Jewish calendar is lunar, meaning that each month begins and ends at the new moon. Jewish holidays therefore fall on a different date each year compared to the Western calendar; however, they do remain roughly fixed about a certain time of the year.

Performance by visiting Shakespearean company at the Jerash Festival

**Jewish girl dressed for Mimouna**

## AVERAGE MONTHLY TEMPERATURE IN JERUSALEM

**Temperature**
*Summers in Jerusalem are hot, temperatures frequently climbing to over 30° C (86° F). In winter, the thermometer can drop to near freezing, with even the occasional snowfall. The chart (left) shows average daily maximum and average daily minimum temperatures for each month.*

## AUTUMN

In terms of the weather, autumn is the ideal time to visit Jerusalem. However, several major Jewish holidays occur in September and October, seriously disrupting public transport and reducing opening hours for shops and restaurants. It is also necessary to make hotel reservations well in advance.

## SEPTEMBER

**Sukkoth booths, in which meals are taken for the feast's duration**

**Rosh ha-Shanah**. The Jewish New Year. It marks the start of ten days of prayer that end with Yom Kippur. On the penultimate day some Jews perform Kaparot, a ceremony in which a live fowl is waved over the head to absorb sins. The *shofar*, ram's horn, is sounded at services.

**Yom Kippur**. The Day of Atonement, the holiest day of the year, which Jews observe by fasting for 26 hours, not having sex and

not using cosmetics, the whole country coming to a virtual standstill.

**Sukkoth**. Commemoration of the Israelites' 40 years in the wilderness after leaving Egypt. Makeshift "booths" are built outside where meals are eaten for seven days. The ultra-orthodox even sleep in them.

**Haifa International Film Festival**, Haifa, Israel. Held annually during the holiday of Sukkoth *(see above)*, the biggest and most

important film event in Israel hosts more than 200 screenings over eight days.

## OCTOBER

**Fringe Theatre Festival**, Akko *(see pp178–9)*. This festival in the ancient city of Akko involves local and inter-national avant-garde groups performing in various venues.

## NOVEMBER

**Jerusalem Marathon** *(late Oct/early Nov)*. One of the major sports events in Israel with hundreds of Israelis and foreigners participating.

## WINTER

Christmas is obviously a good time to visit Bethlehem and Nazareth, especially if you can attend one of the special church services. It does occasionally snow in Jerusalem, and snow on the Golan Heights sees the ski-lifts operating.

## MUSLIM FESTIVALS

**Muslim at prayer**

Eid el-Fitr and Eid el-Adha are the major feasts, both lasting two or three days, and celebrated by the slaughter of sheep. The former marks the end of Ramadan, the month of fasting, observed by all devout Muslims. Other significant days include the Prophet's Birthday (Moulid en-Nabi) and Islamic New Year (Ras el-Sana). The Islamic year is lunar and 11 days shorter than the Western year. This means that in terms of the Western calendar Islamic festivals fall 11 days earlier each year. Hence, in 2007 Ramadan begins on 13 September, and the following year on 2 September.

## AVERAGE MONTHLY RAINFALL IN JERUSALEM

**Rainfall**
*There is virtually no rainfall in Jerusalem from April to October. Showers begin to occur in autumn and winter, and during January and February skies are often filled with threatening grey clouds. Visitors at this time would be wise to go armed with an umbrella.*

## DECEMBER

**Hanukkah.** The Jewish Festival of Lights, this commemorates the reconsecration of the Temple in 164 BC *(see p42).* It lasts eight days, and is celebrated by the lighting of candles in a special eight-branched menorah.

**Christmas** *(24–25 Dec).* A Christmas Eve procession from Jerusalem arrives in Bethlehem for midnight mass at the Church of the Nativity *(see pp194–5).* To attend this service you must book in advance at the Christian Information Centre in Jerusalem *(see p101).* The mass is also projected on a huge screen in Manger Square. The service at Abu Ghosh *(see p139)* is also impressive. In Nazareth a procession is held on the afternoon of Christmas Eve,

**Hanukkah candles**

**Skiing on Mount Hermon, possible during January and February**

which ends with services held in the town's six churches.
**International Choir Festival** *(26 Dec),* Nazareth. In the days following the choir festival, the town plays host to sacred music concerts.
**Tiberias Marathon** *(Dec–Feb).* Less well-known than the Jerusalem Marathon, this attracts many runners because of the scenery along the route *(see pp182–3).*

## JANUARY

**Orthodox Christmas** *(7 Jan),* Jerusalem. This is celebrated on Christmas Eve with a service at the Holy Trinity Church in the Russian Compound *(see p124).*
**Armenian Christmas** *(19 Jan),* Jerusalem. This is celebrated with a Christmas Eve mass at St James's Cathedral in Jerusalem's Old City *(see pp106–7).*

## FEBRUARY

**Purim.** This festival celebrates the salvation of the Jews in Persia from threatened genocide (related in the Old Testament Book of Esther). The Scroll of Esther is read publicly in the morning and on the evening of Purim. Children wear fancy dress costumes, while adults participate with the giving of gifts to the poor and to friends, feasting and drinking.

**Jewish children dressed up as part of Purim festivities**

# THE HISTORY OF THE HOLY LAND

*S*ince prehistoric times the fertile plains and scattered oases between the Nile and the rivers of Mesopotamia have been colonized by countless different peoples. The ebb and flow of nations continues to this day; as independent countries, both Israel and Jordan are barely half a century old, with the Jewish state composed of a great many nationalities, all united by their shared faith.

Much of our knowledge of the early prehistory of the Holy Land comes from the site of Jericho, just north of the Dead Sea. Excavations have uncovered a series of settlements dating back to about 10,000 BC, when Stone Age hunters first abandoned their nomadic way of life. In settling, these people took the all-important step which led to cultivating crops and domesticating animals – a process known as the "Neolithic revolution". During the following 3,000 years small farming villages sprang up all over the region.

**Philistine sarcophagus lid, 12th century BC**

In the 3rd millennium BC the coastal plains witnessed the rise of a fairly uniform culture, known as the Canaanite civilization. There may never have been a single Canaanite nation; rather the Canaanites were probably organized in a series of city-states. A Canaanite army was defeated at Megiddo by the pharaoh Thutmose (1468 BC) and all the city-states were then subject to Egypt. The Canaanites nevertheless survived for two millennia – during which time they developed the world's first alphabet – until their culture was brought to an end by the rise of two new peoples. The first were invaders who came from the sea around 1200 BC; these were the Philistines, after whom the area was called Palestine ("land of the Philistines"). The second were the Hebrew tribes, who, between about 1200 and 1000 BC, coalesced into a political entity known as Israel.

There are several theories as to how the Hebrews came to control Palestine: through hard-won battles, or possibly by peaceful infiltration. There are no historical sources to verify events, but the Old Testament tells how these tribes formed a confederation that eventually led to the birth of a united kingdom whose first sovereign was Saul. His successors, David (whose rule is traditionally given as from around 1010 to 970 BC) and Solomon (c.970–930 BC), laid the foundations for the Jewish nation. It was David, according to the Bible, who captured Jerusalem and made it the Israelite capital, and Solomon who built the Jews' First Temple there.

## TIMELINE

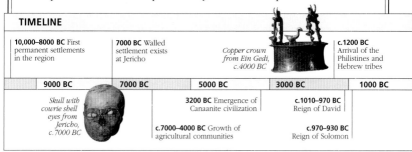

**10,000–8000 BC** First permanent settlements in the region

**7000 BC** Walled settlement exists at Jericho

*Copper crown from Ein Gedi, c.4000 BC*

**c.1200 BC** Arrival of the Philistines and Hebrew tribes

| 9000 BC | 7000 BC | 5000 BC | 3000 BC | 1000 BC |
|---|---|---|---|---|

*Skull with cowrie shell eyes from Jericho, c.7000 BC*

**3200 BC** Emergence of Canaanite civilization

**c.7000–4000 BC** Growth of agricultural communities

**c.1010–970 BC** Reign of David

**c.970–930 BC** Reign of Solomon

◁ **Medieval European map, showing the holy city of Jerusalem as the centre of the world**

### BABYLONIAN CAPTIVITY

According to the Bible, after Solomon died, conflicts led to the division of the Jewish nation into two separate parts: the Kingdom of Israel in the north and the Kingdom of Judaea in the south. Two centuries later, the Assyrians conquered the north, and many of the Jews of Israel were deported. When Judaea withheld tribute, it too was invaded and defeated at the battle of Lachish. The Assyrians, in turn, were defeated by the Babylonians who, in 587 BC, captured Jerusalem and destroyed Solomon's Temple, forcing the Jews of Judaea into exile. During the brief period of Babylonian captivity the Jews maintained and even strengthened their cultural and religious identity. Defeated by the Persians under Cyrus the Great in 538 BC, the Babylonians disappeared from history and the Jews were allowed to return to their land.

Israelite prisoners leaving Lachish after its fall to the Assyrians in 701 BC

### THE SECOND TEMPLE

Returning to Jerusalem, in the 6th century BC, the Jews built a new temple on the same site as the first. This event in the history of Jerusalem marks the beginning of what is referred to as the "Second Temple" period.

The Persians remained dominant in the region until their empire was torn apart by the armies of Alexander the Great. Judaea was swallowed up in the wake of the Macedonian's triumphant progress into Egypt. On the death of Alexander, his empire was split between three generals; the dynasties they founded proceeded to fight over the spoils, with Palestine eventually going to the Syria-based Seleucids. The culture of the Greeks spread throughout the region. This era saw the rise of the Decapolis ("ten cities" in Greek), a loose grouping of Hellenistic city-states in an otherwise Semitic landscape, which included Philadelphia (Amman), Gerasa (Jerash) and Scythopolis (Beth Shean). But Jerusalem resisted. The response of the Seleucid king Antiochus IV Epiphanes (175–164 BC) was to rededicate the Jews' temple in Jerusalem to Zeus and make observance of Hebrew law punishable by death. Led by Judas Maccabeus, a priest of the Hasmonean family, the Jews rebelled in 164 BC. They defeated the Seleucids, took complete control of Jerusalem and reconsecrated their Temple.

Rule of Judaea was assumed by the Hasmoneans. However, independence for the Jews did not ensure peace. There was bitter conflict between the Hasmoneans and the Pharisees, a rival priestly sect who propounded strict observance of Hebrew religious tradition. In the struggle for influence,

The recapture of the Temple by Judas Maccabeus in his successful revolt against the Seleucids, 164 BC

## TIMELINE

**722 BC** Assyria conquers the Kingdom of Israel and sends the Israelites into exile

**587 BC** The Babylonians conquer Jerusalem and destroy the First Temple

**515 BC** The founding of the Second Temple

*Alexander the Great, whose successors Hellenized Palestine*

| 800 BC | 700 BC | 600 BC | 500 BC | 400 BC |

*The seal of Jeroboam, a 9th-century Jewish king*

**538 BC** Cyrus the Great frees the Jews in exile in Babylon

**332 BC** Alexander the Great conquers Palestine

both factions asked for help from the new political and military power of the period – Rome.

## THE ROMANS AND JEWISH UPRISINGS

The Romans lost no time in taking advantage of this opportunity: in 63 BC their legions took Jerusalem. The Hasmoneans were superseded by a series of Roman governors, known as procurators. Anxious not to offend local religious sensibilities, the Romans had the Jewish Herod (the Great) rule as a client king in Palestine (37–4 BC). Allowed a relatively free hand in domestic affairs, the ambitious Herod expanded his frontiers and promoted architectural projects such as the Masada and Herodion fortress complexes, the port-city of Caesarea and the grand reconstruction of the Jews' Second Temple in Jerusalem.

Jerash, a former Decapolis city which flourished under the Romans

On Herod's death his kingdom was ruled for a brief period by his three sons before being governed directly by the Romans. A heavy tax burden, insensitive administration and the imposition of Roman culture were responsible for growing discontent among the Jews. Large numbers of Messianic claimants, revolutionary prophets and apocalyptic preachers only served to inflame the situation further. This was the political climate into which Jesus Christ was born, as described in the biblical New Testament.

Jewish clashes with Rome broke out repeatedly, culminating in a full-scale revolt in AD 66. It took the Romans four years to gain victory in this First Jewish War. When in AD 70 they finally captured Jerusalem, they destroyed the city and demolished the Temple (*see pp44–5*). The final subjugation of the Jews occurred three years later at Masada. Judaea once again became a Roman province, but the Jews refused to be subdued and before long a second major revolt broke out.

## THE EXILE OF THE JEWS

After the Second Jewish War (AD 132–5), Hadrian rebuilt Jerusalem as Aelia Capitolina, a Roman city, which Jews were forbidden to enter. Their communities were broken up and great numbers were sold into slavery and sent to Rome. Others fled, south into Egypt and across North Africa, or east to join the existing Jewish community in Babylon who had settled there after the destruction of the First Temple. This great scattering of the Jews is known as the Diaspora.

**Hadrian, builder of Aelia Capitolina**

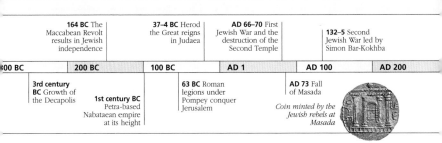

| 164 BC The Maccabean Revolt results in Jewish independence | 37–4 BC Herod the Great reigns in Judaea | AD 66–70 First Jewish War and the destruction of the Second Temple | 132–5 Second Jewish War led by Simon Bar-Kokhba |
|---|---|---|---|
| 300 BC | 200 BC | 100 BC | AD 1 | AD 100 | AD 200 |

| 3rd century BC Growth of the Decapolis | 1st century BC Petra-based Nabataean empire at its height | 63 BC Roman legions under Pompey conquer Jerusalem | AD 73 Fall of Masada | Coin minted by the Jewish rebels at Masada |

# The Destruction of the Second Temple

**Titus**

During the Jewish Revolt of AD 66, the Romans suffered early defeats until the emperor Vespasian sent his son Titus to Jerusalem with four legions. The siege of the city was bitterly fought. Eventually, after five months, on 29 August AD 70, the city's defenders were forced to surrender. In *The Jewish War*, historian Flavius Josephus describes how the Temple was set ablaze in the heat of battle. "When the flames rose up," he writes, "the Jews let out a terrific cry and, heedless of mortal danger, ran to put it out." But it was in vain, and the Second Temple was razed to the ground.

**ROMAN EMPIRE AD 117**

▨ *Maximum extent of the Empire*

**Arch of Titus**
*The Romans built the triumphal Arch of Titus in the Forum in Rome, with friezes showing the victorious troops with their booty from the destroyed Temple.*

**The Antonia Fortress** was built by Herod the Great around 37–35 BC to protect the Temple, and named for his patron, Mark Antony. It was the last stronghold of the Jewish rebels in AD 70.

**Portico**

**The Court of the Gentiles** was as far into the Temple complex as non-Jews could venture.

**The Causeway** linked the Temple with the main city gate to the west. Evidence of it remains today in Wilson's Arch *(see p85)*.

**Ossuary of Caiaphas**
*Carved from limestone, ossuaries held the bones of the dead. This particular ossuary bears the name Caiaphas, which was the name of the Temple High Priest at the time of the crucifixion of Jesus.*

**The Western Wall**
*Herod's engineers created the Temple platform by building four walls around a natural hill and filling in. The Western Wall (see p85) is part of one of those retaining walls.*

**Destruction and Sack of the Temple of Jerusalem**
*Painted by Nicolas Poussin in 1625–6, and now in the collection of the Israel Museum (see pp132–7), this shows Roman soldiers, directed by Titus on his white horse, emerging from the Inner Temple carrying the Jewish menorah and other treasures.*

**The Inner Temple** contained the Holy of Holies, an empty chamber meant for the Ark of the Covenant, which was lost when the First Temple was destroyed.

**Bronze Helmet**
*Archaeologists' finds such as this legionary's helmet (c. AD 100) indicate that Rome maintained a strong military presence after the Jewish Revolt.*

**The Hulda Gates**

**The Royal Stoa** was a covered colonnade, 162 columns in length, used for teaching.

**The Lower City Steps** led to the area known as the City of David. Evidence of them exists in Robinson's Arch *(see p85)*.

## THE SECOND TEMPLE

Built in the 6th century BC on the same site as the First Temple, which was destroyed by the Babylonians in 587 BC, the Second Temple was greatly expanded by Herod the Great (37–4 BC). He nearly doubled the size of the Inner Temple.

**"Judaea Capta" Coin**
*A commemorative coin issued after the defeat of the Jewish rebels depicting, on one side, Vespasian and, on the other, Rome standing triumphant over a subdued Judaea.*

**Constantine the Great, the first Christian Roman emperor**

### PALESTINE UNDER ROMAN RULE

Despite the Jews being banned from Jerusalem, during the 2nd and 3rd centuries their religion and traditions remained very much alive in Palestine, and scholars and religious schools were active throughout Galilee. This was the period in which the academies wrote down Jewish oral law and the commentaries on it, known collectively as the Talmud.

In the early 4th century, the Christians, who had also suffered Roman persecution, were granted freedom of worship by the Emperor Constantine (306–37), himself a convert to the religion. Constantine moved his capital from Rome to Byzantium, which was renamed Constantinople. This turn of events opened the doors of the Holy Land to pilgrims – first and foremost the devout Helena, mother of

**Byzantine icon of the Madonna and Child, 6th century**

Constantine – and Jerusalem regained its former importance. The first Christian churches were built on the sites connected with the life of Christ, and monasticism spread both in the towns and in the deserts of Palestine and Egypt. The first Holy Sepulchre church was dedicated in Jerusalem in 335.

During the rule of Theodosius (379–95) Christianity became the official state religion. Not long after the Roman Empire was divided in 395 between Theodosius's two sons, the Latin-speaking Western Empire fell to Germanic invaders but the Greek-speaking Eastern Empire, thereafter known as the Byzantine Empire, survived.

### THE BYZANTINE ERA

Despite a long series of schisms within the Eastern Church over the nature of Christ (see p100), the Byzantine period was an age of relative stability and prosperity in the Holy Land. The flow of pilgrims continued and monastic life drew ever more adherents. The construction of two important religious buildings, St Catherine's Monastery (see pp246–8) in Sinai and the enormous Nea Basilica (see p82) in Jerusalem, reflected the confidence of the era. The Holy Land became the land we can see on the early medieval mosaic map at Madaba (see pp216–17). However, upheaval was to arrive in

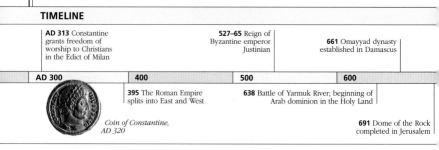

**TIMELINE**

**AD 313** Constantine grants freedom of worship to Christians in the Edict of Milan

**527–65** Reign of Byzantine emperor Justinian

**661** Omayyad dynasty established in Damascus

| AD 300 | 400 | 500 | 600 |
|---|---|---|---|

*Coin of Constantine, AD 320*

**395** The Roman Empire splits into East and West

**638** Battle of Yarmuk River; beginning of Arab dominion in the Holy Land

**691** Dome of the Rock completed in Jerusalem

614 in the form of an invading Persian army. Welcomed and supported by the Jews, who hoped for greater religious freedom, the Persians massacred the Christians and desecrated their holy sites before being driven off in 628 by the forces of the Byzantine Empire.

In the same year that the Byzantines reconquered Palestine, in neighbouring Arabia an army led by the Prophet Muhammad conquered Mecca, marking the emergence of a new force in the Near East which, in a little over ten years, would change the face of the Holy Land.

Pilgrimage scroll showing the Haram esh-Sharif

### THE ARABS AND ISLAM

In AD 638, only six years after Muhammad's death, the troops of his successor, or *caliph*, Omar defeated the Byzantines at the Yarmuk River, in modern-day Syria. The Muslims became the new rulers of Palestine.

Islam recognizes many of the prophets of the Old Testament, such as Abraham (Ibrahim), and so the Arabs regarded Jerusalem as holy in the same way as the Jews and Christians. The Arabs also believed that the Prophet Muhammad had ascended to Heaven on his Night Journey *(see p27)* from the same rock in Jerusalem on which, according to the Bible, Abraham had been about to sacrifice his son, and over which the Jews had built their temples. Consequently, the rubble in the Temple area was cleared and construction of two mosques began there: the Dome of the Rock (691) and El-Aqsa (705). Access to this "sacred precinct" *(Haram esh-Sharif)*, was forbidden to non-Muslims, but Christians and Jews were permitted to live in the city of Jerusalem on payment of an "infidels" tax.

Groups of Christian pilgrims regularly arrived in the Holy Land from Byzantium and Europe and were given safe passage under the successive Arab dynasties of the Omayyads (661–750), Abbasids (750–974) and, initially, the Fatimids (975–1171). This happy state of affairs ended in 1009 when the third Fatimid caliph El-Hakim initiated the violent persecution of non-Muslims and destroyed the Holy Sepulchre. The situation became critical in 1071 when Jerusalem fell to the Seljuk Turks, who forbade Christians access to the Holy City.

The outraged response of Christian Europe was to take up arms and set off on the first of a series of crusades spread over almost 200 years to recapture the Holy City and biblical sites of Palestine *(see pp48–9)*.

Triumphant group of the feared Muslim cavalry

**747** Earthquake drives dwindling populations from Petra and Jerash

*Fatimid jewellery*

**1071** Seljuk Turks capture Jerusalem and bar Christian pilgrims

| 0 | 800 | 900 | 1000 | 1100 |

**1099** The Crusaders take Jerusalem

*Dome of the Rock*

**975** North African Fatimid dynasty rules the Holy Land from Cairo

# The Crusades

"God wills it!" With these words, on 27 November 1095 at the Council of Clermont, Pope Urban II launched an appeal to aid the Byzantines in their wars with the Seljuk Turks and so free the Holy Land. His preachings inspired more than 100,000 men and women from all over Europe to join the armies heading east.

*Crusading emperor Frederick I*

They succeeded in creating a Latin kingdom of Jerusalem, but a series of further Crusades meant to reinforce the Western Christian presence in the east were ever less successful. Within 200 years the Crusaders were gone, leaving a legacy of fine ecclesiastical and military architecture.

**THE HOLY LAND**

▢ *Crusader domains 1186*

Church of the Holy Sepulchre

Scenes from the life of Christ

**The First Crusade**
*Passing through Constantinople, the Crusaders first engaged the Muslim Seljuks in Anatolia (Turkey). They conquered Nicaea and Antioch before marching down through Syria to Palestine.*

Stylized Gothic gates of Jerusalem

**The Second Crusade**
*Most of the Second Crusaders never made it to the Holy Land. Those that did launched a disastrous attack on Damascus and had to withdraw.*

**THE CAPTURE OF JERUSALEM**
On 7 June 1099, the Crusaders laid siege to Jerusalem. The Muslims held out for five weeks until on 15 July the Christian troops breached the walls unleashing a massive slaughter in the streets.

## TIMELINE

**1119** Founding of the Knights Templar

*Templar Knight*

**1148** Second Crusade defeated while besieging Damascus

**1187** Saladin defeats the Crusaders at the Horns of Hattin and takes Jerusalem

| 1100 | 1120 | 1140 | 1160 | 1180 | 1200 |

**1099** Crusaders capture Jerusalem; Godfrey of Bouillon becomes "Protector of the Holy Sepulchre"

*Saladin, founder of the Ayyubid dynasty (1169–1250)*

**1188–92** Third Crusade; after reconquering much of the coast, Richard I fails to retake Jerusalem

### The Third Crusade

*The retaking of Jerusalem by Saladin in 1187 prompted the Third Crusade. The Crusade failed to regain the Holy City, but Richard I "the Lionheart" negotiated the right of access for pilgrims.*

**Richard I and Saladin**

**The Crucifixion** was believed to have taken place on the site occupied by the Holy Sepulchre church.

**The burial of Christ**

**The city walls** were finally breached by the Crusaders in the north, near Herod's Gate, and also on Mount Zion.

**Siege warfare** was a major element of the Crusades; siege engines were built on site.

### The Fall of Akko

*Following a succession of defeats by the Mamelukes, the Crusaders were forced to leave the Holy Land for good in 1291. The last stronghold to fall was Akko, where this coat of arms was discovered.*

### THE TEMPLARS AND HOSPITALLERS

Much of the defence of Crusader gains in the Holy Land fell to two elite Military Orders of monastic knights, the Hospitallers (see p99) and the Templars, so named because they were headquartered in the former Temple area of Jerusalem. The Orders occupied and refortified Crusader castles in the Holy Land, as well as building new ones of their own.

**The Hospitaller castle of Belvoir in the Jordan Valley**

**1244** Jerusalem falls to Muslim mercenaries in the employ of Egypt

**1270** Last major Crusade, led by Louis IX, ends in his death in Tunis

*Louis IX embarking on the last Crusade*

| 1220 | 1240 | 1260 | 1280 | 1300 |
|------|------|------|------|------|

**1217–21** Fifth Crusade

**1249–50** Louis IX of France leads unsuccessful invasion of Egypt

**1260** Mamelukes defeat invading Mongols; Baybars becomes Sultan of Egypt

**1291** Last Latin strongholds in Holy Land, including Akko, fall to Mamelukes

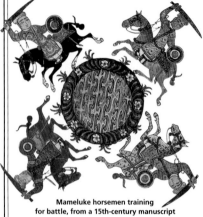

**Mameluke horsemen training for battle, from a 15th-century manuscript**

### PALESTINE UNDER THE MAMELUKES

In the wake of the Crusades, Jerusalem slowly declined to the status of a provincial city. The Mamelukes (former slave guards of Saladin's Ayyubid dynasty) ruled the Holy Land from Egypt, and the Holy City became a place of banishment for officials who fell from court favour in Cairo.

While the Mamelukes had driven the Christian knights from the Holy Land, they did make allowance for Christian pilgrims. In 1333 the Franciscan Friars were permitted a presence in Jerusalem, living in the supposed Hall of the Last Supper. In 1342 Pope Clement VI ratified this mission, which took on the name of the Franciscan Custody of the Holy Land.

The following century saw the beginning of a flow of Jews into Palestine escaping persecution in Europe, a movement that has continued through into the 20th century. In this case, the defeat of the Moors in Spain had given way to the Inquisition and the resultant expulsion of some 100,000 Jews from the country, accused of having too close ties with the vanquished Arabs.

### THE OTTOMAN EMPIRE

Mameluke control of Palestine ended in 1516 with defeat at the hands of the Ottoman army. Originating in northwest Turkey, the Ottoman Turks had captured Constantinople in 1453, renaming it Istanbul. Under the rule of their greatest sultan, Suleyman the Magnificent (1520–66), vast architectural projects were carried out in Jerusalem, most notably the construction of the city walls and gates.

However, a series of weak sultans meant that by the 18th century the enormous Ottoman empire was no longer so secure, particularly in the provinces where corruption was often a system of administration. This was the case in Palestine, where the people frequently suffered heavy taxes and poor government. But the Jews continued to return, largely because they were safer under Turkish rule than they were in Europe. Many chose to settle in Galilee, around Tiberias and Safed, joining the Sephardic Jewish communities that had fled Spain several centuries earlier. At the same time, Europe was making its first real entry into the region since the Crusades; Napoleon landed in Egypt in 1798 and the following year he had to be repelled from invading at Akko by the Ottoman governor, Ahmed Pasha el-Jazzar.

**Suleyman I, the Magnificent, Ottoman sultan, 1520–66**

## TIMELINE

| | | |
|---|---|---|
| **14th century** Development of the area round the Haram esh-Sharif in Jerusalem | **1492** Edict signed by King Ferdinand expelling all professing Jews from Spain | **1516** Ottomans defeat the Mamelukes and seize control of Palestine and Egypt |
| **1300** | **1400** | **1500** | **1600** |
| **1333** Franciscans permitted to settle in Jerusalem | **1400** Mamelukes halt westward advance of Mongol ruler Tamerlane | *Jaffa Gate, one of seven gates built by Suleyman's engineers* | **1537** Suleyman the Magnificent orders the construction of the walls of Jerusalem |

Akko, rebuilt by successive Ottoman governors

## JERUSALEM AND THE COLONIAL POWERS IN THE 19TH CENTURY

With the continuing decline of the Ottoman Empire the European nations, newly empowered by their Industrial Revolution, began to follow in Napoleon's wake – unsuccessful though he had been. When in 1831 the Egyptian ruler Muhammad Ali, the supposed vassal of Istanbul, seized Palestine, it was only with British military help that the Turks regained the territory. A British consul arrived in Jerusalem in 1838, followed closely by diplomatic representatives of France and Prussia. One of the causes of the Crimean War (1854) was a dispute between France and Russia over guardianship of the Holy Places.

All the while, Jewish immigration continued, propelled by virulent anti-Semitism and pogroms in eastern Europe and throughout the Russian Empire. A result of this influx was that in the mid-19th century,

Jerusalem overspilled the bounds of its medieval walls with the establishment of a series of small Jewish settlements outside the city gates. The city began to emerge from the lethargy that had characterized it in the preceding centuries.

Over in Europe there had been a growing, but not yet unified, Jewish national movement. In 1839 the British Jew Sir Moses Montefiore had first called for the creation of a Jewish state. This culminated in 1896 with the publication by an Austro-Hungarian Jewish journalist named Theodor Herzl of *Der Judenstat (The Jewish State)*, which proved a rallying cry for Jews worldwide. The following year saw the formation of the World Zionist Organization, with Herzl at its head. Its stated aim was "to create for the Jewish people a home in Palestine". A Jewish National Fund was set up to purchase land for settlement.

However, the Zionist immigrants were also laying the foundations for a century of conflict to come; slogans such as "A land without a people for a people without a land" ignored the fact that Palestine was already home to a large indigenous Arab population with aspirations to self-rule of its own.

The American Colony, one of a great many Western outposts established in 19th-century Jerusalem

| | | | | |
|---|---|---|---|---|
| *Ottoman janissary, soldier of the sultan's guard* | **1831** Egypt's Muhammad Ali takes control of Palestine | **1839** British Jew Sir Moses Montefiore first proposes the idea of a Jewish state | **1909** Founding of Tel Aviv and first kibbutz | |
| **1700** | **1800** | | **1900** | *Theodor Herzl* |
| | **1812** Petra rediscovered by Swiss explorer Jean Louis Burckhardt | **1860** Jerusalem's first new Jewish settlements since the Diaspora | **1896** Herzl publishes *The Jewish State* | |

## THE COLLAPSE OF THE OTTOMANS AND THE BRITISH MANDATE

Turkish rule in Palestine ended in 1917, during World War I, when British troops under the command of General Allenby took Jerusalem. The Arabs, under their leader Faisal, had fought alongside the British and expected Palestine in return. However, with the Balfour Declaration of 1917 the British had let it be known that "His Majesty's government favourably views the creation of a national Jewish home in Palestine". In the event, peace talks in 1920 put Palestine under British authority and this was ratified by the League of Nations on 24 July 1922.

Zionist poster soliciting funds for a homeland in Palestine

The following year, in order to placate Arab discontent, the British recognized Trans-Jordan as an autonomous Arab emirate, ruled by the emir Abdullah, the eldest brother of Faisal, with Amman as its capital. Initially under the supervision of the British in Jerusalem, the territory became totally independent in 1946, with Abdullah confirmed as its king.

### ARAB-JEWISH CONFLICT

At the time of World War I, some 500,000 Palestinian Arabs and about 85,000 Jews were living in the Holy Land. In the 20 years between then and the outbreak of World War II about 250,000 more Jews arrived at the ports of Jaffa and Haifa to settle in Palestine. Each new wave of immigrants served to increase the tension between the Palestinian and Jewish communities.

In 1929 Palestinian riots culminated in a series of pogroms in Jerusalem, Hebron and Safed. An Arab "revolt" proclaimed in 1936 led to a six-month general strike that brought the country to a standstill.

The *Theodor Herzl* about to dock at Haifa, decks crowded with Jewish immigrants, 1947

**TIMELINE**

*TE Lawrence "of Arabia"*

**1916** Faisal and the Arabs, encouraged by TE Lawrence, join the British in a desert war against the Turks

**24 July 1922** League of Nations ratifies British mandate in Palestine

| 1900 | 1905 | 1910 | 1915 | 1920 | 1925 |
|------|------|------|------|------|------|

**1909** Founding of Tel Aviv and first kibbutz in Palestine

**1914** War breaks out in Europe; the Ottoman Turks side with Germany

**1917** General Allenby captures Jerusalem from the Ottoman Turks

*General Allenby*

## PROPOSALS FOR PARTITION

By this time, the British were finding rule in Palestine extremely uncomfortable. In 1937, following the deliberations of the Peel Commission, they proposed ending the Mandate and partitioning the country. The Jews accepted but the Arabs refused, claiming that the proposed Jewish homeland occupied the region's most fertile zones.

Elsewhere, the world was much more concerned with developments in Europe, where war seemed inevitable. In a brazen attempt to improve relations with its potential allies, the Arabs, in 1939, on the eve of war, Britain published a "White Paper" drastically limiting Jewish immigration to Palestine. However, faced with the dangers of Nazism, tens of thousands of Jews continued to arrive, often sneaking in clandestinely by sea. British attempts to check the immigration were, for the most part, in vain.

One effect of this new post-war situation was to inspire extremists to attacks on the British. On 22 July 1946 the Jewish military organization Irgun – one of whose leaders was the future prime minister Menachem Begin – bombed British headquarters at the King David Hotel in Jerusalem, killing more than 80 and wounding hundreds more.

Trapped in a no-win situation, the British placed the "Palestine question" before the newly-formed United Nations. On 29 November 1947 the UN voted for the partition of the Holy Land into an Arab state and a Jewish state, with Jerusalem under international administration. Britain announced its intention to pull out of Palestine on 15 May 1948 and leave the Arabs and Jews to fight among themselves.

Allenby Street, in the rapidly expanding Jewish Tel Aviv of the 1930s

Ben Gurion witnessing the departure of British troops from Haifa port in 1948

## THE CREATION OF ISRAEL

Skirmishing between the Palestinians and Jews escalated as both sides manoeuvred to control as much territory as possible before the end of the Mandate. Jewish extremists attacked Palestinian villages (most infamously at Deir Yassin, on the road between Tel Aviv and Jerusalem), while armed Palestinians made similar raids against Jewish settlements.

As the British prepared to leave, the Jews were ready to replace them. On 14 May 1948, the eve of departure, David Ben Gurion declared the birth of the State of Israel.

**1934** Jews flee central Europe and the threat of Hitler's Germany

**1936** Arab Revolt in Palestine

**1939** Great Britain publishes the "White Paper"

**1947** Discovery of the Dead Sea Scrolls at Qumran

**1930** | **1935** | **1940** | **1950**

**1929** Arab attacks on Jews in Jerusalem, Hebron and Safed

**1937** Peel Commission proposes partition of Palestine

**14 May 1948** State of Israel declared in Tel Aviv

*One of the Dead Sea Scrolls*

**Refugees crossing the border into Jordan in 1967**

## THE 1948 WAR

The Arab reaction to the creation of Israel was swift. Lebanon, Syria, Iraq, Jordan and Egypt launched a combined attack with the avowed aim of casting the new-born state into the sea. Fighting continued until an armistice was signed in December 1949. At the cease of hostilities, the Israelis had made great territorial gains at the expense of the Palestinians. Prior to 1948 the Jews owned less than seven per cent of Palestine but at the war's end they occupied about 80 per cent. As a result, some 500,000 to 750,000 Palestinians were made refugees in neighbouring Arab countries and in camps in the Egyptian-controlled Gaza Strip and in the Jordanian-held territories on the west bank of the Jordan River.

One of the main objectives of the opposing sides had been the capture of Jerusalem. Neither side had achieved this; the Israelis held the modern quarters of West Jerusalem,

Pre-1967 poster, with the West Bank shown as part of Jordan

the Jordanians held the Old City and East Jerusalem. The city was to remain divided, along what came to be known as the Green Line, for almost 20 years.

## THE ARAB-ISRAELI WARS AFTER 1949

After the violent birth of Israel, the infant state sought to strengthen its position by passing the Law of Return. This extended to all Jews throughout the world the right to live in Israel. The first to heed the invitation were communities of Jews from the Arab world, followed by displaced Jews from Europe. Those that followed came from everywhere, from the then-Soviet Union to South America.

Relations with the Arabs remained on a war footing. In 1956, the Israeli army swept into Sinai as part of the French and British plan to seize the Suez Canal, nationalized by Egypt's President Nasser. On this occasion, under pressure from the United States and the United Nations, they were forced to retreat. Eleven years later, in 1967, Israeli tanks rolled into Sinai once again. Alarmed by a build-up of Egyptian forces on the border, Israel launched a pre-emptive attack. Despite then facing the combined forces of all its Arab neighbours, in six days Israel's army had taken the Golan Heights from Syria, the Gaza Strip and Sinai from Egypt, and the West Bank from Jordan. The Israelis also captured the whole of Jerusalem. In what amounted to a face-saving exercise, on 6 October 1973, the Jewish feast of Yom Kippur, Egypt and Syria

**TIMELINE**

**1951** Assassination of King Abdullah of Jordan in Jerusalem by Palestinian extremists

*Hussein, crowned king of Jordan in May 1953*

**6 October 1973** Yom Kippur War breaks out

| 1950 | 1955 | 1960 | 1965 | 1970 | 1975 |

**14 May 1948** On the declaration of the State of Israel war breaks out with the Arabs

**1956** Suez crisis

**5–11 June 1967** Six Day War results in reunification of Jerusalem under the Israelis

*Golda Meir, Israeli prime minister 1969–74*

**1979** Camp David peace treaty signed between Egypt and Israel

The Israeli-built wall, designed to stop Palestinian bombers

launched a surprise attack on Israeli positions. Caught off guard, the Israelis suffered initial losses but they counterattacked and reversed early Arab gains. At the cease of hostilities the action had not altered the territorial state of affairs set six years previously.

The 1973 War did, however, pave the way for the first talks between Egypt and Israel. In 1979 the two countries formally agreed to peace by signing the Camp David agreement. In 1982 Sinai was returned to Egypt.

### THE QUEST FOR PEACE

The peace treaty was not welcomed by all parties. The Palestinians saw it as undermining their campaign for self-rule. Groups such as the Palestine Liberation Organisation (PLO) stepped up their anti-Israel guerrilla war. Their tactics won them little sympathy with the international community. That changed in late 1987 with the beginning of the *intifada* ("shaking off"), a grass-roots Palestinian revolt against Israeli occupation in the Gaza Strip and West Bank. Television screens worldwide were filled with images of stone-throwing young Arab boys facing up

to well-armed Israeli soldiers. In the wake of 1991's Gulf War, the Americans brokered a meeting between Israeli and Palestinian delegations in Madrid. This seemed to achieve little, but in 1993 it was revealed that the two parties had been meeting in Norway where agreement had been reached. The signing of the "Oslo Accords" was capped that year by a handshake between Israeli prime minister Yitzhak Rabin and PLO president Yasser Arafat on the lawn of the White House. The following year saw Jordan and Israel formally end the state of war that had existed between the two countries since 1948.

Since then, Rabin has been assassinated by a Jewish extremist and Arafat has died. Israel has celebrated 50 years of statehood but the Palestinians remain stateless. The Israelis have built a giant wall between themselves and the Palestinians in an attempt to halt the terror bombings that have been a fact of daily life since the 1990s. The cycle of violence continues, but so do the attempts to find a solution that will bring a lasting peace to the region.

Activists on both sides unite for peace

| 1980 | 1985 | 1990 | 1995 | 2000 | 2005 | 2010 |
|---|---|---|---|---|---|---|

**1982** Sinai returned to the Egyptians

**1993** Oslo Accords lead to Rabin and Arafat shaking hands

**1995** Israeli prime minister Yitzhak Rabin assassinated

**1999** King Hussein of Jordan dies

*Yasser Arafat, first president of the Palestinian Authority dies, November 2004*

**1987** Eruption of Palestinian *intifada* against Israeli occupation

**1994** Palestinians granted limited autonomy

*First issue of Palestinian stamps, 1994*

**2005** Israel withdraws Jewish settlements from the Gaza Strip

# JERUSALEM
# AREA BY AREA

# Jerusalem at a Glance

The old city of Jerusalem has a history that
stretches back more than 3,000 years,
although the present street plan dates largely
from Byzantine times, and the encircling walls
are from the 16th century. Within the walls,
the Old City divides into four vaguely defined
quarters – one each for the Christians, Jews
and Muslims, and the fourth occupied by the
Armenians. East and south of the Old City are
the Mount of Olives and Mount Zion, both
places traditionally linked with the last acts of
Jesus Christ. To the north and west is modern
Jerusalem, liberally endowed with fine examples
of late 19th-century architecture.

**The Church of the Holy Sepulchre**
(see pp92–5) *is the most important
of the Holy Land's Christian sites.
Tradition has it that the church occupies the site of Golgotha, where Jesus
Christ was crucified and buried.*

**The Citadel** (see
pp102–4) *is an
impressively restored,
fortified complex, which
has its origins in the
2nd century BC. It now
houses an excellent
museum devoted to the
history of Jerusalem.
There are also splendid
views of the city from
its ramparts.*

**MODERN
JERUSALEM**
(See pp118–127)

**THE CHRISTIAN
AND ARMENIAN
QUARTERS**
(See pp88–107)

**The Israel Museum** (see pp132–7) *was
purpose-built in the 1960s to house the
country's most significant archaeological
finds, including the Dead Sea Scrolls, which
are displayed in this uniquely shaped hall.
The museum is situated a short distance
west of the city centre.*

**Yemin Moshe** (see pp120–1) *is one of several
attractive old quarters in modern Jerusalem,
developed in the mid-19th century to escape
overcrowding in the Old City. It is distinguished
by its windmill and by this communal housing
block, known as Mishkenot Shaananim.*

◁ The Dome of the Rock, with Dominus Flevit Chapel and the Mount of Olives behind

**The Haram esh-Sharif** (see pp68–73) *is the focus of the Muslim faith in Jerusalem. A large plateau on the eastern edge of the Old City, it contains some fine Islamic buildings, including the 8th-century El-Aqsa Mosque, and the magnificent Dome of the Rock, with its dazzling interior.*

**THE MUSLIM QUARTER**
*(See pp60–75)*

**The Western Wall** (see p85) *is Judaism's holiest site. It is believed to be part of the great Temple enclosure built by Herod in the 1st century BC. The plaza in front is busy, day and night, with supplicants at prayer.*

**THE JEWISH QUARTER**
*(See pp76–85)*

**THE MOUNT OF OLIVES and MOUNT ZION**
*(See pp108–117)*

**The Sephardic Synagogues** (see p82) *are a group of four synagogues which were at the heart of the 17th-century Sephardic community, once the largest Jewish group in Jerusalem. The Ben Zakkai Synagogue, shown here, was built in 1610.*

**The Mount of Olives** (see pp108–13) *has several fine churches, including the richly decorated Russian Orthodox Church of St Mary Magdalene.*

| 0 metres | 300 |
| --- | --- |
| 0 yards | 300 |

# THE MUSLIM QUARTER

This is the largest and most densely populated quarter of the Old City. It was first developed under Herod the Great and delineated in its present form under the Byzantines. In the 12th century it was taken over by the Crusaders, hence the quarter's wealth of churches and other Christian institutions, such as the

**Street sign for a Quranic recitation school**

Via Dolorosa (see pp30–31). In the 14th and 15th centuries the Mamelukes rebuilt extensively, especially in the areas abutting the Haram esh-Sharif. The quarter has been in decay since the 16th century. Today it contains some of the city's poorest homes. It is also one of the most fascinating and least explored parts of Jerusalem.

## SIGHTS AT A GLANCE

**Historic Streets, Buildings and Gates**
Chain Street ⑥
Damascus Gate ⑧
Ecce Homo Arch ②
Herod's Gate ⑨
Lady Tunshuq's Palace ④
St Stephen's Gate ⑪
Via Dolorosa ③

**Souks and Markets**
Central Souk ⑦
Cotton Merchants' Market ⑤

**Holy Places**
Haram esh-Sharif
pp68–73 ⑫
Monastery of the Flagellation ①
St Anne's Church ⑩

**GETTING THERE**
The Muslim Quarter is served by Damascus, Herod's and St Stephen's gates. There are buses from the New City to Damascus Gate (see p311). Alternatively, for visitors with their own transport, there is a car park just inside St Stephen's Gate.

### KEY

▨ Street-by-Street map
See pp62–3

— City wall

---

◁ **Muslim women entering the Dome of the Rock, centrepiece of the Haram esh-Sharif**

# Street-by-Street: The Muslim Quarter

**Studium Museum artifact**

The main routes through this busy quarter are along the Via Dolorosa and up and down El-Wad. Both streets are lined with a gaudy array of shops, whose salesmen eagerly press on visitors all manner of ornaments and kitsch, from plastic crucifixes to glass-bowled water pipes. Few people stray from the main thoroughfares, but those who do are richly rewarded. The quiet, winding back alleys contain a wealth of fine medieval Islamic architecture, much of it dating from the Mameluke era (1250–1516). Not all of it is in good condition, but many of these buildings still perform the functions for which they were intended.

**The Austrian Hospice** was built in 1869 to accommodate Christian pilgrims.

**Damascus Gate**

VIA DOLOROSA

EL-WAD

### Via Dolorosa
*Crossing the quarter from east to west, this street is revered by Christian pilgrims as the route taken by Christ as he was led to his crucifixion* ❸

**Holy Sepulchre church and the Christian Quarter**

**Abu Shukri restaurant (see p272)**

### El-Takiya Street
*A narrow, stepped street at the heart of the quarter, El-Takiya contains some of the city's finest examples of Mameluke architecture.*

### Lady Tunshuq's Palace
*The banding of different coloured stone and panels of intricate marble inlay typify the decorative style of the Mamelukes* ❹

**KEY**

– – – Suggested route

**STAR SIGHTS**

★ Monastery of the Flagellation

★ Ecce Homo Arch

### ★ Monastery of the Flagellation

*Built on the site traditionally associated with the flogging of Christ, this Franciscan complex includes two attractive chapels and the Studium Museum* ❶

**LOCATOR MAP**
*See Jerusalem Street Finder, map 4*

St Stephen's Gate and the Mount of Olives →

BARQUQ

ALLAH-E-DIN

BAB

EL-WAD

↓ Jewish Quarter

### Convent of the Sisters of Zion

*The convent, which runs a pilgrims' hospice, dates from the 19th-century Christian building boom.*

### ★ Ecce Homo Arch

*The arch, which spans the Via Dolorosa, is the main section of a Roman triple arch. One of the smaller, flanking arches (left) is incorporated into the structure of the Convent of the Sisters of Zion* ❷

Madrasa el-Araghonia (1358)

EL-HADID

### Bab el-Hadid Street

*Though badly neglected, this street has a number of* madrasas *(see p71) from the 14th and 15th centuries.*

0 metres    50

0 yards    50

Monastery of the Flagellation, with the Via Dolorosa behind

## Monastery of the Flagellation ❶

Via Dolorosa. **Map** 4 D2. **Tel** (02) 627 0444. ◯ 8am–6pm (winter: 5pm) daily. **Studium Museum** ◯ 9–11:30am Mon–Sat.

Owned by the Franciscans, this complex embraces the simple and striking Chapel of the Flagellation, designed in the 1920s by the Italian architect Antonio Barluzzi, who was also responsible for the Dominus Flevit Chapel on the Mount of Olives (see p113). It is located on the site traditionally held to be where Christ was flogged by Roman soldiers prior to his Crucifixion (Matthew 27: 27–30; Mark 15: 16–19).

On the other side of the courtyard is the Chapel of the Condemnation, which also dates from the early 20th century. It is built over the remains of a medieval chapel, on the site popularly identified with the trial of Christ before Pontius Pilate.

The neighbouring monastery buildings house the Studium Biblicum Franciscanum, a prestigious institute of biblical, geographical and archaeological studies. Also part of the complex, the **Studium Museum** contains objects found by the Franciscans in excavations at Capernaum, Nazareth, Bethlehem and various other sites. The most interesting exhibits are Byzantine and Crusader

objects, such as fragments of frescoes from the Church of Gethsemane, precursor of the present-day Church of All Nations (see p114), and a 12th-century crozier from the Church of the Nativity in Bethlehem (see pp194–5).

Crusader-era angel's head, Studium Museum

## Ecce Homo Arch ❷

Via Dolorosa. **Map** 4 D2. **Convent of the Sisters of Zion** Tel (02) 643 0887. ◯ 9am–noon & 2–6pm (winter: 5pm) Mon–Thu. 🎥 🎫

This arch that spans the Via Dolorosa was built by the Romans in AD 70 to support a ramp being laid against the Antonia Fortress, in which Jewish rebels were barricaded (see p44). When the Romans

The Ecce Homo Arch bridging the Via Dolorosa

rebuilt Jerusalem in AD 135 in the wake of the Second Jewish War (see p43), the arch was reconstructed as a monument to victory, with two smaller arches flanking a large central bay. It is the central bay that you see spanning the street.

One of the side arches is also still visible, incorporated into the interior of the neighbouring **Convent of the Sisters of Zion**. Built in the 1860s, the convent also contains the remains of the vast Pool of the Sparrow (Struthion), an ancient reservoir which collected rainwater directed from the rooftops. The pool was originally covered with a stone pavement (lithostrothon) and it was on this flagstone plaza, Christian tradition has it, that Pilate presented Christ to the crowds and uttered the words "Ecce homo" (Latin for "Behold the man"). However, archaeology refutes this, dating the pavement to the 2nd century AD, long after the time of Christ. Within a railed section you can see marks scratched into the stone. Historians speculate that they may have been carved by bored Roman guards as part of some kind of street game.

## Via Dolorosa ❸

**Map** 3 C3 & 4 D2.

The identification of the Via Dolorosa (see pp30–31) with the ancient "Way of Sorrows" walked by Christ on the way to his Crucifixion has more to do with religious tradition than historical fact. It nevertheless continues to draw huge numbers of pilgrims every day. The streets through which they walk are much like any others in the Muslim Quarter, lined with small shops and stalls, but the route is marked out by 14 "Stations of the Cross", linked with events that occurred on Christ's last, fateful walk. Some of the Stations are commemorated only by wall plaques, which can be difficult to spot among the religious souvenir stalls. Others are located inside buildings. The last five Stations are all within the Holy Sepulchre church *(see pp92–5)*.

Friday is the main day for pilgrims, when, at 3pm, the Franciscans lead a procession along the route.

In fact, the more likely route for the original Via Dolorosa begins at what is now the Citadel *(see pp102–103)* but was at the time the royal palace. This is where Pontius Pilate resided when in Jerusalem, making it a more likely location for the trial of Christ. From here, the condemned would probably have been led down what is now David Street, through the present-day Central Souk *(see p66)*, out of the then city gate and to the hill of Golgotha, the presumed site of which is now occupied by the Holy Sepulchre church.

**Stalactite stone carvings above a window on Lady Tunshuq's Palace**

## Lady Tunshuq's Palace ❹

El-Takiya St. **Map** 4 D3.
⬤ *to public.*

Lady Tunshuq, of Mongolian or Turkish origin, was the wife, or mistress, of a Kurdish nobleman. She arrived in Jerusalem some time in the 14th century and had this edifice built for herself. It is one of the loveliest examples of Mameluke architecture in Jerusalem. Unfortunately the narrowness of the street

**An unusually quiet Via Dolorosa, leading down from Ecce Homo Arch to El-Wad Road**

prevents you from standing back and appreciating the building as a whole, but you can admire the three great doorways with their beautiful inlaid-marble decoration. The upper portion of a window recess also displays some fine carved-stone, stalactite-like decoration, a form known as *muqarnas*. The former palace now serves as an orphanage and is not open to the public.

When Lady Tunshuq died, she was buried in a small tomb across from the palace. The fine decoration on the tomb includes panels of different coloured marble, intricately shaped and slotted together like a jigsaw – a typical Mameluke feature known as "joggling".

If you head east and across El-Wad Road, you will enter a narrow alley called Ala ed-Din, which contains more fine Mameluke architecture. Most

of the façades are composed of bands of different hues of stone, a strikingly beautiful Mameluke decorative technique known as *ablaq*.

## Cotton Merchants' Market ❺

Off El-Wad Rd. **Map** 4 D3.

Known in Arabic as the Souk el-Qattanin, this is a covered market with next to no natural light but lots of small softly-lit shops. It is possibly the most atmospheric street in all the Old City. Its construction was begun by the Crusaders. They intended the market as a free-standing structure but later, in the first half of the 14th century, the Mamelukes connected it to the Haram esh-Sharif *(see pp68–73)* via a splendidly ornate gate facing the Dome of the Rock. (But note, non-Muslims are not allowed to enter the Haram esh-Sharif by this gate, although you can depart this way.)

As well as some 50 shop units, the market also has two bathhouses, the Hammam el-Ain and the Hammam el-Shifa. One of these has been undergoing restoration with a view to its being eventually opened to the public. Between the two bathhouses is a former merchants' hostel called Khan Tankiz, also being restored.

Less than 50 m (160 ft) south of the Cotton Merchants' Market on El-Wad Road is a small public drinking fountain, or *sabil*, one of several such erected during the reign of Suleyman the Magnificent.

**The tunnel-like interior of the Cotton Merchants' Market**

# Chain Street ❻

**Map** 4 D4.

The Arabic name for this street is Tariq Bab el-Silsila, which means "Street of the Gate of the Chain". The name refers to the magnificent entrance gate to the Haram esh-Sharif *(see pp68–73)* situated at its eastern end. The street is a continuation of David Street, and together the two streets run the width of the Old City from Jaffa Gate to the Haram esh-Sharif.

Chain Street has several noteworthy buildings commissioned by Mameluke emirs in the 14th century. Heading eastwards from David Street, the first is the Khan el-Sultan caravanserai, a restored travellers' inn. Further along on the right is Tashtamuriyya Madrasa, with its elegant balcony. It houses the tomb of the emir Tashtamur, and is one of many final resting places built here in the 14th and 15th centuries in order to be close to the Haram esh-Sharif. On the same side of the street is the tomb of the brutal Tartar emir Barka Khan, father-in-law of the Mameluke ruler Baybars, who drove the Crusaders out of the Holy Land *(see pp48–9).* This building, with its intriguing façade decoration, now houses the Khalidi Library.

Opposite the Khalidi Library are two small mausoleums. Of the two, that of emir Kilan stands out for its austere, well-proportioned façade. Further

**Window on Khalidi Library**

along on the same side is the tomb of Tartar pilgrim Turkan Khatun, easily recognizable by the splendid arabesques on its façade. Opposite the Gate of the Chain is the impressive entrance to the 14th-century Tankiziyya Madrasa. In the inscription, three symbols in the shape of a cup show that emir Tankiz, who built the college, held the important office of cupbearer. Nearby is a drinking fountain, or *sabil*, from the reign of Suleyman the Magnificent, which combines Roman and Crusader motifs.

# Central Souk ❼

David St/Chain St. **Map** 3 C4.
◯ 8am–7pm Sat–Thu.

The Central Souk consists of three parallel covered streets at the intersection of David Street and Chain Street. They once formed part of the Roman Cardo *(see p80)*. Today's markets sell mostly

clothes and souvenirs, although the section called the Butchers' Market (Souk el-Lakhamin in Arabic), restored in the 1970s, still offers all the excitement of an eastern bazaar. It is not for the faint-hearted, however, as the pungent aromas of spices and freshly slaughtered meat can be overwhelming.

# Damascus Gate ❽

**Map** 3 C1. 🚌 1, 2, 23. **Roman Square Excavations** ◯ 9am–5pm Sat–Thu, 9am–3pm Fri. 🞖

Spotting this gate is easy, not only because it is the most monumental in the Old City, but also because of the perpetual bustle of activity in the area outside the gate.

Arabs call it Bab el-Amud, the Gate of the Column. This could refer to a large column topped with a statue of the emperor Hadrian *(see p43)* which, in Roman times, stood just inside the gate. For Jews it is Shaar Shkhem, the gate which leads to the biblical city of Shechem, better known by its Arabic name – Nablus.

The present-day gate was built over the remains of the original Roman gate and parts of the Roman city. Outside the gate and to the west of the raised walkway, steps lead down to the excavation area. In the first section are remains of a Crusader chapel with frescoes, part of a medieval roadway and an ancient sign marking the presence of the Roman 10th Legion. Further in, metal steps lead down to the single surviving arch of

Some of the many and varied spices on sale at the Central Souk

Crowds of visitors and market traders outside Damascus Gate

*For hotels and restaurants in this area see p256 and p272*

the Roman gate, which gives access to the **Roman Square Excavations**. Here, the fascinating remains of the original Roman plaza, the starting point of the Roman Cardo, include a gaming board engraved in the paving stones. A hologram depicts Hadrian's column in the main plaza. It is possible to explore the upper levels of the gate as part of the ramparts walk *(see pp142–3)*.

## Herod's Gate ❾

**Map** 4 D1.

The Arabic and Hebrew names for this gate, Bab el-Zahra and Shaar ha-Prakhim respectively, both mean "Gate of Flowers", referring to the rosette above the arch. It came to be known as Herod's Gate in the 1500s, when Christian pilgrims wrongly thought that the house inside the gate was the palace of Herod the Great's son. It was via the original, now closed, entrance further east that the Crusaders entered the city and conquered it on 15 July 1099 *(see pp48–9)*.

## St Anne's Church ❿

2 Shaar ha-Arayot St. **Map** 4 E2.
**Tel** *(02) 628 3285.* ◯ *8am–noon & 2–6pm (winter: 5pm) daily.* 🖼

This beautiful Crusader church is a superb example of Romanesque architecture. It was constructed between 1131 and 1138 to replace a previous Byzantine church, and exists today in more or less its original form. It is traditionally believed that the church stands on the spot where Anne and Joachim, the

The 16th-century St Stephen's Gate, in the Old City's eastern wall

parents of the Virgin Mary, lived. The supposed remains of their house are in the crypt, which is also noted for its remarkable acoustics.

Shortly after the church was built, it was made larger by moving the façade forwards by several metres. The connection with the original church can still be seen in the first row of columns. In 1192, Saladin *(see pp48–9)* turned the church into a Muslim theological school. There is an inscription to this effect above the church's entrance. Later abandoned, the church fell into ruins, until the Ottomans donated it to France in 1856 and it was restored.

Next to the church are two cisterns that once lay outside the city walls. They were built in the 8th and 3rd centuries BC to collect rainwater. Some time later, under Herod the Great they were turned into curative baths. Ruins of a Roman temple, thought to have been to the god of medicine, can be seen here, as can those of a later Byzantine church built over the temple. It is also widely believed that this is the site of the Pool of Bethesda, described in St John's account of Christ curing a paralysed man (John 5: 1–15).

**Lion detail from St Stephen's Gate**

## St Stephen's Gate ⓫

**Map** 4 F2.

Suleyman the Magnificent built this gate in 1538. Its Arabic name, Bab Sitti Maryam (Gate of the Virgin Mary), refers to the Tomb of the Virgin in the nearby Valley of Jehoshaphat *(see p115)*. The Hebrew name, Shaar ha-Arayot, or Lions' Gate, refers to the two emblematic lions on either side of the gateway, although one school of thought insists that they are panthers. There are many different stories to explain the significance of the lions. One is that Suleyman the Magnificent had them carved in honour of the Mameluke emir Baybars and his successful campaign to rid the Holy Land of Crusaders. The name St Stephen's Gate was adopted in the Middle Ages by Christians who believed that the first Christian martyr, St Stephen, was executed here. Prior to that, however, it had been generally accepted that St Stephen had been stoned to death outside Damascus Gate.

The gate is also significant because of its more recent history, for it was through it that the Arab Legion penetrated the Old City in 1948 *(see p54)* and where Israeli paratroopers entered in 1967 *(see p54)*. It is an excellent starting point for the walk along the Via Dolorosa *(see p64)*.

**Archaeological site in front of St Anne's Church**

# Haram esh-Sharif ⑫

**Dome of the Prophet**

Haram esh-Sharif, the "Noble Sanctuary" or Temple Mount, is a vast rectangular esplanade in the southeastern part of the Old City. Traditionally the site of Solomon's Temple, it later housed the Second Temple, enlarged by Herod the Great and destroyed by the Romans *(see pp44–5)*. Left in ruins for more than half a century, the site became an Islamic shrine in AD 691 with the building of the Dome of the Rock. Over the centuries other buildings have been added to this, the third most important Islamic religious sanctuary.

**★ Dome of the Rock**
*This is the crowning glory not just of the Haram esh-Sharif but of all Jerusalem (see pp72–3).*

**Madrasa el-Omariyya** is one of several Mameluke-era schools on the Haram.

**Madrasa el-Isardiyya**

**Dome of the Prophet**

**Sabil of Qaitbey**
*This public fountain was built on the order of the Mameluke sultan Qaitbey (ruled 1468–98). It has a superb carved stone dome, the only one of its kind in the Holy Land.*

**Cotton Merchants' Gate** is a strikingly decorated Mameluke portal giving access to the market of the same name *(see p65)*.

**Chain Gate (Ha-Shalshelet)**

**Western Wall** *(see p85)*

**Moors' Gate** (Bab el-Maghariba) is one of only two gates that non-Muslims may use to enter the Haram.

**Grammar College**
*Also known as "The Dome of Learning", this still serves as a Quranic teaching school. The doorway on the north side is flanked by some unusual candy-twist columns dating from the Ayyubid era (1169–1250).*

**Museum of Islamic Art**
*This engraved Mameluke vessel is part of a collection of artifacts, largely from the Middle Ages, that includes Qurans, textiles, ceramics and weaponry (see p70).*

### ★ Dome of the Chain

*This small dome (see p71) stands at the approximate centre of the Haram esh-Sharif, which, according to one theory, equated to the centre of the world. The 13th-century tiling on the interior surpasses even that of the Dome of the Rock.*

**Asbat Minaret**

**Gate of the Tribes** (Bab el-Asbat) leads to the Via Dolorosa.

### Qanatir

*Each of the eight flights of steps up to the platform of the Dome of the Rock is topped by a qanatir, or free-standing arcade (see p70). Some of the column capitals were recycled from Roman-era buildings.*

**Golden Gate** is one of the original city gates *(see p71)* but was sealed up by the Muslims in the 7th century. The area is out of bounds.

### ★ El-Aqsa Mosque

*Originally built in the early years of the 8th century (see p70), El-Aqsa remains the main place of Islamic worship in Jerusalem and draws huge crowds of devout Muslims each Friday for noon prayer.*

**Crusader-built tower**

**Women's mosque**

### El-Kas Fountain

*Carved from a single block of stone and dating from 1320, this is the largest of the Haram's many old but still functioning ablutions fountains.*

### STAR FEATURES

★ Dome of the Rock

★ Dome of the Chain

★ El-Aqsa Mosque

# Exploring the Haram esh-Sharif

Stone
window,
El-Aqsa

Although the undoubted main attraction is
the Dome of the Rock, the Haram esh-
Sharif has a great many other features that
are worthy of attention. The esplanade acts
as a virtual museum of Islamic architecture,
beginning with the Dome, which dates back
to the Omayyad era and is the earliest
structure, and running through the Ayyubid
(Grammar College), Mameluke (numerous
*madrasas*) and Ottoman periods. Visitors
should be aware that certain parts of the Haram esh-
Sharif are out of bounds, notably the area south of the
Gate of the Tribes and east of El-Aqsa.

Antiquity-strewn area in front of
the Museum of Islamic Art

The much reconstructed interior of the El-Aqsa Mosque

## EL-AQSA MOSQUE

Construction of El-Aqsa
was begun less than 20 years
after the completion
of the Dome of the Rock.
However, unlike the Dome,
whose structure and interior
have remained intact over the
centuries, El-Aqsa has under-
gone great changes. In the
first 60 years of its existence
the mosque was twice razed
to the ground by earthquakes.
Its present form dates from the
early 11th century. When the
Crusaders captured Jerusalem
in 1099, El-Aqsa became the
headquarters of the Templars
*(see p49)*; their legacy remains
in the three central bays of
the main façade. As it appears
today, the façade has seven
bays; in the mid-14th century
the Mamelukes added an
extra two on either side of
the original Crusader porch.
 The interior is dominated
by mid-20th century addi-
tions, notably ranks of marble

columns, donated by Benito
Mussolini, and an elaborately
painted ceiling paid for by
King Farouk of Egypt. Older
elements include the mihrab,
decorated in 1187 under the
patronage of Saladin, and the
mosaics above the central
aisle arch and around the
drum of the dome, dating
from 1035. Until 1969, the
mosque had a fine carved
pulpit *(minbar)*, also dating
from the time of Saladin, but
this was lost in a fire started
by a deranged visitor.

A *qanatir*, topping a flight of steps up to the Dome

## MUSEUM OF ISLAMIC ART

Housed in the Crusader-era
refectory of the Knights
Templar, this sparsely-filled
museum contains objects
donated to the Haram esh-
Sharif over the centuries, as
well as architectural remnants
from many of the Haram's
buildings. Worthy of mention
are the precious large Qurans,
with pages adorned by fine
Islamic calligraphy; part of a
carved cypress-wood ceiling
from El-Aqsa, dating from the
7th century and removed in
1948; and fine 15th-century
copper doors from the Dome
of the Rock. Admission to the
museum is included in the
fee for the Dome of the Rock
and El-Aqsa Mosque.
 Visitors with an interest in
Islamic art should also visit
the LA Mayer Museum in the
new city *(see p130)*.

## THE QANATIRS

Eight short flights of steps
lead up to the platform on
which the Dome of the Rock
sits. All these stairways are of
different sizes and lengths,
and they all date from
different periods. The flight
opposite the Sabil of Qaitbey,
leading up to the main
entrance of the
Dome, is unique
in that it is carved
out of the stone
of the platform.
Each flight is
crowned by a
slender arcade
known as a
*qanatir*. An
alternative name
for the arches is
*mawazin*, or
scales, because
according to a

widely-accepted Muslim belief, on the day of the Last Judgment, the scales used by God to weigh the souls of humankind will be hung from these arches on the Haram.

## DOME OF THE CHAIN

Beside the dome of the Rock, the Haram has many other, smaller domes. The most impressive is the Dome of the Chain, immediately to the east of the Dome of the Rock. It is a simple structure of a domed roof supported on 17 columns. It originally had 20 columns but was remodelled to its current form by the Mameluke emir Baybars in the 13th century. The interior tiling is splendid (see p69). Some mystery exists over the purpose of the dome, but it is likely that it was a treasury. Its name derives from the legend that a chain once hung from the roof, and whoever told a lie while holding it would be struck dead by lightning.

## THE MADRASAS

Most of the buildings fringing the Haram are madrasas – Islamic colleges. Of these, the **Ashrafiyya** on the western side of the Haram, built in 1482 by Sultan Qaitbey, is a masterpiece of Islamic architecture. It has an especially ornate doorway exhibiting all the best elements of Mameluke design, including bands of different

coloured stone, stalactite carvings above the doorway and, on the benches on either side, intricate, interlocking stones known as "joggling".

Adjoining the Ashrafiyya to the north, close to the Sabil of Qaitbey, is another madrasa, the **Uthmaniyya**. Its upper section has beautiful wheel-shaped decorations formed by inlays of yellow and red stone. Along the northern edge of the Haram are two more, the triple-domed **Isardiyya** and adjacent **Malekiyya**. Both date from the 14th century. West of these two, in the corner, is the **Omariyya** college, which is held to contain the First Station of the Cross, but can only be entered from the Via Dolorosa (see pp30–31).

## JERUSALEM AND ISLAM

The Dome of the Rock and neighbouring El-Aqsa Mosque represent the first great religious complex in the history of Islam. Although Muslims venerate many of the same prophets as the Jews and Christians, notably Abraham (Ibrahim to the Muslims), Jerusalem itself is never mentioned in the Quran. The choice of this site was more likely a political issue. In locating his mosque on the site of the Temple, the caliph Abd el-Malik meant to reinforce the idea that the new religion of Islam, and its worldly empire, was the successor and continuation of those of the Jews and the Christians. It was only later that Jerusalem came to be tied into Islamic tradition through the story of the Night Journey (see p27). In this, Muhammad visits el-masjid el-aqsa, which means literally "the most distant mosque", and this name was retroactively applied to the whole Haram esh-Sharif before later being restricted to the mosque only.

**Angel with Muhammad's robe on the Night Journey**

## GOLDEN GATE

Also known as the Gate of Mercy (Bab el-Rahma), the Golden Gate was one of the original Herodian city gates. According to Jewish tradition, the Messiah will enter Jerusalem through this gate, which is said to be the reason why the Muslims walled it up in the 7th century. The existing structure dates to the Omayyad period and is best viewed from outside the city walls.

The domed fountain, the Sabil of Qaitbey, with part of the Ashrafiyya Madrasa in the background

# Dome of the Rock

**Tile above the south entrance**

One of the first and greatest achievements of Islamic architecture, the Dome of the Rock was built in AD 688–91 by the Omayyad caliph Abd el-Malik. Intended to proclaim the superiority of Islam and provide an Islamic focal point in the Holy City, the majestic structure now dominates Jerusalem and has become a symbol of the city. More a shrine than a mosque, the mathematically harmonious building echoes elements of Classical and Byzantine architecture, including the rotunda of the Holy Sepulchre *(see pp92–5)*.

View of the Dome of the Rock with the Muslim Quarter in the background

**The drum** is decorated with tiles and verses from the Quran which tell of Muhammad's Night Journey.

★ **Tilework**
*The multicoloured tiles that adorn the exterior are faithful copies of Persian tiles that Suleyman the Magnificent added in 1545 to replace the badly damaged original mosaics.*

**Quranic verses**

**The octagonal arcade** is adorned with original mosaics (AD 692) and an inscription inviting Christians to recognize the truth of Islam.

**Marble panel**

**Inner Ambulatory**
*The space between the inner and outer arcades forms an ambulatory around the Rock. The shrine's two ambulatories recall the ritual circular movement of pilgrims around the Qaaba in Mecca.*

**STAR FEATURES**

★ Interior of Dome

★ Tilework

**Dome**
The dome was originally made of copper but is now covered with gold leaf thanks to the financial support of the late King Hussein of Jordan.

**★ Interior of Dome**
The dazzling interior of the cupola has elaborate floral decoration as well as various inscriptions. The large text commemorates Saladin, who sponsored restoration work on the building.

**Green and gold mosaics** create a scintillating effect on the walls below the dome.

**Outer ambulatory**

**Well of Souls**
This staircase leads down to a chamber under the Rock known as the Well of Souls. The dead are said to meet here twice a month to pray.

**Stained-glass window**

**Each outer wall** is 20.4 m (67 ft) long. This exactly matches the dome's diameter and its height from the base of the drum.

**South entrance**

**The Rock**
The Rock is variously believed to be where Abraham was asked to sacrifice Isaac, where Muhammad left the Earth on his Night Journey (see p27), and the site of the Holy of Holies of Herod's Temple (see pp44–5).

Geometric tiling and verses from the Quran on the exterior of the Dome of the Rock ▷

# THE JEWISH QUARTER

In Herodian times this area abutted the Temple enclosure (*see pp44–5*) and was occupied by the priestly elite. In the late Roman period, Jews were forbidden from living in Jerusalem, but under the more tolerant Arab rule a small community was re-established here. The district became prevalently Jewish during Ottoman rule, when it acquired its present name. By the 16th century, pilgrimage to the Western Wall – the only surviving remnant of the Temple – had become a strong tradition. After the destruction wrought in the 1948 War and the subsequent years of Jordanian occupation, the Jewish Quarter was taken by Israeli troops in 1967, and reconstruction work began soon afterwards. A great many ruins from ancient periods were uncovered below more recent buildings. These remains were made accessible to the public, so that the Jewish Quarter of today stands as a fascinating, living mix of more than 2,000 years of Jerusalem Jewry.

**Ark in a Jewish Quarter synagogue**

## SIGHTS AT A GLANCE

**Archaeological Sites**
The Broad Wall ②
The Cardo ①
Israelite Tower ⑩
Jerusalem Archaeological
    Park ⑮
St Mary of the Germans ⑬

**Museums**
Ariel Centre for Jerusalem in
    the First Temple Period ⑪
The Burnt House ⑫
Old Yishuv Court Museum ⑨
Wohl Archaeological
    Museum ⑥

**Holy Places**
Dung Gate ⑭
Ramban Synagogue ④
The Sephardic Synagogues ⑧
The Western Wall ⑯

**Streets and Squares**
Batei Makhase Square ⑦
Hurva Square ③
Tiferet Yisrael
    Street ⑤

**KEY**

Street-by-Street map
See pp78–9

Taxi rank

Bus station

City wall

0 metres 100
0 yards 100

## GETTING THERE

The Jewish Quarter is most easily reached on foot via Jaffa Gate and the Armenian Quarter. Buses No. 1 and 2 stop at Western Wall Plaza. Drivers can enter the Old City by Jaffa, Zion or Dung gates and park at the bottom of Khabad St.

◁ **Orthodox Jews praying at the Western Wall**

# Street-by-Street: Around Hurva Square

Jewish Quarter sign

Extensively reconstructed since 1967 and largely residential, the Jewish Quarter is noticeably more orderly than the rest of the Old City. It is also relatively free of large groups of tourists. The focal point for the local community is Hurva Square. This has a few small shops and cafés with outdoor seating. Most of the interesting sights in the quarter are just a few minutes' walk from here. Another hub of the district is the Cardo and Jewish Quarter Road area, which is filled with souvenir shops and more places to eat.

Looking towards Hurva Square from Jewish Quarter Road

Cardo shopping arcade

The Sidna Omar minaret is all that remains of a 14th-century mosque.

★ **The Cardo**
*This is an excavated and partially reconstructed section of the main street of Byzantine-era Jerusalem* ❶

**The Sephardic Synagogues**
*Two of these four synagogues date back to the early 17th century. They all contain much ornate decoration* ❽

Rothschild House

**Batei Makhase Square**
*A small secluded square, this is favoured by local children as a play area. Its most notable feature is the elegant 19th-century Rothschild House, with its arcaded façade* ❼

BATEI MAKHASE SQUARE

Shelter Houses
(see p82)

**Ramban Synagogue**
*Founded around 1400, the Ramban was the first major synagogue to be built here since the Romans expelled the Jews from Jerusalem* ➍

**The Broad Wall**
*Archaeologists have dated these remains to the 8th century BC* ➋

**LOCATOR MAP**
See Jerusalem Street Finder, maps 3 and 4

Hurva Synagogue (see pp80–1)

Muslim Quarter

★ **Hurva Square**
*The area's main square is dominated by Hurva Synagogue, which is currently undergoing extensive and lengthy renovations* ➌

Western Wall

**Tiferet Yisrael Street**
*This lively street heads towards the Western Wall, passing the ruined 19th-century Tiferet Yisrael Synagogue* ➎

Western Wall and St Mary of the Germans

★ **Wohl Archaeological Museum**
*Located under a modern housing block, the Wohl contains archaeological remains of Jewish dwellings from the era of Herod the Great* ➏

**KEY**

– – – Suggested route

**STAR SIGHTS**

★ The Cardo

★ Hurva Square

★ Wohl Archaeological Museum

0 metres    25
0 yards     25

# The Cardo ❶

**Map** 3 C4.

Now in part an exclusive shopping arcade, the Cardo was Jerusalem's main thoroughfare in the Byzantine era. It was originally laid by the Romans, then extended in the 4th century as Christian pilgrims began to flock to Jerusalem and the city expanded accordingly. The Byzantine extension, which remains in evidence today, linked the two major places of worship of the time, the Church of the Holy Sepulchre *(see pp92–7)* in the north and the long-since-vanished Nea Basilica *(see p82)* in the south.

The central roadway of the Byzantine Cardo was 12.5 m (41 ft) wide. This was flanked by broad porticoed pavements and lined with shops. Visitors can get a good idea of how the area once looked by descending to a reconstructed section, which runs for almost 200 m (650 ft) alongside Jewish Quarter (Ha-Yehudim) Road. At the southern end are the remains of original shops that were partly hewn out of the rock on the west side of the street.

The Cardo's continued importance during the reign of Justinian in the 6th century is attested to by its prominent appearance on the famous Madaba map *(see pp216–17)*. Some 500 years later, in the Crusader era, the Cardo was converted into a covered market, which is how the northern section has now been preserved, as an arcade of smart galleries and boutiques.

The Broad Wall, part of the city's 8th-century BC fortifications

# The Broad Wall ❷

Plugat ha-Kotel Street. **Map** 3 C4.

The Jewish quarter was largely destroyed during the 1948 War and allowed to deteriorate further under Jordanian occupation. Following the 1967 Israeli victory, a vast reconstruction programme resulted in many significant archaeological finds. One of these was the unearthing of the foundations of a wall 7 m (22 ft) thick and 65 m (215 ft) long. This was possibly part of fortifications built by King Hezekiah in the 8th century BC to enclose a new quarter outside the previous city wall. The need for expansion was probably brought about by a flood of refugees after the Assyrian invasion of 722 BC.

On the building next to the exposed wall, a clearly visible line indicates what archaeologists think was the original height of the wall. Also visible are the remains of housing from the same period, demolished to make way for the wall, as described in the Book of Isaiah (22: 10), "And ye have numbered the houses of Jerusalem, and the houses have ye broken down to fortify the wall".

# Hurva Square ❸

**Map** 3 C4.

This is the heart and social centre of the present-day Jewish Quarter. In the maze of narrow, winding streets which, though modern, follow the topography of the quarter before its destruction, Hurva Square is one of the few open spaces in the area. It has cafés, souvenir shops and a few snack bars that have small tables outside when the weather is good. Also here is the **Jewish Students' Information Centre**, which provides help with accommodation and invitations to Shabbat (Sabbath) dinners for visiting young Jews.

On the west side of the square is the minaret of the long-since vanished 14th-century Mameluke **Mosque of Sidna Omar**, along with the historic Hurva and Ramban synagogue complexes. Hurva means "ruins" and the history of the **Hurva Synagogue** more than justifies its name. In the 18th century a group of a few hundred Ashkenazi Jews from Poland came to Jerusalem and founded a synagogue on this site. However, it was burnt down by creditors angered by the community's unpaid debts. The synagogue was rebuilt in 1864 in a Neo-Byzantine style. However, during the fighting that took place in 1948 between the Arab and Jewish armies, the synagogue was destroyed. After the Israelis recaptured

**Sidna Omar minaret**

The Cardo, the main street of Byzantine-era Jerusalem

Hurva Square, the social and commercial hub of the Jewish Quarter

the Old City in 1967, a single arch of the synagogue's main façade was reconstructed. Currently, work on the structure is underway again and it is expected that by 2010 the renovations will have been completed.

# Ramban Synagogue ❹

Hurva Square. **Map** 3 C4. ☐ *for morning and evening prayers.* ♿

When the Spanish rabbi and scholar Moses Ben Nahman (Nahmanides) arrived in Jerusalem in 1267, he was shocked to find only a handful of Jews in the city. He dedicated himself to nurturing a Jewish community and bought land near King David's Tomb on Mount Zion in order to build a synagogue. Some time around 1400, the synagogue was moved to its present site. It was perhaps the first time there had been a Jewish presence in this quarter of the Old City since the exile of the Jews in AD 135. The synagogue had to be rebuilt in 1523 after it collapsed. It is believed that, at this time, it was probably the only Jewish place of worship in what was then Ottoman-controlled Jerusalem. In 1599 the authorities banned the Jews from worship in the synagogue and the building became a workshop. It was not until the Israelis took control of the Old City in 1967 that it was restored as a place of worship.

# Tiferet Yisrael Street ❺

**Map** 4 D4.

This is one of the busiest streets in the Jewish Quarter. It connects Hurva Square with the stairs that descend towards the Western Wall. Partway along is the shell of the ruined **Tiferet Yisrael Synagogue**, destroyed in the 1948 War and left gutted as a memorial. Sectarian feelings run high around here, and local souvenir shops stock contentious items such as Israeli Army T-shirts and postcards of the Haram esh-Sharif with its mosques replaced by the "future Third Temple". The street ends in an attractive tree-shaded square which has several

Tiferet Yisrael Street, one of the liveliest thoroughfares in the Jewish Quarter

snack bars and cafés, including the popular Quarter Café, which serves kosher food and offers great views of the Haram esh-Sharif and Dome of the Rock from its terrace.

# Wohl Archaeological Museum ❻

1 Ha-Karaim Street. **Map** 4 D4. *Tel* (02) 628 3448. ☐ 9am–5pm Sun–Thu, 9am–1pm Fri. 🖼 🚫

In the era of Herod the Great (37–4 BC), the area of the present-day Jewish Quarter was part of a wealthy "Upper City", occupied for the most part by the families of important Jewish priests. During post-1967 redevelopment, the remains of several large houses were unearthed here. This rediscovered Herodian quarter now lies from 3 to 7 m (10 to 22 ft) below street level, underneath a modern building, and is preserved as the Wohl Archaeological Museum.

The museum is remarkable for its vivid evocation of everyday life 2,000 years ago. All the houses had an inner courtyard, ritual baths, and cisterns to collect rain, which was the only source of water at the time. The first part of the museum, called the Western House, has a mosaic in the vestibule and a well-preserved ritual bath (*mikveh*). Beyond this is the Middle Complex, the remains of two separate houses where archaeologists found a maze-pattern mosaic floor covered in burnt wood; this, they surmised, was fire damage from the Roman siege of Jerusalem in AD 70. The most complete of all the Herodian buildings is the Palatial Mansion, with more splendid mosaic floors and ritual baths.

The entrance fee to the Wohl Museum also covers admission to the Burnt House (*see p84*).

## Batei Makhase Square ❼

**Map** 4 D5.

This quiet square is named after the so-called Shelter Houses (Batei Makhase), which lie just south of it. They were built in 1862 by Jews from Germany and Holland for destitute immigrants from central Europe. Tenants were chosen by lottery and charged little or no rent. Severe damage in the 1948 and 1967 wars made restoration necessary.

The work brought to light the first remains of the Nea (New) Basilica, whose existence had previously been known only from the Madaba map *(see pp216–17)* and literary sources. Built by Byzantine emperor Justinian in AD 543, it was at the time the largest basilica in Palestine. The remains of one of the apses can be seen near the square's southwest corner. Although other remains are sparse, archaeologists have now been able to trace the basilica's full extent – an enormous 100 m (328 ft) by 52 m (171 ft).

The handsome, arcaded building on the western side of the square was built for the Rothschild family in 1871. In front of it are parts of Roman columns, whose original provenance is unknown.

The 17th-century Ben Zakkai Synagogue

## The Sephardic Synagogues ❽

Ha-Tupim Street. **Map** 3 C5. **Tel** *(02) 628 0592.* ⭘ *9:30am–4pm Sun–Thu, 9:30am–12.30pm Fri.* 📷

The four synagogues in this group became the spiritual centre of the area's Sephardic community in the 17th century. The Sephardim were descended from the Jews expelled from Spain in 1492 and Portugal in 1497. They had first settled in the Ottoman Empire and then moved to Palestine when the latter was conquered by the Turks in 1516. When the first two synagogues were built, the Sephardim formed the largest Jewish community in Jerusalem. The synagogue floors were laid well below street level to allow sufficient

*Bimah from the Istambuli Synagogue*

height for the buildings, as Ottoman law stated that synagogues should not rise above the surrounding houses.

The **Ben Zakkai Synagogue** was built in 1610. Its courtyard, with a matroneum, or gallery for women worshippers, was converted into the **Central Synagogue**, whose present form dates from the 1830s. The **Prophet Elijah Synagogue**, created from a study hall built in 1625, was consecrated in 1702. Legend has it that during prayers to mark Yom Kippur, Elijah appeared as the 10th adult male worshipper needed for synagogue prayer – hence the building's name. The **Istambuli Synagogue** was built in 1857 and, like the other three, contains furnishings salvaged from Italian synagogues damaged in World War II.

## Old Yishuv Court Museum ❾

6 Or ha-Khayim Street. **Map** 3 C5. **Tel** *(02) 627 6319.* ⭘ *10am–3pm Sun–Thu, 10am–1pm Fri.* 📷 🚫

This small museum, devoted to the history of the city's Jewish community from the mid-19th century to the end of Ottoman rule in 1917, occupies one of the oldest complexes of rooms in the Jewish Quarter. Of Turkish construction, thought to date from the 15th or 16th centuries, it was once part of a private home. The exhibits, consisting largely of reconstructed interiors, memorabilia and photographs, also include the Ari Synagogue on the ground floor. This was used by a Sephardic congregation during most of the Ottoman period. Badly damaged in the fighting of 1936, it fell into disuse until 1967, when it was restored. On the top floor is the

Rothschild House and a Roman column base and capital in Batei Makhase Square

**Household objects on display at the Old Yishuv Court Museum**

18th-century Or ha-Khayim Synagogue, used by Ashkenazi Jews in the 19th century. Closed between 1948 and 1967, it is now a functioning synagogue once more.

## Israelite Tower ⑩

Shonei Halakhot Street. **Map** 4 D4. ◯ 9am–5pm Sun–Thu, 9am–1pm Fri. ✎

Steps at the corner of Shonei Halakhot and Plugat ha-Kotel streets lead underneath a modern apartment block to the remains of a tower of the 7th century BC. The tower, the walls of which are over 4 m (13 ft) thick and survive to a height of 8 m (26 ft), is believed to have been part of a gateway in the Israelite city wall. At its foot were found

the heads of Israelite and Babylonian arrows, as well as evidence of burning. These finds are thought to date from the Babylonian conquest of Jerusalem in 586 BC (see p42) and may identify the gate as the one through which Babylonian troops entered the city (Jeremiah 39: 3). The other visible remains belong to the 2nd-century BC Hasmonean city wall, another section of which can be seen at the Citadel (see pp102–5).

The apartment block above was built on stilts, as were other modern buildings in the Jewish Quarter, to allow access by archaeologists. However, the need to rebuild rapidly after the 1948 War meant that there was insufficient time to uncover many of the remains and draw a complete plan of the area's fortifications.

## Ariel Centre for Jerusalem in the First Temple Period ⑪

Bonei Hahomah Street. **Map** 4 D4. **Tel** (02) 628 6288. ◯ 9am–4pm Sun–Thu (Jul & Aug 9am–6pm Sun–Thu, 9am–1pm Fri). ✎ **www**.ybz.org.il

The principal exhibit here is a model of all the archaeological remains of First Temple Period Jerusalem (around the 8th century BC). It illustrates the relationship between remains, which can be difficult to interpret when they are seen on the ground surrounded by other buildings. It also shows the original topography of the area before valleys were filled in and occupation layers built up. An audiovisual show describes the city's history from 1000 to 586 BC.

There is also a display of finds from a secret dig carried out in 1909–11 by English archaeologist Captain Montague Parker. His team of excavators penetrated underneath the Haram esh-Sharif in search of a chamber that reputedly contained King Solomon's treasure. When news of the dig got out, violent demonstrations by Jews and Muslims, united in their opposition to the desecration of their holy site, forced Parker to flee the city.

---

### JEWISH QUARTER ARCHITECTURE

Heavily damaged during the 1948 War, the Jewish Quarter has been almost totally reconstructed in recent times. While there is no distinct "Jewish style", the quarter's modern architecture belongs to a well-defined Jerusalem tradition. First and foremost, everything is constructed of the pale local stone. Use of this stone has been mandatory in Jerusalem since a law to this effect was passed by the British military governor, Ronald Storrs, in 1917. Buildings and street patterns are deliberately asymmetrical to evoke haphazard historical development. Streets are also narrow and cobbled, with many small courtyards and external staircases to upper levels. Buildings make great use of traditional Middle Eastern elements such as arches, domes and oriels (the high bay windows supported on brackets, much favoured by Mameluke builders). A jumble of

**Modern additions harmonise with traditional styles**

different heights means that the roof of one building is often the terrace of another. The result is a very contemporary look, which is at the same time firmly rooted in the past.

# The Burnt House

Tiferet Yisrael Street. **Map** 4 D4.
*Tel (02) 628 7211.* 9am–4:20pm Sun– Thu, 9am–12:20pm Fri. *phone in advance.*

In AD 70 the Romans took Jerusalem and destroyed the Temple and Lower City to the south. A month later they rampaged through the wealthy Upper City, setting fire to the houses. The charred walls and a coin dated to AD 69 discovered during excavations show that this was one of those houses.

A stone weight found among the debris bears the inscription "son of Kathros", indicating that the house belonged to a wealthy family of high priests. They are known from a subsequent reference to them in the Babylonian Talmud, written between the 3rd and 6th century AD.

The rooms on view, introduced by a slide show with commentary, comprise a kitchen, four rooms that may have been bedrooms, and a bathroom with a ritual bath. It is believed that these formed part of a much larger residence, but further excavations cannot be undertaken as the remains lie beneath present-day neighbouring houses.

The entrance fee also covers the Wohl Archaeological Museum *(see p81).*

Surviving walls of the Crusader-built St Mary of the Germans

## St Mary of the Germans

Misgav la-Dakh Street. **Map** 4 D4. *daily.*

Immediately below the terrace of Tiferet Yisrael's Quarter Café are the original walls of St Mary of the Germans. This early 12th-century Crusader church was part of a complex that included a pilgrims' hospice (no longer in existence) and a hospital. It was built by the Knights Hospitallers *(see p49)* and run by their German members. This was in response to the influx of German-speaking pilgrims unfamiliar with French, the lingua franca, or Latin, the official language, of the new Latin Kingdom of Jerusalem. Activity ceased when Jerusalem fell to the Muslims in 1187, but the church and the hospital were again used during the brief period when Jerusalem was once more under Christian rule (1229–44).

Today the church is roofless. However, the walls survive to a considerable height, showing clearly the three apses of the typical basilica plan so widely used in the Holy Land from early Byzantine times.

Dung Gate, leading to the Western Wall

Beside the church is a flight of steps down to the Western Wall Plaza. These provide wonderful views of the Western Wall, the Dome of the Rock and the Mount of Olives behind.

## Dung Gate

**Map** 4 D5.

In old photographs the Dung Gate is shown to be hardly any larger than a doorway in the average domestic house. Its name in Hebrew is Shaar ha-Ashpot, and it is mentioned in the Book of Nehemiah (2: 13) in the Old Testament. It is probably named after the ash that was taken from the Temple to be deposited outside the city walls. The Arab name is Bab Silwan, because this is the gate that leads to the Arab village of Silwan.

The gate was enlarged by the Jordanians in 1948 to allow vehicles to pass through. It is now the main entrance and exit for the Jewish Quarter, but it still remains the smallest of all the Old City gates. It retains its old Ottoman carved arch with a stone flower above.

## Jerusalem Archaeological Park

See pp86–7.

The outline of rooms and some of the artifacts unearthed at the Burnt House

# The Western Wall ⑯

Western Wall Plaza. **Map** 4 D4.
🚌 *1, 2, 38.* ♿ 📷 *on Sabbath.*
**Chain of the Generations Centre**
**Tel** *(1-599) 515 888.* ⏲ *8am–8pm
Sun–Thu, 8am–noon Fri. Visits must
be booked in advance.* ◑ *Jewish
hols.* 📷 📹 *compulsory.* **Western
Wall Tunnel Tel** *(1-599) 515 888.*
⏲ *8am–evening Sun–Thu; 8am–
12:30pm Fri. Visits must be booked
in advance.* ◑ *Jewish hols.* 📷 📹
*compulsory.* **www**.thekotel.org

A massive, blank wall
built of huge stone blocks,
the Western Wall (Ha-Kotel
in Hebrew) is Judaism's
holiest site, and the plaza
in front of it is a permanent
place of worship. The wall
is part of the retaining wall
of the Temple Mount and
was built by Herod the Great
during his expansion of the
Temple enclosure *(see
pp44–5)*. The huge, lower
stones are Herodian, while
those higher up date from
early Islamic times.

During the Ottoman period,
the wall became where
Jews came to lament the
destruction of the Second
Temple. For this reason it
was for centuries known as
the Wailing Wall.

Houses covered most of
what's now the Western Wall
Plaza until relatively recently.
When the Israelis gained
control of the Old City after
the 1967 war, they levelled
the neighbouring Arab district.

---

## WORSHIP AT THE WESTERN WALL

The Western Wall Plaza
functions as a large,
open-air synagogue
where groups gather to
recite the daily, Shabbat
(Sabbath) and festival
services of the Jewish
faith. Special events are
also celebrated here, such
as the religious coming
of age of a boy or girl
(Bar or Bat Mitzvah).

Prayers inserted into gaps between
the stones of the Western Wall

Some worshippers visit the wall daily to recite the entire
Book of Psalms; others, who believe that petitions to God
made at the wall are specially effective, insert written
prayers into the stones. On Tisha B'Av, the ninth day of
the month of Av, which falls in either July or August, a fast
is held commemorating the destruction of both Temples
*(see pp42–5)*. People sit on the ground reciting
the Book of Lamentations and liturgical
dirges called *kinot*. Since the plaza is
essentially a public space, conflicts arise
over such issues as the relative size of the
men's and women's sections and the wish of
non-Orthodox groups to hold services in which
men and women participate together.

Orthodox Jew at prayer beside the Western Wall

---

Non-Jews can approach
the wall, provided they dress
appropriately and cover their
heads *(see pp298–9)*.

At the left-hand corner of
the men's prayer section is
Wilson's Arch (named after a
19th-century archaeologist).
Now contained within a
building that functions
as a synagogue, it originally
carried the Causeway to the
Temple. From the arch,

archaeologists have dug the
**Western Wall Tunnel** to explore the wall's foundations.
It follows the base of the
outside face of the Temple
wall along a Herodian street,
below today's street level, and
emerges on the Via Dolorosa.
The **Chain of the Generations
Centre** tells the story of the
Jewish people. Access to this
and the Tunnel is by tour
only; book well in advance.

The Western Wall Plaza, with the men's prayer section to the left and women's to the right

# Jerusalem Archaeological Park ⑮

**Exhibit at the Davidson Center**

The area south of the Western Wall and Haram esh-Sharif is one of the most important archaeological sites in all Jerusalem. Excavations, ongoing here since 1968, have uncovered remains dating back to the First and Second Temple periods (*see pp41–2*), and through Byzantine times to the Omayyad era. In this one small, L-shaped site, the entire sweep of the history of the ancient city is revealed. The new Davidson Center provides a multi-media introduction to the site and contextualizes the archaeologists' findings.

**The Western Wall Plaza** *(see p85)*

**Robinson's Arch**
*A row of stones projecting from the wall is the remains of an arch that once supported a flight of stairs, as shown in this model at the Tower of David Museum (see pp102–5).*

**Ritual Bath (Mikveh)**
*The baths are where worshippers purified themselves before approaching the Temple. The divider, running down the centre of the stairs, ensured the separation of the clean and the unclean.*

**The Western Wall** is a part of the retaining wall of the Temple Mount, which runs south into the Archaeological Park.

**Dung Gate**

**Herodian Street**
*At the base of the Temple Mount is a flagged street dating from the time of the Second Temple. It would have been lined with shops – four small doorways have been reconstructed.*

**★ Davidson Center**
*This new subterranean exhibition centre contains artifacts from the site and screens two informative films, plus a computer-animated recreation of the Second Temple.*

## EARLY EXCAVATORS

Before the archaeologists, the Temple Mount area drew the attentions of 19th-century biblical scholars. The American Edward Robinson (1794–1863) was the first to identify the huge arch that is now named after him. The first serious excavations were made by the British officer Captain Charles Warren, who discovered a series of underground tunnels, as well as the nearby water shaft that carries his name *(see p115).*

**Charles Warren, 1840–1927**

### VISITORS' CHECKLIST

Batei Makhase Street, Jewish Quarter. *Tel (02) 627 7550.* www.archpark.il ◯ 8am–5pm Sun–Thu, 8am– 2pm Fri. ● Sat & Jewish holidays. 🖼 📷 💳 Guided tours last 1 hr and must be booked in advance. The computer-animated reconstruction of the Second Temple screened in the Davidson Center may only be viewed as part of a guided tour.

### Temple Mount
*The great retaining wall of the Temple Mount dates from the reign of Herod (37–4 BC). To see what the complex would have looked like at this time, turn to pages 44–5.*

**El-Aqsa Mosque**

**Crusader-era tower** partially obscuring the Double Gate *(see below).*

### ★ Hulda Gates
*At the top of a monumental flight of steps, a Double Gate and Triple Gate (together known as the Hulda Gates) provided access to the precincts of the Second Temple. They were later walled up by the Romans.*

**Old City walls, from the reign of Suleyman the Great**

### Omayyad Palace
*A canopy covers what was the central courtyard of an Omayyad-era palace. The building would have filled the area between the Temple Mount and the city walls.*

### STAR SIGHTS

★ Davidson Center

★ Hulda Gates

# THE CHRISTIAN AND ARMENIAN QUARTERS

Under Byzantine rule the Christian community of Jerusalem expanded rapidly. Settlement was concentrated in the northwest corner of the city, in the shadow of the great basilica of the Holy Sepulchre. Bounded by Souk Khan el-Zeit and David Street,

**Old City sign made of Armenian tiles**

the modern quarter remains filled with the churches, patriarchates and hospices of the city's many Christian denominations. To the south is the area traditionally inhabited by the Armenians, who have a long history in Jerusalem. It is one of the quietest parts of the Old City.

## SIGHTS AT A GLANCE

### Museums
The Citadel pp102–4 **9**
Mardigian Museum **14**
Museum of the Greek
   Orthodox Patriarchate **7**

### Churches
Alexander Hospice **2**
Church of the Holy Sepulchre
   pp92–5 **1**
Church of St John
   the Baptist **5**
Lutheran Church of
   the Redeemer **3**
St James's Cathedral **13**
St Mark's Church **12**

### Historic Areas, Streets and Gates
Christian Quarter Road **6**
Jaffa Gate **8**
Muristan **4**
Omar ibn el-Khattab Square **10**
Zion Gate **15**

### Walks
A Walk on the Roofs **11**

## GETTING THERE
These two quarters are served mainly by Jaffa Gate; a great many buses from the New City halt just outside. The area can also be entered from Zion and New gates. Zion Gate has parking just outside.

## KEY

| | |
|---|---|
| ▨ | Street-by-Street map See pp90–1 |
| ℹ | Tourist information |
| 🚖 | Taxi rank |
| — | City wall |

Christian Quarter

Armenian Quarter

0 metres 150
0 yards 150

◁ **Pilgrims crowding outside the main doorway of the Church of the Holy Sepulchre**

# Street-by-Street: The Christian Quarter

**Capital from the Church of the Redeemer**

The most visited part of the Old City, the Christian Quarter is a head-on collision between commerce and spirituality. At its heart is the Church of the Holy Sepulchre, the most sacred of all Christian sites. It is surrounded by such a clutter of churches and hospices that all one can see of its exterior are the domes and entrance façade. The nearby streets are filled with shops and stalls that thrive on the pilgrim trade. Respite from the crowds can be found in the cafés of Muristan Road.

The Christian Quarter, centred on the Holy Sepulchre

**Church of St John the Baptist**
*The founding of the Crusader Knights Hospitallers is connected with this small church. A carved stone cross echoes the order's historic emblem* ❺

**Christian Quarter Road**
*Along with David Street, this is the quarter's main shopping thoroughfare. It specializes in religious items and quality handicrafts* ❻

**David Street**
*From the Jaffa Gate area, David Street is the main route down through the Old City. This cramped, stepped alley doubles as a busy tourist bazaar.*

Jaffa Gate

**★ Muristan**
*The intersecting avenues of the Muristan were created when the Greek Orthodox Church redeveloped the area in 1903* ❹

| 0 metres | 30 |
| 0 yards | 30 |

For hotels in this area see p256

**★ Church of the Holy Sepulchre**
*The Stabat Mater Altar is one of numerous chapels and shrines that fill the church, which commemorates the Crucifixion and burial of Christ* ❶

**Omar Mosque**
*(see p99)*

**Khanqa Salahiyya**
*(see p99)*

**LOCATOR MAP**
*See Jerusalem Street Finder, map 3*

**Souk el-Dabbagha**
*With the Holy Sepulchre church at the end of the street, the few shops here have no shortage of customers for their religious souvenirs.*

**Ethiopian Monastery**
*(see p95)*

**Zalatimo's** is a famed confectionery shop; its storeroom contains remains of the doorway of the original 4th-century Holy Sepulchre church.

**Alexander Hospice**
*Belonging to the Russian Orthodox Church, the hospice is built over ruins of the early Holy Sepulchre church* ❷

SOUK EL-DABBAGHA

SOUK KHAN EL-ZEIT

**KEY**

– – – Suggested route

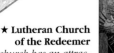

**★ Lutheran Church of the Redeemer**
*This church has an attractive medieval cloister, but most people visit for the views from the bell tower* ❸

**STAR SIGHTS**

★ Church of the Holy Sepulchre

★ Lutheran Church of the Redeemer

★ Muristan

# Church of the Holy Sepulchre ●

Built around what is believed to be the site of Christ's Crucifixion, burial and Resurrection, this complex church is the most important in Christendom. The first basilica here was built by Roman emperor Constantine between AD 326 and 335 at the suggestion of his mother, St Helena. It was rebuilt on a smaller scale by Byzantine emperor Constantine Monomachus in the 1040s following its destruction by Fatimid sultan Hakim in 1009, but was much enlarged again by the Crusaders between 1114 and 1170. A disastrous fire in 1808 and an earthquake in 1927 necessitated extensive repairs.

The mosaic of roofs and domes of the Church of the Holy Sepulchre

**The Rotunda,** heavily rebuilt after the 1808 fire, is the most majestic part of the church.

### ★ Christ's Tomb

*For Christians, this is the most sacred site of all. Inside the 1810 monument, a marble slab covers the rock on which Christ's body is believed to have been laid.*

**The Crusader bell tower** was reduced by two storeys in 1719.

### Stone of Unction

*This is where the anointing and wrapping of Christ's body after his death has been commemorated since medieval times. The present stone dates from 1810.*

**Chapel of the Franks**

**The main entrance** is early 12th century. The right-hand door was blocked up late in the same century.

### Courtyard

*The main entrance court-yard is flanked by chapels. The disused steps opposite the bell tower once led to the Chapel of the Franks, the Crusaders' ceremonial entrance to Golgotha.*

## THE HOLY FIRE

On the Saturday of Orthodox Easter, all the church's lamps are put out and the faithful stand in the dark, a symbol of the darkness at the Crucifixion. A candle is lit at Christ's Tomb, then another and another, until the entire basilica and courtyard are ablaze with light to symbolize the Resurrection. Legend says the fire comes from heaven.

**The Easter ceremony of the Holy Fire**

## VISITORS' CHECKLIST

Entrance from Souk el-Dabbagha. **Map** 3 C3. **Tel** (02) 627 3314. ☐ summer: 5am–9pm daily; winter: 4am–7pm daily.

**The Seven Arches** of the Virgin are the remains of an 11th-century colonnaded courtyard.

**Catholikon Dome**
*Rebuilt after the 1927 earthquake and decorated with an image of Christ, this dome covers the central nave of the Crusader church. This part of the building is now used for Greek Orthodox services.*

**The Centre of the World**, according to ancient map-makers *(see p40)*, is marked here by a stone basin.

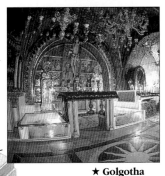

★ **Golgotha**
*Through the glass around the Greek Orthodox altar can be seen the outcrop of rock venerated as the site of the Crucifixion.*

**Chapel of Adam** *(see p94)*

**Rock of Golgotha** *(see p94)*

**The Chapel of St Helena** is now dedicated to St Gregory the Illuminator, patron of the Armenians.

**Ethiopian Monastery**
*A cluster of small buildings on the roof of the Chapel of St Helena is inhabited by a community of Ethiopian monks.*

## STAR FEATURES

★ Christ's Tomb

★ Golgotha

**Stairs to the Inventio Crucis Chapel (see p95)**

# Exploring the Church of the Holy Sepulchre

**Chapel door, main courtyard**

The reconstructions and additions that have shaped this church over the centuries make it a complex building to explore. Its division into chapels and spaces allotted to six different denominations adds a further sense of confusion. The interior is dimly lit, and queues often form at Christ's Tomb, so that the time each person can spend inside the shrine may be limited to just a few minutes. Nonetheless, the experience of standing on Christianity's most hallowed ground inspires many visitors with a deep sense of awe.

show that the site lay outside the city walls until new ones encompassed it in AD 43; that in the early 1st century it was a disused quarry in which an area of cracked rock had been left untouched; and that rock-hewn tombs were in use here in the 1st centuries BC and AD. This all tallies with Gospel accounts of the Crucifixion.

## CHAPEL OF ADAM

Immediately beneath the Greek Orthodox chapel on Golgotha, this chapel is built against the Rock of Golgotha. It is the medieval replacement of a previous Chapel of Adam that was part of Constantine's 4th-century basilica. It was so called because tradition told that Christ was crucified over the burial place of Adam's skull – a tradition first recorded by the Alexandrian theologian Origen (c.AD 185–245).

The crack in the Rock of Golgotha, clearly visible in the apse, is held by believers to have been caused by the earthquake that followed Christ's death (Matthew 27: 51).

**The Greek, Stabat Mater and Roman Catholic altars on Golgotha**

## GOLGOTHA

Just inside the church's main entrance, on the right, two staircases lead up to Golgotha, which in Hebrew means "Place of the Skull" and was translated into Latin as Calvary. The space here is divided into two chapels. On the left is the Greek Orthodox chapel, with its altar placed directly over the rocky outcrop on which the cross of Christ's Crucifixion is believed to have stood. The softer surrounding rock was quarried away when the church was built and the remaining, fissured, so-called Rock of Golgotha can now be seen through the protective glass around the altar. It can be touched through a hole in the floor under the altar. The 12th Station of the Cross (see p30) is commemorated here.

To the right is the Roman Catholic chapel, containing the 10th and 11th Stations of the Cross. The silver and bronze altar was given by Ferdinand de Medici in

1588. The 1937 mosaics encircle a Crusader-era medallion of the Ascension on the ceiling. The window looks into the Chapel of the Franks (see p92).

Between these altars is the Altar of the Stabat Mater, commemorating Mary's sorrow as she stood at the foot of the cross. It marks the 13th Station of the Cross. The wooden bust of the Virgin is 18th century.

Archaeological evidence that the church rests on a possible site of the Crucifixion is scant, but positive. Excavations

**11th-century apse, Chapel of Adam, built against the Rock of Golgotha**

---

## THE STATUS QUO

Fierce disputes, lasting centuries, between Christian creeds (see p100) over ownership of the church were largely resolved by an Ottoman decree issued in 1852. Still in force and known as the Status Quo, it divides custody among Armenians, Greeks, Copts, Roman Catholics, Ethiopians and Syrians. Some areas are administered communally. Every day, the church is unlocked by a Muslim keyholder acting as a "neutral" intermediary. This ceremonial task has been performed by a member of the same family for several generations.

**Coptic priest in ceremonial vestments**

## CHRIST'S TOMB

The present-day shrine around the tomb of Christ was built in 1809–10, after the severe fire of 1808. It replaced one dating from 1555, commissioned by the Franciscan friar Bonifacio da Ragusa. Before that, there had been a succession of shrines replacing the original 4th-century one destroyed by the sultan Hakim in 1009. Constantine's builders had dug away the hillside to leave the presumed rock-hewn tomb of Christ isolated and with enough room to build a church around it. They had also had to clear the remains of an AD 135 Hadrianic temple from the site, as well as the material with which an old quarry had been filled to provide the temple's foundations. In so doing, the Rock of Golgotha was also found.

Today the shrine, owned by the Greek, Armenian, Coptic, and Roman Catholic communities, contains two chapels. The outer Chapel of the Angel has a low pilaster incorporating a piece of the stone said to have been rolled from the mouth of Christ's Tomb by angels. It serves as a Greek Orthodox altar. A low door leads to the tiny inner Chapel of the Holy Sepulchre with the 14th Station of the Cross. A marble slab covers the place where Christ's body was supposedly laid. The slab was installed here in the 1555 reconstruction and purposely cracked to deter Ottoman looters.

### SITE OF CHRIST'S TOMB

In the first century AD, this site consisted of a small, rocky rise just outside the city walls and a disused stone quarry into whose rock face tombs had been cut.

**The hillside** was dug away in the 4th century to allow a church to be built around the tomb.

**Burial chambers** existed here in the 1st centuries BC and AD.

**Christ's Tomb**

**Present church**

**Rock of Golgotha**

In the Coptic chapel behind the shrine, a piece of polished stone is shown as being part of the tomb itself, but it is granite and not limestone, as the tomb here is known to be.

### ROTUNDA AND SYRIAN CHAPEL

The Rotunda is built in Classical Roman style. The outer back wall (now hidden by interior partitions) survives from the 4th-century basilica up to a height of 11 m (36 ft). The 11th-century dome was replaced after the 1808 fire and the two-storey colonnade built. The first two columns on the right, standing with your back to the nave, are replicas of two that survived the fire, but were

**Carvings in St Helena's Chapel**

judged unstable. The originals were made in the 11th century from the two halves of a single, gigantic Roman column – part either of the 4th-century basilica or of the previous Hadrianic temple.

In the Rotunda's back wall is the Syrian Chapel. It contains Jewish rock tombs (c.100 BC– AD 100), marking the limit to which the hillside was dug away when the first church was built.

### CHAPELS OF ST HELENA AND THE INVENTIO CRUCIS

From the ambulatory in the Crusader-period apse, now the choir in the Greek Catholikon, steep steps lead down to St Helena's Chapel. The crosses on the walls were carved by pilgrims. Although this crypt was built by the Crusaders, who reused Byzantine columns, the side walls are, in fact, foundations of the 4th-century basilica. More stairs go down to the Inventio Crucis (Finding of the Cross) Chapel, a former cistern, in which St Helena is said to have found the True Cross. The statue of her is 19th century.

### ETHIOPIAN MONASTERY

This simple monastery is approached either through the Coptic chapel in the corner of the courtyard, to the right of the main entrance, or from Souk Khan el-Zeit *(see p91)*, up steps beside Zalatimo's, a famous pastry shop.

It occupies a series of small buildings on the roof of St Helena's Chapel, among the ruins of the former Crusader cloister. The Ethiopians were forced up here in the 17th century, when, unable to pay Ottoman taxes, they lost ownership of their chapels in the main church to the Copts.

**People queuing to enter the shrine containing Christ's Tomb in the church's Rotunda**

View of the Holy Sepulchre church from the roof of St Helena's Chapel ▷

## Alexander Hospice ❷

Souk el-Dabbagha. **Map** 3 C3.
*Tel* (02) 627 4952. **Excavations**
◯ *9am–1pm & 3–5pm Mon–Sat;
ring the bell.* 🖼 ♿ ✓

Home to St Alexander's
Church, the central place of
worship for Jerusalem's
Russian Orthodox community,
the Alexander Hospice also
 houses some
important exca-
vations. When
the hospice
was founded in
1859, the site
was already
known to con-
tain ruins of the
original church
of the Holy
Sepulchre,
built in AD
335. In 1882,

**Alexander
Hospice doorway**

however, excavations revealed
remains of a Herodian city
wall. This finally proved that
the site of the Holy Sepulchre
church was outside the ancient
city walls, which added cre-
dence to the claim that it was
on the true site of Christ's
crucifixion *(see pp92–7)*.

Also preserved here are remnants of a colonnaded street
and, in the church, part of a
triumphal arch from Hadrian's
forum, begun in AD 135. The
excavations are open to the
public, but only parts of the
church can be visited.

## Lutheran Church of the Redeemer ❸

24 Muristan Rd. **Map** 3 C3.
*Tel* (02) 627 6111. ◯ *9am–1pm &
1:30–5pm (winter: 4pm) Mon–Sat.*
🖼 *for bell tower only.*

This Neo-Romanesque church
was built for the German
Kaiser Wilhelm II, and completed in 1898. Renewed
interest in the Holy Land by
Europe during the late 19th
century had ushered in a period of restoration and church
building, with many nations
wanting to establish a religious presence in Jerusalem.
The Lutheran Church of the
Redeemer was constructed
over the remains of the 11th-
century church of St Mary of
the Latins, built by wealthy
merchants from Amalfi in
Italy. An even earlier church
is thought to have existed on
the site from the 5th century.
Many details from the medieval
church have been incorporated
into the new building, and
the entrance way, decorated
with the signs of the zodiac
and symbols of the months, is
largely original. The attractive
cloister, which is inside the
adjacent Lutheran hospice,
has two tiers of galleries and
dates from the 13th–14th
centuries. Perhaps the most
interesting part of the church
though is the bell tower. After
climbing the 177 steps, visitors
are rewarded with some great
views over the Old City.

One of the many souvenir shops in
the Muristan

## Muristan ❹

Muristan Rd. **Map** 3 C3.

The name Muristan derives
from the Persian word for a
hospital or hospice for
travellers. For centuries the
area known as the Muristan,
south of the Holy Sepulchre,
was the site of just such a
hospice for pilgrims from
Latin-speaking countries. It
was built by Charlemagne in
the early 9th century, with
permission from the caliph
Haroun el-Rashid. Partly
destroyed in 1009 by the
Fatimid caliph El-Hakim, it
was restored later in the 11th
century by merchants from
Amalfi. They also built three
churches here: St Mary Minor
for women, St Mary of the
Latins for men, and St John
the Baptist for the poor.
  St John the Baptist still
stands today, and was where
the Knights of the Hospital
of St John (or the Knights
Hospitallers) were founded.
They were to take over much
of the Muristan area as their

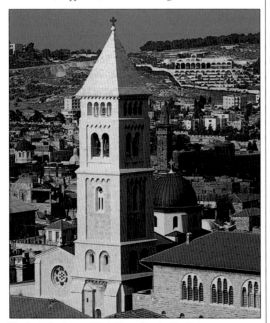

The dominating tower of the Lutheran Church of the Redeemer

*For hotels in this area see p256*

The fountain square, at the heart of the Muristan

headquarters, later building their own huge hospital to the north of the church. During the Crusades it was reported that there could often be up to 2,000 people under their care here at any one time.

By the 16th century the Muristan had fallen into ruins and Suleyman the Magnificent had its stones used to rebuild Jerusalem's city walls.

Today the Muristan is very different from how it once looked, most traces of the original buildings having long since disappeared. It is now characterized by its quiet lanes and attractive pink-stone buildings. The lanes converge at the ornate fountain in the main square – site of the original hospice. The surrounding streets are packed with small shops selling souvenirs, handicrafts and antiques. Along the nearby Muristan Road you will also find a number of outdoor cafés where you can sit and absorb the atmosphere.

The distinctive dome of the Church of St John the Baptist

## Church of St John the Baptist ❺

Christian Quarter Rd. **Map** 3 C4.
🔲 *to the public.*

The silvery dome of the Church of St John the Baptist is clearly visible above the rooftops of the Muristan, but the entrance is harder to spot among the hordes of people along busy Christian Quarter Road. A small doorway leads into a courtyard, which in turn gives access to the neighbouring Greek Orthodox monastery and the church proper.

Founded in the 5th century, the Church of St John the Baptist is one of the most ancient churches in Jerusalem. After falling into ruin, it was extensively rebuilt in the 11th century, and aside from the two bell towers which are a later addition, the modern church is little changed.

In 1099 many Christian knights who were wounded during the siege of Jerusalem were taken care of in this church. After their recovery they decided to dedicate themselves to helping the sick and protecting the pilgrims visiting Jerusalem. Founding the Knights of the Hospital of St John, they later developed into the military order of the Hospitallers and played a key role in the defence of the Holy Land (*see pp48–9*).

## Christian Quarter Road ❻

**Map** 3 B3.

Together with David Street, which runs from Jaffa Gate towards the Muristan, Christian Quarter Road is one of the main streets in the Christian Quarter. Marking off the Muristan zone, it passes by the western side of the Holy Sepulchre, and parallel to Souk Khan el-Zeit. This busy road is lined with shops selling antiques, Palestinian handicrafts (embroidery, leather goods and Hebron glass), and religious articles (icons, carved olive-wood crucifixes and rosaries).

Midway up the road on the right, down an alley signposted for the Holy Sepulchre, a short stairway descends to the modest **Omar Mosque**, with its distinctive square minaret. Its name commemorates the caliph Omar, the person generally credited with saving the Holy Sepulchre from falling into Muslim control after Jerusalem passed under Muslim dominion in February 638. Asked to go and pray inside the church, which would almost certainly have meant its being converted into a mosque, he instead prayed on the steps outside, thus allowing the church to remain a Christian site. The Omar mosque was built later, in 1193, by Saladin's son Aphdal Ali, beside the old Hospital of the Knights of St John.

The unassuming **Khanqa Salahiyya** is at the top of Christian Quarter Road. Built by Saladin between 1187 and 1189 as a monastery for Sufi mystics, it is on the site of the old Crusader Patriarchate of Jerusalem. Its ornate entrance way may be as close as you are allowed, however, as it is not open to non-Muslims. Along the north side of the mosque is El-Khanqa Street. This attractive, old, stepped street is lined with interesting shops, and runs up one of the Old City's many hills.

Glassware on sale on Christian Quarter Road

# Museum of the Greek Orthodox Patriarchate ❼

Greek Orthodox Patriarchate Road.
**Map** 3B3. **Tel** (02) 628 2048.
⬜ 8am–3pm Mon–Sat. 🖼 **Greek Catholic Patriarchate Tel** (02) 627 1968. ⬜ 8am–noon Mon–Sat. 🖼

Tucked away in the back alleys of the Christian Quarter, this museum houses a collection of ecclesiastical items that includes icons, embroidered vestments, mitres, chalices and filigree objects. It also has a fine array of archaeological finds. Of most interest are two white-stone sarcophagi found at the end of the 19th century in a tomb near the present-day King David Hotel. They are considered to belong to the family of Herod the Great *(see p120)*, and are covered in wonderfully elaborate floral decoration, which represents some of the finest Herodian-era funerary art ever found. The museum also displays Crusader objects, including a 12th-century carved capital from Nazareth, and artifacts found in the tomb of Baldwin I (king of Jerusalem, 1100–18) in the Church of the Holy Sepulchre.

Among a collection of historical firmans (imperial edicts), is one that purports to have been issued by the caliph

Omar in AD 638, granting the Greek Orthodox Church custody Jerusalem's holy places.

The nearby **Greek Catholic Patriarchate**, on the street of the same name that leads towards Jaffa Gate, has a small museum containing a collection of religious vestments and liturgical objects.

**Codex from the Greek Patriarchate Museum**

## Jaffa Gate ❽

**Map** 3 B4. 🚌 1, 13, 20.

This is the busiest of the seven Old City gates. It is the main gate for traffic and pedestrians coming from modern West Jerusalem. Despite the gate's

**Jaffa Gate, the main way into the Old City from West Jerusalem**

great size, the entrance tunnel is narrow; it is also L-shaped – both measures meant to slow attackers. It was constructed during the reign of Suleyman the Magnificent – an exact date of 1538 is given in a dedication within the arch on the outside of the gate. The breach in the wall through which cars now pass was made in 1898, in order to allow the visiting Kaiser Wilhelm II of Germany to enter the city in his carriage.

Immediately inside the gate, set into the wall behind some railings on the left, are two graves. Tour guides like to tell how these belong to Suleyman's architects, executed because they failed to incorporate Mount Zion within the city walls. An alternative legend has it that they were killed to prevent them ever building such grand walls for anyone else. In fact, they are the graves of a prominent citizen and his wife.

Jaffa Gate is one of the places where visitors can access the ramparts to walk along the city walls *(see pp142–3)*. To the Arabs this gate is known as Bab el-Khalil, from the Arabic name for Hebron (El-Khalil). The old road to the town started here.

## EASTERN CHRISTIANITY AND THE PATRIARCHATES

**Jerusalem's Greek Orthodox Patriarch**

There are no fewer than 17 churches represented in Jerusalem, a result of a great many historical schisms. As Christianity spread in the 2nd and 3rd centuries, patriarchates were established in Alexandria, Antioch, Constantinople, Jerusalem and Rome. Their heads, the patriarchs, claimed lineage from the Apostles, which gave them the authority to pronounce on correct doctrine. The first major schism came when the Council of Chalcedon (AD 451) proclaimed the dual "divine and human" nature of Christ, and in so doing estranged the Armenian, Ethiopian, Coptic and Syrian churches from the Roman Catholic and mainstream Orthodoxy. Eastern and Western Christianity split in 1054, when the Eastern churches refused to acknowledge the primacy of the Pope and the Roman church. Today there are four patriarchs (a position akin to that of an archbishop) resident in Jerusalem: those of the Greek Orthodox, Armenian, Greek Catholic and Latin (Roman Catholic) churches. The Ethiopians and Copts have a building called a patriarchate, but without the figure of the patriarch.

**Syrian Orthodox priest**        **Armenian priest**

Omar ibn el-Khattab Square, just inside Jaffa Gate

## The Citadel **9**

*See pp102–5.*

## Omar ibn el-Khattab Square **10**

**Map** 3 B4.

Not so much a square as a widening of the road as it passes around the Citadel, this area just inside Jaffa Gate is a focal point of Old City life. Arab boys selling street food solicit black-garbed Orthodox Jews heading for the Western Wall, and priests in cassocks pose for the cameras of the tourist groups, who pick up their tour guides here.

The square takes its name from the caliph Omar, who captured Jerusalem for Islam in AD 638. The Muslim name is misleading, as most of the property around the square is owned by the Greek Orthodox Patriarchate. In the late 19th century, the patriarchate built the hotels and shops on the north side, including the Neo-Classical **Imperial Hotel**. These days the hotel suffers badly from neglect and has appeal only for those who value atmosphere over comfort.

At a street junction behind the hotel is a **Roman column**, erected around AD 200 in honour of the prefect of Judaea and commander of the 10th Legion. This was one of the legions that participated in the recapture of Jerusalem in AD 70 *(see p43)*, and was

subsequently quartered in the city. The column now supports a street light.

Several cafés with pavement tables fringe the east side of the square. Next to the cafés is the Christian Information Centre, and, opposite the entrance to the Citadel, the Anglican Christ Church compound. Its Neo-Gothic church (1849) was the first Protestant building in the Holy Land.

## A Walk on the Roofs **11**

**Map** 3 C4.

At the corner of St Mark's Road and Khabad Street, in an area where the Jewish, Christian and Muslim Quarters all overlap, an iron staircase leads up to the Old City rooftops. From here it is possible to walk above the central souk area, peering down through ventilation grilles to the

bustling street below. It is possible to walk for some distance, between satellite dishes and dividing walls. There is even a ramshackle children's playground up here. Locals use the rooftops as a short cut; for visitors the appeal is in the unusual views the terrace affords of the Church of the Holy Sepulchre and Dome of the Rock. It is also worth coming up here in the evening to see the rooftop skyline thrown into silhouette by moonlight. A second set of stairs leads down past a *yeshiva* (Jewish religious school) onto El-Saraya Street in the Muslim Quarter.

## St Mark's Church **12**

5 Ararat Street. **Map** 3 C4. **Tel** (02) 628 3304. ◯ 8am–5pm (winter: 4pm) daily.

This small church is the centre of the Syrian Orthodox community in Jerusalem. It is a place rich in biblical associations, albeit of suspect authenticity. According to tradition the church was built on the site of the house of Mary, mother of St Mark the Evangelist. A stone font in the church is supposedly that in which the Virgin Mary was baptized, and the church also has a painting on parchment of the Virgin and Child that is often attributed to St Luke. Of course, historians identify it as dating from a much later period. Some scholars do believe, however, that a small cellar room here was the true site of the Last Supper, not Mount Zion *(see p117)*.

Orthodox Jews cross the rooftops of the Old City

# The Citadel

Now occupied by the Tower of David Museum of the History of Jerusalem *(see p104)*, the Citadel is an imposing bastion just inside the city wall. The present-day structure dates principally from the 14th century and includes additions made in 1532 by Suleyman the Magnificent. However, excavations have revealed remains dating back to the 2nd century BC, and indicate that there was a fortress here from Herodian times. This supports the view that this is the most likely site of Christ's trial and condemnation.

**Ruined arch in the courtyard**

**View of the Citadel and the Dome of the Rock behind, from the New City**

**The Hasmonean** city wall (2nd century BC) is one of the oldest finds. Part of the same wall can be seen in the Jewish Quarter *(see p83)*.

**Base of an early Islamic tower**

**The mosque** was built by the Mamelukes above a Crusader hall.

**Southeast Tower**

**East Tower**

**The entrance** was built with an L-shaped hallway to impede the progress of attackers.

**Open-air mosque**

**Tower of David**
*The Citadel is also called the Tower of David. The misnomer dates back to Byzantine confusion over the geographical layout of the city. Today it is also applied to this minaret, added in 1655.*

**Triple-arched Gateway**
*This ornamental gate was built in the 16th century. It was on the steps in front that General Allenby accepted the city's surrender in 1917 (see p52).*

### ★ Ramparts

*The crenellated walls have the same outline as in Crusader times, but date largely from the 14th century. It is possible to walk almost the whole circuit, taking in views of the city in all directions.*

### VISITORS' CHECKLIST

Jaffa Gate. **Map** 3 B4.
*Tel* (02) 626 5333. ⬜ 10am–4pm Sun, Thu & Sat; 10am–2pm Fri; call in advance during hols.

**An 1873 model** of Jerusalem is on display in an underground cistern.

**The courtyard** within the Citadel has archaeological remains from almost every era from the 2nd century BC to the 12th century AD.

**Entrance to café**

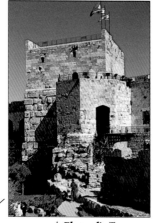

### ★ Phasael's Tower

*Herod the Great built a huge defensive tower here, naming it after his brother Phasael. It was demolished by Hadrian in AD 135 and partly rebuilt in the 14th century. The top offers spectacular views of the Old City.*

**Traces of the Byzantine** city wall can be seen at the base of this section of wall.

**The massive blocks** at the base of Phasael's Tower are part of the original Herodian structure. This section is solid all the way through.

**Moat**

### Mameluke Cupola

*This small cupola and the hexagonal room beneath are part of the Mameluke rebuilding that took place around 1310. The tour of the museum starts on this rooftop.*

### STAR FEATURES

★ Phasael's Tower

★ Ramparts

# Exploring the Citadel

**Statue of a Crusader**

There is a lot to see in the Citadel's Tower of David Museum. To help the visitor, there are three well-signposted routes: the Observation Route runs along the ramparts for the best panoramic views of the city, both Old and New; the Excavation Route concentrates on the archaeological remains in the courtyard; and the Exhibition Route takes visitors through a series of rooms tracing the history of the city. This takes the form of displays, dioramas and models, rather than a collection of historical artifacts. Visitors can join a free English tour of the route departing at 11am Sunday to Friday, and lasting one and a half hours.

**Three-dimensional representation of the Second Temple**

## PHASAEL'S TOWER

The Exhibition Route begins in Phasael's Tower with a short, animated film. From here, exit to the roof of the octagonal entrance chamber where there is the first in a series of models placed throughout the museum that depict Jerusalem at various stages during its history. This one shows the topography of the site before the founding of the city. If you then ascend Phasael's Tower, you can see the pattern of hills and valleys for yourself.

## THE CANAANITES AND THE FIRST TEMPLE

Heading clockwise from Phasael's Tower, the first two sections deal with the origins of Jerusalem, covering the period from 3150 to 587 BC, the year the First Temple was destroyed. The Canaanite era is explained in three display boards outside the East

Tower, while the First Temple-era exhibits are inside the tower. These include a model of a 19th-century BC Egyptian statuette bearing the first written reference to Jerusalem. There is also a model of the 10th-century City of David, prior to the building of the Temple, a hologram of the Temple itself, and an informative animation showing how the ancient city's water system worked. The latter is very useful for any-one who intends visiting Hezekiah's Tunnel and the Pool of Siloam (*see p115*).

## RETURN TO ZION AND THE SECOND TEMPLE

The next series of rooms, in a lower level of the East Tower, traces the return of the Jews

**Verrochio's statue of David**

to Jerusalem from exile in Babylon – illustrated in the form of copies of Persian friezes from the British Museum – and also the period of rule of the Roman and Byzantine empires. One room features a three-dimensional portrait of the Second Temple, which is worth studying closely by anyone who intends visiting the Ophel Archaeological Park (*see pp86–7*). There is also an illustration of the three Herodian towers – one of these forms the base of the Phasael Tower visited at the start of this route. The destruction of the Temple is represented by a reproduction of a frieze from the Arch of Titus, erected in Rome in AD 81 to celebrate the triumph over the Jews 11 years earlier. It shows Roman soldiers carrying off Jewish treasures.

Between here and the next exhibition room is a bronze copy of Verrochio's *David*, a Renaissance sculpture of the young king for whom the museum is named. David, in fact, had nothing to do with the Citadel or the tower that bears his name (*see p102*), as the fortress dates from the time of Herod, a thousand years after the time of David. The statue was a gift to Jerusalem from the city of Florence.

**Phasael's Tower (left) seen across the Citadel's courtyard**

## LATE ROMAN AND BYZANTINE PERIODS

A small room in the Southeast Tower deals with the creation of Aelia Capitolina, the Roman city, built on the ruins of Second Temple-era Jerusalem. The room has floors based on mosaics from Hadrian's Villa in Rome and the St Martyrius Monastery near Jerusalem. There is also a splendid model, 1.5 m (5 ft) long, of the Church of the Holy Sepulchre as it is thought to have looked when it was first built in the 4th century, on the orders of Helena, mother of the Emperor Constantine.

**The prayer niche and pulpit in the Citadel's former mosque**

## EARLY ISLAM AND THE CRUSADES

Appropriately enough, the early Islamic exhibits are housed in the Citadel's former mosque. This is the most striking room in the whole Citadel complex, with a still intact *mihrab* (niche indicating the direction of Mecca) and *minbar* (pulpit). At the centre of the room is a large, detailed, sectioned model of the Dome of the Rock. The model apparently took two years to construct. A pewter model at the centre of

**The sabil of Suleyman in a finely detailed model in the Ottoman room**

the room shows that by this time the Old City had taken on the form in which it appears today. There is also a model of the Crusader Church of St Anne's and life-size statues of the Western knights, as well as a brightly coloured diorama depicting the famed conqueror of the Crusaders, Saladin (Salah ed-Din in Arabic), in his tent outside the city walls.

## THE MAMELUKES AND OTTOMANS

The final exhibition rooms are housed in the large, northwest tower. The Mamelukes (1260-1516), a dynasty of former slaves who ruled from Egypt, endowed Jerusalem with some of its most distinctive and beautiful buildings. Their contribution is represented by drawings and a scale reconstruction of a street of distinctive striped-stone *(ablaq)* architecture. You can see similar examples today at Lady Tunshuq's Palace in the Old City *(see p65).* Illustrating Ottoman Jerusalem is a large-scale model of a fountain *(sabil)* erected by Suleyman the Magnificent – the real thing survives today on Chain Street in the Muslim Quarter.

**Members of Saladin's retinue**

## END OF THE OTTOMANS AND THE BRITISH MANDATE

This last room is a brief race through the last century and a quarter of the city's history. The story it tells is of the mass influx of Christian pilgrims and Jewish immigrants who began to settle for the first time outside the security of the walls of the Old City and, in doing so, established what is now the modern city of Jerusalem. In addition to the photos and illustrations is some rare 1896 Lumière Brothers footage of the Jerusalem–Jaffa railway.

The chronological sequence ends in a separate hall with a vast and superb model of Jerusalem as it was at the time, made by a Hungarian artist in 1873. It was exhibited throughout Europe before going into storage and being forgotten for a century until its rediscovery and removal here in the early 1980s.

**Detail of the enormous model of Jerusalem constructed in 1873**

**Wrought-iron gate framing the ornate main entrance to St James's Cathedral**

# St James's Cathedral ⓭

Armenian Patriarchate Rd. **Map** 3 B5.
**Tel** (02) 628 2331. ◯ 6:30–7:30am &
3–3:40pm Sun–Fri, 6:30–9:30 am Sat.

The Armenian Cathedral is one of the most beautiful of all Jerusalem's sacred buildings. It was originally constructed in the 11th and 12th centuries over the reputed tomb of St James the Great, the Apostle, killed by Herod Agrippa I (AD 37–44). Many alterations and additions have since been made, most notably in the 18th century, when much of the existing decoration was added.

Entrance to the cathedral is via a small courtyard with a 19th-century fountain. On the western wall of the courtyard are inscriptions in Armenian, one of which dates from 1151. Hanging in the vaulted porch are wooden bars. Each afternoon a priest strikes these with a wooden mallet known as a *nakus*, to signal the start of the service.

The cathedral interior is enchanting. It is only dimly illuminated by a forest of oil lamps hung from the ceiling. There are no seats; instead the floors are thickly laid with Oriental rugs. Four great square piers divide the main space into three aisles. These piers, along with the walls, are covered in blue-and-white tiles with floral and abstract patterns. In the apses at the end of each of the three aisles are altars, separated from the rest of the church by the iconostasis screen. Two thrones stand in the choir; the one nearest the pier is said to be that of St James the Less, traditionally held to have been a step-brother of Christ and the first bishop of Jerusalem. It is used only once a year, in early January, on the occasion of his feast day. The other throne is the one normally used by the patriarch.

The cathedral contains many small shrines and chapels. The third on the left as you enter is the most important: it supposedly holds the head of St James the Great. Off to the right, the Etchmiadzin Chapel has some beautiful tiling.

# Mardigian Museum ⓮

Armenian Patriarchate Rd. **Map** 3 B5.
**Tel** (02) 628 2331. ◯ 10am–4:30pm
Mon–Sat. 🖼

Dating from 1863, this was originally the seminary of the nearby Armenian patriarchate. It is now a museum dedicated to the history and culture of the Armenian people. The building is attractive, with a long central courtyard flanked by porticoes. The oldest finds in the collection are fragments of 1st-century frescoes from the courtyard of the so-called House of Caiaphas on Mount Zion, and remains from Byzantine-period Armenian

**17th-century jug, Mardigian Museum**

churches unearthed near Damascus Gate. The pride of the museum is its collection of early manuscripts. In addition, there are also a great many liturgical objects, many of which were donated to St James's Cathedral by Armenian pilgrims. There are also examples of the pottery for which the Armenians have always been famous.

Other interesting objects are examples of the first books printed in the first print shop in Jerusalem, which has been active since 1833 inside the Armenian monastery.

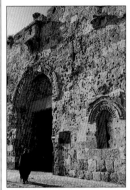

**Battle-scarred Zion Gate**

# Zion Gate ⓯

**Map** 3 C5.

Zion Gate was constructed by Suleyman the Magnificent's engineers *(see p105)* in 1540. It allowed direct access from the city to the holy sites on Mount Zion. Fighting was particularly fierce here in 1948, when Israeli soldiers were desperate to breach the walls to relieve the Jewish Quarter inside, under siege by the Jordanians. The outside of the gate is terribly pockmarked by bulletholes. A short distance to the west of the gate there is conspicuous damage to the base of the wall where soldiers tried to blast their way through with explosives.

In Arabic, the gate is known as Bab el-Nabi Daud (Gate of the Prophet David), because of its proximity to the place traditionally known as King David's Tomb *(see p117)*.

# The Armenians in Jerusalem

The kingdom of Armenia was the first country to make Christianity the state religion, when in AD 301 its king was converted. Armenian pilgrims began to visit the Holy City soon after. In the 12th century they purchased St James's Cathedral from the Georgians, and this became the focal point of their community in Jerusalem. The Armenian Quarter grew to its current size in the 17th and 18th centuries, during the rule of the Turks. In the early 20th century Armenian numbers were

**Detail from an Armenian carpet**

swollen by refugees who had fled from the 1915 persecution in Turkey, a terrible genocide in which some one and a half million Armenians were exterminated. But from a peak of around 16,000 in 1948, the Armenian population of Jerusalem has since dwindled to less than 2,000, largely due to emigration. After the 1967 war, the Jews also started to encroach into the area, and the fear now is that other than in name, the Armenian Quarter may one day disappear altogether.

**Tiling** *adorns the interior of St James's Cathedral. The tiles were made in the early 18th century in Kütahya, a town around 125 km (75 miles) southeast of Constantinople, and renowned as the foremost Armenian ceramic centre in the Ottoman Empire.*

**The Armenian Church** *is one of the three major guardians of the Christian places in the Holy Land. Among the sites they have at least partial jurisdiction over are the Church of the Holy Sepulchre, the Tomb of the Virgin Mary at the foot of the Mount of Olives, the Church of the Nativity in Bethlehem and, of course, St James's Cathedral (above).*

**Mosaics represent** *the finest legacy of ancient Armenian art. This 5th- or 6th-century example was unearthed just outside Damascus Gate.*

**Armenian-language manuscripts,** *such as this 13th-century example, are held in huge numbers at the Gulbenkian Library, next to St James's Cathedral.*

**Giant pots** *for wine or oil, dating from around 1700, are displayed at the Mardigian Museum.*

TCHEQUE

Otče náš
jenž jsi na nebesích,
posvěť se jméno tvé.
Přijď království tvé.
Buď vůle tvá, jako
v nebi tak i na zemi.
Chléb náš vezdejší
dej nám dnes A odpusť
nám naše viny, jako
i my odpouštíme našim
viníkům. A neuveď nás
v pokušení, ale zbav
nás od zlého.

Amen

# THE MOUNT OF OLIVES AND MOUNT ZION

he Mount of Olives is the hill that rises to the east of the Old City. Its slopes have been used as a place of burial since the 3rd millennium BC. The hill is also dotted with sites connected with the last days of Jesus Christ, but the highlight for many visitors is the superb view of the Old City from the summit. Between the city walls and the hill is the Valley of Jehoshaphat, with several tombs from the 1st and 2nd centuries BC. At the southern end of the valley is the site of the 3,000-year-old settlement that was to become Jerusalem (the City of David). The land rises again to the west to Mount Zion, an area of the city traditionally linked with the Last Supper.

**Belfry at the Tomb of the Virgin**

## SIGHTS AT A GLANCE

**Holy Places**
Church of All Nations ❼
Church of the Dormition ⓭
Church of the Paternoster ❸
Church of St Mary Magdalene ❻
Dominus Flevit Chapel ❺
Hall of the Last Supper ⓮
Mosque of the Ascension ❷
Russian Church of the Ascension ❶
St Peter in Gallicantu ⓫
Tomb of the Virgin ❽

**Historic Areas**
Mount Zion ⓬

**Tombs**
King David's Tomb ⓯
Schindler's Tomb ⓰
Tombs of the Prophets ❹
Valley of Jehoshaphat ❾

**Archaeological Sites**
City of David ❿

## KEY

■ Mount of Olives
    See pp110–11

## GETTING THERE

The best way to see the Mount of Olives is to take a bus (No. 75 from the station on Sultan Suleyman Street) or a taxi to the summit and walk down. Walking from the Old City involves a strenuous uphill climb. Mount Zion is most easily reached via Zion Gate in the Old City.

0 metres        400
0 yards        400

◁ **The cloister of the Church of the Paternoster, which displays the Lord's Prayer in over 60 languages**

# The Mount of Olives

**Mosaic, Dominus Flevit Chapel**

Rising on the eastern side of Jerusalem, the Mount of Olives offers magnificent views of the Dome of the Rock and the Old City. Now best known as the scene of Christ's Agony and betrayal in the Garden of Gethsemane and his Ascension into Heaven, this prominent hill has always been a holy place to the inhabitants of the city. The Jebusites dug tombs here as early as 2400 BC, as later did Jews, Christians and Muslims. To take in all the sights it is wisest to start at the top, near the Mosque of the Ascension, and walk downhill to the Tomb of the Virgin. The Old City views are best in the morning.

**Dominus Flevit Chapel**
*The chapel's west window frames a breathtaking view of the Old City* ❺

**The Cave of Gethsemane** is the traditional site of Christ's betrayal by Judas.

**Garden of Gethsemane**

**★ Tomb of the Virgin**
*An impressive flight of Crusader steps leads into the cruciform underground church. Tradition says this is where the Virgin Mary was laid to rest* ❽

**★ Church of All Nations**
*Mosaics, predominantly in blues and greens, decorate the 12 domes of this church, built in 1924 with donations from many countries* ❼

**Jericho Road**

**Church of St Mary Magdalene**
*This Russian Orthodox Church, with typically Muscovite gilded onion domes, was built by Tsar Alexander III in memory of his mother, whose patron saint was Mary Magdalene* ❻

### STAR SIGHTS

★ Tomb of the Virgin

★ Church of All Nations

★ Church of the Paternoster

*For hotels in this area see p256*

**This road** leads to Bethphage, the village from which Christ rode in triumph to Jerusalem on Palm Sunday.

**Mosque of the Ascension**
*Sacred to Muslims and Christians, this medieval chapel, now part of a mosque, is on the supposed site of Christ's Ascension* ❷

**MODERN JERUSALEM**

**MUSLIM QUARTER**

**MOUNT OF OLIVES AND MOUNT ZION**

**LOCATOR MAP**
*See Jerusalem Street Finder, map 2*

**Benedictine convent**

**Village of El-Tur**

**★ Church of the Paternoster**
*Its name meaning "Our Father", this church was built above a grotto where Christ is believed to have taught the Lord's Prayer* ❸

**Seven Arches Hotel** *(see p256)*

**Tombs of the Prophets**
*Revered as the burial place of three Old Testament prophets, this catacomb in fact dates from a much later period, the 1st century AD* ❹

**Jewish Cemeteries**
*Many Jews wish to be buried on the Mount of Olives so as to be close to the Valley of Jehoshaphat, where it is said mankind will be resurrected on the Day of Judgment.*

**Church of the Ascension's bell tower in the quiet convent gardens**

# Russian Church of the Ascension ❶

Off Ruba el-Adawiya St, Mount of Olives. **Map** 2 F3. **Tel** (02) 628 4373. ☐ 9am– noon Tue & Thu. 📷

This is the church of a still active Russian Orthodox convent built between 1870 and 1887. The bell tower, a prominent landmark on the Mount of Olives, was built tall enough to allow pilgrims too infirm to walk to the River Jordan to see it from afar. The 8-tonne bell was hauled from Jaffa by Russian pilgrims.

Two Armenian mosaics were found during construction. A small museum was built over the most beautiful, which is fragmentary and dates from the 5th century AD; the other, complete and of slightly later date, is in the Chapel of the Head of John the Baptist, inside the church. An iron cage on the floor shows where John's head was supposedly found.

# Mosque of the Ascension ❷

Off Ruba el-Adawiya St, Mount of Olives. **Map** 2 F3. ☐ daily (if closed, ring bell). 📷

Poemenia, a Christian noble-woman, built the first chapel here around AD 380 to commemorate Christ's Ascension. It had three concentric porticoes around an uncovered space, where the dust miracu-

lously formed the image of Christ's footprints. The Crusad-ers rebuilt the chapel as an octagon and the column bases of a surrounding Crusader por-tico are still visible outside. By this time, the footprints, now set in stone, were venerated here and the right imprint re-mains to this day. The capitals were carved in the 1140s and the two depicting animals and leaves are particularly beautiful.

The chapel became a Muslim shrine after Saladin's conquest in 1187. In 1200 it was roofed with a dome, the arches were walled in, a mihrab added and a surrounding wall built. The outer wall today is largely re-built. The adjacent minaret and mosque are 17th century.

The underground tomb near the entrance is venerated by Jews as belonging to the Old Testament prophetess Huldah, by Christians as St Pelagia's and by Muslims as that of the holy woman Rabia el-Adawiya.

# Church of the Paternoster ❸

Mount of Olives. **Map** 2 F4. **Tel** (02) 626 4904. ☐ 8:30am–noon & 2:30–4:30pm Mon–Sat.

This church stands next to the partly restored ruins of one commissioned by the Emperor Constantine, who sent his mother, St Helena, to supervise construction in

**Site of Christ's footprint in the Mosque of the Ascension**

AD 326. Called Eleona (*elaion* in Greek meaning "of olives"), it was sited above a grotto where the Ascension was commemorated. By Crusader times, the church had been rebuilt three times and the grotto was known as the place where Christ had taught the Disciples the Paternoster (meaning "Our Father"), or Lord's Prayer.

The present church and a Carmelite monastery were built close by between 1868 and 1872 by the French Princesse de la Tour d'Auvergne. Excava-tions of the Byzantine church in 1910–11 unearthed a marble plaque engraved in Latin with the Paternoster. In 1920, the grotto was restored, but plans to reconstruct the Byzantine church were never realized through lack of funds.

Today, the 19th-century church and its cloister are famous for the tiled panels inscribed with the Paternoster in more than 60 languages.

**Panels inscribed with the Lord's Prayer, Church of the Paternoster**

*For hotels in this area see p256*

## Tombs of the Prophets ❹

Mount of Olives. **Map** 2 F4.
⬤ *9am–3:30pm Mon–Fri.*

The southwestern slope of
the Mount of Olives, facing
the Kidron Valley (also known
along this stretch as the Valley
of Jehoshaphat – *see p115*), is
densely occupied by Jewish
cemeteries. At the top of the
slope, an unusual, fan-shaped
catacomb containing *kokhim*
(oven-shaped) graves is held
by Christian and Jewish tradition to enclose the tombs of
the 5th-century BC prophets
Haggai, Malachi and Zechariah.
The graves actually date from
the 1st century AD and were
reused in the 4th or 5th.

## Dominus Flevit Chapel ❺

Mount of Olives. **Map** 2 F4.
***Tel*** *(02) 626 6450.* 💷 *99.*
*8am–5pm daily.*

Its name meaning "The Lord
Wept", this chapel stands
where medieval pilgrims identified a rock as the one on
which Jesus sat when he wept
over the fate of Jerusalem. The
chapel was designed in the
shape of a teardrop by Italian
architect Antonio Barluzzi and
built in 1955 over a 7th-century
chapel. Part of the original apse
is preserved in the new one.
The view of the Dome of the
Rock from the altar window is
justly famous. A mosaic floor
preserved in situ outside is
from a 5th-century monastery.
The graves on view nearby

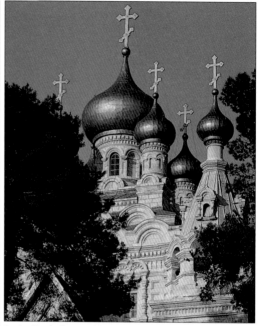

**Russian Church of St Mary Magdalene, built in Muscovite style**

show the types found in the
1950s in a vast cemetery here,
in use periodically from 1600
BC to AD 70. Also on show are
some carved stone ossuaries.

## Church of St Mary Magdalene ❻

Mount of Olives. **Map** 2 E3. ***Tel*** *(02)
628 4371.* 💷 *99.* ⬤ *10am–noon
Tue, Thu & Sat.*

In 1885, Tsar Alexander III
had this Russian Orthodox
church built in memory of his
mother, Maria Alexandrovna.

It is pleasantly set among trees,
and the seven gilded onion
domes are among the most
striking features of Jerusalem's
skyline when viewed from
the Old City. The domes and
other architectural and decorative features are in 16th–17th-
century Muscovite style.

The church was consecrated
in 1888 by Grand Duke Sergei
Alexandrovich (Tsar Alexander
III's brother) and his wife,
Grand Duchess Elizabeth
Feodorovna. In 1920, after her
murder during the Russian
Revolution, her remains were
brought here for burial.

---

### THE RUSSIANS IN JERUSALEM

Russia's Christians belong to the Eastern
Orthodox church, the centre of which was
once Constantinople. In the 19th century,
when the European powers were
competing to stake their claims on
pieces of the crumbling Ottoman
Empire, the Russians thus
presented themselves as the
successors to the Byzan-
tine Empire and the true
"defenders of Christianity
and the Holy Places". At
this time some 200,000
Russian pilgrims were

**Russian Orthodox nuns embroidering
vestments, Church of the Ascension**

visiting Jerusalem each year. The Russian
government purchased land on a grand scale,
notably on the Mount of Olives and just west
of the Old City, where they built
a great cathedral, a consulate, a
hospital and several hospices,
all enclosed in a walled compound *(see p124)*. In World
War I Britain captured
Jerusalem and confiscated all
Russian property as "enemy
institutions". Although some
White (Tsarist) Russians did
remain after the war.

Mosaic-decorated, vaulted ceiling in the Church of All Nations

# Church of All Nations ❼

Jericho Rd. **Map** 2 E3. **Tel** (02) 626 6444. ▣ 99. ◯ 8am–noon & 2:30–5pm (summer: 6pm) daily.

The Church of All Nations is also known as the Church of the Agony because it is built over the rock in the Garden of Gethsemane on which it is believed Christ prayed the night before he was arrested.

The 4th-century church built here was destroyed in an earthquake in 747. The Crusaders built a new one, aligned differently to cover three outcrops of rock, recalling Christ's three prayers during the night. It was consecrated in 1170, but fell into disuse after 1345.

After excavation of the site in the early 20th century, the present church was designed by Antonio Barluzzi (see p113) and built in 1924 with financial contributions from 12 nations – hence the church's name and its 12 domes decorated with national coats of arms. In the centre of the nave is the rock of the Byzantine church, surrounded by a wrought-iron crown of thorns. The mosaic in the apse represents Christ's agony, while others depicting his arrest and Judas's kiss are at the sides. The plan of the Byzantine church is traced in black marble on the floor, and sections of Byzantine mosaic pavement can also be seen.

Outside, the gilded mosaic scene decorating the pediment also depicts the Agony. Next to the church is the surviving part of the Garden of Gethsemane with its centuries-old olive trees.

# Tomb of the Virgin ❽

Jericho Rd. **Map** 2 E3. **Tel** (02) 628 4054. ▣ 99. ◯ 8am–noon & 2:30–5pm daily. **Cave of Gethsemane** ◯ 8:30am–noon & 2:30–5pm (winter: 3:30pm) daily.

Believed to be where the Disciples entombed the Virgin Mary, this underground sanctuary in the Valley of Jehoshaphat is one of the most intimate and mystical holy places in Jerusalem. The façade, the impressive flight of 47 steps and the royal Christian tombs in side niches half-way down all date from the 12th century. The tomb on the right, going down, was originally the burial place of Queen Melisande of Jerusalem, who died in 1161. Her remains were moved into the crypt in the 14th century and the tomb has been venerated since about that time as that of St Anne and St Joachim, Mary's parents.

The first tomb was cut in the hillside here in the 1st century AD. The cruciform crypt as seen today, much of it cut into solid rock, is Byzantine. By the 5th century, an upper chapel had also been built. This was destroyed by the Persians in 614, rebuilt by the Crusaders,

The 12th-century entrance to the atmospheric Tomb of the Virgin

but again destroyed by Saladin in 1187. He left the crypt, however, largely intact.

The Tomb of Mary stands in the eastern branch of the crypt, which is decorated with icons and sacred ornaments typical of Orthodox Christian tradition. Today, religious services are held here by Greek, Armenian, Coptic and Syrian Christians.

In the southwestern wall beside the Tomb of Mary is a mihrab installed after Saladin's conquest. The place was sanctified by Muslims because, according to the 15th-century scholar Mujir al-Din, Muhammad saw a light over the tomb of his "sister Mary" during his Night Journey to Jerusalem (see p27). In the opposite wall, a 1st-century tomb is evidence of the site's earliest use for burials.

Outside, to the right of the façade, is the **Cave of Gethsemane**, or Cave of the Betrayal, the traditional place of Judas's betrayal. It was once used for oil pressing, but fragments of 4th–5th-century mosaics bear

The Church of All Nations in the Garden of Gethsemane

The Tomb of Bnei Hezir (left) and the pyramid-roofed Tomb of Zechariah in the Valley of Jehoshaphat

witness to its transformation into a place of worship. The stars on the vaults were painted in Crusader times.

# Valley of Jehoshaphat **9**

**Map** 2 E3.

The Kidron Valley separates the Old City from the Mount of Olives. Near Gethsemane the valley is also known by its Old Testament name, the Valley of Jehoshaphat (meaning "Yahweh judges", Yahweh being the Hebrew name for God), where it was believed the dead would be resurrected on the Day of Judgment (Joel 3: 1–17). For this reason, the valley sides are densely covered with Christian, Jewish and Muslim cemeteries.

At the southern end are several Jewish rock-hewn tombs of the 1st and 2nd centuries BC. Four are particularly fine. Absalom's Tomb, like an inverted funnel, was ascribed in medieval times to King David's rebellious son, Absalom. The so-called Tomb of Jehoshaphat (the 9th-century BC King of Judah) behind it has a carved frieze above the doorway. The pyramid-topped Tomb of Zechariah is actually the above-ground monument of the adjacent Tomb of Bnei Hezir. The latter has a rectangular opening with two Doric columns and was identified by an inscription referring to the "sons of Hezir", a Jewish priestly family.

# City of David **10**

Maalot Ir David. **Map** 2 D4. *Tel* 1 800 25 24 23. 🕐 8:30am–5pm (last entrance: 3pm) Sun–Thu (Shaft & Tunnel: 4pm in winter), 8:30am–1pm (last entrance: 11am) Fri. 🌐 for Shaft & Tunnel. 📞 phone ahead (English-speaking guides Mon, Wed & Fri).

South of the Temple Mount (Haram esh-Sharif) a rocky ridge runs beside the Kidron Valley. Its summit was already settled by the Jebusites, a Canaanite (*see p41*) people, in the 20th century BC, making this the oldest part of Jerusalem. It was from them that David supposedly took the city for his capital around 1000 BC (2 Samuel 5: 6–17).

On the site are remains of buildings up to the city's capture by the Babylonians in 586 BC. They include 13th-century BC walls belonging to the Jebusite acropolis, fragments of a palace attributed to David, and houses burnt in the Babylonian attack. About 100 m

The Pool of Siloam, which stored the City of David's water supply

(330 ft) from the entrance to the acropolis excavations is **Warren's Shaft**, named after Charles Warren, its 19th-century English discoverer. A sloping tunnel, reached by spiral stairs, leads to the vertical shaft at the bottom of which is a pool fed by the Gihon Spring. The system was built by the Jebusites to ensure a water supply during sieges. Nearby is their 18th-century BC city wall, identified by the large, uncut stone blocks used in its construction. It was sited to bring the entrance to Warren's Shaft within the confines of the city.

In the 10th century BC a tunnel, later attributed to Solomon, was dug to take water from the Gihon Spring to fields in the Kidron Valley. In the face of Assyrian invasion in about 700 BC, King Hezekiah had a new tunnel built to bring the spring water right into the city, so concealing the source of the supply. **Hezekiah's Tunnel** ran 533 m (1,750 ft) from the spring to a large, new storage pool – the Pool of Siloam – in the south of the city. Not far from the Siloam end an inscription, carved by the engineer, describes the tunnel's construction. The pool is now smaller than it was originally and was rebuilt after the Romans sacked Jerusalem in AD 70 and burnt it "as far as Siloam", as told by contemporary historian Flavius Josephus.

Visitors can wade through the tunnel in thigh-deep water from the Gihon Spring – wear shoes and bring a flashlight.

**The beautifully painted interior of St Peter in Gallicantu**

# St Peter in Gallicantu ⓫

Malki Tsedek Rd. **Map** 2 D5. *Tel (02) 673 4812.* 38. ☐ *8:30am–5pm Mon–Sat.* ♿

Standing to the east of Mount Zion, on the slopes overlooking the City of David *(see p115)* and the Kidron Valley, this church commemorates the traditional site of St Peter's reported denial of Christ which fulfilled the prophecy, "Before the cock crow twice, thou shalt deny me thrice" (Mark 14: 72). Built in 1931, the church has a modern appearance. In the crypt, however, are ancient caves where, it is said, Christ spent the night before being taken to Pontius Pilate. The remains of some Herodian architecture have been discovered under the church and, in the garden, there still exists part of a Hasmonean stairway, in use in Christ's time, which once connected the city with the Kidron Valley. Mosaics from a previous 5th–6th-century Byzantine church and monastery have also been unearthed.

# Mount Zion ⓬

**Map** 1 C5. 1, 2.

A short walk from Zion Gate is the hill synonymous with biblical Jerusalem and the Promised Land. Believed by many to be the site of King David's tomb and associated

with the final days of Christ, Mount Zion is revered by Jews, Muslims and Christians alike.

The hill is bounded to the east by the Kidron Valley, to the south and west by the Hinnom Valley and to the north by the city walls. This makes it seem like an island outside the confines of the Old City. This was not always the case, however, for on the Madaba mosaic map in Jordan *(see pp216–17)* it is shown inside the walls. It appears to have been excluded in 1542 when the walls were rebuilt. Legend has it that Suleyman the Magnificent's architects left it outside by mistake.

Christians began assembling here some time after Christ's death to worship in the Hall of the Last Supper and later at the stone where the Virgin Mary is said to have died. Now the site of the Church of the Dormition, this point marked the ceasefire border from 1949 to 1967 *(see p54)*.

# Church of the Dormition ⓭

Mount Zion. **Map** 1 C5. *Tel (02) 671 9927.* 38, 20. ☐ *9am–noon & 12:30–6pm Mon–Thu, 9am–noon & 2–6pm Fri, 10:30am–noon & 12:30– 6pm Sun.* ♿

Crowned by a tall bell tower and a dome with four small corner turrets, the Neo-Romanesque Church of the Dormition dominates the Mount Zion hilltop. The large, airy, white-stone church stands on the site where the Virgin Mary is said to have fallen into an "eternal sleep". After Christ's death, according to Christian tradition, his mother went to live on Mount Zion until she herself died.

The hill soon became a holy site, available information suggesting that there may have been a church here as early as the 4th century AD. It is known with more certainty that around the 6th century a large basilica was built on the site which later fell into ruins. When the Crusaders came, they too erected a church with chapels devoted to the Dormition of the Virgin and the Last Supper.

The present-day church, which includes the Chapel of the Dormition and Dormition Abbey, was built in the early 20th century for Kaiser Wilhelm II and was inspired by the Carolingian cathedral in Aachen, Germany.

During the 1948 and 1967 wars the church was used as a strategic outpost by Israeli soldiers and was damaged in

**The conical dome and bell tower of the Church of the Dormition**

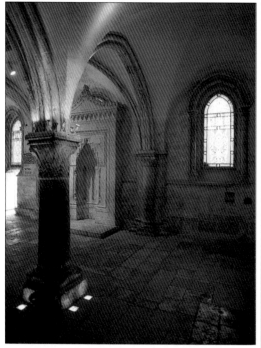

The Crusader-built Hall of the Last Supper, with fine Gothic details

the crossfire of several battles. The main part of the church boasts a fine mosaic floor featuring zodiac symbols and the names of saints and prophets. In the crypt is a wood and ivory sculpture of the "sleeping" Virgin, while the walls are adorned with images of women from the Old Testament, including Eve, Judith, Ruth and Esther. In the rooms on the mezzanine are some of the remains from the site's previous churches.

## Hall of the Last Supper ⓮

Mount Zion. **Map** 1 C5.
◯ 8am–8pm (winter: 6pm) daily.

On the first floor of a Gothic building – all that remains of the large church constructed by the Crusaders to commemorate Mary's Dormition and overshadowed slightly by the more recent Church of the Dormition – is the Hall of the Last Supper, or Coenaculum. Christian tradition maintains that it is

on the site of Christ's last meal with his Disciples. The room is unadorned apart from the Gothic arches dividing it.

In the Middle Ages it became part of the adjacent Franciscan monastery, while in the 15th century it was turned into a mosque by the Turks, who added a mihrab and some stained-glass windows.

## King David's Tomb ⓯

Mount Zion. **Map** 1 C5. **Tel** (02) 671 9767. ▦ 1, 2. ◯ summer: 8am–8pm Sat–Thu & hols, 8am–2pm Fri; winter: 8am–sunset Sun–Thu, 8am–1pm Fri.

Beneath the Hall of the Last Supper, on the lower floor of the Crusader building, are some small chambers venerated as King David's Tomb. The main chamber is bare apart from a cenotaph covered by a drape. The site was first identified as David's tomb in the 11th century AD and in the 15th century was incorporated into a mosque by the Muslims,

who consider David one of the true prophets. In spite of recent doubts about the tomb's authenticity, it is one of the most revered Jewish holy sites. It was particularly so between 1948 and 1967, when the Old City was under Jordanian control. As the Western Wall was inaccessible to Jews, they came here to pray. Today the entrance hall is still used as a synagogue. From the 4th to the 15th centuries, the tomb was associated with Pentecost and the death of the Virgin, and, according to tradition, it was here that Christ washed his Disciples' feet after the Last Supper (John 13: 1–17).

## Schindler's Tomb ⓰

Mount Zion. **Map** 1 C5. ▦ 1, 2.

Straight down the hill from Zion Gate, the path forks left past the Chamber of the Holocaust, a small museum commemorating the thousands of Jewish communities wiped out by the Nazis. Across the road at the end of the path is a Christian cemetery. It is here that the grave of German-born Oskar Schindler is located.

Schindler was an industrialist who, during World War II, went out of his way to use Jewish prisoners as labourers in his factory. By doing this, he saved over 1,000 people from the death camps. He became a symbol of the fight against the Holocaust and before he died, in 1974, he asked to be buried in Jerusalem. The story of his courageous stand against the Nazis was told in Steven Spielberg's successful 1993 movie, *Schindler's List*.

Schindler's tomb in the Christian cemetery on Mount Zion

# MODERN JERUSALEM

**B**y the 1860s the Old City had become overcrowded, and the need for more space gave rise to a period of unrestricted building activity outside the walls. The earliest developments, such as Yemin Moshe, Nakhalat Shiva and Mea Shearim, were Jewish community projects or, like the Russian Compound, intended

*Young Israelis in the lively district around Ben Yehuda Street*

to cater for Holy Land pilgrims. The architecture of the new city became increasingly eclectic as colonial builders imported their own national styles. As a result, exotic features such as Muscovite domes and Florentine towers form the backdrop to the equally multi-cultural bustle on the streets of the modern city.

## SIGHTS AT A GLANCE

**Historic Districts**
Ben Yehuda and
    Nakhalat Shiva ④
Ha-Neviim Street ⑨
Mea Shearim ⑪
Russian Compound ⑧

**Holy Places**
Italian Synagogue ⑤
St Etienne Monastery ⑭
St George's Cathedral ⑮

**Tombs**
Garden Tomb ⑬
Kings' Tombs ⑯

**Museums and Historic Buildings**
American Colony Hotel ⑰
Italian Hospital ⑩
Jerusalem Time Elevator ③
King David Hotel ②
New City Hall ⑦
Rockefeller Museum ⑱
Ticho House ⑥
YMCA ①

**Archaeological Sites**
Solomon's Quarries ⑫

**KEY**

| | |
|---|---|
| ▦ | Street-by-Street map *See pp120–1* |
| ℹ | Tourist information |
| 🚌 | Bus station |
| 🚕 | Taxi rank |

0 metres — 500
0 yards — 500

## GETTING THERE
There are buses to most of the sights from Ha-Emek Street, just outside Jaffa Gate, from Nablus Road, just north of Damascus Gate, and from Jaffa Road, in front of the New City Hall. Taxis can be convenient, but also expensive *(see p310).*

◁ **The Bloomfield Gardens' Lion Fountain in the Yemin Moshe district**

# Street-by-Street: Yemin Moshe

Sir Moses Montefiore, a rich British Jewish philanthropist was so shocked by the living conditions in the squalid Old City that he decided to improve the Jews' lot by building new homes outside the walls. The first project was Mishkenot Shaananim ("Dwellings of Tranquillity"), a communal block of 16 apartments, completed in 1860. Initially, people were afraid to move outside the security of the walls because of bandits, but by the end of the century a small community called Yemin Moshe had been established nearby and was thriving. From this core, the vast spread of modern Jerusalem has grown. Yemin Moshe survives as its beautifully renovated historic heart.

**Public Sculptures**
*Outdoor sculptures, such as these buried cubes, are found all around Yemin Moshe.*

Jaffa Road

ABA SIKRA

KING DAVID STREET (DAVID HA-MELEKH)

BLOOMFIELD

KING DAVID STREET (DAVID HA-ME

**★ YMCA**
*Even if a room is beyond your budget, as one of Jerusalem's most elegant and beautiful buildings, both inside and out, the YMCA is well worth looking around* ❶

**King David Hotel**
*Still the premier hotel in Jerusalem, and all Israel, the King David has been hosting royalty, politicians and international celebrities since it first opened its doors in the 1930s* ❷

**KEY**

- - - Suggested route

0 metres          100
0 yards           100

**Herod's Family Tomb**
*The splendour of this 1st-century BC tomb, discovered in 1892, suggests that it may be that of Herod's family. The king himself was supposedly buried at the Herodion (see p192).*

## STAR SIGHTS

★ YMCA

★ Yemin Moshe

★ Montefiore's Windmill

### ★ Yemin Moshe

*Built on the slope of the valley facing the Old City walls, these early, attractive Oriental-style houses are now some of the most sought-after and exclusive residences in all Jerusalem.*

**LOCATOR MAP**
See Jerusalem Street Finder, map 1

### ★ Montefiore's Windmill

*Montefiore meant Mishkenot Shaananim to be self-sufficient, hence a windmill to grind the settlement's own flour. Unfortunately, there was rarely enough wind to turn the sails.*

### Mishkenot Shaananim

*In the earliest days, lodging in this block had to be offered rent-free in order to attract tenants. Now the place serves as a guesthouse for artists and writers. Saul Bellow, Marc Chagall and Simone de Beauvoir have all been accommodated here.*

### Bloomfield Gardens

*Grassy parks fringe Yemin Moshe. Attractive in their own right, and dotted with ornament, such as the Lion Fountain (right), the parks also afford great views across the valley to the Old City.*

## YMCA ❶

24 King David St. **Map** 1 A4.
***Tel*** *(02) 569 2692.* 7, 8, 30, 38.
**Tower** *8am–6pm daily.*

Built in 1926–33 by Arthur
Loomis Harmon, who also
created New York's Empire
State Building, Jerusalem's
YMCA *(see p257)* is one of the
city's best-known landmarks. It
consists of three sections – the
central body, dominated by a
bell tower offering extraordinary
views of the city, and the
two side wings. The stone and
wrought-iron decorative
elements on the outside of the
building, including the 5-m
(16.5-ft) bas-relief of one of the
six-winged seraphim described
in the Old Testament (Isaiah 6:
2–3), reflect a stylized form of
Oriental Byzantine design,
combined with elements of
Romanesque and Islamic art.
   Yet the exterior, splendid as
it is, does not prepare the
visitor for the fabulously
elaborate decor on the inside.
Here design elements from
three different cultures are
woven through with symbols
from the three main monotheistic
religions.
In the concert
hall, the dome's
twelve windows
represent the
Twelve Tribes of
Israel, the Twelve
Disciples of Christ
and the Twelve
Followers of
Muhammad,
while depicted on
the chandelier are the Cross,
Crescent and the Star of David.
The entire creation has a kind
of Art Deco gloss, while the
ethos of its eclectic design is
clearly one of peace and
tolerance
between
faiths and
cultures.

The distinctive bell tower of
Jerusalem's YMCA

## King David Hotel ❷

23 King David St. **Map** 1 B4. ***Tel***
*(02) 620 8888.* 7, 8, 30, 38.

Eye-catching not least for its
pink stone walls and green
windows, this impressive 1930s
hotel *(see p258)* is a grandiose
display of colonial
architecture. It
was designed by
Swiss architect
Emile Vogt for the
Jewish-Egyptian
Mosseri family.
   Inside, the
spacious lobbies
and public areas,
with their discreet
period wooden
furnishings, reflect a sense of
splendour from an altogether
different era. The richly
ornamental style is achieved
through a mixture of various

**Inside the elegant lobby of
the King David Hotel**

ancient architectural and
decorative elements, including
Egyptian, Phoenician, Assyrian
and Greek, as well as aspects
of Islamic art. The hotel boasts
an impressive list of former
guests, including Winston
Churchill and Haile Selassie,
and for a long time, part of
the British Mandate administration
*(see p52)* was housed
here. In 1946 it was the target
of a bomb attack perpetrated
by the Zionist paramilitary
terrorist group Irgun, led by
Menachem Begin *(see p53)*. It
was rebuilt and the two top
floors were added later.

## Jerusalem Time Elevator ❸

Beit Agron, 37 Hillel St. **Map** 1 A3.
***Tel*** *(02) 625 2227.* *10am–8pm
Thu–Sun.*

On the southern edge of the
neighbourhood of Nakhalat
Shiva *(see p123)*, this is a
themepark-style ride through
3,000 years of Jerusalem's
often-turbulent history. The
audience is belted into their
seats and given surround-sound
headphones for an
audiovisual journey enhanced
by computer-generated
animation and other special
effects. It begins in the times
of King David and Solomon,
and rattles through dramatic
highlights of conquest,
destruction, earthquake and
fire, ending with the Six Day
War of 1967 and reunification.
   The special "motion" seats
jolt and sway through the
experience, which culminates
in an "aerial" ride over the
Jerusalem of today. It is a
useful introduction to the city's
complicated chronology,
especially if
visited in

**The square-set form of the King David Hotel, the choice of many rich and famous visitors to Jerusalem**

*For hotels and restaurants in this area see pp257–8 and pp272–4*

The Italian Synagogue and Museum of Italian-Jewish Art in a quiet square

conjunction with the Tower of David Museum at the Citadel *(see p104)* – buy a discounted joint ticket. The ride lasts about 30 minutes, with shows at 40-minute intervals. It is not recommended if you do not enjoy rollercoasters.

## Ben Yehuda and Nakhalat Shiva ❹

**Map** 1 A3. 🚍 20, 23, 27.

One of the popular streetside cafés and restaurants in Ben Yehuda

At the heart of modern Jerusalem are the pedestrianized precincts of Ben Yehuda Street and Nakhalat Shiva. They constitute one of the liveliest parts of the city, with shops, restaurants, street vendors and musicians coming together to create a rich and varied atmosphere. In the minds of local people, Ben Yehuda Street and Nakhalat Shiva are the embodiment of secular Jerusalem. The contrast with the Orthodox city, just a short distance to the north in Mea Shearim *(see p125)*, could not be more marked.

Ben Yehuda Street was built in the 1920s, and has since been the traditional meeting place for Jewish intellectuals, politicians and journalists.

South of Ben Yehuda Street is a series of narrow lanes, with low houses and connecting courtyards. These are collectively known as Nakhalat Shiva, meaning "the Domain of the Seven", which refers to the seven families who built them. Dating back to 1869, this area was the third Jewish residential quarter to appear outside the Old City walls. Despite being threatened with demolition on more than one occasion, the area was finally renovated in the 1980s. Today it is filled with shops, workshops, bars, restaurants and cafés and is invariably busy until the early hours.

Other streets in this locality also have much to interest the visitor. Buildings of varied architectural styles reflect the diverse cultural influences that have shaped the city.

## Italian Synagogue ❺

27 Hillel St. **Map** 1 A3. **Tel** *(02) 624 1610.* 🚍 *18, 21, 22, 30.* ⏲ *9am–5pm Sun, Tue, Wed, 9am–2pm Mon, 9am– 1pm Thu, Fri.* ● *Jewish hols.* 🌐 **www**.jija.org

Originally a German college constructed in the late 19th century, this building now houses an 18th-century synagogue from Conegliano Veneto, near Venice in Italy. In 1952, with no more Jews living there, the synagogue had fallen into disuse. It was decided to dismantle the interior and bring it here. It is arguably the most beautiful synagogue in Israel, and on

Saturdays and Jewish holidays the Italian-Jewish community worships here. The building also houses the Museum of Italian-Jewish Art, which has some fascinating items, such as medieval ritual objects. On the lower floor is the Centre of Studies on Italian Judaism and a library on the same subject.

## Ticho House ❻

9 Ha-Rav Kook St. **Map** 1 A2. **Tel** *(02) 624 5068.* 🚍 *11, 13, 18, 20, 35, 48.* **Museum** ⏲ *10am–5pm Sun, Mon, Wed & Thu, 10am–10pm Tue, 10am–2pm Fri.* ● *Jewish hols.* 📷

Built in the 19th century as the luxurious residence of a wealthy Jerusalem family, this is one of the city's loveliest examples of an Arab mansion. Its large central drawing room is the focal point of both the architecture and the social life of the building. In the early 20th century the house was bought by Dr Abraham Ticho, a famous Jewish ophthalmologist who used to give the poor free treatment, irrespective of their ethnic origin or religion. Dr Ticho's Viennese wife, Anna, was an artist. By day the house was a clinic and by night it was the centre of Jerusalem's social and intellectual life.

Nowadays the house is administered by the Israel Museum *(see pp132–7)*, to which Anna Ticho left more than 2,000 watercolours and drawings. Some of these are exhibited here. The house also has a charming and very popular café overlooking a delightful garden.

View over the beautiful garden at the back of Ticho House

## New City Hall ⑦

Jaffa Rd. **Map** 1 B3. **Tel** (02) 629 7777
or (02) 629 6666. 🚌 6, 13, 18, 20,
27. 🕐 8:30am–4pm Sun–Thu,
8:30am–noon Fri. 📠 (02) 629 6672.

Completed in 1993, the New
City Hall complex is sited
just outside the Old City walls,
where Jewish West Jerusalem
meets Arab East Jerusalem. Its
architecture displays an appropriate spirit of synthesis – the
complex includes ten renovated historical buildings, along
with two modern blocks that
refer subtly to historical
models (for example, the
banding of different coloured
stone echoes the Mameluke
buildings of the Old City).
    One of the renovated build-
ings, on Jaffa Road, is the old
City Hall. It is still pocked with
bullet holes from its days as a
frontline Israeli army post
when, between 1948 and 1967,
the city was divided (see p53).

## Russian Compound ⑧

Kheshin St. **Map** 1 B3. 🚌 13, 18,
20, 23. **Underground Prisoners'
Museum 1918–48 Tel** (02) 523
3166. 🕐 9am–5pm Sun–Thu. 📷

The Russians were some of
the first people to settle
outside the Old City in the
19th century (see p113).
The process began around
1860 when a few acres of
land were acquired a short
distance outside the city
walls. The Russians built a
virtually self-contained
compound to provide
lodgings for the city's
growing number of
Russian pilgrims, and
erected a cathedral
for services.

The New City Hall, seen through the palms of Safra Square

Consecrated in 1864, the
Cathedral of the Holy Trinity
is fashioned in an unmistak-
ably Muscovite style, with
eight drums topped by green
domes. Unfortunately, it is
closed to the public. Across
the plaza, under a pavement
grille, is what is known as
Herod's Column, a 12-m (40-ft)
stone pillar, which historians
believe was intended for the
Second Temple before it
cracked and was abandoned.
    These days the Russians own
only the cathedral, as many of
the other buildings belonging
to the compound were sold
off by the Soviet
Union in exchange
for shipments of
Israeli oranges.
    The building with
the crenellated
tower – the
grandest of the
former pilgrims'
hostels – is now
home to the Agriculture
Ministry. The street on which
it stands, Heleni ha-Malka,
is one of the city's
nightlife centres, filled
with bars and cafés.
The former women's
hostel, behind the
cathedral, now
houses the

**Royal lion above the
door, Ethiopian Church**

**Underground Prisoners'
Museum 1918–48**, which is
dedicated to Jewish resistance
fighters, some of whom were
jailed in this building during
the period of the British
Mandate (see pp52–3).

## Ha-Neviim Street ⑨

**Map** 1 B2. 🚌 1, 27.

One of the oldest streets
outside the Old City,
Ha-Neviim (Street of the
Prophets) roughly marks the
dividing line between the
religious and
secular halves of
modern Jerusalem
(ultra-Orthodox
Mea Shearim lies
just to the north;
the drinking and
dining scene of
the Russian Com-
pound is to the
south). Once a prestigious
address, Ha-Neviim is lined
with some grand buildings. At
No. 58 is Thabor House, the
self-designed home of Conrad
Schick, a German who arrived
in the Holy Land a Protestant
missionary and became the
city's most renowned architect
of the late 19th century. The
house now belongs to the
Swedish Theological Institute,
but visitors can admire the
eccentric fortress-like main
gate. Someone will usually
answer the bell and admit the
curious into the courtyard to
admire the building's façade,
complete with embedded
archaeological finds.
    A few steps west at No. 64
is the house once occupied
by the Victorian painter

The Cathedral of the Holy Trinity, in the Russian Compound

William Holman Hunt *(see p33)*. It is now a private residence and closed to the public. A couple of minutes' walk to the north, along narrow, leafy Etyopya Street, is Ben Yehuda House, named after the man responsible for reviving popular usage of the Hebrew language. This was his residence in the early years of the 20th century.

A little further up the lane is the striking, round form of the Ethiopian Church, which sits in beautifully tended gardens. It was built between 1873 and 1911, and is modelled after churches in Ethiopia, with its sanctuary clearly separated from the main body of the church. Just five minutes' walk away, back on Ha-Neviim Street, the Ethiopians also have their consulate. It is notable for a vivid blue and gold mosaic on the façade depicting the Lion of Judah.

## Italian Hospital ⓾

Corner of Ha-Neviim and Shivtei Yisrael Sts. **Map** 1 B2. 🚌 *27.* 🚫 *to public.*

The grandest building of all on Ha-Neviim Street is the Italian Hospital. It was built just before World War I to underscore Italian presence in the Holy City, at a time when the colonial powers were using architecture to assert their influence and status. Designed by prolific architect Antonio Barluzzi, the hospital is clearly inspired by the Palazzo Vecchio in Florence. The building now houses the Ministry of Education.

**The extravagant Italian Hospital**

**Mea Shearim, the heartland of Jerusalem's insular ultra-Orthodox community**

## Mea Shearim ⓫

**Map** 1 A1. 🚌 *1.*

Possibly the most unusual district in all Jerusalem, Mea Shearim is a perfectly preserved, living model of 18th-century Jewish Eastern Europe. It is a quarter inhabited exclusively by ultra-Orthodox Jews, where the influence of the outside world is kept to an absolute minimum. Dress is traditional in the extreme; many men wear black stockings and long black coats, and women keep their hair covered beneath a snood. The streets either side of main Mea Shearim Street are narrow alleyways, which squeeze between long, narrow two-storey dwellings, occasionally opening out into washing-strewn communal courtyards. The area is completely self-contained, with its own bakeries, markets, synagogues and, although no longer in use, its own huge cistern.

Mea Shearim was founded in the late 19th century and built in three stages, to a design by Conrad Schick, for Jews from Poland and Lithuania. Until well into this century the quarter was shut off from the rest of the city each night by six gates.

The gates are gone but visitors should bear in mind that this is still a very insular community. Skirts should reach below the knee, and men must not wear shorts or T-shirts. Discretion is advised when taking photographs.

Northwest of Mea Shearim is the Bukharan Quarter, founded in the late 19th century by wealthy Central Asian Jews. Traces of its former grandeur remain in some elegant, if dilapidated, mansions.

### ULTRA-ORTHODOX JEWS

The life of the ultra-Orthodox *(haredim)* is grounded in rigorous observance of Judaic law and study of the Torah. Their lifestyle involves an uncompromising rejection of modern life and all its trappings, which means no television, no cars and minimum intrusion by technology. The ultra-Orthodox live and dress strictly according to traditions practised in Eastern Europe several centuries ago. This lifestyle means that they segregate themselves from less observant Jews. More radical factions are opposed to the common use of Hebrew, the "Holy tongue", and instead speak Yiddish; some do not recognize the State of Israel or its laws, even refusing to pay taxes. They claim that there can be no true Jewish state until the coming of the Messiah.

**Ultra-Orthodox Jews dressed in everyday attire**

# Solomon's Quarries ⑫

Sultan Suleyman St. **Map** 4 D1.
🚌 23, 27. ◷ 9am–4pm Sun–Thu,
9am–2pm Fri. 🖼

This is an enormous empty
cave stretching under the Old
City, with its entrance at the
foot of the wall between
Damascus and Herod's gates.
Despite the popular name, historians are not convinced that
the cave has any connection
with Solomon, but it is likely
that Herod took stone from
here for his many building
projects, including his modi-
fication of the Second Temple.

The quarry is also known
as Zedekiah's cave, after the
last king of Judaea who,
legend has it, hid here during
the Babylonian conquest of
Jerusalem in 586 BC.

# Garden Tomb ⑬

Conrad Schick St. **Map** 3 C1.
*Tel* (02) 627 2745. 🚌 1, 3.
◷ 2–5:30pm Mon–Thu.
**www**.gardentomb.com

Towards the end of the 19th
century the British general,
Charles Gordon, of Khartoum
fame, was visiting Jerusalem
and started a dispute among
archaeologists. He argued that
this skull-shaped hill was the
Golgotha referred to in the
New Testament (Mark 15: 22)
and that the real burial site
of Jesus Christ was here and
not at the Holy Sepulchre

**The simple Neo-Romanesque chapel
at St Etienne Monastery**

**Tourists visiting the ancient Garden Tomb in its attractive setting**

*(see pp92–5)*. Excavations
carried out in 1883 did in fact
unearth some ancient tombs,
but further study found them
to date back to the 9th–7th
century BC, with an entirely
different configuration from
those in use in Christ's time.
However, regardless of its
authenticity, this place is
well worth a visit if only for
the lovely garden.

# St Etienne Monastery ⑭

Nablus Rd. **Map** 1 C2. *Tel* (02) 626
4468. 🚌 23, 27. ◷ open all day;
ring the bell.

The name of this site relates
to the belief that in AD 439
Cyril of Alexandria interred
the remains of St Stephen (St
Etienne in French), the first
Christian martyr, in a basilica
built on this spot. The basilica
was destroyed by the Persians
in AD 614, and a subsequent
7th-century chapel on the
same site was also destroyed,
this time by the Crusaders
holding Jerusalem, who feared
Saladin would use it as a base
for assaults on the city.

The present monastery was
built between 1891 and 1901
by the French Dominicans. Its
eclectic design includes an
Oriental tower, Romanesque
walls and Neo-Gothic flying
buttresses. Within are remains
of the mosaic floor of the
original Byzantine church,
as well as the Ecole Biblique,
the Holy Land's first school
of biblical archaeology.

# St George's Cathedral ⑮

53 Nablus Rd. **Map** 1 C1. *Tel* (02)
628 3261. 🚌 6, 23, 27. ◷ not
generally open for visitors so call first.

This Archetypal Middle
England church, with its
pretty, cloistered courtyard and
connotations of vicars, tweeds
and cucumber sandwiches,
stands in startling contrast to
the chaotic Arab streets of its
East Jerusalem neighbourhood.

The cathedral dates from
1910 and is named for the
patron saint of England, who
was actually a Palestinian
conscript in the Roman army,
executed in AD 303 for tearing
up a copy of the emperor
Diocletian's decree forbidding
Christianity. He is supposedly
buried at Lod (ancient Lydda),
now better known as the site
of Ben Gurion airport.

In World War I the cathedral
was the local headquarters of
the Turkish army, and the
1917 truce sanctioning British
presence in Palestine was
signed in the bishop's quarters.

**St George's Cathedral, part of
Jerusalem's colonial heritage**

## Kings' Tombs 16

Salah ed-Din St. **Map** 1 C1. 23, 27. 8am–5pm Mon–Sat.

Despite the name, this single-but elaborate tomb is thought to have been that of Queen Helena of Adiabene. In the 1st century AD she converted to Judaism and moved to Jerusalem from her kingdom in Mesopotamia. The tomb was named by early explorers who believed that the magnificent tomb housed members of the dynasty of David. A small entrance leads down into a dimly lit maze of chambers with stone doors.

The tomb is one of the places of interest on the East Jerusalem walk (see pp146–7).

**Well-worn steps leading to the deceptively named Kings' Tombs**

## American Colony Hotel 17

2 Louis Vincent St. **Map** 1 C1. **Tel** (02) 627 9777. 23, 27.

This elegant hotel (see p258) built in 1865–76 has long been a favourite of diplomats and journalists. It started life as the home of a rich Turkish merchant. The name American Colony came about in the late 19th century when Anna and Horatio Spafford of Chicago bought the building and made it the centre of an American religious community dedicated to good works. When the community broke up in the early 20th century, a Baron Ustinov, related to the actor Peter Ustinov, suggested converting the building to accommodate pilgrims to the Holy Land. Soon after, it was turned into a beautiful hotel,

**The Rockefeller Museum courtyard**

which it remains today. If you cannot afford to stay here, it is definitely worth coming for lunch, taken out in the tree-shaded courtyard.

## Rockefeller Museum 18

27 Sultan Suleyman St. **Map** 2 D2. **Tel** (02) 628 2251. 1, 2. 10am–3pm Sun, Mon, Wed, Thu, 10am–2pm Sat.

This museum was made possible by a substantial financial gift made in 1927 by the American oil magnate John D Rockefeller. British

architect Austin Harrison designed the building along Neo-Gothic lines. It is vaguely reminiscent of the Alhambra in Spain and runs around a central courtyard. Constructed from the white stone typical of Jerusalem buildings, the Rockefeller has Byzantine-and Islamic-type decorative motifs. It was once one of the most important museums in the Middle East and the first to make a systematic collection of finds from the Holy Land. These days, it is a branch of the Israel Museum (see pp132–7), but still houses a very impressive collection.

Among its many remarkable objects are the stuccowork from Hisham's Palace in Jericho, beams from the Holy Sepulchre church and wooden panels from El-Aqsa mosque. Other exhibits worth seeing include a fascinating portrait modelled on an 8,000-year-old cranium discovered in Jericho; a lovely Bronze Age bull's head; a Canaanite vase in the shape of a human head; sculptures from the time of the Crusades; and Hellenistic and Roman objects found in Judaean desert caves. The museum also holds a number of the Dead Sea Scrolls (see p137).

**The delightfully secluded courtyard of the American Colony Hotel**

# FURTHER AFIELD

Since the creation of the state of Israel in 1948, the boundaries of Jerusalem have greatly expanded in all directions. The city has also been endowed with a great many significant new buildings. Two stand out as being of particular importance: the Israel Museum, a world-class institution that incorporates several collections of priceless treasures, including the famous Dead Sea Scrolls; and the Knesset, the seat of national government.

Another cornerstone in the psyche of Israeli society is Yad Vashem, the moving – and, in parts, harrowing – memorial complex that honours the more than six million Jews who died at the hands of the Nazis during the Holocaust. The site of this memorial is Mount Herzl, named after Theodor Herzl, the founding father of Zionism (*see p51*). The grassy slopes here are also home to an extensive military cemetery, in which many figures of national importance are buried.

As Jerusalem has expanded, what, not too long ago, were small, isolated villages are now virtually suburbs of the city. They have not, however, lost their character. Places such as Ein Kerem, nestled in the valley below Mount Herzl, and Abu Ghosh, further to the northwest, have a great deal of rural charm, as well as several attractive religious buildings linked with biblical events.

**A memorial statue at Yad Vashem**

## SIGHTS AT A GLANCE

**Museums**
Bible Lands Museum ④
Biblical Zoo ⑧
*Israel Museum pp132–37* ③
LA Mayer Museum of Islamic Art ①
Mount Herzl and Herzl Museum ⑩

**Memorials**
Yad Vashem ⑨

**Holy Places**
Monastery of the Cross ②

**Modern Buildings**
Hadassah Hospital Synagogue ⑫
Knesset ⑤
Supreme Court ⑥

**Districts**
Mahane Yehuda and Nakhlaot ⑦

**Towns and Villages**
Abu Ghosh ⑬
Ein Kerem ⑪

**GREATER JERUSALEM**

### JERUSALEM AND ENVIRONS

**KEY**

| | |
|---|---|
| ▨ | Main sightseeing area |
| ▢ | Built-up area |
| ▬ | Major road |
| ═ | Minor road |

0 kilometres  2

0 miles  2

◁ **Crusader church complex at Abu Ghosh, 13 km (8 miles) west of Jerusalem**

The refectory at the Monastery of the Cross

# LA Mayer Museum of Islamic Art **1**

2 Ha-Palmakh St, Talbiya. *Tel* (02) 566 1292. 13, 15. 10am–3pm Sun, Mon, Wed & Thu, 10am–6pm Tue, 10am–2pm Fri & Sat.

While the cream of Islamic artifacts collected in the Holy Land are to be found in the Rockefeller Museum *(see p127)* and the Museum of Islamic Art on the Haram esh-Sharif *(see p70)*, this modern, purpose-built museum offers a beautifully presented collection of pieces from the greater Islamic world. Especially attractive are the examples of Persian tiling and Indian Moghul miniatures, and there is a very informative section on Arabic calligraphy.

# Monastery of the Cross **2**

Shalom St, Neve Granot. *Tel* (02) 679 0961. 18, 31, 32. 10am–4pm Mon–Sat.

Stranded in the middle of a large area of scrubland, ringed at its outer perimeters by main roads and modern buildings, this solitary Byzantine monastery has the look of a place that time forgot and urban planners ignored. Its high, buttressed walls emphasize still more its seclusion and reflect its once precarious position outside the Old City.

There was a church here in the 5th century, but it was destroyed by the Persians in 614. Part of its mosaic floor can still be seen on one side of the main altar in the present church. The monastery which exists today was built in the 11th century by monks from Mount Athos, with financial backing from King Bagrat of Georgia. According to tradition, it marks the spot where the tree grew that was used to make Christ's cross.

In the 13th century the Georgian poet Shota Rustaveli lived here and commissioned the frescoes in the main church. They were repainted in the 17th century respecting the original style.

By the 14th century the monastery had become the centre of Jerusalem's Georgian community and a major centre of Georgian culture in the region. Gradually, however, their standing declined and by 1685 the monastery had been taken over by the Greek Orthodox Patriarchate.

The church is largely in its original, 11th-century form, while many other parts of the complex have been altered or added to. The courtyard and the late Baroque bell tower display clear signs of 19th-century changes. In the late 1990s large-scale restoration was undertaken. The simple dome is one of the church's most beautiful features. Also remarkable are the frescoes, which show an unusual combination of Christian, pagan and worldly images. Visitors

Babylonian tablet, **Bible Lands Museum**

are permitted to wander freely around the complex. Particularly evocative of monastic life are the refectory on the upper floor and the kitchen.

# Israel Museum **3**

*See pp132–7.*

# Bible Lands Museum **4**

25 Avraham Granot St, Givat Ram. *Tel* (02) 561 1066. 9, 17, 24, 99. 9:30am–5:30pm Sun–Tue & Thu, 9:30am–9:30pm Wed, 9:30am–2pm Fri & eves of Jewish hols. Sat & Jewish hols. English-speaking guides available (phone for times).

Opposite the Israel Museum is this rather unremarkable building which houses an outstanding collection of archaeological finds that reflect the different cultures of the Holy Land region in biblical times. The museum was inaugurated in 1992 with the private collection of Elie Borowski, a passionate scholar of ancient Middle Eastern civilizations. The collection features many finely crafted objects from ancient Egypt, Syria, Anatolia, Mesopotamia and Persia. Among these are a great number of artifacts that shed light on the culture of the Mesopotamian region in

The Bible Lands Museum, covering the early history of the Middle East

The sculpted menorah near the entrance to the Knesset

the millennia before the Christian era. The many fascinating and unique objects include ancient inscriptions, jewellery, mosaics, seals, ivory carvings and scarabs.

The exhibits are displayed in a way that enables the visitor to build a clear and illuminating picture of the cultural context in which the biblical texts were written. The items are arranged according to both chronology and region. The result is a clear illustration of the way in which different cultures influenced each other and new societies evolved.

## Knesset ❺

Rothschild St, Givat Ram. *Tel (02) 675 3333.* 9, 24, 99. 8:30am–2pm Sun & Thu. *compulsory (ring in advance to book).*

The Knesset (Assembly) is the seat of the Israeli Parliament. It takes its name from the Knesset ha-Gedola (Great Assembly) of 120 men that governed the political and civic life of Jews in the Second Temple period *(see p42)*. The building, inaugurated in 1966, was designed by Joseph Klarwin. His design makes use of classical elements and is inspired by the Parthenon in Athens and various reconstructions of the Temple.

Opposite the entrance is a large, seven-branched menorah (candelabrum), symbol of the State of Israel. It is the work of British sculptor Benno

Elkan and was a gift from the British parliament. The relief work on its branches depicts crucial moments in Jewish history and is accompanied by biblical quotations. Nearby is a monument with an eternal flame, commemorating the dead of the Holocaust and Israel's wars *(see pp53–5).*

The reception area inside the Knesset was designed and decorated by the Russian-Jewish artist Marc Chagall *(see p33).* It is adorned with his mosaics and a triple tapestry which depicts the creation of the world, the exodus of the Israelites from Egypt, and the city of Jerusalem. The main chamber ends in a stone wall that is a very clear reference to the Western Wall *(see p85).*

The Supreme Court, one of the city's architectural highlights

## Supreme Court ❻

Shaarei Mishpat St, Givat Ram. *Tel (02) 675 9612.* 9, 24, 99. 8:30am–2:30pm Sun–Thu. *noon daily in English (ring in advance to book).*

In the absence of a formal constitution, Israel's Supreme Court plays a pivotal role in the lives of ordinary citizens. Its significance is reflected in

the building's design – by Ram Karmi and Ada Karmi-Melamed – which manages to depict the concept of justice in architectural terms. The two copper pyramids on the roof are powerful symbols of the immutable nature of the principles of law. The long sweeping stairway seems to represent the accessibility of the law to ordinary people, and at the top it offers an all-embracing view of Jerusalem.

Motifs from the past, such as the Islamic elements in the inner courtyard and the Byzantine-era mosaic outside the entrance, recall the cultural and historical influences that have shaped contemporary Israel. They are given a modern context to link the past with the present and reflect the universality of justice.

## Mahane Yehuda and Nakhlaot ❼

6, 8, 13, 14, 18, 21.

The district of Mahane Yehuda, which means Field of Judah, was built in 1929 to house Jewish immigrant workers. It is famous for its vibrant and very colourful market, selling mainly foodstuffs. It is also home to a large number of popular local restaurants, which specialize in Middle Eastern salads and kebabs. To the south of Mahane Yehuda is the older district of Nakhlaot. This lively, warren-like jumble of low houses and narrow alleyways is fascinating to explore.

Displays of fruit and vegetables at the market in Mahane Yehuda

# Israel Museum ❸

★ **Shrine of the Book**
*This innovatively designed underground hall houses the Dead Sea Scrolls. It is the most visited part of the museum (see pp136–7).*

Built in 1965 on a ridge overlooking West Jerusalem, the Israel Museum contains some of the country's finest art and archaeology. Its modular design, by Israeli architects A Mansfeld and D Gad, consists of a series of pavilions echoing the layout of traditional Arab villages. Inside, the collection includes entire synagogue interiors from Europe and India, a stunning array of regional art and archaeology and the world-famous Dead Sea Scrolls. Much of the museum is currently closed for renovation, so call in advance.

**Apple Core (1992), Claes Oldenburg**

★ **Beth Shean Mosaic**
*This 6th-century mosaic floor, from a synagogue at Beth Shean (see p185), shows the Ark of the Covenant (see p19) flanked by two menorahs.*

**Ibex Sceptre**
*This copper sceptre decorated with ibex heads is part of a hoard of treasure found in the Judaean Desert. The workmanship is remarkable for its era (late 5th millennium BC).*

**Open-air plaza**

**Anthropoid sarcophagi** *(see p135)*

**To Youth Wing**

**Café**

**Walkway from entrance pavilion**

## KEY TO FLOORPLAN

|   |   |
|---|---|
| ▨ | Judaica and Jewish Ethnography |
| ▢ | Art collections |
| ▢ | Archaeology |
| ▨ | Temporary exhibitions |
| ▨ | Non-exhibition space |

**Billy Rose Art Garden**
Woman Combing Her Hair (1914), by Ukrainian-born Alexander Archipenko, is one of the art garden's striking sculptures.

## PLAN OF MUSEUM

**KEY**

|   |   |
|---|---|
| ▨ | Entrance pavilion |
| ▨ | Main museum block |
| ▨ | Ruth Youth Wing |
| ▨ | Billy Rose Art Garden |
| ▨ | Shrine of the Book |
| ▨ | Temporary exhibitions |

**Café**

**Entrance to main block**

**Model of Ancient Jerusalem**

**Walkway**

*For hotels and restaurants in this area see p258 and p274*

### Red Blue Chair (1918)

*The design collection includes this famous chair by Gerrit Rietveld. Like others in the Dutch De Stijl art movement, Rietveld used primary colours and simple geometric shapes.*

Entrance to main block

Coin gallery

Upper level

Lower level

Rothschild Room (see p134)

Asian and Islamic art

Auditorium

Israeli art

### VISITORS' CHECKLIST

Ruppin Rd, Givat Ram. *Tel* (02) 670 8811. 🚌 9, 17, 24. ⬜ 10am–4pm Mon, Wed, Sat & hols, 4–9pm Tue, 10am–9pm (Shrine of the Book closes 4pm) Thu, 10am–2pm Fri & hol eves. ⬤ Sun, Yom Kippur. 📷 ♿ 🍴 🛍 📷 www.imj.org.il

### The Rabbi (1912–13)

*Russian-Jewish artist Marc Chagall painted this figure after moving to Paris – it shows Cubist influence.*

### Yemenite Prayer Stand

*This 18th-century prayer stand (tevah) would have been used for reading the Torah in the synagogue.*

### MUSEUM GUIDE

*The main block is on two levels. The upper (entrance) level concentrates on contemporary art and design. The lower level displays Judaica, archaeology and the rest of the art collection. The complex also has a sculpture garden, a space for children's activities and the Shrine of the Book.*

### ★ Horb Synagogue

*This richly painted synagogue interior from Horb in Germany dates from 1735. The decoration includes flowers, animals and excerpts from traditional prayers.*

### STAR EXHIBITS

- ★ Shrine of the Book
- ★ Beth Shean Mosaic
- ★ Horb Synagogue

# Exploring the Israel Museum

Thanks to its wide variety of sources, the collection is extraordinarily eclectic. Its core was inherited from the Bezalel School and Museum (Israel's first arts academy) and the Israel Department of Antiquities, and this has been supplemented by gifts, loans and acquisitions from around the globe. The biggest draw, though, for most visitors is the Shrine of the Book, which houses the Dead Sea Scrolls *(see pp136–7)*.

Byzantine-era oil lamp

**Jeanne Hebuterne, Seated (1918), by Amedeo Modigliani**

## JUDAICA AND JEWISH ETHNOGRAPHY

Jewish culture is represented by two separate sections. The Judaica section, one of the largest of its kind in the world, displays objects connected with Jewish religious practice *(see pp22–3)*. It spans the period from the Middle Ages to the present, and has exhibits from as far afield as Spain and China. Among the most precious objects are the medieval illuminated manuscripts. These include a 14th-century German *Haggadah* (the story read at Passover of the Israelites' liberation from Egypt) and the Rothschild Miscellany, a 15th-century collection of biblical, legal and other pieces.

**The Rothschild Miscellany**

Elaborate silverwork on display includes *hadassim* (spiceboxes used during the ceremony of separation between the Sabbath and the start of the week) and the *rimonim* (pomegranates that decorate Torah scrolls in the synagogue). Another highlight is the large collection of *Hannukkiot* – the oil lamps that are lit for Hanukkah *(see p39)*. There are also three beautiful, complete synagogue interiors, from Italy, Germany and India.

The ethnographic section covers the culture and daily life of various Jewish communities around the world. It exhibits textiles, clothing, jewellery, reconstructions of rooms and ritual articles connected with life events such as birth, circumcision and marriage.

## ART COLLECTIONS

The museum's various art collections cover a wide range of periods and artistic disciplines. In consecutive rooms visitors can take in Chinese porcelain, African figurines, Impressionist masterpieces and even an entire 18th-century French salon.

Rooms on the lower level house the modern art collection, which has international works from the 1890s to the 1960s. These include paintings by figures such as Gauguin, Cézanne, Chagall, Matisse and Modigliani. Twentieth-century sculpture is also represented,

**The Rothschild Room, an 18th-century Parisian salon donated by Baron Edmond de Rothschild**

both here and outdoors in the Billy Rose Art Garden *(see p136)*. On the upper level, the rooms are devoted to design, architecture and contemporary art. The exhibits on this level are rotated regularly.

One of the largest collections of Israeli art in the country is exhibited in a series of rooms on both floors. It begins with paintings and drawings produced in the 19th century, at the beginning of Jewish resettlement *(see p51)*. The 1920s and 30s are represented by figurative pieces by artists such as Reuven Rubin and Yitzhak Danziger. The contemporary Israeli art on display mirrors, and sometimes anticipates, tendencies seen elsewhere in the world.

Other lower-floor rooms are devoted to prints and drawings, photography, Old Master paintings (including a large work by Poussin depicting the sacking of the Second Temple; *see p45*), Islamic and East Asian art and the art of Africa, Oceania and the Americas.

**Anthropoid sarcophagi, a highlight of the archaeology collection**

## ARCHAEOLOGY

The archaeology collection constitutes the largest section of the museum. Most pieces are on loan from the Israel Antiquities Authority and come from excavations carried out all over the country, which has the highest concentration of digs in the world. The digs cover a vast period of history – from as far back as 1.5 million BC – and have revealed artifacts from an impressive number of civilizations, from Palaeolithic flint

utensils, through Canaanite and Israelite figurines, to Byzantine mosaics and Islamic jewellery. The museum's collection represents most aspects of this cultural spectrum, and visitors will require at least two hours to fully appreciate the range of pieces on display.

The artifacts are arranged chronologically, starting in the gallery that leads from the main staircase. Objects to look out for in the first section (Palaeolithic to Chalcolithic periods, 1.5 million–3500 BC) include the jewellery and sculpted figures of the Natufian culture (10th–9th millennium BC), the 6,000-year-old, house-shaped ossuaries at the end of the first gallery and the elegant copperware of the so-called Judaean Desert Treasure (5th millennium BC). Highlights of the following rooms, the Canaanite Period (3500–1200 BC), are the sophisticated gold jewellery and, particularly, the anthropoid sarcophagi found in a cemetery at Deir el-Balah, in the Gaza Strip.

The Israelite Period (1200–586 BC) starts with the rise of the Israelites in the region and ends with the destruction of Solomon's Temple. In these rooms, look out for the beautiful Philistine pottery, the ivory pomegranate inscribed with ancient Hebrew (believed to be the only object ever found relating to worship in Solomon's Temple) and the priestly benediction written on a tiny silver amulet – the earliest known fragment of biblical text (7th century BC).

**Mosaic from floor of 6th-century AD synagogue at Gaza, showing King David playing the lyre**

Finds from the next 300 years are relatively scarce but the Hellenistic, Roman and Byzantine periods (332 BC–AD 636) offer fascinating objects, such as the sarcophagi and ossuaries from various Jewish catacombs, the bronze statue of the emperor Hadrian and the beautiful mosaics from Tsipori (Sepphoris), Kisufim, Gaza and Beth Shean.

In the last room are objects from neighbouring Middle Eastern and Mediterranean civilizations that had some bearing on the history of the Holy Land. The artifacts here include Egyptian cult and game objects, Assyrian and Babylonian reliefs, Greek vases and Roman jewellery.

Throughout the section are interesting models and reconstructions of some of the most important sites in this part of the world. The permanent exhibition is also flanked by temporary displays based on historical themes or particular archaeological sites.

### JEWISH ART OF THE DIASPORA

During the many centuries of the Diaspora, Jews around the world directed their artistic talents primarily to ritual objects connected with the life cycle and synagogue liturgy. They produced fine examples of applied art, especially in the fields of gold- and silverware, other metalwork and manuscript decoration. Naturally, the motifs and techniques reflect the place and time in which the objects were produced, but many elements, both functional and iconographic, recur again and again. These recurring themes and local variations can be appreciated among the many exhibits in the museum's Judaica section.

**18th-century silver spicebox from Germany**

## RUTH YOUTH WING

This section of the museum is devoted to interactive art activities. The idea behind it was to introduce children to art and culture. The largest of its kind in the world, the centre has now extended its reach to adults. With ten classrooms, an auditorium, library, recycling workshop and exhibition space, it provides a stimulating environment for children and adults to learn about creative processes. There are regular "hands on" exhibitions, art courses and summer schemes for all ages, as well as tours for groups with special needs.

**Children participating in creative activities in the Ruth Youth Wing**

## BILLY ROSE ART GARDEN

The garden was designed by the American sculptor Isamu Noguchi. It is an extraordinary combination of elements from local history and landscape, motifs from the traditional Zen garden and significant works of modern sculpture. It is laid out as a series of semi-circular terraces echoing those made for centuries by farmers in the Judaean Hills. Indigenous plants such as olive trees, cypresses and rosemary bushes are dotted around the garden.

The garden offers an overview of sculpture through the 20th century. There are stunning early works by Rodin, Maillol, Picasso and Bourdelle. The curvaceous shapes in Henry Moore's pieces contrast with the angular composition of David Smith's *Cubi VI* (1963). Contemporary sculptures include James Turrell's intriguing installation with a large rectangular opening in the top for observing the sky, and Claes Oldenburg's "rotting" apple core, rich in symbolism and existential allusions.

## SHRINE OF THE BOOK

Built to house the Dead Sea Scrolls and other important artifacts, the intriguingly shaped Shrine of the Book has become a symbol of the whole museum. The unusual design, by American architects F Kiesler and A Bartos, is inspired by the scrolls themselves. The distinctive dome is intended to imitate the lids of the jars in which the scrolls were found. Near the entrance is a black granite wall. The contrast between the black of the wall and the white of the dome is a reference to the decisive battle between the Children of Darkness and the Children of Light, described in the scroll known as the War Scroll. This final confrontation between good and evil would, the authors believed, herald the coming of the Messiah.

Inside, a long, subtly lit passageway, designed to evoke the catacomb-like environment in which the scrolls were found, has a permanent exhibition on life in Qumran at the time the scrolls were written. It leads into the main chamber under the dome. The imposing showcase directly beneath the dome contains a facsimile of the Great Isaiah Scroll, the only biblical book that survived in its entirety. Its 66 chapters were written on several strips of parchment, which were then sewn together, making it more than 7 m (23 ft) long. One of the surrounding display cases contains part of the real scroll. Also on show are the Psalms Scroll, 28

**Magdalena Abakonowicz's *Negev* (1987), Billy Rose Art Garden**

columns of text consisting of psalms, hymns and a prose passage about the psalms; the War Scroll; the Manual of Discipline; the Temple Scroll; and the 10th-century Aleppo Codex – not one of the Dead Sea Scrolls, but the oldest complete Bible in Hebrew.

On the Shrine's lower level are 2nd-century AD articles, such as keys and baskets, found in the Cave of Letters, south of Ein Gedi *(see p197)*. Adjacent to the Shrine of the Book is a Second Temple-era model of Jerusalem. Originally constructed on the grounds of the Holyland Hotel on the outskirts of the city, this large-scale model was relocated to the museum in 2006. It offers visitors a three-dimensional view of the landscape of Jerusalem during the 1st century. Mainly built from local limestone, the model covers almost one acre and was constructed at a scale of 1:50, with 2 cm of the model representing one metre of the city.

**Symbolic clash of darkness and light at the Shrine of the Book entrance**

# The Dead Sea Scrolls

In 1947, a Bedouin shepherd, in search of a lost goat near the Dead Sea, entered a cave and discovered jars containing seven ancient scrolls. Over the next two decades fragments of some 800 more were found in 11 caves. At the same time, archaeologists, looking for signs of habitation, uncovered the nearby settlement of Qumran *(see p191)*. The scrolls had been written in the Late Second Temple period, between the 3rd century

**Jar in which scrolls were found**

BC and AD 68. Some contain the oldest existing versions of biblical scriptures. Others are tracts on history, daily life and the messianic predictions of a Hebrew sect generally identified with the separatist and monastic Essenes. Since the discovery of the scrolls, their interpretation, the identity and mission of their authors and the significance of nearby Qumran have been the subject of passionate academic and theological debate.

**The Shrine of the Book** *is dominated by a dramatic display case, which contains a copy of the Great Isaiah Scroll. It was designed to look like the wooden rods around which the Torah scrolls are rolled for readings at synagogue services.*

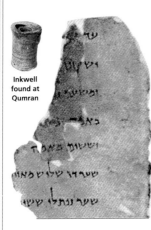

**Inkwell found at Qumran**

**The reconstruction** *of thousands of scroll fragments is still being carried out by researchers hoping to unravel the mysteries surrounding the scrolls.*

**The parchment** *on which the scrolls were written was made from sheepskin. Inkwells found near a table at Qumran suggest a scriptorium – a room for copying manuscripts.*

**The Great Isaiah Scroll** *is the largest and best preserved of the scrolls. Written around 100 BC, it is 1,000 years older than the oldest biblical manuscript known before the finds at Qumran.*

**Qumran was excavated** *by Roland de Vaux, a French Dominican friar. He believed that the settlement was a communal retreat used by the Essenes.*

# Biblical Zoo ❽

Manahat. *Tel* (02) 675 0111. 🚌 26,
33, 99. ⭕ 9am–5pm (7pm Jun–Aug)
Sun–Thu, 9am–4:30pm Fri, 10am–5pm
(6pm Jun–Aug) Sat. 🖼

The Jerusalem Biblical Zoo,
also known as the Tisch
Family Zoological Gardens,
is famous for its collection of
wildlife featured in the Bible.
This group of animals, many
of which are no longer
naturally present in the Holy
Land, includes bears, lions,
Arabian oryx and Nile
crocodiles. There are also
other endangered species
from around the world. The
zoo occupies an attractive site
in the southwestern suburbs
of the city, surrounded by
green hills. Visitors can gain an
overview of the zoo on a train
ride around the grounds.

# Yad Vashem ❾

Mount Herzl. *Tel* (02) 644 3400.
🚌 13, 21, 23, 27. ⭕ 9am–5pm
Sun–Thu, 9am–2pm Fri. 🖼
**www.**yadvashem.org

Yad Vashem, meaning "a name
and a place" (from Isaiah 56:
5), is an archive, research
institute, museum and, above
all, a monument to perpetuate
the memory of the more than
six million who died in the
Nazi Holocaust. More than 20
monuments occupy this
hillside site.

Entrance to Yad Vashem is
along the Avenue of the
Righteous Among Nations,
which is lined with plaques
bearing the names of Gentiles

who helped Jews and, in
doing so, put their own
lives at risk. Some 16,000
people are recognized,
including Oskar
Schindler (*see p117*).
The avenue leads to the
new Historical Museum,
which was designed by
Jewish architect Moshe
Safdie and inaugurated
in 2005. The museum
is one long corridor,
carved into the
mountain, with 10
exhibition halls, each
dedicated to a different
chapter of the
Holocaust. Its exhibits
include some 2,500
personal items donated
by survivors, adding a
harrowing first-person
dimension to the horrors that
began with the rise of the
Nazis in 1933 and culminated
in the death camps.

The Hall of Remembrance
beside the museum is a stark,
tomb-like chamber that bears
the names of 21 of the main
camps on flat, black basalt
slabs. At the centre of
the vast chamber is
a casket of ashes
from the cremation
ovens; above it is
an eternal flame.
The nearby Hall of
Names is devoted
to recording the
names of all those
Jews who perished,
along with as much
biographical detail
as possible.

Visitors to Yad Vashem
are expected to dress
appropriately; shorts and
miniskirts are not acceptable.

**Grave of Rabin, Mount Herzl**

# Mount Herzl and Herzl Museum ❿

Mount Herzl. *Tel* (02) 643 3266.
🚌 13, 17, 18, 20, 23.
⭕ 9am–3:30pm Sun–Thu, 9am–
12:30pm Fri. 🖼

Mount Herzl (in Hebrew *Har
Hertzel*) is a high hill north of
central Jerusalem,
named after Theodor
Herzl, the man
considered to have
been the founder of
Zionism (*see p51*). The
slopes serve as a large
cemetary and Herzl's
tomb lies at the top of
the hill. At the
entrance to the site is
the new Herzl
Museum, which
opened in 2005. It
offers a crash course in Zionist
history, with audiovisual
presentations and recreations
of the founding father's study
and library. Mount Herzl is also
the burial place of three of
Israel's prime ministers and the
country's presidents. It is
also the site of Israel's main
military cemetary.

**Janusz Korczak
Memorial, Yad Vashem**

# Ein Kerem ⓫

7 km (4 miles) W of central
Jerusalem. 🚌 17, 184.

A picturesque village, Ein
Kerem ("the vineyard
spring") has strong biblical
associations. According to
Christian tradition, John the

**Memorial to the Victims in Camps, Yad Vashem**

Baptist was born and lived here. The village boasts several fine churches and monasteries connected with his life. Recognizable by its tall, thin tower, the Franciscan **Church of St John the Baptist** dates from the 17th century, but is built over the ruins of earlier Byzantine and Crusader structures. Steps inside the church lead down into a natural cave, known as the Grotto of the Nativity of St John, which tradition connects with the birth of the Baptist.

The other church of note is the two-tiered **Church of the Visitation**, completed in 1955 to a design by Antonio Barluzzi, architect of the Dominus Flevit Chapel (see p113) and the Chapel of the Flagellation (see p64). It commemorates the Virgin Mary's visit to Elizabeth, mother of John the Baptist, who was then pregnant, an episode depicted in mosaic on the church's façade. Within is a natural grotto, in front of which are the remains of Roman-era houses. According to tradition, the grotto is where Elizabeth hid with her infant son to escape from the Massacre of the Innocents (the killing of all first-born sons, ordered by King Herod). The courtyard walls are lined with tiled panels inscribed with the *Magnificat* (Luke 1: 46–55), Mary's hymn of thanks, in 42 languages.

At the bottom of the hill below the church is a small, abandoned mosque. Beside it surfaces the spring (popularly known as the Spring of the Virgin) from which the village takes its name.

One of the other pleasures to savour in Ein Kerem is its tranquil, wooded, valley setting. This can be best appreciated on a beautiful scenic walk that starts beside the sculpture at the beginning of the access road to Yad Vashem, and winds through the trees.

Church of St John the Baptist, Ein Kerem

## Hadassah Hospital Synagogue ⑫

Ein Kerem. **Tel** (02) 677 6271.
🚌 19, 27. ⏰ 8am–1pm & 2–3:30pm Sun–Thu, 8am–12:30pm Fri. 📷 🎥 🚫

A splendid cycle of 12 stained-glass windows decorates the synagogue at the otherwise unremarkable Hadassah Hospital. The windows were created in 1960–61 by the Russian-Jewish artist Marc Chagall (see p33), and installed the following year for the inauguration of the building. Each of the windows represents one of the 12 tribes of Israel (Genesis 49). Tradition associates each of the tribes with a symbol, a precious stone and a social role, and these elements are all represented in Chagall's imagery and choice of colour.

Several of the windows were damaged by shrapnel during the 1967 War (see p54) and had to be repaired by the artist. However, one of the windows (a green one) bears a small symbolic bullet hole in the lower half, deliberately left there as a testimony to the fighting.

## Abu Ghosh ⑬

13 km (8 miles) W of central Jerusalem. 🚌 185, 186.

This Arab village just north of the main Jerusalem-Tel Aviv highway was considered by the Crusaders to be Emmaus, where Christ appeared to two disciples in the days after his Resurrection. The beautiful Romanesque **Crusader Church** was built in the early 12th century by the Knights Hospitallers and stands almost complete in its original form. Its 12th-century frescoes are lovely, but in a poor state of repair. The adjacent early 20th-century monastery belongs to French Olivetan Benedictine monks, who produce pottery. Up on the hill above the village stands the **Church of Notre Dame de l'Arche de l'Alliance**, built in 1924 over the remains of a 5th-century church, whose mosaics are still visible. It is said to occupy the site of the house of Abinadab, where the fabled Ark of the Covenant (see p21) rested for 20 years (1 Samuel 7: 1–2) until David took it to Jerusalem.

The modern Church of Notre Dame de l'Arche de l'Alliance, Abu Ghosh

# THREE GUIDED WALKS

**Jerusalem shield at New City Hall**

Jerusalem is a perfect city to explore on foot: it is small and compact, traffic is light, the pavements are rarely crowded, and there are plenty of sites to see and places to sit and rest. This is particularly true in the Old City, which, with the exception of just one or two roads, doesn't allow for motor vehicles at all. Most streets are simply too narrow and meandering, and there are too many steps. It is a place perfectly described by the over-used adjective "labyrinthine"; a place in which getting lost is inevitable. However, this is no bad thing because wandering aimlessly around the Old City is a highly pleasurable and rewarding activity. For that reason, we have avoided describing any walks within Jerusalem's ancient fortified walls.

Instead, we suggest you get up on the walls themselves, which is something few visitors do, largely because they remain unaware that the opportunity exists.

Similarly, few visitors spend any time exploring the more modern parts of the city and so miss out on some attractive old quarters and some fine architecture. Much of this is non-indigenous, raised at the end of the 19th century, when the great powers of Europe were all vying for political influence in the Holy City. This was expressed through ostentatious examples of their own national architectures. Muscovite churches, English Gothic cathedrals, German hospices and Italian insurance offices all serve as reminders of the central role Jerusalem has always played in the Western consciousness.

## CHOOSING A WALK

**Three Walks**
*The routes of the three walks are marked on this map, which shows the main areas of Jerusalem.*

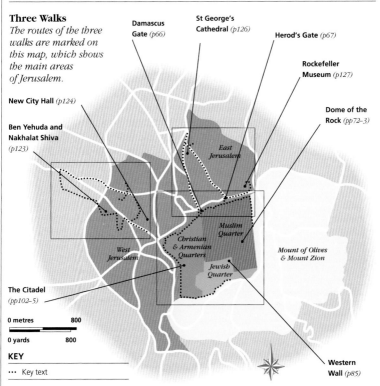

St George's Cathedral (p126)

Damascus Gate (p66)

Herod's Gate (p67)

Rockefeller Museum (p127)

New City Hall (p124)

Ben Yehuda and Nakhalat Shiva (p123)

Dome of the Rock (pp72–3)

East Jerusalem

The Citadel (pp102–5)

Muslim Quarter

Christian & Armenian Quarters

West Jerusalem

Jewish Quarter

Mount of Olives & Mount Zion

| 0 metres | 800 |
| 0 yards | 800 |

**KEY**

••• Key text

Western Wall (p85)

◁ Snow covers graves on the Mount of Olives, which faces the Old City across the Kidron Valley

# A 60-Minute Walk around the Old City Walls

The Old City of Jerusalem may occupy a relatively small area geographically, but its compactness and uneven topography make it a frequently confusing place to explore. One good way to gain an overview is to take to the ramparts and view the crush of alleys, domes and towers from the top of the walls that enclose them. Visitors can walk along two sections of wall: from Jaffa Gate clockwise to St Stephen's Gate, and from Jaffa Gate anti-clockwise to the Dung Gate. The section between St Stephen's Gate and the Dung Gate is closed to the public. Many steep flights of steps mean that this is not a walk for the elderly or infirm.

The city walls wrap around the Tower of David

**Clockwise from Jaffa Gate**
Jerusalem's walls were built in the first half of the 16th century (in part on the line of earlier walls) on the order of the Ottoman sultan Suleyman the Magnificent. They are pierced by eight gates, of which seven remain in use. Until as recently as 1870, the gates were all closed from sunset to sunrise.

A section of the ramparts just east of New Gate ②

### TIPS FOR WALKERS

*Starting point:* Jaffa Gate.
*Length:* Jaffa Gate to St Stephen's Gate 1.5 miles (1 km); Jaffa Gate to Dung Gate 0.75 miles (0.5 km).
*Open:* 9am–4pm Sat–Thu; 9am–2pm Fri. There is a separate admission fee for each of the two sections of wall.
*Stopping-off points:* There are several small cafés on Omar ibn el-Khattab Square, just inside the Jaffa Gate. Otherwise, when you descend at St Stephen's Gate, walk west along the Via Dolorosa and then left onto El-Wad Road for Abu Shukri, which serves the best houmous in town.

Start the walk by climbing the steps that are immediately inside the **Jaffa Gate** ① (*see p100*), to your left as you enter the Old City. After paying admission, you pass through a gate and ascend a steep flight of steps leading to the top of the gatehouse. Heading north brings you to the first of some 35 watchtowers that punctuate the circuit of the walls. This one has a raised platform which allows walkers to step up for a view of the large new shopping and office development that is currently taking shape outside the city walls. Looking into the Old City, you will see the backs of buildings belonging to the Latin Patriarchate, the centre of Roman Catholicism in Jerusalem.

A short distance on and you'll notice that the third watchtower along has been reinforced with side walls; this was done by the Jordanians when they were in occupation of the Old City between 1948 and 1967, and Jerusalem was divided between Arabs and Jews. After skirting around three sides of a crescent-topped dome, the ramparts pass over **New Gate** ②. This was added in 1889 to allow pilgrims in the compounds outside the walls direct access to the Christian Quarter.

From here the ramparts drop, following the slope of the land. Notice the profusion of aerials and satellite dishes inside the walls, evidence of the large number of people who continue to live in the Old City. At a certain point the level of the rooftops falls below that of the ramparts, affording a fine view of the golden Dome of the Rock.

### KEY

••• Walk route

🔆 Viewpoint

## Damascus Gate to St Stephen's Gate

The ramparts now climb over **Damascus Gate** ③ (*see p66*), the grandest of all the Old City gates. From up here you can survey the vaulted roof over the gate's defensive dogleg entrance tunnel and the crowds on El-Wad Road. Continuing east, you will encounter a rapid succession of

The view from the ramparts between New Gate and Damascus Gate

0 metres      200
0 yards      200

towers, because attacks on Jerusalem have traditionally always come from the north, where the approach is flattest (the approaches to the east, south and west are protected by deep valleys).

It was the north wall, just east of the next gate, **Herod's Gate** ④ (*see p67*), that the Crusader army breached on 15 July 1099 to capture Jerusalem from the Muslims. Look outwards from the gate and you are facing down Salah ed-Din Street, the main street of Arab East Jerusalem.

At **Storks' Tower** ⑤, with its views to the northeast of the Hebrew University's Mount Scopus campus, the wall swings through 90° to run due south. From the ramparts here, you overlook the tombs that fill the Kidron Valley below and the slopes of the Mount of Olives (*pp110–111*). As you approach the final gate, to your right, just inside the walls, are the remains of the complex of the biblical Pool of Bethseda and, beside them, the Crusader-built St Anne's Church (*see p67*).

Crenellations on Damascus Gate ③

The walk ends at **St Stephen's Gate** ⑥ (*see p67*), where you descend to street level. The beginning of the Via Dolorosa (*see pp30–31*) is just ahead, which, if followed, will lead back towards the Jaffa Gate area. Energy permitting, you can then embark on another short ramparts walk.

The modern amphitheatre outside Damascus Gate ③

## Anti-clockwise from Jaffa Gate

The access to this section of the ramparts is from outside the city walls, just south of the **Citadel** ⑦ (*see pp102–5*). The initial stretch southwards is like a trench, with a high stone wall on either side of the walkway. This arrangement was fashioned by the Jordanian army between 1948 and 1967. Occasional vantage points allow you to look out across the Hinnom Valley below to the red rooftops of the early Jewish settlement of Mishkenot Shaananim (*see p121*) and the cliff-like bulk of the King David Hotel (*see p122*). At the southwestern corner you have a good view of Sultan's Pool, an ancient reservoir, now dry and used as an outdoor concert venue.

As the ramparts run east, they pass close by the Church of the Dormition (*see p116*) before passing over the **Zion Gate** ⑧ (*see p106*). The gate is riddled with bulletholes from the fighting in 1948, although, of course, you can't see this from above.

The final stretch affords wonderful views of the Arab village of Silwan, before the rampart walk ends on Batei Makhase Street, which you can follow down to the **Dung Gate** ⑨ (*see p84*). This is the smallest of the city gates, despite being widened for cars by the Jordanians. The name indicates that what is now the main access to the Western Wall was probably once the site of a refuse tip.

# A 90-Minute Walk around West Jerusalem

The heart of West Jerusalem, centred on Jaffa Road, was largely developed during the years of the British Mandate (1917–1948). So, while it is nowhere near as ancient as the Old City, it does carry a weight of recent history related to the founding of the Jewish state of Israel. Aside from the scattering of historic buildings and monuments, this is also the heart of the modern city, with pedestrianised streets of cafés, restaurants and shops, cultural centres and busy markets. It is a highly rewarding area to explore.

**Passing time on pedestrianised Ben Yehuda Street ⑤**

**Water sculpture on Safra Square at the New City Hall ①**

## Jaffa Road

Until Tel Aviv got its own port in the 1930s, Jews arriving in Palestine would disembark at Jaffa, entering Jerusalem on the Jaffa Road. It ran right up to the Old City and the correspondingly named Jaffa Gate. The road now ends just short of the city walls, which is where this walk begins, at the rounded façade of the **Former Barclays Bank** ① (look for the "BB" in the iron window grilles). The building was on the line that divided Arabs and Jews between 1948 and 1967 and still bears the scars left by bullets.

Walk west, past two British Mandate-era post boxes, and almost immediately you come to palm-filled Safra Square, forecourt to the **New City Hall** ② *(see p124)*, also home to the main tourist information office. Cross to the lefthand side of the road at the next junction to pass **Feingold House** ③, built in 1895, with its series of arched shop fronts and one arched entrance to a passageway containing the fine bar-restaurant Barood *(see p150)*. Look back to spot the winged lion on top of the Generali Building, trademark of the Italian insurance company that once had its offices here.

Continue along Jaffa Road, taking the next left into Rivlin Street and **Nakhalat Shiva** ④ *(see p123).* This is one of the oldest parts of the modern city (founded 1869) but also one of the liveliest. Its attractive two-storey buildings are home to trendy eateries and late-night bars. At the bottom of Rivlin turn right,

**KEY**

∙∙∙  Walk route

then head up Salomon to Jaffa Square, the traditional gathering point for protests and demonstrations. Running west from here, **Ben Yehuda Street** ⑤ *(see p123)* is one of the city's main shopping streets. Take the third right into Ben Hillel, cross over main King George V Street and you will be standing in front of Felafel & Shwarma King, which makes supposedly the best felafels in the city.

**A balcony in the historic neighbourhood of Nakhalat Shiva ④**

*For hotels and restaurants in this area see pp257–8 and pp272–4*

## Mahane Yehuda

Continue west along **Agrippas Street** ⑥, passing on the right a passage that leads to top restaurant Arcadia. This has traditionally been a poor area with cheap rents that have proved attractive to recent immigrants, hence all the signs in Cyrillic. Agrippas is also the southern boundary of **Mahane Yehuda Market** ⑦, the city's colourful prime source of fresh produce, from fruit and vegetables to fish and meat *(see p148)*.

Exit the market back onto Jaffa Road, now returning east. Pass by a building on your right that has a doorway flanked by two lions on pillars – the former residence of the British Consul, 1863–90

The garden terrace at Ticho House, open daily for lunch ⑪

– before arriving at a major junction marked by a small monument of a mortar on a plinth; this is a **Davidka** ⑧, a weapon that played a large role in the 1948 War. The Hebrew inscription is from the Old Testament Book of Isaiah and reads, "For I will defend this city to save it".

Fork left at the monument to follow historic **Ha-Neviim Street** ⑨ *(see p124)*, which during the 19th century was one of Jerusalem's main avenues. It is lined by some notable buildings, including at No. 64 a fine house once occupied by the English Victorian painter William Holman Hunt and, at No. 58, Thabor House, designed and once occupied by the German Conrad Schick, one of the city's foremost early architects.

Just past Thabor House, a pretty, high-walled lane on the left leads to the **Ethiopian Church** ⑩, a modest basilica with an interior painted in nursery blues and pinks, and filled with glittery, golden icons and smoky incense.

Return to Ha-Neviim and cross over to head south down Ha-Rav Kook Street looking for the signs for **Ticho House** ⑪ *(see p123)*. This is an historic Arab residence

Decorative panel, Ethiopian Church ⑩

that has been turned into a lively cultural centre hosting art exhibitions and regular jazz, folk and classical recitals; it also has a pleasant garden terrace.

Returning to Ha-Neviim, take the next right and walk straight over the roundabout; the end point of the walk is visible ahead in the form of the three Muscovite-styled domes of the **Cathedral of the Holy Trinity** ⑫ *(see p124)*. Consecrated in 1872, the church was built to cater to Russian pilgrims, who at the time far outnumbered pilgrims from any other country. From here, it's just a short step back to Jaffa Road and the start of the walk.

### TIPS FOR WALKERS

***Starting point:*** *Jaffa Road.*
***Length:*** *2 miles (3 km).*
***Best time to walk:*** *Any time, but avoid Friday afternoon and Saturday, when everything is closed.*
***Stopping-off points:*** *In addition to the places mentioned in the walk, there are dozens of food stalls around Mahane Yehuda Market, including some selling "meorav Yerushalmi", literally "Jerusalem meats", a mix of chopped livers, kidneys, hearts and beef, fried and served in pockets of bread. At the end of the walk, there are two good cafés at the junction of Heleni Ha-Malka and Jaffa Road, and many more cafés and restaurants in Nakhalat Shiva, which is just across Jaffa Road.*

A stall in one of the covered lanes of Mahane Yehuda Market ⑦

# A 90-Minute Walk around East Jerusalem

East Jerusalem is the Palestinian Arab part of the city.
It lies north of the Old City and east of the main
north–south road Derekh Ha-Shalom, swelling over
the Mount of Olives and down the other side. The
main street is Salah ed-Din Street, which is visited as
part of this walk. High-profile tourist sights are few,
but it is a vibrant area with many points of interest,
including Christian pilgrimage sights and the Holy
Land's most atmospheric old hotel.

**A fruit stall on the corner of Nablus Road**

### Nablus Road

The walk starts at **Damascus
Gate** ① *(see p66)*, the largest
and one of the busiest of
the Old City gates. Taking
advantage of the perpetual
crowds, small traders
spread their wares on
sheets around the
amphitheatre-like
space in front of
the gate so that it
operates as a small
makeshift market.
Cross the busy road
that runs parallel with
the city walls to the
junction with Nablus
Road, which is also
busy with street
traders selling breads
and fruit. Some of
these traders stand
in the shadow of
**Schmidt's Girls' College**
②, part of the St Paul's
Hospice complex, designed
in fine Germanic style by the
same architect responsible for
Mount Zion's Church of the
Dormition *(see p116)*.
Walk north up Nablus Road
and shortly you come to an
alley enclosed between high
walls off to the right: this
leads to the **Garden Tomb** ③
*(see p126)*. The claims for it
as the burial place of Jesus
Christ have been dismissed by

**An elderly
Palestinian**

archaeologists, but that does
not seem to deter the coach-
loads of Christian pilgrims
who flock here each day to
engage in open-air prayer
sessions in what is,
admittedly, a lovely
garden setting. Stroll on,
passing on your left the
Arab bus station for
services to West
Bank towns and
Gaza. At the next
traffic junction,
marked by the modest
little Sadd and Said
Mosque, continue north
as Nablus Road becomes
a narrow, leafy lane
squeezed beside the
fortified bulk of the local
US Consulate. On
your right at No.
14 is **Palestinian
Pottery** ④,
founded on this site
back in 1922 by the
Balians, one of three
Armenian families
brought over by the
British authorities from
Kuthaya, Turkey, to
renovate the ceramic
tiles on the Dome of the
Rock. Ring the bell to enter
and visit the showrooms
and a small museum on
the history of ceramics in
Jerusalem. You can also
watch the craftspeople
at work hand-painting
designs onto the pottery
prior to firing.
Further along, on
the left, are several fine
examples of late 19th-
and early 20th-century
buildings, including a
villa that houses the East
Jerusalem offices of the
British Council. On the
right is the high wall
that rings St George's
Cathedral, which is
visited later in the walk.

**Handpainting a ceramic tile at the
Palestinian Pottery workshop** ④

**KEY**

••• Walk route

Nablus Road now joins
with Salah ed-Din Street,
but continue on, taking the
second right, Louis Vincent
Street, a short cul-de-sac
leading to the **American
Colony Hotel** ⑤ *(see p127)*.
Originally built (1865–76) as

a home by a wealthy Arab merchant, the building was subsequently sold to pilgrims from Chicago, hence the name, before later becoming a hospice and then a hotel. It boasts a beautiful courtyard café and equally welcoming cellar bar. Opposite the main entrance to the hotel, beside an attractive little giftshop, steps leads up to the excellent Bookshop at the American Colony Hotel (*see p149*).

### Salah ed-Din Street
Return the way you came, taking a quick detour left down Abu Obeida Street to take a look at **Orient House** ⑥, an elegant 1897 villa that

Lobby area of the historic American Colony Hotel ⑤

0 metres 250

0 yards 250

The Gothic bell tower of St George's Cathedral ⑧

served as the headquarters of the Palestinian Authority in Jerusalem until it was shut down by the Israeli government in 2001.

Back on Salah ed-Din Street an easily missed, plain door in a wall gives access to the **Kings' Tombs** ⑦ (*see p127*) – actually the tomb of a single queen, dating from the 1st century AD. From here, cross over the street to the main gate of **St George's Cathedral** ⑧ (*see p126*) and buzz for admittance. Visitors are usually free to wander the gardens and courts of what is a surprisingly large compound. It is worth finding your way into the cathedral for its admirably restrained interior, which contains the royal arms formerly displayed in Government House during the time of British rule and deposited here when the Mandate came to an end in 1948. Services are still held throughout the week, although the language of mass these days is Arabic.

South of the cathedral, **Salah ed-Din Street** ⑨ becomes a busy high street with a clutter of low-rise shops, moneychangers, pharmacies and snack joints. Although vibrant, the scene is very visibly poorer than the corresponding main streets over in West Jerusalem. At its southern end Salah ed-Din Street terminates opposite the city walls and **Herod's Gate** ⑩, which to the Arabs is the far more poetic Bab el-Zahra,

or "Flower Gate". At this point you can enter the Old City; or turn left and follow the walls down to the very worthwhile **Rockefeller Museum** ⑪ (*see p127*) and its archaeological finds from the Holy Land; or bear right and follow Sultan Suleyman Street, past rows of small clothes and jewellery shops, and eateries, back to the Damascus Gate area.

Decorative sarcophagus at the Rockefeller Museum ⑪

### TIPS FOR WALKERS

***Starting point:*** *Damascus Gate.*
***Length:*** *1.5 miles (2.4 km).*
***Palestinian Pottery:*** *Open 9am–4pm Mon–Sat.*
***Stopping-off points:*** *The American Colony Hotel serves lunch in the courtyard garden or indoors in Val's Brasserie Lounge. Café Europe, at 9 El-Zahra Street, just off Salah ed-Din, offers good value Western-style cuisine, including ham and eggs, in premises that resemble an English tearoom.*

# Shops and Markets

When it comes to shopping, the main attractions in Jerusalem are the souks (markets) of the Old City. In comparison with the great bazaars of Istanbul or Cairo, Jerusalem's souks are perhaps a little small, and the array of goods on offer is largely limited to souvenir items such as T-shirts and religious articles, but they still reward exploration. There is better shopping elsewhere, however, notably in the modern centre of West Jerusalem, where you'll find high-street shopping and malls, and areas of interesting boutiques: see Where to Shop, below. For more information on methods of payment and bargaining, see pp284–5.

Sacks of spices at a shop on the Old City's Souk Khan el-Zeit Street

Religious souvenirs are popular throughout the Old City

## OPENING HOURS

Shops in the Muslim Quarter of the Old City and in East Jerusalem are open daily except for Friday morning – Friday being the Islamic holy day. Many shops and stalls in the souks of the Old City are also closed all day Sunday, as many of the shop owners are Christian. Shops in the Jewish Quarter of the Old City and throughout West Jerusalem are open Sunday to Thursday from around 9am to 7pm, Friday from 9am to 3pm, and closed Saturday. Beware of local religious holidays (see pp36–9): during the holy month of Ramadan Muslim shops close 30 minutes to one hour before sunset. All Jewish-owned businesses close for Jewish holidays.

## WHERE TO SHOP

Away from the Old City, visit King George V Street around the intersection with Jaffa Road for general high-street shopping. For boutique shopping, visit nearby Ben Hillel and Bezalel Streets. However, for the most diverse selection of interesting shops you need to take a taxi south to Emek Refa'im Street in the German Colony (it is just five minutes from the King David Hotel/YMCA), which boasts a mile-long stretch of chic boutiques and cafés.

## MARKETS

The streets in the Muslim and Christian Quarters of the Old City form a single large market, or souk. In the traditional Middle Eastern manner, different areas specialise in specific wares. David Street, for example, which runs east from the Jaffa Gate area, is almost entirely devoted to tourist trinkets and is the place to buy Christian-themed kitsch. Christian Quarter Road, off David Street, is more upmarket and, in addition to more religious souvenirs, also sells items such as richly coloured Palestinian rugs, covers and dresses. Many of the shops in the Muristan (see pp90–91) specialise in leather, while the Via Dolorosa is strong on religious items. Most diverse of all is Souk Khan el-Zeit, where stores sell everything from CDs and clothes to live chickens and honey-drenched Arabic pastries.

West Jerusalem has an excellent covered central market in **Mahane Yehuda**, which runs between Agrippas Street and Jaffa Road. Many stalls sell fruit and vegetables, but there are also fishmongers, butchers, sellers of dairy produce, olives, nuts and dried fruits, plus clothing stalls. There are a handful of cafés and even a couple of small jewellery and designer apparel boutiques. The market is open Monday to Thursday from 9am to 8pm, and Friday 9am to one hour before Shabbat.

## ANTIQUES

In Jerusalem (and Israel in general), unlike other parts of the Holy Land, you may buy antiques and objects from excavations, but to take them

A typical antiques shop in the Christian Quarter of the Old City

out of the country you must obtain a permit from the Israeli Antiquities Authority (see pp284–5). Only certain shops are authorised to deal in antiques of this kind; buy from a non-accredited source and there is a chance that you may be buying looted goods. **Tzadok** in West Jerusalem is an authorised specialist that often has items for sale garnered from recent digs. Founded in 1938, **Baidun** is one of the better known of a great many antique dealers along the Via Dolorosa. It sells pieces from the Chalcolithic era to early Islamic times. The **Via Dolorosa Rest House**, in addition to antiques, always has a good selection of lovely, high-quality Russian icons.

## BOOKS

Israel's oldest and largest bookstore chain is **Steimatzky**, founded in Jerusalem in 1925. It still has several branches in the city (including on Jaffa Road, Ben Yehuda Street and King George V Street), all of which sell English-language newspapers and magazines, fiction and non-fiction, and books about Jerusalem and Israel. However, the best selection on the history and politics of the city, and the Middle East in general, is found at the **Bookshop at the American Colony Hotel**.

It also carries a well chosen selection of general English-language literature.

## CERAMICS

Distinctive items of pottery are sold in shops throughout the Old City but for the best quality visit **Palestinian Pottery** (see p146). Its show-rooms are filled with displays of the company's trademark hand-painted cups, bowls, tiles and vases, with prices starting from a few dollars.

In West Jerusalem, the narrow lanes of Nakhalat Shiva are full of pottery-stocked gift stores, including the **Guild of Ceramists Gallery Shop**, which has different collections of unique pieces by a variety of Israeli artisans.

**Distinctive items of handpainted ceramics at Palestinian Pottery**

## JEWELLERY

Israeli-jewellery designer **Michal Negrin**, whose whimsical designs are sold in her own-brand boutiques across the world, has several stores in Jerusalem; the most central of these is located in Nakhalat Shiva. **Goldtime** is another respected local chain store with several branches in Jerusalem. For more one-off and highly decorative designs visit **Puenta**, which is also in Nakhalat Shiva.

## RELIGIOUS ARTICLES

For Christian religious items there is a plethora of shops along the Old City's David Street and the Muristan area of the Christian Quarter, specialising in crucifixes, rosaries and biblical scenes crafted from olive wood. Shops selling exquisitely crafted items of Judaica are found all throughout the Old City's Jewish Quarter, particularly on the ancient Cardo, which is where you'll find **Ot Ezra** and **Chabad**. In the new city they cluster on King David Street, near the King David Hotel and YMCA. Try **Tzadok**, which carries everything from simple silver candlesticks to chalah dishes and menorahs, and shofars, the traditional Jewish trumpet made from a ram's horn.

# Entertainment

For a relatively small city, Jerusalem offers a wide range of high-quality entertainment, especially in the fields of theatre and classical music. It enjoys several months of dynamic artistic and cultural activity a year, focused on summer and the Christmas season. Every May and June there is the Israel Festival, the country's most important cultural jamboree, and in April/May there is the Jerusalem Arts Festival. The Jerusalem Film Festival is in July and there is an annual Jewish Film Festival. For information on what's on, consult the daily *Jerusalem Post* or the free monthly *Time Out Jerusalem*, available at hotels and tourist offices.

The Armenian Tavern, a lone drinking spot in the Old City

## BARS & PUBS

Apart from a small but characterful bar in the corner of the **Armenian Tavern** restaurant, just south of the Citadel, there is nowhere to drink in the Old City. You need to go to West Jerusalem and, specifically, the district of narrow lanes known as Nakhalat Shiva. This small neighbourhood has become the centre of nightlife in the city, with dozens of bars, whose patrons spill outside in the warmer months. Among them, **Barood** stands out for its superb selection of spirits and liqueurs, including shelves of absinthes, schnapps and home-made flavoured vodkas. Nearby **Stardust** is the place for terrific music on the sound system, sports on the big screen, and a happy hour that lasts four hours.

Also in West Jerusalem, just off King George V Street is **Link**, a bar-restaurant with a pleasant garden terrace. One block north and west in the premises of the Bezalel Art School, **Mona** is another good bar-restaurant, beloved of the city's secular population for being one of the few places open on Shabbat (the Jewish day of rest).

Predominantly Muslim East Jerusalem is naturally thin on venues serving alcohol, but a drink at the **Cellar Bar** of the American Colony Hotel is a signature experience every bit as essential as a stroll along the Via Dolorosa. It's the place to meet UN officials, international correspondents, NGO workers and Palestinian entrepreneurs. Otherwise, the **Kan Zaman** garden restaurant at the Jerusalem Hotel serves Palestinian beers, wine and *nargilehs* (waterpipes).

## CHILDREN

The **Jerusalem Biblical Zoo** *(see p138)* brings together all the animals that the Bible mentions as living in the Holy Land. It is beautifully designed and kids love it. The **Bloomfield Science Museum** is devoted to acquainting children with science via lots of interactive exhibits. It's fun for adults too. In the Liberty Bell Gardens (Ha-Pa'amon), just south of the Bloomfield Gardens *(see p121)*, an old railway carriage acts as a summer **Puppet Theatre**. The park itself is also very child friendly, with basketball courts, ping-pong tables and a rollerblade rink.

## CINEMA

Jerusalem's cinemas screen both local Israeli films plus international and Hollywood hits. Non-Hebrew films are usually screened in the original language with subtitles. For mainstream fare, the best bet is the **Gil** cinema complex in the Malkha Mall in the southwest of the city. The **Jerusalem Cinematheque**, on the slopes of the Hinnon Valley just outside the Old City walls, screens seasons of classics and retrospectives, as well as recent world cinema releases. Every July it hosts the Jerusalem Film Festival. **Lev Smador** in the German Colony is another quality art-house cinema, specialising in European and independent films. The nearby **Third Ear** is a courtyard book, DVD and CD store that also screens films in its small auditorium.

## MUSIC

The **Henry Crown Concert Hall** at the Jerusalem Centre for the Performing Arts is the major venue for classical performances and home to the Jerusalem Symphony

Creative advertising for the Cinematheque Film Festival

Orchestra. Organ and choral concerts are held regularly at the **Church of the Dormition** (*see p116*) on Mount Zion, while the **YMCA** and **Ticho House** host regular classical recitals by soloists and ensembles, and regular folk evenings. In East Jerusalem, the **Kan Zaman** restaurant has Friday night performances of classical Arabic music.

## ROCK, POP & JAZZ

The city's premier live music venue is **Yellow Submarine**, which features nightly acts performing blues, jazz, rock and folk. It is in an industrial district south of the centre, but it's only a short taxi ride from the Jaffa Road area. At the heart of West Jerusalem,

**Syndrome** also has nightly live blues, jazz and rock, while nearby **Art-L Jazz** is the city's first dedicated jazz club. When the occasional big name plays town, the venue is the **Sultan's Pool** on Hebron Road, a now-dry ancient reservoir, which, when not in use, resembles an abandoned quarry, just outside the city walls.

## THEATRE & DANCE

The **Jerusalem Centre for the Performing Arts** is the city's largest and most active cultural centre. In addition to the main Sherover Theatre, it has an additional three concert spaces and is a busy venue for both local and foreign productions. Smaller,

but housed in a beautifully renovated old Ottoman structure, the **Khan Theatre** has two performance spaces, kept busy with a lively programme of international productions. The **Gerard Bahar Performance Centre**, which is just west of central King George V Street, hosts regular theatre and dance events (it's the home of the respected Vertigo and Kombina dance companies), as well as occasional music concerts. **Ha-Ma'abada** (The Lab) is a beautifully designed modern performance space that is used for avant-garde theatre and dance. Over in East Jerusalem is **El-Hakawati Palestinian National Theatre**, with performances in Arabic, often of a political nature.

## DIRECTORY

### BARS & PUBS

**Armenian Tavern**
79 Armenian Patriarchate Road, Armenian Quarter, Old City. **Map** 3 B4.
*Tel* (02) 627 3854.

**Barood**
31 Jaffa Street, Nakhalat Shiva, West Jerusalem.
**Map** 1 A3.
*Tel* (02) 625 9081.

**Cellar Bar**
American Colony Hotel, 2 Louis Vincent Street, off Nablus Road, East Jerusalem. **Map** 1 C1.
*Tel* (02) 627 9777.

**Kan Zaman**
Jerusalem Hotel, Nablus Road, East Jerusalem.
**Map** 1 C1.
*Tel* (02) 628 3282.

**Link**
3 Hama'alot Street, West Jerusalem.
*Tel* (02) 625 3446.

**Mona**
12 Shmuel Ha-Nagid, West Jerusalem.
*Tel* (02) 622 2283.

**Stardust**
6 Rivlin Street, Nakhalat Shiva, West Jerusalem.
**Map** 1 A3.
*Tel* (02) 622 2196.

### CHILDREN

**Bloomfield Science Museum**
Hebrew University, Givat Ram, West Jerusalem.
*Tel* (02) 654 4888.

**Jerusalem Biblical Zoo**
Manahat, West Jerusalem.
*Tel* (02) 675 0111.

**Puppet Theatre**
King David Street, West Jerusalem. **Map** 1 B5.
*Tel* (02) 561 8514.

### CINEMA

**Gil**
Malkha Mall, Manahat, West Jerusalem.
*Tel* (02) 678 8448.

**Jerusalem Cinematheque**
11 Hebron Road, West Jerusalem. **Map** 1 B5.
*Tel* (02) 565 4333.

**Lev Smador**
4 Lloyd George Street, German Colony, West Jerusalem.
*Tel* (02) 561 8618.

**Third Ear**
8 Emek Refa'im Street, German Colony, West Jerusalem.
*Tel* (02) 563 3093.

### MUSIC

**Church of the Dormition**
Mount Zion, Old City.
**Map** 1 C5.
*Tel* (02) 565 5330.

**Henry Crown Concert Hall**
Jerusalem Centre for the Performing Arts, 20 David Marcus Street, Rehavia, West Jerusalem.
*Tel* (02) 560 5757.
**www**.jso.co.il

**Kan Zaman**
See Bars & Pubs.

**Ticho House**
9 Ha-Rav Kook Street, West Jerusalem. **Map** 1 A2. *Tel* (02) 624 4168.

**YMCA**
26 King David Street, West Jerusalem. **Map** 1 A4.
*Tel* (02) 569 2692.

### ROCK, POP & JAZZ

**Art-L Jazz**
9 Heleni Ha-Malka Street, Russian Compound, West Jerusalem. **Map** 1 A3.
*Tel* (077) 962 0165.

**Syndrome**
18 Ben Hillel Street, West Jerusalem. **Map** 1 A3.

**Yellow Submarine**
13 Ha-Rechavim Street, Talpiot, West Jerusalem.
*Tel* (02) 679 4040.

### THEATRE & DANCE

**Gerard Bahar Performance Centre**
11 Bezalel Street, Nakhla'ot, West Jerusalem.
*Tel* (02) 625 1139.

**Ha-Ma'abada (The Lab)**
28 Hebron Road, West Jerusalem. **Map** 1 B5.
*Tel* (02) 629 2000.
**www**.maabada.org.il

**El-Hakawati Palestinian National Theatre**
El-Nuzha Street, East Jerusalem. **Map** 1 C1.
*Tel* (02) 628 0957.

**Jerusalem Centre for the Performing Arts**
20 David Marcus Street, Rehavia, West Jerusalem
*Tel* (02) 560 5757.
**www**.jerusalem-theatre.co.il

**Khan Theatre**
2 David Remez Square, West Jerusalem.
*Tel* (02) 671 8281.

# JERUSALEM STREET FINDER

The map references that are given throughout the Jerusalem chapters of this guide refer to the maps on the following pages. References are also given in the listings for hotels *(see pp256–8)* and restaurants *(see pp272–4)*. Some of the many small streets and alleys may not be named on the maps. Many streets and monuments have two or even three names: one in Hebrew, one in Arabic and, occasionally, a commonly used English-language form,

too. What we call Damascus Gate is also known as Shaar Shkhem to Israelis and Bab el-Amud to Arabs. In this guide and on the following maps, where there is a sufficiently well-recognized English name, we have used it; otherwise, we have used the Arabic names for predominantly Arab areas (for example, the Muslim Quarter of the Old City) and Hebrew names for Jewish areas. Spellings in this guide may vary from those you see on street signs.

## KEY TO JERUSALEM STREET FINDER

| | | | |
|---|---|---|---|
| ▪ | Major sight | 🄲 | Mosque |
| ▨ | Other sight | ···· | Route of Via Dolorosa |
| ▪ | Other important building | **IV** | Station of the Cross |
| 🚌 | Bus station | ▦ | Police station |
| 🚕 | Taxi rank | ⊠ | Post office |
| 🅿 | Parking | ✚ | Hospital with casualty unit |
| 🛈 | Tourist information | ▬ | City wall |
| ✿ | Synagogue | ▬ | Covered street |
| 🛆 | Church | 25» | Street number |

**SCALE OF MAP ABOVE**

| 0 metres | 1000 |
|---|---|
| 0 yards | 1000 |

**SCALE OF MAPS 1 – 2**

| 0 metres | 250 |
|---|---|
| 0 yards | 250 |

**SCALE OF MAPS 3 – 4**

| 0 metres | 100 |
|---|---|
| 0 yards | 100 |

# THE HOLY LAND REGION BY REGION

# The Holy Land at a Glance

The Holy Hand is rich in historical sights far beyond its biblical associations. In Petra it has one of the most unusual and magical ruined cities in the world, and the Roman-era remains at sites such as Jerash in Jordan and Beth Shean in northern Israel are similarly stunning. The scenery that the visitor encounters while travelling can also be dramatic, especially in the region of the Dead Sea (a geographic marvel in itself) and in the Sinai peninsula. Off the coast of Sinai, the Red Sea conceals underwater scenery every bit as spectacular as that on dry land.

Waterfront at Jaffa, a virtual suburb of Tel Aviv and a favourite place for city-dwellers to dine at weekends

**THE DEAD SEA AND THE NEGEV DESERT**
*(See pp186–205)*

Beautiful sandstone cloisters at the Church of the Nativity in Bethlehem

**THE RED SEA AND SINAI**
*(See pp236–249)*

St Catherine's Monastery, Sinai, one of the world's oldest continuously functioning monasteries

◁ Spectacular desert scenery at Wadi Rum in Western Jordan

THE COAST
AND GALILEE
*(See pp164–185)*

WESTERN
JORDAN
*(See pp206–235)*

View from the shore of the Sea of Galilee, rich in associations with
the miracles and teachings of Jesus Christ

The ruined main street of Jerash, the best-preserved
Roman city in the Holy Land

The mountaintop fortress of Masada on the Dead
Sea, the most visited site in Israel after Jerusalem

The incredible shaping of the landscape in the
carved rock façades of Petra

0 kilometres      50

0 miles            50

# THE COAST AND GALILEE

*fertile corridor squeezed between the sea and the desert, this is the Promised Land of the Old Testament. The green hills and fresh waters of Galilee provided the setting for many episodes in the early life and ministry of Christ. Beside all its religious associations this is very much a secular paradise too, the heartland of modern Israel and a sun-drenched scenic magnet for tourists.*

The wealth of ancient sites along this stretch of coast bears witness to the fact that for centuries this has been an important land corridor connecting Africa, Europe and Asia. The great empires of ancient Egypt to the south and Assyria and Babylon to the east met here in trade and battle. Later, the Romans exploited this coastline with the laying of a great highway, the Via Maris, and Herod built a magnificent port in Caesarea *(see p176)*, one of the grandest and most important in the eastern Mediterranean. Ports such as this formed the nuclei of the Latin Kingdoms when the Crusaders came conquering in the Middle Ages. The Muslim Arabs eventually drove out the Christian knights but their legacy remains in some superb muscular architecture, especially at Akko, which retains one of the most charming old towns in the whole of the Holy Land.

When in the 19th century the first major waves of Jewish immigrants began arriving, it was on the fertile coastal plains and rolling hills of Galilee that they chose to settle. They planted wheat and cotton in the fields, orange groves and vineyards on the slopes, and cities overlooking the sea. The capital they founded, Tel Aviv, has become a vibrant centre of culture and commerce, while Haifa, attractively tumbling down Mount Carmel to the sea, is a thriving economic powerhouse. Inland Galilee remains rural and idyllic, equally pleasing to pilgrims on the trail of Christ and to seekers after relaxation and the picturesque.

**The harbour at Akko, stronghold of the Crusaders and one of the Holy Land's best preserved old cities**

◁ **A vaulted street in Jaffa, an important ancient port now part of metropolitan Tel Aviv**

# Exploring the Coast and Galilee

Northern Israel is arguably the most attractive region in the Holy Land. The coast has long white sandy beaches, while Galilee is a landscape of rolling green hills, forested valleys and clear freshwater lakes. The Golan even has mountains that are capped with snow for part of each year. Places of interest include the hilltop Jewish holy town of Safed, Nazareth, traditionally held to be where Jesus spent his childhood, and many fine archaeological sites, including Crusader castles and Roman towns. With such a concentration of beauty spots and picturesque vistas, this is an area ideally explored by car.

## SIGHTS AT A GLANCE

*Akko pp178–9* **4**
Belvoir Castle **13**
Beth Alpha **14**
Beth Shean **15**
Caesarea **2**
Capernaum **10**
Golan Heights **8**
Haifa and Mount Carmel **3**
Megiddo **5**
Nazareth **6**
Safed **7**
*Sea of Galilee pp182–3* **9**
Tabkha **11**
*Tel Aviv pp168–73* **1**
Tiberias **12**

Herod the Great's port of Caesarea, now an impressive set of ruins beside the sea

## GETTING AROUND

Jerusalem and Tel Aviv are linked by a good motorway. Buses depart roughly every 15 minutes and the journey takes less than an hour. Northbound services along the coastal highway from Tel Aviv to Caesarea and Haifa are only slightly less frequent. Trains link Tel Aviv and Jerusalem, and there is a coastal line from Tel Aviv to Nahariya.

0 kilometres 20

0 miles 10

*Beirut*

Kfar Rosh ha-Nikra

Nahariyya

Shavei Tsiyon

Shomrat

**AKKO** **4**

*Bay of Haifa*

Kfar Masaryk

Kiryat Yam

Kiryat Bialik

**HAIFA** **3**

Kiryat Ata

Shfar'am

Tirat Carmel

Nesher

Kiryat Tiv'on

Daliyat el-Carmel

Neve Yam

Yokne'am

Geva Karmel

Nakhsholim

Fureidis

Mishmar ha-Emek

Bat Shlomo

**MEGIDDO** **5**

Zikhron Ya'akov

Binyamina

Musmus

Um el-Fahm

**CAESAREA** **2**

Pardes Khana-Karkur

Sdot Yam

Ya'bad

Khadera

*Dotan Valley*

Mikhmoret

Baqa el-Gharbiya

Nazlat Isa

Yama

Kafr Ra'i

Ma'abarot

**Netanya**

Kfar Yona

Tul Karem

Nitsanei Oz

Deir Sharaf

Udim

Kur

Kalkilya (Qalqilya)

Ra'anana

Imatin

Herzliya

Kfar Saba

Ramat ha-Sharon

Yarkhiv

Mas'ha

Salfit

**TEL AVIV** **1**

Ramat Gan

Rosh Ha-ayin

Old Jaffa

**Petakh Tikva**

Or Yehuda

Rantis

Kholon

Rishon le-Tsiyon

*Jerusalem*

MEDITERRANEAN SEA

**The Sea of Galilee viewed from the Church of the Beatitudes, Tabkha**

**KEY**

| | |
|---|---|
| ═══ | Motorway |
| ═ ═ | Motorway under construction |
| ──── | Major road |
| ·········· | Minor road |
| ──── | Scenic route |
| ━━━ | Railway |
| ▪▪▪▪ | International border |
| ▪ ▪ | Disputed border/Cease-fire line |

**SEE ALSO**

• *Where to Stay* pp258–61

• *Restaurants, Cafés and Bars* pp274–8

**Old Jaffa, where the Gan ha-Pisga Gardens crown a hilltop with splendid views of seafront Tel Aviv**

# Tel Aviv ➊

Tel Aviv represents the modern face of the Jewish state – a brash, confident centre of commerce and contemporary culture. It is also a true Mediterranean resort city, with a long, sandy beach fringed by cafés, bars and shops. Away from the seafront are gracious palm-filled avenues, lined with elegant buildings in the international Bauhaus style *(see p171)*. All this has been created since 1909, when the Jewish National Fund purchased land among the dunes north of the old Arab port of Jaffa *(see pp174–5)* on which to build a new city, to be called Tel Aviv ("Hill of the Spring").

Mosaic flooring at the Eretz Israel Museum in northern Tel Aviv

### 🏛 Museum of the Jewish Diaspora (Beit Ha-Tefutsoth)
University Campus, Gate 2, Klausner Street, Ramat Aviv. **Tel** *(03) 640 8000.* ⬜ *10am–4pm Sun–Tue, Thu; 10am–6pm Wed; 9am–1pm Fri.* 🅿 www.bh.org.il

When it opened in 1978, this was regarded as one of the world's most innovative museums. It is still worth setting aside several hours to visit. Instead of showing historical artifacts, it uses thematically arranged dioramas, interactive displays and short videos to illustrate aspects of life in the Jewish diaspora, past and present, throughout the world, and the influence of Jewish arts and literature on other cultures. One of the highlights is a display of beautifully made scale models of synagogues from various countries. The permanent

**Museum of the Jewish Diaspora**

collection is supplemented by temporary exhibitions. There is also a genealogy centre, where Jews from around the world can trace their lineage.

### 🏛 Eretz Israel Museum
2 Haim Levanon, Ramat Aviv. **Tel** *(03) 641 5244.* ⬜ *9am–3pm Sun–Thu; 10am–2pm Fri & Sat.* 🅿 www.eretzmuseum.org.il

Built around the site of Tel Qasile, where excavations have revealed layers of human habitation dating back to 1200 BC, this museum depicts the history and culture of the land of Israel. It comprises a number of themed pavilions, all containing permanent exhibitions. One has a very fine collection of ancient and Islamic-era glass; others are devoted to coins, ancient pottery, Judaica, copper mining, postal history and philately, and to ancient crafts, with demonstrations by artisans. Additionally there's a square with a collection of beautiful mosaic floors from early synagogues, churches and mosques; an old olive oil press; a reconstructed flour mill; and a 1925 fire engine given by the city of New York to the Tel Aviv volunteer fire brigade in 1947.

Historical Jewish personages – part of a display at the Museum of the Jewish Diaspora

### 🚰 Old Port
North of the centre, at the point at which the Yarkon River empties into the Mediterranean, Tel Aviv's port was developed in the late 1930s to lessen Jewish dependence on the Arab port of Jaffa. It was

## SIGHTS AT A GLANCE

Beachfront Promenade ④
Bialik Street ⑧
Dizengoff Street ⑤
Eretz Israel Museum ②
Manshiye ⑫
Museum of the Jewish Diaspora
  (Beit Ha-Tefutsoth) ①
Neve Tzedek ⑬
Old Port ③
Rabin Square ⑥
Rothschild Avenue ⑪
Shalom Tower ⑩
Tel Aviv Museum of Art ⑦
Yemenite Quarter ⑨

**A café on the boardwalk in the fashionable Old Port area**

**Key to Symbols** *see back flap*

## VISITORS' CHECKLIST

**Road Map** B3. 🏙 *370,000.*
✈ *Ben Gurion, 22 km (14 miles)
SE.* 🚆 *Arlosoroff Station,
Arlosoroff Rd, (03) 577 4000.* 🚌
*New Central Bus Station, Levinsky
St, (03) 639 4444 (local buses),
(03) 694 8888 (long-distance
buses).* 🛈 *7 Mendale Street,
(03) 570 7600.* 🎭 *Beach Festival
(Jul & Aug).* 🛥 *daily.*

Many of the businesses
are on the boardwalk
facing the sea; many
also have a view of the
disused power plant just
across the river, which
serves as the venue for
the Ha'aretz Art Festival
every autumn.

### 🚻 Beachfront Promenade

A white-sand beach
stretches right along
the seafront of central
Tel Aviv, backed by
a long promenade,
modern hotels and
Miami-style condo-
miniums. It is possible
to walk all the way
from the Old Port in
the north down
to Jaffa in the south
(*see pp174–5*) along
the promenade. At
its northern end this
takes the form of a
big, rolling wooden
deck, which in parts gently
undulates like sand dunes.
This is a favourite area for
fishermen and for wedding
couples, who have their
photographs taken with
the Mediterranean Sea as
a backdrop.

Further south, in the
vicinity of **Independence
Park** (Gan Ha-Atzmaut),
there's a small children's
playground. Beside this, a
section of beach is screened
off for the use of Orthodox
Jews (men and women on
different days).

The city centre stretch of
beach is dominated by the
huge, pink **Opera Towers**,
with shops and restaurants at
street level, and a distinctive
stepped profile. The beach
here is crowded all summer
with sun-seekers and, after
dark, with open-air concert-
and disco-goers. Strong sea
currents mean that you should
swim only where you see
white flags. Red flags mean
that it is dangerous; black
flags that it is forbidden.

decommissioned in 1965,
when bigger facilities were
created in Ashdod to the
south, and lay neglected for
around 30 years until the site
was revitalised in the 1990s.
It is now a lively area of bars,
cafés, restaurants, nightclubs
and shops. There is even an
antiques market on Saturdays.

**The beachfront parade in central Tel Aviv, part of a well-maintained
promenade that stretches the length of the city**

# Exploring Tel Aviv

North central Tel Aviv is where the money is. Visit Basel Street for chic cafés and boutiques. The real heart of the city, however, lies south of Ben Gurion Avenue, which is named for Israel's first prime minister *(see p53)*; his former home at No. 17 is now a museum. The main streets run north–south and are Ben Yehuda Street and Dizengoff Street (see below), both of which run almost the whole length of the city centre. South again is the Yemenite Quarter and the districts of Manshiye and Neve Tzedek, which are some of the oldest parts of Tel Aviv.

Dizengoff Square with a performing fountain at its centre

### ⊞ Dizengoff Street
The city's main shopping street is named after Tel Aviv's first mayor, Meir Dizengoff. It is at its liveliest around the junction with Frishmann Street, where there are plenty of street cafés with pavement seating and a large branch of the Israeli chain bookstore Steimetzky's. Also here is the **Bauhaus Center**, which is dedicated to raising awareness of Tel Aviv's unique architectural heritage *(see p171)*. To this end, the Center runs two-hour English-language tours at 10am each Friday visiting some of the city's Bauhaus buildings.

One block south of the Bauhaus Center is **Dizengoff Square**, an irregularly shaped concrete platform raised above a traffic underpass. It sports a drum-like fountain by Israeli artist Yaakov Agam that has water jets programmed to perform hourly light and music shows. At the weekend, the square is host to a flea market. On the east side are two beautifully renovated Bauhaus buildings, one of which is now the **Hotel**

**Cinema Eden**; it's possible to take the elevator up to the fifth-floor roof terrace to enjoy the city views.

### ⊞ Bauhaus Center
99 Dizengoff Street. **Tel** (03) 522 0249. ☐ 10am–7:30pm Sun–Thu; 10am–2:30pm Fri. **www.**bauhaus-center.com

### ⊞ Rabin Square
A large, rectangular plaza in the eastern part of central Tel Aviv, Rabin Square is overlooked by **City Hall**, a brutal concrete block that is only slightly softened by

Modern large-scale sculpture outside the Tel Aviv Museum of Art

having its windows painted in different colours. The square is a venue for demonstrations, celebrations and concerts. It was at one such gathering – a peace rally on 4 November 1995 – that the then Israeli Prime Minister Yitzhak Rabin was assassinated. The basalt stones of the **Rabin Memorial** on Ibn Givrol Street, beside City Hall, occupy the very spot where he was shot. Nearby is a wall covered with graffiti drawn by mourning citizens and now preserved behind glass.

At the centre of the square is another memorial, the **Monument of Holocaust and Resistance**, a huge glass and iron structure erected in the 1970s and designed by well-known and often controversial Israeli artist Yigal Tumarkin.

There are some good shops on the west side of the square, notably Tola'at Seferim, a bookshop with a pleasant café, and Mayu, a youthful fashion boutique. Across on the east side is Brasserie, an excellent Art Deco, French-style restaurant.

### ⊞ Tel Aviv Museum of Art
27 Ha-Melekh Shaul Avenue. **Tel** (03) 607 7000. ☐ 10am–4pm Mon, Wed, Sat; 10–10pm Tue, Thu; 10am–2pm Fri. 🈺 **www.**tamuseum.com
Israel's most important collection of 19th- and 20th-century art includes works representing the major trends of modernism: Impressionism (Degas, Renoir, Monet), Post-Impressionism (Van Gogh, Gauguin, Cézanne), Cubism (Braque, Leger, Metzinger) and Surrealism (Miró), as well as key pieces by Pablo Picasso. Other works range from 17th-century Flemish to modern Israeli. In addition to the permanent collections, there are excellent temporary exhibtions. A ticket also covers entrance to the **Helena Rubenstein Pavilion** on Habima Square, where additional contemporary art shows are held.

*For hotels and restaurants in this region see pp258–9 and pp275–9*

# Tel Aviv's Bauhaus Architecture

Tel Aviv has the world's largest assemblage of buildings in the International Modern style, also known as Bauhaus. Altogether there are some 4,000 examples within the city. These buildings, largely erected in the 1930s and 1940s, were designed by immigrant architects trained in Europe, particularly in Germany, home of the modernist Bauhaus School between 1919 and 1933. The simplicity and functionality of the style, which aimed to unify art with technology, was considered highly appropriate to the socialist ideals of Zionism that underpinned the founding of the new city.

**Rounded balconies on a Bauhaus building**

In 2003, Tel Aviv's unique and bountiful Bauhaus legacy was recognised by the United Nations cultural agency UNESCO, who declared the "White City" on the Mediterranean a World Heritage Site.

**Horizontals** Characteristics of Bauhaus architecture include asymmetrical façades with "ribbons" of windows running horizontally. Balconies are often curbed and have overhanging ledges to provide shade for the rooms below.

**Verticals** The sole vertical element in the typical Bauhaus building is provided by the internal stairwell; this appears on the façade as a ladder-like arrangement of windows.

**Ships** Some of the most striking buildings were inspired by the superstructure of the ships that brought the Jewish immigrants to Palestine. Windows shaped like maritime portholes are a common feature.

**Where to look** The highest concentration of Bauhaus buildings is on Rothschild Boulevard and neighbouring Ahad Ha'am Street. The Bauhaus Centre, on Dizengoff Street (see p170) is a source of books and information on the subject, as well as a place to find some unusual souvenirs.

**Rounded forms** Although initially Bauhaus buildings were completely rectilinear, later architects began to introduce more rounded forms. This was decried by purists who regarded curves as heretical because of their supposed impracticality: "How do you hang a picture on a curved wall?" they asked.

Nahum Gutman's colourful, mosiac-covered fountain on Bialik Street

### 🚏 Bialik Street

Bialik is one of the city's most historic streets. At No. 14 is the **Rubin Museum**, the former residence of one of Israel's most famous painters, Reuven Rubin (1893–1974). It now contains a permanent collection of 45 of his works, as well as a historical archive of his life. Changing exhibits feature other Israeli artists. A few doors along, **Bialik House** (Beit Bialik) is the former home of Haim Nahman Bialik (1873-1934), Israel's national poet. The house has been kept as it was during Bialik's time, and includes a library and paintings by some of Israel's best-known artists.

At the end of the street is a striking mosaic-covered fountain by Nahum Gutman (see p173).

A little south of Bialik, **Bezalel Street** is home to a street market famed for cut-price fashion. South again, **Sheinkin Street** was a centre of alternative culture in the 1980s. That is no longer the case, but it still boasts many independent shops and cafés.

🏛 **Rubin Museum**
14 Bialik Street. *Tel* (03) 525 5961.
◯ *10am–3pm Mon, Wed, Thu; 10am–8pm Tue; 11am–2pm Sat.* 📷
www.rubinmuseum.org.il

🏛 **Bialik House**
22 Bialik Street. *Tel* (03) 525 4530.
◯ *9am–5pm Sun–Thu; 10:45am–2pm Sat.*

### 🚏 Yemenite Quarter

A masterplan for Tel Aviv was drawn up by Scottish urban planner Sir Patrick Geddes at the request of Mayor Dizengoff in 1925. This influenced the growth of the city for decades to come. The Yemenite Quarter (Kerem Ha-Temanim), however, predates the Geddes plan, and its maze of small streets contrasts sharply with the orderly layout of the rest of the city. The architecture also predates the arrival of the Bauhaus style that characterises much of the rest of Tel Aviv. Here, buildings instead employ motifs from Classical, Moorish and Art Nouveau styles. This is most apparent on **Nakhalat Binyamin Street**, which boasts many curious, if slightly faded, examples of this eclectic architecture. The street is especially worth visiting on Tuesdays and Fridays, when it hosts a busy craft market. This is also one of the busiest nightlife streets, in particular the area around the junctions with Rothschild Avenue and Lilienblum Street.

The other local landmark is **Carmel Market** (open 8am–5pm Sun–Fri), which is on Ha-Carmel Street and is the city's largest and busiest open-air market. It begins near the junction with Allenby Street with stalls selling cheap clothing and household items, before switching to fresh fish, meat, fruit and vegetables, spices and herbs, breads and biscuits, and nuts and seeds. Many of the side streets off Ha-Carmel specialise in different food produce.

Street performer on Nakhalat Binyamin

### 🚏 Shalom Tower

**Observatory** 9 Ahad Ha'am Street. *Tel* (03) 517 7304. ◯ *10am–6:30pm Sun-Thu; 10am–2pm Fri; 11am–4pm Sat.* 📷
One block west of Nakhalat Binyamin Street, this austere, 1960s office building sits on the former site of Israel's first secular Hebrew school. At the time of its construction, the tower was the tallest structure in Israel (it is now surpassed by the radio tower near the Tel Aviv Museum). There are impressive mosaics in the lobby area, shops on the first and second floors, and a wax museum on the third, but the main attraction is the observation area on the 34th (top) floor. On a clear day, the view stretches all the way north to Mount Carmel near Haifa and inland to Jerusalem and the Judaean Desert.

### 🚏 Rothschild Avenue

This is one of Tel Aviv's most elegant old thoroughfares, lined with palm trees and some of the city's finest examples of Bauhaus buildings (see p171).

Twice-weekly craft market on Nakhalat Binyamin in the Yemenite Quarter

**Attractive Hassan Bek Mosque, founded by a local governer**

**Independence Hall** (Beit Ha-Tanakh) at No. 6 was once the residence of the first mayor, Meir Dizengoff. This is also where Ben Gurion declared the independence of Israel on 14 May 1948. The museum's Hall of Declaration remains as it was on that day, with original microphones on the table and a portrait of Herzl, the Zionist leader. Nearby 23 Allenby Street is now the **Haganah Museum**. The Haganah was the clandestine pre-1948 military organisation that later became the Israeli army.

🏛 **Independence Hall**
16 Rothschild Boulevard. *Tel (03) 517 3942.* ⬛ *9am–2pm Sun–Thu.*

🏛 **Haganah Museum**
23 Rothschild Boulevard. *Tel (03) 560 8624.* ⬛ *9am–4pm Sun–Thu.*

🕌 **Manshiye**
Manshiye is the coastal neighbourhood that acts as a buffer between the twin municipalities of Tel Aviv and Jaffa *(see pp174–5)*. Its most distinguished landmark is the little **Hassan Bek Mosque** on the main seafront road, built in 1916 by a governor of Jaffa of the same name. During the 1948 War, Arab soldiers used the mosque's minaret as a firing position; this is one of the episodes recorded in the nearby **Etzel Museum 1947–1948**, which is dedicated to the Israeli defence forces and their role in this particular conflict. Historical documents, photos, newspaper clippings and weapons are exhibited in a purpose-built, black-glass structure in attractive **Charles Clore Park** on the seafront. The park is a venue for many of the city's big open-air events, including the annual Love Parade.

**Etzel Museum 1947–1948**
South Herbert Samuel Promenade. *Tel (03) 517 2044.* ⬛ *8:30am–4pm Sun–Thu.*

🕌 **Neve Tzedek**
Neve Tzedek is where Tel Aviv began. The settlement was founded on empty sandy flats in the late 1880s by a group of Jewish families keen to escape overcrowding in the port of Jaffa. Today, the area retains the feel of a small village, with narrow lanes lined by high walls and a strange mix of architectural styles. Decades of neglect are currently being reversed by an energetic programme of renovation and restoration.

At the heart of the district is the **Suzanne Dellal Centre** for dance and drama. It boasts four performance halls in a building that was once a local school. The main courtyard, with orange trees and tiled murals, is a popular place to meet and relax.

Nearby, the **Rokach House Museum** occupies the former home of Shimon Rockach, one of the founding fathers of Neve Tzedek. Inside, photos and documents illustrate the daily life of the community at the end of the 19th century.

A few doors away, the **Nahum Gutman Museum** is dedicated to another of Israel's best-known artists, a Russian-born painter who was also admired for his children's books. As well as displaying a small collection of Gutman's work, the galleries are used for temporary exhibitions.

🏛 **Suzanne Dellal Center**
6 Yehieli Street. *Tel (03) 510 5656.*

🏛 **Rokach House Museum**
36 Shimon Rockach Street. *Tel (03) 510 0655.* ⬛ *10am–2pm Fri, Sat.* www.rokach-house.co.il

🏛 **Nahum Gutman Museum**
21 Shimon Rokach Street. *Tel (03) 516 1970.* ⬛ *10am–4pm Sun–Wed; 10am–7pm Thu; 10am–2pm Fri; 10am–5pm Sat.* www.gutmanmuseum.co.il

**The history of Neve Tzedek in tiled murals at the Suzanne Dellal Centre**

# Street-by-Street: Old Jaffa

Artists'
Quarter
mural

According to the Bible, Jaffa (then called Joppa) was founded in the wake of the great flood by Noah's son Japheth. Archaeologists have unearthed remains dating back to the 20th century BC, establishing Jaffa as one of the world's oldest ports. However, with the growth of Tel Aviv, Jaffa, which had flourished under the Ottomans, went into decline. Following Jewish victory in the 1948 War it was absorbed into the new city to the north. The core of the old town has since been revived as an attractive arts, crafts and dining centre.

The seafront of Old Jaffa, with its warehouses reborn as restaurants

**Ha-Pisga open-air amphitheatre** is used for concerts during the summer.

**Archaeological Museum**
*Housed in an elegant 18th-century local government building, this museum holds finds from digs in the area.*

To Flea Market

To Clock Tower

**The Mahmoudiya Mosque** dates from 1812 and remains in use by the local Muslim community.

**A 19th-century** *sabil (fountain)*

To the Promenade

MIFRAZ SHLOMO

**Clock Tower**
*Built in 1901 to mark the 25th anniversary of the then Turkish sultan, the clock tower has since been heavily restored and now serves as a symbol of modern Jaffa.*

**Napoleonic cannons**

HA–ALIYAH HA–SHNIYA

**The Sea Mosque** was the mosque of local fishermen.

| 0 metres | 50 |
| 0 yards | 50 |

**KEY**

– – – Suggested route

**Gan ha-Pisga**
*Ha-Pisga garden lies on top of the ancient 'tel' (mound) of Jaffa. An observation area, marked by the curious Statue of Faith, offers good views across to Tel Aviv.*

For hotels and restaurants in this region see pp258–9 and pp275–8

### ★ Artists' Quarter

*A compact area of old Arab houses and narrow stone-flagged alleys, in recent times this has been transformed into residences, studios and galleries for artists and craftspeople.*

**Ha-Simta Theatre**

**Ilana Goor Museum of Ethnic and Applied Art**

**Synagogue**

MAZAL DAGIM

NATIV HA-MAZALOT

**The House of Simon the Tanner** is traditionally held to be where the apostle Peter once stayed (Acts 9: 43).

### ★ Kedumim Square

*Underneath the picturesque main square of Old Jaffa is the Visitors' Centre, with exposed Roman-era exhibits and a light and sound show about the old city.*

### St Michael's Church

*Dating from the 19th century, this small Greek Orthodox church has recently been renovated.*

**The Monastery of St Nicholas**, built around 1667, still serves Jaffa's Armenian community.

**The Wishing Bridge** has recently been renovated. It is said to bring true the wish of anyone crossing it if they touch the bronze statue of their zodiac sign while looking at the sea.

### STAR SIGHTS

★ Artists' Quarter

★ Kedumim Square

### Monastery of St Peter

*Built in Latin American Baroque style, this Roman Catholic monastery and church was dedicated in 1891. It stands on a site formerly occupied by a Crusader citadel.*

**The impressive Roman aqueduct at Caesarea**

# Caesarea ❷

**Road map** B2. 🚌 76 and 77 from Khadera. 🛈 (04) 617 4444/6550.

At the height of his power, in 29–22 BC, Herod the Great (*see pp43–5*) built a splendid city over the site of an ancient Phoenician port and dedicated it to Augustus Caesar, the Roman emperor. The splendour of this city is attested to by the lavish description of it by Flavius Josephus in his book *The Jewish War.* Until the many recent excavations, this had been seen by many scholars as wild exaggeration.

This period of prosperity lasted in Caesarea until AD 614, after which its history became more unstable. During the early 12th century and the Crusades, Caesarea again became an important city, and was used once more as a port. By the late 13th century however, it had been destroyed by the Mamelukes and was left to be reclaimed by the sand, with only a small Arab village remaining. The importance of these great hidden ruins was not realized until the 1940s, and now Caesarea is one of Israel's major archaeological sites.

Most of the main sights lie in the **Caesarea National Park**. If entering from the south, you will first see the huge Roman theatre. With seats for 4,000 spectators, it has been restored, and hosts summer concerts. A short distance to the west, on a small coastal promontory, a group of half-submerged walls indicate the site of Herod's palace. Further inland are the neglected ruins of one of the largest hippodromes in the Roman Empire.

On the coast by the inner harbour is the Crusader citadel, still surrounded by walls which date back to around AD 1250. Enclosing this whole area are the ruins of the much larger Crusader city walls. Within these ruins lies the unique **Underwater Archaeological Park**. The four diving complexes at this new park enable divers to see the techniques used to build the ancient port, as well as remnants of wrecked ships.

North of the ancient city is the extraordinary Roman aqueduct dating from the Herodian period. Extending for 17 km (11 miles), it carried water from the foothills of Mount Carmel to Caesarea. A short way to the south of the site, the **Caesarea Museum** has interesting artifacts from the Roman city.

🏛 **Caesarea National Park**
🕐 8am–4pm daily. 🖼 ♿

🏛 **Underwater Archaeological Park**
Caesarea Harbour. **Tel** (04) 626 5898.
🕐 6am–dark daily. 🖼 ♿

🏛 **Caesarea Museum**
Kibbutz Sdot Yam. **Tel** (04) 636 4367. 🕐 daily. 🖼 📷 ♿

## RUINS OF CAESAREA

Byzantine street ④
Crusader citadel ⑤
Crusader wall ⑥
Herod's palace ②
Hippodrome ③
Roman aqueduct ⑦
Roman theatre ①
Underwater Archaeological Park ⑧

Byzantine wall

Herodian amphitheatre

Herodian wall

To modern Caesarea

Entrance

Outline of Herodian harbour

0 metres     300
0 yards       300

To Khadera

Entrance

↓ To Caesarea Museum

**The magnificent ruins of the Roman theatre at Caesarea**

# Haifa and Mount Carmel ❸

The city of Haifa lies on the Mediterranean coast at the foot of Mount Carmel. Israel's third largest city, it is a major industrial centre. Away from the busy port, steep slopes rise up the mountain, providing quiet, attractive suburbs for the wealthy. A small trading port for most of its history, Haifa was conquered by the Crusaders in the early 12th century *(see pp48–9)*, and later fortified under Ottoman rule. In the late 19th century it became an important refuge for Jewish immigrants. Between 1918 and 1948 Haifa was taken over by the British in the occupation of Palestine. Today it is a mixed, non-religous city, and the only one where buses run on Saturdays.

The spectacular Baha'i Temple and gardens in Haifa

## 🏛 National Museum of Science and Technology
Old Technion, 12 Balfour St. *Tel* (04) 862 8111. ◯ *Daily.* 
www.mustsee.co.il
The former Technology Institute in the city centre is one of Haifa's most important buildings. Founded by German immigrants in the early 1900s, it was Israel's first institute of higher education. Renovated many times, it is now home to the National Museum of Science and Technology, which has many interesting interactive exhibits, exploring the latest innovations in Israeli science.

## 🄲 Baha'i Temple and Gardens
Ha-Ziyonut St. *Tel* (04) 835 8358. ◯ *daily (temple: am only).* 
On the edge of the city centre towards Central Carmel is Haifa's most striking landmark, the impressive golden-domed Baha'i Temple. Standing imperiously on the hillside, it is surrounded by a splendidly manicured park,

and is the headquarters of the Baha'i faith. Its followers believe that no religion has a monopoly on the truth, and aim to integrate the teachings of all holy men. The ornate temple houses the tomb of the Bab, the herald of Bahaulla. Bahaulla (1817–92) is the central figure of the Baha'i faith and is considered by his disciples to have been the most recent of God's messengers.

## Central Carmel
South of the temple, Central Carmel spreads up the slopes of the mountain. A largely wealthy residential area, it manages to resist the onslaught of traffic and busy modern life. Its many parks, cafés, and stylish bars make it a relaxing detour.

## Bat Galim
Northwest of Central Carmel is the popular coastal area of Bat Galim. Close to the city centre, its beach and busy seafront promenade have made it a favourite with tourists. For those wanting more extensive beaches, however, try the attractive Carmel Beach. This is 6 km (4 miles) to the south, away from the busy city.

## 🄰 Carmelite Monastery
Stella Maris St. *Tel* (04) 833 7758. ◯ *daily.* 
On much of the upper slopes of Mount Carmel are wide stretches of vegetation, the remnants of an ancient forest. On these slopes, to the southwest of Bat Galim, is the Stella Maris Carmelite Monastery, which can be reached by cable car or on foot. Built in an area that for centuries was frequented by hermits, this was a place of worship where the Carmelite order was founded. The beautiful church here dates from the early 1800s.

## ⛰ Elijah's Cave
Stella Maris St. *Tel* (04) 852 7430. ◯ *Sun–Fri (Fri: am only).* 
Below the monastery is Elijah's Cave, with its small altar, where Elijah is said to have lived and meditated before defeating the pagan prophets of Baal on Mount Carmel. Today it is a pilgrimage site for all three monotheistic religions.

Dome of the Stella Maris Carmelite Monastery

# Akko ❹

**Khan el-Umdan clocktower**

Outside of Jerusalem Akko (the historic Acre) has the most complete and charming old town in all of the Holy Land. Its origins date back to Canaanite times, but the form in which it survives today was set by the Arabs and their Crusader foes. After the Crusaders took Jerusalem in 1099, they seized Akko as their main port and lifeline back to Europe. Lost at one point to the Muslim armies under Saladin, it was regained by Richard I "the Lionheart". For most of the 13th century, with Jerusalem in the hands of the Muslims, Akko was the Crusaders' principal stronghold. As the Christian armies steadily lost ground, it was the last bastion to fall. Akko's fortunes were revived under a series of Ottoman governors, one of whom, Ahmed Pasha el-Jazzar, successfully defended the city against an invasion by Napoleon in 1799.

The harbour at Akko, in continuous use since Canaanite times

## Exploring Akko

Crusader Akko was destroyed by the victorious Arab armies in 1291 and what can be seen today is largely an 18th-century Turkish town built on the site of the old. The heavy defensive **walls** are rebuildings of the original Crusader walls, fragments of which are still discernible. The tight, warren-like street pattern within the walls is interrupted by three great khans, or merchants' inns: the **Khan el-Umdan** (Khan of the Columns) with its distinctive clocktower; the **Khan el-Faranj** (Khan of the Franks or Foreigners); and the **Khan el-Shohada** (Khan of the Martyrs). While the khans date from the Ottoman era they echo the fact that in Crusader times Akko had autonomous quarters given over to the merchants of Italy and Provence. Such was the rivalry between these colonies that at one point open warfare erupted between the Venetians and Genoese, who fought a sea battle off Akko in 1256. The khans are no longer in commercial use but Akko does have a lively **souk**, selling fruit and vegetables and household items – no tourist knick-knacks here. You'll also find plenty of fresh fish, which you can see being brought ashore at the town's picturesque harbour early each morning.

## 🇨 Mosque of El-Jazzar

El-Jazzar St. **Tel** (04) 991 3039 ◯ daily. ● during prayers. 🖼

Akko lay semi-derelict for more than 400 years after its destruction in 1291. Its rebirth came with the rule of the emir Dahr el-Amr and his successor, Ahmed Pasha el-Jazzar ("the Butcher"), both of whom governed the city for the Ottomans in the second half of the 18th century. El-Jazzar, in particular, was a prolific builder. Among his legacy is the attractive Turkish-style mosque (built 1781) that bears his name and continues to dominate the old town skyline. Its courtyard contains recycled columns from the Roman ruins of Caesarea and, at the centre, a small, elegant fountain used for ritual ablutions. Inside the mosque are the sarcophagi of El-Jazzar and his son, while underneath (and accessed from the courtyard cloisters) are the remains of a Crusader church that El-Jazzar had transformed into a cistern to collect rainwater.

## ♟ Crusader City

El-Jazzar St. **Tel** (04) 995 6706. ◯ 8:30am–4pm Sun–Thu, 8:30am–2pm Fri. 🖼

When the Ottoman governors rebuilt Akko they did so on top of the ruins of the Crusader city. The Crusader-era street level lies some 8 m (25 ft) below that of today. Part of it has been excavated revealing a subterranean wealth of well-preserved examples of 12th- and 13th-century streets and buildings.

Akko's dominant landmark, the Turkish-style Mosque of el-Jazzar

Akko in 1148. One of Akko's other well-known visitors was Marco Polo and it is quite possible that he dined in this very room. Below the refectory is a network of underground passageways that lead to an area known as El-Bosta (from the Arabic for "post office", which is what the Turks used this space for); divided by columns into six sections, it was probably the Crusaders' infirmary.

### 🏛 Citadel

Off Ha-Hagannah St. **Tel** (04) 995 6707. ◯ Sun–Fri (Fri: am only). ✍
Akko's Citadel was built by the Turks in the 18th century on top of Crusader foundations. During the British Mandate it served as a prison for Jewish activists and political prisoners, some of whom were executed in the gallows room. These events are commemorated in the Citadel's **Museum of Underground Prisoners**.

**Gothic-arched halls of the former Crusader city in Akko**

There are some amazingly grand Gothic knights' halls, each belonging to one of the nations represented in the crusading Order of the Knights Hospitallers: Auvergne, England, France, Germany, Provence and Spain. From the halls, a narrow passage leads to a large refectory with huge columns; in two corners you can still see carved lilies that may indicate building work done in the period of Louis VII of France, who arrived at

### VISITORS' CHECKLIST

Road map B2. 🚶 46,000. 🚌
Ha-Arbaa St. 🚉 David Remez
St, (04) 856 4444. 🛈 El-Jazzar
St, (04) 995 6706. 🛥 daily. 🎭
Fringe Theatre Festival (Sep–Oct).
**www**.akko.org.il

### 🏛 Municipal Museum

Off El-Jazzar St. **Tel** (04) 995 1088.
◯ daily (Fri: am only). ✍
This is not a museum as such, but a Turkish bathhouse dating to 1780 and the rule of El-Jazzar (hence the alternative name of Hammam el-Pasha, meaning "Bathhouse of the Governor"). It was in use until as recently as the 1940s and remains in an excellent state of repair. The floors and walls are composed of panels of different coloured marble, and the fountain in the "cold room" (where patrons would relax after bathing) retains most of its beautiful majolica decoration.

**Fountain from the Hammam el-Pasha**

### THE OLD CITY OF AKKO

Citadel ④
Crusader City ②
El-Jazzar's Wall ⑤
Khan el-Faranj ⑦
Khan el-Shohada ⑧
Khan el-Umdan ⑥
Lighthouse ⑩
Mosque of El-Jazzar ①
Municipal Museum
  (Hammam el-Pasha) ③
Souk ⑨

Railway Station
1km (0.6 mile)
Bus Station
1km (0.6 mile)

Burj el-Kommander
El-Jazzar's Wall ⑤
Daher el-Omar's Wall
Museum of Heroism
Citadel ④
Crusader City ②
Majdla Mosque
El-Jazzar ① Mosque
Souq el-Abyad
Shazalia Mosque
Municipal Museum (Hammam el-Pasha) ③
Sea Wall
Souk ⑨
Ramal Mosque
Khan ⑧ el-Shohada
Babal-Ard (Land Gate)
St. George's Church
Bahai House
Khan el-Faranj ⑦
Acre Bay
Burj el-Chadid
Maronite Church
Mu'allek Mosque
Sinan Basha Mosque
VENEZIAN SQUARE
St Andrew's Church
Khan el-Shuna
Khan el-Umdan ⑥
Church of St John
Burj el-Sanjak
Lighthouse ⑩

0 metres 50
0 yards 50

**Key to Symbols** see back flap

Aerial view of the ruined hilltop city of Megiddo

## Megiddo ❺

**Road map** B2. Route 66, 35 km (22 miles) SE of Haifa. **Tel** (04) 659 0316. 🚌 from Haifa & Tiberias. ⭕ 8am–4pm (winter: 3pm) daily. 🏛

This ancient town at the head of the Jezreel valley was the scene of so many battles that the Book of Revelation in the New Testament says that it is where the final battle between Good and Evil will take place at the end of the world. The biblical name of "Armageddon" derives from "Har Megedon", or mountain of Megiddo.

The settlement controlled the main communication routes between the East and the Mediterranean, and in the 3rd millennium BC it was already a fortified city. In 1468 BC its Canaanite fortress was destroyed by the troops of the Egyptian pharaoh Thutmose III, and became an Egyptian stronghold. Megiddo was subsequently conquered and again fortified, possibly by Solomon, and in the 8th century BC came under Assyrian rule, after which it fell slowly into decline.

Extensive excavation of the spectacular mound (or "tel") has, over the years, revealed 20 successive settlements, each built over the other. The visible remains include defensive walls, a temple, an enormous grain silo and the foundations of many buildings. On the eastern side of the "tel"

is an old reservoir, at the base of which a tunnel leads to a spring that lies outside the city walls. Visitors can go through the tunnel at the end of their tour of the site.

In 2005, the remains of what is thought to be a 3rd-century church and a large, well-preserved mosaic were found in the grounds of a military prison. Also in this year, the site joined UNESCO's World Heritage list.

## Nazareth ❻

**Road map** B2. 🏘 60,000. 🚌 ℹ Casa Nova St, (04) 601 1072.

Lying on the rise between the Jordan Valley and the Jezreel plain, Nazareth consists of two parts. The old town is inhabited by Christian and

Mosaic of Joseph, Basilica of the Annunciation, Nazareth

Muslim Palestinians, and contains all of the major sights. To the north is Nazareth Illit, a large Jewish district founded in 1957 by colonists as part of the plan to settle all Galilee.

Famous as the site of the Annunciation and the childhood of Jesus, Nazareth has had a colourful history. The village suffered at the hands of the Romans during the Jewish Revolt of AD 66 (see p43), then flourished under the Byzantines, and later became an important Christian site with the Crusader conquest of the Holy Land in 1099. After the resurgence of Muslim power in the 12th and 13th centuries, Christians found it increasingly dangerous to visit. Improving relations by the 18th century allowed the Franciscans to acquire the Basilica, and they have maintained a Christian presence here ever since. Today the town is a pilgrimage site, with its many Christian churches attracting large numbers of visitors. Recent restoration projects and modern hotel developments have helped Nazareth to cope with the crowds. Unfortunately though, such high levels of tourism have done little to preserve the city's magical atmosphere. The old town is still fascinating however, with much of its traditional architecture remaining. The souk, the heart of local life, is a maze of narrow alleys where you can find a wide range of unusual goods.

Built in 1969 over the ruins of the original Byzantine church, and the successive Crusader one, the **Basilica of the Annunciation** is the major focal point in Nazareth. A bold, modern church, its large dome towers over the town. The crypt includes the Cave of the Annunciation, where the angel Gabriel is said to have appeared to Mary. A peaceful garden leads to **St Joseph's**, a small church, rebuilt in 1914 on what is thought to be the site of Joseph's home and workshop.

### Environs

The main attraction of the ruined fortified town of **Tsipori** (Sepphoris), northwest of Nazareth, is its splendid 3rd-century AD mosaics. The hilltop site includes a Roman theatre that seated 5,000, the remains of a Crusader citadel and sections of the ancient water supply. Tsipori is also famous as being the supposed birthplace of the Virgin Mary.

On **Mount Tabor**, 10 km (6 miles) east of Nazareth, is a beautiful basilica, built here in 1924 to commemorate the Transfiguration (Mark 9: 9–13). It lies within the ruins of a 12th-century Muslim fortress.

**⋔ Tsipori**
Route 79, 3 km (2 miles) NW of Nazareth. **Tel** (04) 656 8272. ◯ 8am–3pm (summer:4pm) daily.

## Safed ❼

**Road map** C2. 🏔 26,000. 🚍
ℹ️ Town Hall, (04) 680 1465.

The highest town in Israel, Safed is also one of the four holy cities of the Talmud, together with Jerusalem, Hebron and Tiberias. In the Middle Ages Safed became a popular meeting place for many groups of Sephardic Jews who had been driven out of Spain in the course of the Christian Reconquest. Religious schools were founded and many interpreters of the Kabbalah lived in the town. To this day Safed has remained an important centre of Jewish religious studies.

Safed covers a number of small hilltops, with its attractive old town centre located around the slopes of Gan ha-Metusda, once the site of a Crusader citadel. The old quarters of the town centre are best explored on foot, via their narrow streets and steep stairways. The Synagogue Quarter has many interesting Kabbalist synagogues including those of Itzhak Luria, Itzhak Abuhav and Joseph Caro. The former Arab Quarter (which became Jewish in 1948) is now home to a large colony of artists and is known as the Artists' Quarter. In the narrow streets and alleys between the area's picturesque houses, artists display their paintings and sculptures. Many also use their own homes as galleries.

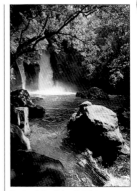
**Banias Falls, Golan Heights**

## Golan Heights ❽

**Road map** C2. 🚍 to Katsrin.
ℹ️ (04) 685 1010.
**www**.tour.golan.org.il

This region of long-running historical conflict has nevertheless got much to recommend it. A high fertile plateau, dominated by Mount Hermon, it borders Israel, Syria, Jordan and Lebanon. This unique geography, aside from making it strategically important, also makes it a spectacular place to visit, with incredible vistas all around.

A major source of the Jordan River, one of the most popular places to visit is **Banias**, 15 km (9 miles) east of Kiryat Shmona. Here a large spring cascades downstream to the attractive Banias Falls nearby. **Nimrud Castle**, a short way to the northeast, originates from biblical times, though it owes its present shape to the rule of the Mameluke sultan Baybars I (1260–77). Nine of the defensive towers remain, along with much of the outer wall, a keep, and the moat.

In the south of the Golan is the administrative capital of **Katsrin**. Founded as an Israeli settlement in 1974, the town itself is unremarkable, but is a good base for exploring the beautiful countryside around. This is ideal hiking country, and the spectacular **Yehudiya Reserve** to the south of Katsrin is well worth a visit.

**⋔ Nimrud Castle**
26 km (16 miles) E of Kiryat hmona. **Tel** (04) 694 9277. ◯ daily.

**Old quarter of Nazareth, dominated by the Basilica of the Annunciation**

# Sea of Galilee ❾

Israel's chief source of water, the Sea of Galilee (Lake Tiberias/Kinneret) lies 212 metres (696 feet) below sea level and is fed and drained by the Jordan River. It is 21 km (13 miles) long, and 9 km (6 miles) wide, and since biblical times has been famous for its abundance of fish. Many of Jesus's disciples were fishermen here, and he did much of his preaching by its shores. Today, this beautiful area is one of Israel's most popular tourist centres, with a mix of fascinating historical and religious sites, and a varied selection of hotels and outdoor activities.

**Statue of Saint Peter, Tiberias**

Speedboating on the Sea of Galilee, one of many water sports available

## KEY

- 〓 Major road
- ＝ Minor road
- 🚢 Ferry
- 🚤 Excursion boat
- 🏊 Water sports
- 🏕 Camping site
- 🏖 Beach
- ✳ Viewpoint

**Mount of the Beatitudes** (see p184)    To Safed

**Church of the Primacy of St Peter** (see p184)    Capernaum

**Church of the Multiplication of the Loaves and the Fishes** (see p184)

Tabkha

**Kibbutz Ginosar** is home to a fishing boat from Jesus's time, found here in 1986 (see p29).

Kibbutz Ginosar

Migdal

*HAR ARBEL*

90

TIBERIAS

77    To Nazareth

*HAR MENORIM*

**The Hammat Tiberias Hot Springs** have long been renowned for their curative properties, and are said to date from the time of Solomon.

Poriya

90

Kibbutz Kinneret

## Tiberias
*The largest town on the Sea of Galilee, Tiberias is a popular resort with many hotels, bars and restaurants. The busy lakeside offers beaches and water sports.*

**Kibbutz Kinneret's** cemetery, with great views of the sea, is resting place to many spiritual leaders of the Zionist movement.

## Yardenet Baptism Site
*The Jordan River has always been an important Christian site since Christ was supposedly baptized here. At Yardenet, large crowds of pilgrims gather to be baptized in the river themselves.*

**A View of the Sea of Galilee**
*This view is taken from the hills above the northeastern shore.*

To Katsrin

Jordan River

87

92

Ramot

Kursi

92

Kibbutz Ein Gev

92

Mevo Khama

98

HAR NIMRON

Kibbutz Haon

92

Kibbutz Degania

98

90

To Beth Shean

Hammat Gader

0 kilometres 4

0 miles 2

**VISITORS' CHECKLIST**

**Road map** C2. from Tel Aviv and Jerusalem. 19 Habanim St, Tiberias, (04) 672 5666. for groups only from Tiberias to Kibbutz Ein Gev (daily in summer), (04) 665 8008. Holyland Sailing for Pilgrim Groups, Tiberias (all year round), (04) 672 3006; Lido Kinneret Sailing Co, Tiberias (all year round), (04) 672 1538. Kibbutz Ein Gev Music Festival (Apr), Galilee Song Festival (May).

**THE FIRST KIBBUTZ – DEGANIA**

Conceived by Eastern European Jews, the first kibbutz was founded at Degania in 1909. The guiding ideals behind Israel's kibbutzim are self-sufficiency and equality, with everyone working for the common good. Rural farming communities, they are highly productive, and hold their own plenary meetings to decide on community matters. There are now two kibbutzim here, with the original called Degania Alef (A). By the main gate to the kibbutz is a Syrian tank, stopped here by the kibbutzniks when they famously defeated an entire armoured column during the 1948 war.

**Typical kibbutz house at Degania**

**Kibbutz Ein Gev** is renowned for its fish restaurants, good beaches and its annual international music festival.

**Hammat Gader Alligator Farm**
*The large alligator farm at Hammat Gader is open to the public. The town is also famous for its ancient Roman hot springs, which have now been largely restored. You can still bathe in their relaxing waters.*

## Capernaum  ⑩

**Road map** C2. Route 87, 12 km (7.5 miles) N of Tiberias. ▮ from Tiberias. **Tel** (04) 672 1059. ◯ daily. ▮

Capernaum, on the northern shoreline of the Sea of Galilee, was an important Roman town and one of the focal points of Christ's teachings in Galilee. It was also home to a number of his Disciples, including Simon Peter. In Capernaum's fascinating archaeological precinct there are surviving houses from the period, as well as a church, built over the ruins of what is said to have been **Simon Peter's house**. There are also the remains of a synagogue that has been dated to the 4th century AD.

**Carved relief, Church of the Multiplication**

## Tabkha ⑪

**Road map** C2. Route 87, 10 km (6 miles) N of Tiberias. ▮ from Tiberias to junction of routes 90 and 87.

Just to the southwest of Capernaum, Tabkha (Ein Sheva) is one of the most important sites of Christ's ministry in Galilee, where he did much of his preaching. Heading from the bus-stop, a short way along Route 87 you will come to the **Church of the Multiplication of the Loaves and the Fishes**. Built in the 1980s, it boasts the remains of a 5th-century Byzantine basilica and fragments of splendid mosaics. This original church was built over the supposed spot from which Christ fed 5,000 followers with five loaves and two fish.

Nearby to the east, on the lakeside, is the **Church of the Primacy of Peter**. A black basalt Franciscan chapel, it is built on the site where Jesus Christ is said to have appeared to the Apostles after his Resurrection. The area has various other ruins, including a 4th-century chapel.

On top of the hill behind, known as the Mount of the Beatitudes, is the modern **Church of the Beatitudes**. The hill is so called, because it is thought that here, over looking the lake, Christ gave his Sermon on the Mount. This famously began with his blessings or "beatitudes".

## Tiberias ⑫

**Road map** C2. ▮ 29,000. ▮ ▮ Archaeological Garden, Rehov ha-Banim, (04) 672 5666.

The busy town of Tiberias (Tverya) is the largest on the shores of the Sea of Galilee. It was founded during Roman times by Herod Antipas, who dedicated it to the Emperor Tiberius and moved the regional capital here from Tsipori. The town has been home to many notable scholars and rabbis, and became one of Israel's holy cities, along with Jerusalem, Hebron and Safed. The **Tomb of Maimonides**, the great medieval Jewish philosopher, can be found on Ben Zakai Street.

Today, Tiberias is a popular tourist centre, with an attractive lakeside setting and in an ideal location for exploring Galilee. The town has a lively atmosphere, especially along the busy lakeside promenade. Just behind here is **St Peter's Church**, built originally by the Crusaders. The current church has a boat-shaped nave, reflecting St Peter's life as a fisherman.

Tiberias is also known for its curative hot springs, of which there are several to visit in the town. There are also some public beaches to the north of town, and the popular **Gai Beach Water Park** is 1 km (half a mile) to the south of Tiberias.

▮ **Gai Beach Water Park**
Sederot Eliezer Kaplan. **Tel** (04) 670 0700. ◯ daily. ● Nov–Mar. ▮

**Ruined arches at Belvoir Castle**

## Belvoir Castle ⑬

**Road map** C2. Off Route 90, 27 km (17 miles) S of Tiberias. ▮ to Beth Shean, then taxi. **Tel** (04) 658 1766. ◯ 8am–4pm (winter: 3pm) daily. ▮

The ruined Crusader fortress of Belvoir, in the Kokhav ha-Yarden nature reserve, offers incomparable views of the Jordan Valley. The impressive fortress is surrounded by two huge walls, the outer one pentagonal and the inner one square. Built by the Knights Hospitallers in 1168, Belvoir was besieged many times by Saladin. It capitulated only in 1189 after a siege of more than a year, with the Muslim leader sparing both the fortress and its defenders' lives, in recognition of their great courage. Belvoir was finally destroyed by troops from Damascus in the 13th century. The area around the fortress is dotted with modern sculpture.

**The modern Church of the Beatitudes near Tabkha**

*For hotels and restaurants in this region see pp258–60 and pp275–6*

Detail from 6th-century mosaic at Beth Alpha, showing signs of the zodiac

## Beth Alpha ⓮

**Road map** C2. Off Route 71, 11 km (7 miles) W of Beth Shean. *Tel* (04) 653 2004. 🖾 ⭕ 8am–4pm (winter: 3pm) daily. 🖾 ♿

The remnants of this 6th-century synagogue were found by chance in 1928 by colonists from the nearby Hefzi-Bah kibbutz. The ruined walls give an idea of the original basilica-shaped building, but the main interest is the magnificent mosaic floor, which has survived largely intact. The upper part of the floor depicts the Ark of the Covenant, with cherubs, lions and religious symbols. The large central patterns represent the zodiac and symbols of the seasons. These show the continuing importance of pagan beliefs at the time, and the need for Judaism to try to accommodate them. The lower part relates the story of Abraham and the sacrifice of his son Isaac.

## Beth Shean ⓯

**Road map** C2. 🏛 18,000. 🚌 from Tiberias.

The best-preserved Roman-Byzantine town in Israel, Beth Shean lay on the old trade routes between Mesopotamia and the Mediterranean. First inhabited 5,000 years ago during the Canaanite era, it later became the main city in the region during the period of Egyptian occupation (see p41). Falling to the Philistines in the 11th century BC, it then became part of Solomon's kingdom. After the conquest of Alexander the Great it was renamed Scythopolis, and became a flourishing Hellenistic city. The Roman conquest in the 1st century BC saw Scythopolis further prosper as one of the ten city states of the Decapolis. It later retained its economic importance under the Byzantines, also becoming a major centre of Christianity. An economic collapse, then an earthquake in AD 749, eventually left only a small remaining Jewish community.

The archaeological sites at Beth Shean are in two areas. The main site comprises the Roman-Byzantine city, and the archaeological mound, or 'tel'. These are both within the Beth Shean National Park, 1 km (half a mile) north of the town. The jewel of this site is the Roman theatre, one of the best preserved in Israel, and once capable of seating 7,000. The old Byzantine baths have surviving mosaic and marble decoration, and tall columns from the ruined temples are equally impressive. The *tel* offers a good overview of the site, and consists of 16 or more superimposed towns. It is difficult however to understand the details of its complex archaeology.

The other site focuses on the ruined Roman amphi-theatre, a short way to the south. Used for gladiatorial contests, it was connected to the main town by a paved street. Some of this street survives today, paved with huge blocks of basalt.

**🏛 Beth Shean National Park**
*Tel* (04) 658 7189. ⭕ daily.
🖾

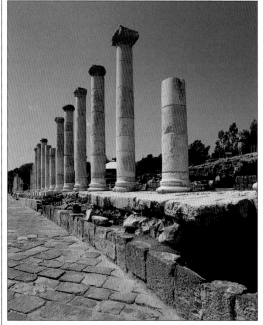

Ruined colonnade along an old Byzantine street, Beth Shean

# THE DEAD SEA AND THE NEGEV DESERT

*I*n this the most arid and inhospitable region of the Holy Land, even the waters of its great lake are incapable of supporting life, hence the "Dead Sea". But in times past, the harsh remoteness of the hills and desert was prized by reclusive communities and rebels, and so the area is dotted with ancient ruins charged with biblical significance.

Today, the Dead Sea is no longer so remote – just a 20-minute ride from Jerusalem on an air-conditioned bus. Tourists flock to its shores to test its incredibly buoyant waters. The lowest body of water in the world, it has such a high salt content it is impossible to sink. Its mineral-rich mud is also claimed to have therapeutic qualities and a string of lakeside spas do good business out of the black, sticky silt. Away from the water, high up on the rocky hillsides are the caves in which the Dead Sea Scrolls were discovered, while on a mountain top to the south is Herod the Great's fortress of Masada, one of the most stunning attractions in all Israel.

Where the Dead Sea ends, the Negev Desert begins. Here, the only signs of life, apart from the odd convoy of tourists exploring canyons and craters, are a few groups of Bedouin *(see p249)* tenaciously clinging to traditional nomadic ways.

Over the centuries, there have been many attempts to cultivate the desert. More than 2,000 years ago, the Negev was the final stage for caravans on the spice and incense route from India and southern Arabia to the Mediterranean; the Nabataeans who controlled the route perfected irrigation and cultivation techniques and established flourishing cities, such as Ovdat *(see p202)*. More recently, Israel has initiated programmes for the economic development of the region in the form of desert kibbutzim.

In spite of this desire to tame the desert, more and more people these days come in search of all that remains wild and undeveloped. In this respect, the Negev still has much to offer.

The secluded retreat of St George's Monastery, hidden in a desert canyon near Jericho

◁ Masada on the Dead Sea, one time rebel fortress, now the most visited archaeological site in Israel

# Exploring the Dead Sea and the Negev Desert

All the sites as far south as Masada can be visited in a series of day trips from Jerusalem. Heading south beyond Masada or Beersheva and into the Negev Desert is more of an undertaking. There are only two main routes through this vast wedge of sun-baked wilderness: along the border with Jordan on Route 90; or straight down the centre of the country via Ein Ovdat and Mitspe Ramon. This latter route is by far the more interesting.

The mountain-top fortress of Masada, conveniently visited as a day trip from Jerusalem

## SIGHTS AT A GLANCE

Beersheva 15
*Bethlehem pp193–5* 6
The Dead Sea 9
Eilat 19
Ein Gedi 8
Ein Ovdat 12
Hebron 14
Herodion 5
Jericho 2
Khai Bar Biblical Wildlife Reserve 17
Makhtesh Ramon 16
Mar Saba Monastery 4
*Masada pp200–1* 10
Nebi Musa 3
Ovdat 13
Qumran 7
Sodom 11
St George's Monastery 1
Timna National Park 18

0 kilometres          25

0 miles          20

Tel Aviv
Bat Yam
Rekhovot
Gedera
Ashdod
Nitsanim
Ashkelon
Kiryat Gat
MEDITERRANEAN SEA
Gaza
Sderot
GAZA STRIP
Sa'ad
Netivot
Re'im
Rahat
Khan Yunis
Magen
Ofakim
Rafah (Rafi'akh)
BEERSHEVA 15
Kerem Shalom'
Tse'elim
ISRAEL
Agur Sands
Mash'abei Sade
Nitsana
Sde Boker
EIN OVDAT 12
OVDAT 13
Mitspe Ramon
MAKHTESH 16
Negev

Ein Gedi, where waterfalls and greenery provide respite from the heat and dust

Bethlehem and surrounding hills, viewed over the roof of the Church of the Nativity

### GETTING AROUND

The easiest way of getting from Jerusalem to Jericho, Bethlehem and Hebron is a shared taxi from Damascus Gate *(see p310)*. From Bethlehem you can take a taxi on to the Herodion or Mar Saba. For longer trips, the Israeli bus company Egged serves all Dead Sea and Negev locations *(see pp312–13)*. For those who only want to visit the Negev Desert, there are direct flights to Eilat with Arkia *(see pp308–9)*.

### KEY

| | |
|---|---|
| ═══ | Motorway |
| ≡ ≡ | Motorway under construction |
| ▬▬ | Major road |
| ⋯⋯ | Minor road |
| ─── | Scenic route |
| ⋯⋯⋯ | Railway |
| ▬▬▬ | International border |
| ▪ ▪ | Disputed border/Cease-fire line |

### SEE ALSO

- *Where to Stay* pp261–2
- *Restaurants, Cafés and Bars* p278–9

The volcano-like mound of the Herodion, a 1st-century BC hilltop fortress

The waters of the Dead Sea, the most saline on earth and at their saltiest at the southern end, where crystalline pools are formed

# St George's Monastery ❶

**Road map** C3. Route 1, 27 km
(17 miles) E of Jerusalem. **Tel** (050)
259 949. 🚌 from Jerusalem.
⊙ 8–11am & 3–5pm Sun–Fri;
8–11am Sat.

One of the finest hikes in
the region is rewarded by
the spectacle of St George's
Monastery, an ancient retreat
hollowed out of the sheer
rock wall of a deep and
narrow gorge. The monastery
was founded in AD 480
around a cluster of caves
where, according to tradition,
St Joachim learned from an
angel that Anne, his sterile
wife and mother-to-be of the
Virgin Mary, had conceived.

In AD 614 invading Persians
massacred the monks and
destroyed the monastery.
It was partially reoccupied by
the Crusaders in the Middle
Ages but only fully restored
at the end of the 19th
century. Some attractive 6th-
century mosaics remain, and
there is a Crusader-era church
with a shrine containing the
skulls of the martyred monks.

The monastery can be
reached in 20 minutes on foot
via a signposted track off the
old Jerusalem–Jericho road.
From a starting point on the
modern road hikers can take
a more scenic path to the
monastery along the full
length of the Wadi Qelt gorge.

St George's Monastery, built into
the cliff face of Wadi Qelt

Jericho, regarded as perhaps the world's oldest city

# Jericho ❷

**Road map** C3. 🏙 17,000. 🚌 or
taxi from Jerusalem. 🏨 daily.
🎪 Jericho Festival (Feb).

It is best to check with the
authorities first before visiting
the city to make sure it is safe
for tourists as unrest has
returned to the region.

Claimed to be the world's
oldest city and with rich
biblical associations, Jericho
lies just a few miles
north of the Dead
Sea, 258 m (846
ft) below sea
level, in the
middle of the
Judaean desert. It
owes its existence
to the Ain es-
Sultan spring (the     **Islamic-era mosaic from**
biblical Elisha's        **Hisham's Palace**
Spring), the same
one that, 10,000 years ago
in the late Mesolithic period,
attracted a semi-nomadic
population of hunter-
gatherers to first settle here.

According to the Bible,
Jericho was the first town
captured by the Israelites
under the leadership of
Joshua. The Book of Joshua
tells how, in order to possess
the land promised to them by
God, the Israelites brought
down the city walls with a
tremendous shout and a
trumpet blast (Joshua 6).
During Roman times Mark
Antony made a gift of the
oasis town to Cleopatra of
Egypt, who, in turn, leased
the place to Herod the Great.
Being at a lower altitude than
Jerusalem, Jericho is notably
warmer, and Herod wintered

in a palace here, as had the
Hasmonean rulers before him.

The Bible's New Testament
mentions several visits to
Jericho by Jesus, who healed
two blind men and lodged at
the home of the tax collector
Zacchaeus (Luke 19: 1-10).
Near the centre of town
there is still the centuries-
old sycamore tree up which
Zacchaeus was said to have
climbed in order to see Jesus.

Repeated Bedouin raids
led to the decline of
Jericho around the
12th century, and
it wasn't until the
1920s that the
town's former
irrigation
network was
restored and the
area was brought
to bloom again.

In 1948, the town
took in more than 70,000
Palestinian refugees. The
camps have since gone, and
Jericho is now administered
by the the Palestinian
National Authority.

Other attractions include
**Tel Jericho** (also known
as Tell es-Sultan), the sun-
baked earthen mound that
represents something like
10,000 years of continuous
settlement. Most striking of
all is a large stone tower with
great thick walls that dates
back as far as 7,000 BC.

A cable car service connects
Tell es-Sultan with the Greek
Orthodox **Monastery of the
Temptation** 2 km (1 mile) to
the north. Like St George's in
Wadi Qelt, this holy retreat
has a spectacular location,
perched high up on a cliff

face. The views from its terraces are breathtaking. The monastery dates back to the 12th century and is supposedly built around the grotto where the Devil appeared to tempt Jesus away from his 40-day fast (Matthew 4: 1–11).

**Hisham's Palace** (Qasr Hisham) is an early Islamic hunting lodge built in AD 724 for the Omayyad caliph Hisham. It lies in ruins, destroyed centuries ago by an earthquake, but it is worth a visit if only for a gorgeous floor mosaic depicting a lion hunting gazelles grazing under a broad leafy tree.

🏛 **Tel Jericho**
◯ *daily.* 📷 ✦

🏛 **Monastery of the Temptation**
*Tel (02) 232 2827.* ◯ *Mon–Sat.* ♿

🏛 **Hisham's Palace**
*Tel (02) 232 2522.* ◯ *daily.* 📷

# Nebi Musa ❸

**Road map** C4. Route 1, 10 km (6 miles) S of Jericho. 🚌 *to Jericho, then taxi.* ♿

Although the claim is heavily disputed, Muslims revere the desert monastery of Nebi Musa as the burial place of Moses. There has been a mosque on the site since 1269, built under the patronage of the Mameluke emir Baybars. In 1470–80 a two-storey hospice was added to accommodate visiting pilgrims. However, the attractive whitewashed

**Nebi Musa, regarded by Muslims as the burial place of Moses**

structures of the present day date from around 1820 and the days of Ottoman rule. The disputed cenotaph of Moses, covered with a traditional Islamic green drape, occupies the spartan, domed tomb chamber of the mosque.

Although the five-day festival of feasting and prayer that used to occur here each year now no longer happens, many Muslims still desire to be laid to rest in the large cemetery that covers the hills around the complex.

# Mar Saba Monastery ❹

**Road map** C4. Off Route 398, 17 km (11 miles) E of Bethlehem. *Tel (02) 277 3135.* 🚌 *Bethlehem, then taxi.* ◯ *8am–5pm daily. Ring bell. No women allowed.*

Located out in the wilds of the Judaean desert, Mar Saba is one of the dozens of retreats built in this area from the 5th century on by hermits seeking an austere life of solitude and prayer. This particular monastery was founded in AD 482 by St Saba, a monk born in Cappadocia, Turkey, whose preachings were said to have impressed the Byzantine emperor Justinian. Despite a massacre of the monks by the Persians in the 7th century (the skulls are preserved in a chapel), the monastery survived to bloom in the 8th and 9th centuries, when its thick defensive walls housed up to 200 devotees.

Although only around 20 monks now live in Mar Saba, it remains a functioning desert monastery. As seen today, topped by bright blue domes, the complex largely dates to 1834, when it was rebuilt following a major earthquake.

An ornate canopy in the monastery's main church supposedly shelters the remains of St Saba, which were returned to the Holy Land only in 1965 having being carried off by the Crusaders and kept in Venice for seven centuries. The church walls are hung with icons and a lurid fresco depicting Judgment Day.

Unfortunately, women are not allowed to enter the monastery, but the views of Mar Saba from a neighbouring tower (which women are permitted to climb) are alone worth the trouble of a visit.

**The distinctive blue domes of the gorge-top monastery of Mar Saba**

The hilltop Herodion with sweeping views of the landscape

# Herodion ❺

**Road map** B4. Route 356, 12 km (7 miles) SE of Bethlehem. *Tel (050) 505 007.* 🚍 *Bethlehem, then taxi.* ◻ *8am–4pm (Fri: 3pm) daily.* 🎫 📷 *on Sat but call ahead.* ♿

Dominating the desert landscape south of Bethlehem is the volcano-like mound of the Herodion, named for Herod the Great. He had this circular fortified palace built in 24–15 BC for entertaining, and to mark the defeat of his rival, Antigonus. It was long thought that this might also have been his mausoleum, but despite extensive excavations no tomb has been found.

During the Second Revolt in AD 132–5 the Herodion became the headquarters of the Jewish leader Bar-Kokhba. In expectation of a Roman attack, the rebels turned its cisterns into a network of escape tunnels.

Around the 5th century, the site became a monastery with cells and a chapel, where you can still see carved Christian symbols. Also identifiable are a massive round tower and three semicircular ones, ruins of the palace baths, the *triclinium* (dining room) and fragments of mosaics, all dating from Herod's time.

At the foot of the mound are the remains of the Lower Herodion, with the dry imprint of a large pool that, in Herod's day, served as a reservoir and centrepiece for ornamental gardens.

# Bethlehem ❻

Perched on a hill at the edge of the Judaean desert, Bethlehem is in biblical tradition the childhood home of David, who was named king here as he tended his father's sheep. It is also the birthplace of Jesus Christ and a major site of pilgrimage since the construction of the Church of the Nativity in the 4th century AD. The town flourished until Crusader times, but the following centuries witnessed a great reduction in population, reversed only after the 1948 war with the arrival of thousands of Palestinian refugees.

**Exploring Bethlehem**
Since 1995 Bethlehem has been under the control of the Palestinian National Authority, which has initiated a programme of economic recovery and tourism. Despite the huge number of pilgrims and chaotic urban growth, Bethlehem has retained a certain amount of fascination, especially in the central area around Manger Square and in the souk just to the west. The souvenir shops are filled with kitsch religious objects but also sell the fine carved olive-wood crib scenes that local craftsmen have produced for centuries. No visitor should miss the **Church of the Nativity** *(see pp194–5)* on Manger Square, built in the fourth century over the supposed spot where Jesus Christ was born and, as such, one of the most holy of Christian sites.

Several of the town's other main attractions also deserve attention. The most interesting parts of Bethlehem lie west of Manger Square, on the streets that run up the hill, behind the prominent **Mosque of Omar**. Built in 1860, this is the only Islamic place of worship in the town centre, despite the fact that Muslim residents now outnumber Christians in Bethlehem.

### 🕌 St Catherine's Church
Manger Square. *Tel (02) 274 2425.* ◻ *daily.* ♿
Connected to the Church of the Nativity, St Catherine's faces a heavily-restored, Crusader-period cloister *(see p174)*. The church was built by Franciscans in the 1880s on the site of a 12th-century Augustinian monastery, which had replaced a 5th-century monastery associated with St Jerome.

On the right side of the nave, stairs descend to the grottoes of the Holy Innocents, St Joseph and St Jerome, which connect to the Grotto of the Nativity. These were used as burial places by Christians as early as the 1st century AD and contain the tombs of St Jerome and St Paula.

The 19th-century St Catherine's Church

The church spires and towers of Bethlehem, birthplace of Jesus Christ

**The Virgin Mary and Child, a relationship celebrated at the Milk Grotto**

### The Milk Grotto

Milk Grotto Street. *Tel (02) 274
2425.* daily.

This grotto, only a few minutes' walk from Manger Square, is considered sacred because tradition has it that the Holy Family took refuge here during the Massacre of the Innocents, before their flight into Egypt. While Mary was suckling Jesus, so the story goes, a drop of milk fell to the ground, turning it white. Both Christians and Muslims believe scrapings from the stones in the grotto boost the quantity of a mother's milk and enhance fertility.

The present, rather gaudy, building was put up by the Franciscans in 1872 on the site of a 4th-century church.

### Old Bethlehem Folklore Museum

Paul VI Street. Mon–Sat (Thu: am only).

In an old Palestinian house on the town's main street, the Arab Women's Union has created this small but interesting museum. One room is given over to the embroidery typical of Palestinian women's dress and to silver jewellery, which normally represented a family's fortune. The *diwan* (living room) is furnished with rugs, musical instruments and oil lamps. The kitchen contains old copper utensils and an oven. Examples of traditional handstitched embroidery are usually available to buy.

### Rachel's Tomb

Hebron Road.

On the road to Jerusalem, just before the border checkpoint between Israel and Palestinian territory, is the tomb of Rachel, wife of Jacob and the mother of two of his twelve sons. It is the third most holy site in Judaism, and is also sacred to Muslims. The actual "tomb" consists of a rock covered by a velvet drape with eleven stones on it, one for each of the eleven sons of Jacob who were alive when Rachel died in childbirth. The structure around the tomb was built around 1620 by the Ottomans and restructured in 1860 by Moses Montefiore (*see p51*). The site is visited by Jewish women who come to pray that they will conceive.

## BETHLEHEM TOWN MAP

Church of the Nativity ⑤
Old Bethlehem
  Folklore Museum ③
The Milk Grotto ②
Rachel's Tomb ④
St Catherine's Church ①

Key to Symbols *see back flap*

# Church of the Nativity

**Statue of Mary**

The first evidence of a cave here being venerated as Christ's birthplace is in the writings of St Justin Martyr around AD 160. In 326, the Roman emperor Constantine ordered a church to be built and in about 530 it was rebuilt by Justinian. The Crusaders later redecorated the interior, but much of the marble was looted in Ottoman times. In 1852 shared custody of the church was granted to the Roman Catholic, Armenian and Greek Orthodox churches, the Greeks caring for the Grotto of the Nativity.

Plaza in front of the Church of the Nativity, with the plain façade in the distance

Stairs to main church

**★ Grotto of the Nativity**
*The grotto is the church's focal point. A silver star is set in the floor over the spot where Christ is said to have been born.*

St Catherine's Church *(see p193)*

Altar of the Adoration of the Magi (Manger Altar)

**Nave**
*The wide nave survives intact from Justinian's time, although the roof is 15th-century, with 19th-century restorations. Fragments of high-quality mosaics decorate the walls.*

Other grottoes, reached by these steps, contain the supposed tomb and study of St Jerome *(see p193)*.

Statue of St Jerome

**Cloister of St Catherine's Church**
*Incorporating columns and capitals from the 12th-century Augustinian monastery that previously stood here, this attractive, peaceful cloister was rebuilt in Crusader style in 1948.*

For hotels and restaurants in this region see pp261–2 and pp278–9

### Painted Columns

*Thirty of the nave's 44 columns carry Crusader paintings of saints, and the Virgin and Child, although age and lighting conditions make them hard to see. The columns are of polished, pink limestone, most of them reused from the original 4th-century basilica.*

## VISITORS' CHECKLIST

Manger Square, Bethlehem.
**Tel** (02) 274 2440. ☐ summer:
6:30am–noon & 2–7:30pm
daily; winter: 5:30am–noon
& 2–5pm daily. Grottoes closed
Sun am. ♿

### ★ Mosaic Floor

*Trap doors in the present floor, here and to the left of the altar, reveal sections of mosaic floor surviving from the 4th-century basilica.*

**Wall mosaics**, made in the 1160s, once decorated the entire church.

**The narthex** was originally a single, long porch with three large doors leading into the church and three onto the street.

### ★ Door of Humility

*The Crusader doorway, marked by a pointed arch, was reduced to the present tiny size in the Ottoman period to prevent carts being driven in by looters. A massive lintel above the arch indicates the door's even larger original size.*

### ST JEROME

Born at Stribo (not far from Venice), St Jerome (c.342–420) was one of the most learned scholars of the early Christian Church. He travelled widely and, in 384, settled in Bethlehem, where he founded a monastery. Here, he completed a new version of the Bible (*see p24*), inspired by the pope's suggestion that a single book should replace the many differing texts in circulation. His great work later became known as the Vulgate. Tradition places the saint's study and tomb next to the Grotto of the Nativity.

*St Jerome Writing (c.1604) by Caravaggio*

### STAR FEATURES

★ Grotto of the Nativity

★ Mosaic Floor

★ Door of Humility

Caves at Qumran, where the hot, dry, desert climate helped to preserve the Dead Sea Scrolls

# Qumran ❼

**Road map** C4. Route 90, 20 km (12 miles) S of Jericho. **Tel** (02) 994 2235. 🚌 from Jerusalem. ○ 8am–5pm (winter: 4pm) daily. 🗲 ♿

Qumran is known chiefly as the place where the Dead Sea Scrolls were discovered. From 150 BC to AD 68 this remote site was the home of a radically ascetic and reclusive community, often identified with the Essenes. According to their school of thought, the arrival of the Jewish Messiah was imminent, and they prepared for this event with fasting and purification through ritual ablutions. These activities were rudely brought to a halt through conflict with the Romans.

The Essenes largely vanished from history until 1947 when a Bedouin shepherd boy looking for a lost goat happened upon a cave full of jars. These jars were found to contain a precious hoard of 190 linen-wrapped scrolls that had been preserved for 2,000 years. Following much study by academics some of the scrolls are now on view in a purpose-built hall at the Israel Museum (see pp136–7).

Visitors to Qumran watch a short film on the Essenes and view a small exhibition on the community before being directed to the archaeological site at the foot of the cliffs. Signs indicate the probable uses of different areas of the vaguely defined remains.

From the site you can see the caves above where the scrolls were found. You can scramble up to the caves for a fine view, but you need to allow about two hours and carry a substantial supply of water.

# Ein Gedi ❽

**Road map** C4. Route 90, 56 km (35 miles) S of Jericho. 🚌 from Jerusalem.

Ein Gedi is famous as a lush oasis in an otherwise barren landscape. Several springs provide plentiful water to support a luxuriant mix of tropical and desert vegetation. The site is mentioned in the Bible for its beauty (Song of Songs: 1–14) and as a refuge of David who was fleeing from King Saul (I Samuel: 24).

Protected as **Ein Gedi National Park**, the oasis is a haven for desert wildlife such as ibexes and rock hyraxes, which look like large rodents, while the more remote areas are the abode of the desert leopard. Two gorges, belonging to the Nakhal David and Nakhal Arugot rivers, are at the core of the park; these are crossed by a network of paths. The shortest walking tour takes about an hour and ends at the spectacular Shulamit Falls. A short way from the park entrance are the ruins of a 5th-century BC synagogue with mosaics and inscriptions in Hebrew and Aramaic.

Ein Gedi is also a popular spot with Dead Sea bathers (see p197). For a more luxurious experience, the **Ein Gedi Health Spa**, a further 3 km (2 miles) to the south, has hot sulphur baths and private access to the Dead Sea.

**🏞 Ein Gedi National Park**
Highway 90, Dead Sea **Tel** (08) 658 4285. ○ daily. 🗲

**♨ Ein Gedi Health Spa**
Highway 90, Dead Sea
**Tel** (08) 659 4726. ○ daily. 🗲 ♿

Trail sign for one of the gorges in the Ein Gedi National Park

# The Dead Sea ❾

The Dead Sea (which is actually a lake, not a sea) lies half in Israel, half in Jordan. It is 76 km (47 miles) from north to south and less than 16 km (10 miles) across. At 411 m (1,348 ft) below sea level, it is also the lowest point on earth. The water is so mineral-laden that it is around 26% solid. The therapeutic qualities of the water and its mud have been touted since ancient times, and spas are dotted along its shores. However, the Dead Sea is endangered. Its water level has gone down 12 m (40 ft) since the beginning of the 20th century because its main source, the Jordan River, has been over-exploited for irrigation purposes.

**VISITORS' CHECKLIST**

30 km (18 miles) E of Jerusalem. 🚌 from Jerusalem for Qumran, Ein Gedi, Masada and Neve Zohar; from Amman for Amman Beach, Dead Sea Panorama and Wadi Mujib Nature Reserve. **Dead Sea Panorama Tel** (03) 231 3059. 🕐 7:30am–4:30pm daily. 🅿 **Wadi Mujib Nature Reserve Tel** (03) 231 3059. 🅿 🚹 compulsory. **www.**rscn.org.jo

**Qumran** is where the Dead Sea Scrolls were discovered (see p196).

To Jericho and Jerusalem

To Amman

**Amman beach**
A public beach with showers. There are also several resort hotels a little to the north, where you pay for access to their private beaches.

**Ein Gedi**
The most popular spot with bathers, Ein Gedi has a beach 1 km (half a mile) south of the National Park (see p196), with showers necessary to rinse off the lake's salty residue.

**Dead Sea Panorama**
A lookout, restaurant and museum complex with breathtaking views.

**Masada** Herod's mountain-top fortress, overlooking the Dead Sea (see pp200–201).

**Wadi Mujib nature reserve**
A wildlife sanctuary that also has several guided trails, some of which involve wading through partially submerged canyons. Bookings for the trails must be made in advance through the Wild Jordan Centre in Amman (see p214).

**Ein Bokek**
A waterside spa resort with hotels, a beach and sanatoriums that make good use of Dead Sea mud.

To Sodom and Eilat

**Neve Zohar** A small hot-springs spa resort.

To Petra

ISRAEL

JORDAN

**KEY**

═══ Major road

─── International border

🚻 Beach

☀ Viewpoint

0 kilometres    20

0 miles    10

# Masada ⑩

This isolated mountain-top fortress about 440 m (1,300 ft) above the banks of the Dead Sea was fortified as early as the 1st or 2nd century BC and then enlarged and reinforced by Herod the Great, who added two luxurious palace complexes. On Herod's death the fortress passed into Roman hands but it was captured in AD 66 during the First Revolt by Jews of the Zealot sect. After the Romans had crushed the rebels in Jerusalem, Masada remained the last Jewish stronghold. Held by less than 1,000 defenders, it was under Roman siege for over two years before the walls were breached in AD 73.

**Cable Car**
*The cable car operates daily between 8am and 4pm; otherwise it is a strenuous 45–60-minute climb up the twisting Snake Path.*

Upper terrace

Snake Path

Storerooms

Middle terrace

Lower terrace

**★ Hanging Palace**
*Part of the large Northern Palace complex, the Hanging Palace was Herod's private residence. It was built on three levels; the middle terrace had a circular hall used for entertaining, the lower had a bathhouse.*

**Calidarium**
*Masada's hot baths are one of the best preserved parts of the fortress. The columns remain on which the original floor was raised to allow hot air to circulate underneath and heat the room.*

**The Water Gate**
is at the head of a winding path to reservoirs below.

**STAR FEATURES**

★ Hanging Palace

★ Western Palace

**Synagogue**
*Possibly built by Herod, this synagogue is thought to be the oldest in the world. The stone seats were added by the Zealots.*

*For hotels and restaurants in this region see pp261–2 and pp278–9*

### Cistern

*At the foot of the mountain Herod built dams and canals that collected the seasonal rainwater to fill cisterns on the northeast side of the fortress. This water was then carried by donkey to the cisterns on top of the rock, such as this one in the southern part of the plateau.*

## VISITORS' CHECKLIST

**Road map** C4. Off Route 90,
18 km (11 miles) S of Ein Gedi.
from Jerusalem or Eilat.
**Tel** (08) 658 4207. ◻ 8am–
4pm (winter: 3pm) Sat–Thu;
8am–3pm (winter: 2pm) Fri.
**Sound and Light Show:**
Mar–Oct. **Tel** (08) 995 9333
for reservations.

Southern
Citadel

### Columbarium

*This is a small building with niches for funerary urns; it is thought the urns held the ashes of non-Jewish members of Herod's court.*

Western
Wall

West
Gate

The Roman ramp is
now the western
entrance to the site.

### ★ Western Palace

*Used for receptions and the accommodation of Herod's guests, the Western Palace was richly decorated with mosaic floors and frescoes adorning the walls.*

## THE ROMAN SIEGE OF MASADA (AD 70–73)

According to a 1st-century account by historian Flavius Josephus, the Roman legions laying siege to Masada numbered about 10,000 men. To prevent the Jewish rebels from escaping, the Romans surrounded the mountain with a ring of eight camps, linked by walls; an arrangement that can still be seen today. To make their attack, the Romans built a huge earthen ramp up the mountainside. Once this was finished, a tower was constructed against the walls. From the shelter of this tower the Romans set to work with a batter-ing ram. The defenders hastily erected an inner defensive wall, but this proved little obstacle and Masada fell when it was breached. Rather than submit to the Romans the Jews inside chose to commit mass suicide. Josephus relates how each man was responsible for killing his own family. "Masada shall not fall again" is a swearing-in oath of the modern Israeli army.

**Roman catapult missiles**

Remains of one of the Roman base camps
viewed from the fortress top

## Sodom ⓫

**Road map** C4. Route 90, 50 km
(31 miles) S of Ein Gedi. 🚌 *from
Jerusalem.*

Biblical tradition holds that
the city of Sodom lay on the
southern shore of the Dead
Sea (Genesis 19). Its sinful
inhabitants, along with those
of neighbouring Gomorrah,
angered God, and he
destroyed the cities with
"brimstone and fire".
Archaeologists now favour
Bab ed-Dhra in Jordan as
the likely site, but the name
Sodom remains attached to a
spot on the Israeli side of the
Dead Sea. There is nothing
to visit but nearby are the
two spas of **Ein Bokek** and
**Neve Zohar**, famous for their
therapeutic centres, and a
public beach with fresh-water
showers *(see p197).*

Inland and 9 km (6 miles)
south of Neve Zohar is
**Mount Sodom**, a mountain
composed largely of rock salt.
A well-marked path goes up
to the top, from where you
can enjoy incomparable views
of the Dead Sea and the
Moab mountains in Jordan.
You can also go up by car:
take the dirt road that heads
west off route 90 just north
of the unattractive Dead Sea
Works plant. Another signposted scenic hiking route
leads to what is known as the
**Flour Cave**. The cave gets its
name from the white crumbly
chalk coating that covers the
interior and the clothing of
all who visit.

**A typically barren Dead Sea
landscape near Sodom**

**Spring-fed pool at Ein Ovdat in the
shade of canyon walls**

## Ein Ovdat ⓬

**Road map** B5. Route 40, 52 km
(32 miles) S of Beersheva. **Tel** (08)
655 5684. 🚌 *from Jerusalem.*
🕐 *summer: 8am–4pm (3pm Fri &
hol eves); winter: 8am–3pm (2pm Fri
& hol eves) daily.* 🎫

At Ein Ovdat a white-walled
gorge gouged 200 m (656 ft)
deep into the desert floor
shades two icy-cold pools.
The larger of the pools is fed
by a waterfall with its source
in the rock face high above.
Archaeologists have found
traces of human presence
in this area that date back
perhaps 35,000 years,
suggesting that the springs
were known in antiquity.

A well-marked trail through
the gorge begins at a roadside
viewpoint 2 km (1 mile) south
of the turn-off for Kibbutz
Sde Boker. The trail ends with
a set of rough rock-cut steps
ascending the cliffs; the views
from these back down the
gorge are spectacular. From
the clifftop a path leads to
a roadside car park 7 km (4
miles) south of the viewpoint.

## Ovdat ⓭

**Road map** B5. Route 40, 60 km
(37 miles) S of Beersheva. **Tel** (08)
655 1511. 🚌 *from Jerusalem.*
🕐 *summer: 8am–4pm (3pm Fri
& hol eves); winter: 8am–3pm (2pm
Fri & hol eves) daily.* 🎫

Located on a flat hilltop,
the ancient town of Ovdat
was built by the Nabataeans
in the 2nd century BC as a

stopover on the trade route
between Egypt and Asia
Minor. It continued to prosper
under the Byzantines, and
most of what you see today
dates from the 4th or 5th century, including the remains
of houses, baths and two
churches. The smaller of
these has its original apse
and bishop's throne; a white
line divides the original and
reconstructed parts. The
views across the desert are
excellent. Below the hill you
can make out evidence of the
network of dams built by the
Nabataeans to channel rainwater towards the dry land,
enabling them to plant vineyards and fruit orchards.
Ovdat was abandoned after
the Persian invasion of 620.
The Visitors' Centre has an
exhibition of archaeological
finds from the ancient site.

**Partially reconstructed Byzantine-
era ruins at Ovdat**

## Hebron ⓮

**Road map** B4. 🏠 120,000. 🚌
🏨 *daily.*

Nestled among hills 40 km
(25 miles) south of Jerusalem,
Hebron is one of the most
densely populated towns in
the West Bank. Its fame rests
on its glassmaking, which
began in the Middle Ages and
has always been managed by
one single family.

This coloured glassware
can be found for sale in
another of Hebron's major
attractions, its medieval Arab
souk, which contains some
imposing Crusader-era
vaulted passageways.

However, Hebron is a town
undermined by troublesome
political tensions. It is divided

**The Tomb of the Patriarchs, mosque and burial site of Sarah, Isaac and Jacob**

Crusaders attempted to reclaim the site for Christianity and built much of the present-day construction, but it was completed by Saladin as a mosque. In the 13th century the Mameluke ruler Baybars forbade non-Muslims from entering the building.

After the 1967 war the mosque remained Muslim, but access was granted to Jews as well. Today, the complex, known as the **Tomb of the Patriarchs** (Haram al-Khalil in Arabic), is divided into a Jewish synagogue and a Muslim mosque, each with its own entrance. It remains a bone of contention between the faiths; in 1994 Jewish colonist Baruch Goldstein entered the mosque and killed 29 Muslim worshippers.

into two zones: the greater area is governed by the Palestinian Authority, but the town centre is occupied by Jewish settlers. Large numbers of Israeli soldiers maintain a constant peace-keeping presence. Friction between the two communities dates back to a 1929 pogrom in which the Arabs massacred Hebron's centuries-old Jewish community. After the Six Day War of 1967 the centre of town was resettled by militant Jewish colonists. Tension continues to erupt into occasional violence. For your personal safety, ask about the situation before making a trip to Hebron.

Hebron is regarded as a sacred place by the Jewish, Christian and Muslim religions alike; it was here they believe that Abraham buried his wife Sarah, in the Cave of Machpelah, purchased from the Hittite Ephron. The cave then became his own tomb and later that of his descendants Isaac and Jacob.

Around 20 BC Herod the Great sealed the cave and built a great hall over it. Under Byzantine rule the structure was turned into a church and then, after the Arab conquest of 638, a mosque. The invading

### Tomb of the Patriarchs
**Tel** (02) 960 602.  8am–4pm Sun–Thu except during prayer times.

## Beersheva ⑮

**Road map** B4.  200,000.  1 Hebron Rd, Beer Abraham, (08) 623 4613.  Bedouin market Thu.

The so-called capital of the Negev is a city that has grown rapidly and chaotically. In the Old Testament it is famous as the place where Abraham made a pact with Abimelech for the use of a well for his animals (Genesis 21: 25–33). Beersheva means "well of the covenant". For centuries it remained little more than a Bedouin well until the Turks transformed the site into an administrative centre (which was the object of a valiant cavalry charge by the Australians in World War I).

Since the Israelis captured Beersheva in 1948, it has attracted many immigrants to become the country's fourth largest city.

There is an attractive grouping of an Ottoman-era mosque and Governor's House in the town centre, but the most interesting thing about Beersheva is the **Bedouin market**. This is held on the edge of town every Thursday from dawn and attracts hundreds of nomads. Besides the livestock and everyday objects bought by the locals, visitors can also buy traditional Bedouin handicrafts such as jewellery and copperwork.

Just outside town is **Tel Beersheva**, a city founded at the end of the 11th century BC and fortified around the time of Solomon. It was destroyed in the 9th century by the Egyptians but was rebuilt, remaining a bulwark of the southern frontier of Judaea until it was razed to the ground by the Assyrians. Remains include a 10th-century BC city gate and a Roman fortress. There is also a museum of Bedouin life.

### Tel Beersheva
6 km (4 miles) NE of Beersheva. **Tel** (08) 646 7286.  daily.

**Bedouin selling sheep at Beersheva's Thursday market**

# Makhtesh Ramon ⑯

**Road map** B5. Route 40, 80 km (50 miles) S of Beersheva. 🚌 *from Beersheba.* **Visitors' Centre** *Tel (08) 658 8691.* ⭘ *8am–5pm Sun–Thu, 8am–4pm Fri (closes 1 hr earlier in winter).* 🏠 ♿

Makhtesh Ramon is Israel's most spectacular natural phenomenon: a crater some 40 km (25 miles) long, 9 km (5 miles) wide, with a depth of 300 m (1,300 ft). It is the largest of three craters in the Negev Desert, which scientists believe were formed more than half a million years ago by a combination of tectonic movement and erosion.

Traffic between Beersheva and Eilat has to cross Makhtesh Ramon, negotiating switchback roads that wind down to the crater floor and back up again. Nabataean caravans also travelled this way between Petra and Ovdat, and the ruins of an ancient caravanserai stand at the centre of the depression.

On the crater's rim is the town of Mitspe Ramon, the main base for exploring this part of the desert. The town's Visitors' Centre has exhibits on the geology of the great crater and its flora and fauna. It also has hiking maps – but make sure to take plenty of water if you go trekking here. In Mitspe Ramon you can also arrange to tour the crater by camel or jeep.

Spectacular geological scenery at Timna National Park

# Khai Bar Biblical Wildlife Reserve ⑰

**Road map** B6. Route 90, 35 km (22 miles) N of Eilat. **Tel** *(08) 637 6018.* 🚌 *from Eilat.* ⭘ *8:30am–5pm (Fri & Sat: 4pm) Mon–Sat.* 🎫 *Obligatory with departures every hour.* 🏠 ♿

**A caracal, one of the biblical species at Khai Bar**

Khai Bar was founded with the aim of reintroducing some of the creatures named in the Bible, which have since vanished from the Negev. Most of the animals roam freely, safari-park style, in a 40-sq km (15-sq mile) territory in the Arava Valley. Visits can be made only by jeep in the company of a ranger guide. Native species in the reserve (not all of which receive biblical mention) include scimitar-horned oryxes, wild Somali donkeys, ostriches and the addax antelope with their curved horns. A Predator Centre houses wildcats, caracals (desert lynxes), foxes, leopards and hyenas in spacious enclosures.

# Timna National Park ⑱

**Road map** B6. Route 90, 30 km (19 miles) N of Eilat. **Tel** *(08) 631 6756.* 🚌 *from Eilat.* ⭘ *8am–4pm Sun–Fri (Jul &Aug 8am–4pm & 6–8:30pm Mon–Thu, Sat; 8am–1pm Sun, Fri).* 🏠 **www**.timna-park.co.il

Ancient remains indicate working mines at Timna as far back as 3000 BC, and the Egyptians were mining copper here around 1500 BC. They left two temples dedicated to the goddess Hathor, protectress of mines. A hieroglyphic inscription mentions pharaoh Rameses III offering a sacrifice to Hathor. The mines continued to be worked under the Nabataeans and Romans before being abandoned. With the added attraction of some curious mushroom-shaped rock formations created by wind erosion, the area has been preserved as a national park. An underground passage gives access to the ancient mines, and you can see Egyptian graffiti representing ibexes and hunters armed with bows and arrows.

**Modern sculptures set in the natural splendour of Makhtesh Ramon**

*For hotels and restaurants in this region see pp261–2 and pp278–9*

# Eilat ⑲

**Road map** B7. 🏙 50,000. ✈ 🚌
🛈 8 Beit ha-Gesher Street. ◷
8am–6pm Sun–Thu. (08) 630 9111.

Lying at the end of the Gulf
of Aqaba, on a stretch of
Israel's 12 km (7 mile) long
southern coast, Eilat is the only
Israeli town on the Red Sea.
The town is filled with hotels
and tourist villages, and is a
centre for diving and trips into
the desert. Eilat is similar in
many ways to Aqaba, which
faces it from 6 km (4 miles)
away on the other side of the
Gulf. Along with an equally
stunning location, Eilat also
shares a similar history to
Aqaba, due to their close
proximity. Now separated by
political boundaries however,
it is Eilat that has prospered
the most. With the United
Nations partition of Palestine
in 1947, Israel was ceded this
small stretch of coastline, and
Eilat has since developed
rapidly, both as a port and as
a popular holiday resort, with
excellent tourist facilities.

The bottom of the Red Sea
is the main attraction here.
If you don't want to dive to
admire this multicoloured

Coral Island, south of Eilat in the Gulf of Aqaba

ecosystem, there are glass-
bottomed boats as well as the
"Yellow Submarine". This large
23 m (75 ft) long submersible
leaves from Coral World, and
cruises out over the reef,
descending to a depth of
around 60 m (200 ft).

The large **Coral World
Underwater Observatory** is
an oceanographic complex
where you can get a close-
up view of the marvellous
marine life here. It contains
25 tanks with more than
500 species of fish, sponges,
corals and invertebrates. The
most interesting displays are
those with the larger creatures
such as sharks and sea turtles.
The main spectacle though is

at the underwater observatory
itself, which is 6 m (20 ft)
underwater and gives a
spectacular live view of the
local marine life through its
large glass windows.

Divers and expert swimmers
will be delighted at **Dolphin
Reef**, where small groups led
by an instructor can actually
swim with the dolphins and
observe their behaviour as
they play, swim and hunt.

The salt marshes just north
of Eilat are the feeding grounds
of many species of migratory
birds travelling between Africa
and Eurasia every spring and
autumn. The **International
Birdwatching Centre**, at
Kibbutz Eilot, has an interpretation centre, and organizes
guided birdwatching tours.
In season, the skies are filled
with thousands of flamingos,
storks and herons, as well as
eagles, hawks and buzzards.

By boat you can go to
the fabulous reefs off **Coral
Island** (or Pharaoh's Island),
which lies just across the
Egyptian border. Regular trips
are run for divers, but those
wishing to land and visit the
12th-century Crusader fortress
that dominates the island will
need to find a tour that can
arrange a group visa.

### 🐠 Coral World Underwater Observatory
Coral Beach. **Tel** (08) 636 4200.
◷ 8:30am–4pm daily. 📷 ♿
www.coralworld.com/eilat

### 🐠 Dolphin Reef
Southern Beach. **Tel** (08) 637 1846.
◷ daily. 📷 www.dolphinreef.co.il

### 🐠 International Birdwatching Centre
Kibbutz Eilot, 2 km (1 mile) N of Eilat.
**Tel** (08) 633 5339. ◷ Oct– Jun:
Sun–Thu (am only). 📷 ♿ ♿

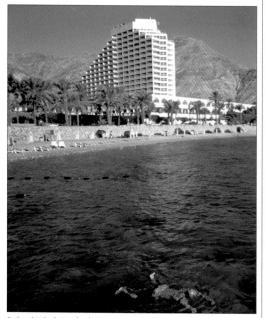

Swimming in the perfectly clear waters off the beach at Eilat

# WESTERN JORDAN

While most visitors to Jordan come for the sole purpose of seeing the magnificent rock-cut city of Petra, many depart with their most treasured experiences being encounters with the gracious and hospitable locals. Beside these two attractions, the western part of the country has a great many fascinating archaeological sites from prehistoric, Roman, Byzantine and Crusader times.

Only partitioned off from Palestine in 1923 and made fully independent in 1946, the nation of Jordan has a maturity that belies its youth. That the kingdom is viewed as an anchor in the often turbulent sea of Middle Eastern politics is due, in large part, to the efforts of the late King Hussein (1953–99) who worked solidly to establish and maintain peace in the region. The extreme warmth and friendliness of the population is an expression of the stability Hussein secured for his country. Day-to-day patterns of life in Jordan are also shaped by a relaxed and tolerant interpretation of Islam. Tourists who have just visited neighbouring Israel may well appreciate the laissez-faire nature of the Jordanian people.

Although Jordan has an area of about 92,000 sq km (36,000 sq miles),

around nine-tenths of this is desert. Consequently, the population of approximately 5.5 million is concentrated in the northwest on a plateau above the Jordan Valley. Watered by the Jordan River and surrounded by mountains, this little pocket enjoys a lush greenhouse-like climate and is entirely devoted to agriculture. But south of Amman the fertile plains abruptly end and give way to the vast stony desert that extends all the way down to the Red Sea. Largely shunned by the local populace, this is the region that visitors come to see. This is where you find the craggy sandstone landscapes out of which Petra was carved. Further south is Wadi Rum with its great cinemascope sandy oceans that provided a dramatic backdrop for the exploits of Lawrence of Arabia.

Perfectly suited to the Jordanian terrain, the camel, pictured here at Mount Nebo

◁ The Treasury at Petra, arguably the single most spectacular sight in the whole Middle East

# Exploring Western Jordan

Though possessing few sites itself, Jordan's modern capital, Amman, makes a very comfortable base from which to explore the northwest of the country. The Arab fortress at Ajlun, the Roman ruins at Jerash, the Byzantine mosaics of Madaba, and further mosaics along with splendid views at Mount Nebo, are all within an hour's drive. If you can spare the time and secure the use of a car (self-drive or a taxi hired by the day), then Amman is certainly worth a couple of days. The Crusader castles of Kerak and Shobak are perhaps best visited while heading south, en route to the site that truly epitomizes the magic of the region, Petra. While it is possible to see the major attractions in just one day, Petra more than repays repeated visits: multiple-day passes are available. Accommodation is easy to find in the neighbouring town of Wadi Musa. Be sure also to leave enough time for the surreal rockscapes of Wadi Rum, full of hidden oases and evidence of prehistoric civilizations.

The impressive stone sweep of the colonnaded Oval Plaza at Jerash

## SIGHTS AT A GLANCE

## GETTING AROUND

Most major tourist destinations can be reached by good, modern roads. There are two main routes south – take the King's Highway (Route 49) for Mount Nebo, Madaba, Kerak and Shobak, and the Desert Highway (Routes 15 and 53) to head directly to Petra and Wadi Rum. It is possible to fly between Amman and Aqaba and an inexpensive bus service connects all areas of the country. For many people, however, coach tours are the most comfortable way to get about.

### SEE ALSO

Wadi Rum, where sandstone mountains rise sheer from the desert floor

AQABA **11**

UMM QAIS ❶

Al Yarmuk

Ma'ad    Irbid    ↑ *Damascus*

Al Husn    Ar Ramtha

Pella

AJLUN ❷    Nadirah

Kurayyimah    JERASH ❸

Bal'ama

Al 'Aluk

Al Hashimiyah

Damiya    Yajuz

As Salt    Az Zarqa'

Suwaylih

Al Karamah    AMMAN ❹

Wadi as Sir

*Jerusalem* ←    Na'ur

MOUNT NEBO ❺    ❻ MADABA

Natl

Mukawir    Dhiban

*Dead Sea*    Ariha

Al Mazra'ah    Al Qasr

Al Qatranah

KERAK ❼    Adir

JORDAN

As Safi    Al Mazar Al Janubi

Fifah    Al 'Ayna

Irhab

At Tafilah    Al Hisa

Al 'Ayn Al Bayda'

Jurf Ad Darawish

Al Husayniyah

SHOBAK ❽

Bi'r Khidad    Adhrui

PETRA ❾    Wadi Musa

Dilaghah    Ma'an

Gharandal    Al Murayghah

Ra's An Naqb

Al Quwayrah

❿ WADI RUM

The Roman theatre in the shadow of modern central Amman

## KEY

═══ Motorway

━━━ Major road

········ Minor road

– – Four-wheel-drive track

━━━ Scenic route

∼∼∼ Railway

▬▬▬ International border

The Royal Tombs at Petra, a site that ranks with the Pyramids as a surviving wonder of the ancient world

# Umm Qais ❶

**Road map** C2. 100 km (62 miles) NW
of Amman. ◯ 7am–sunset daily.

Umm Qais is the site of the
ancient Graeco-Roman city of
Gadara. The ruins lie in lush
hill country overlooking the
Golan Heights and the Sea of
Galilee. The city is well known
from the Bible for Jesus's
miracle of the Gadarene Swine,
when he cast out demons
into pigs (Matthew 8: 28–34).
Since 1974, archaeologists
have uncovered many
impressive Roman remains,
including a colonnaded street,
a theatre and a mausoleum.

# Ajlun ❷

**Road map** C3. 50 km (31 miles) W
of Amman. 📞 (02) 642 0115.
**Fortress** ◯ 8am–5pm daily.

The market town of Ajlun is
dominated by the fortress
of **Qalat ar-Rabad**, a superb
example of Arab military
engineering. Built in 1184–5,
partly in response to Crusader
incursions in the region, it
was later used by the Ottomans
up until the 18th century. At a
height of more than 1,200 m
(4,000 ft), it offers fantastic
views over the Jordan Valley.

**Environs**
About 30 km (19 miles)
northwest of Ajlun is **Pella**.
Water, fertile land and, later,
its location on two major trade
routes were drawing settlers
here well before 3000 BC. Its
Roman-Byzantine ruins are
today's attraction, particularly
the colonnaded atrium.

**The Arab fortress at Ajlun, built
to stem the Crusaders' advance**

**View of Jerash's Cardo, Agora (market place) and unusual Oval Plaza**

# Jerash ❸

**Road map** C3. 50 km (31 miles) N
of Amman. 🚌 from Amman.
**Tel** (02) 635 1272. ◯ Oct–Apr:
8am–4pm; May–Sep: 8am–7pm daily.
**Sound & Light Shows** Jul–Oct:
8:30–10:30pm daily. 🎭 Arts Festival
(late Jul–early Aug). **Tel** (06) 567
5199. www.jerashfestival.com.jo

Excavations of Jerash, known
as Gerasa in Classical
times, began in the
1920s, bringing to
light one of the
best preserved
and most original
Roman cities in the
Middle East. It was
during the Hellenistic
period of the 3rd
century BC that          **Detail of floor mosaic**
Jerash became an          **in St George's Church**
urban centre and a
member of the loose federation
of Greek cities known as the
Decapolis (see p42). From the
1st century BC Jerash drew
considerable prestige from the
semi-independent status it was
given within the Roman
province of Syria. It prospered
greatly from its position on the
incense and spice trade route
from the Arabian Peninsula to
Syria and the Mediterranean.
Jerash lost its autonomy under
Trajan, but his annexation of
the Nabataean capital Petra

(see pp220–31) in AD 106
brought the city even more
wealth. By AD 130 ancient
Gerasa was at its zenith.
Having become a favourite city
of Hadrian (see p43), it
flourished both economically
and socially. After a period of
decline in the 3rd century, it
enjoyed a renaissance as a
Christian city under the Byzantines, notably in the reign of
Justinian (AD 527–65).
The Muslims took over
the city in 635, and it
was badly
damaged by
a series of earth-
quakes in the 8th
century. The final blow
to the city was dealt by
Baldwin II of
Jerusalem in 1112
during the Crusades
(see pp48–9).
The city is reached through
**Hadrian's Arch**, built in honour
of the Roman emperor.
Alongside is the **Hippodrome**,
where Gerasa's chariot races
and other sporting events took
place, and a little way down
the track is the **South Gate**,
part of the 4th-century AD city
wall. To its left, and on a
prominent rise is first the
**Temple of Zeus**, and then the
**South Theatre**, which nowadays is used as a venue for the
Jerash Festival (see p37). The

most unusual feature of the Roman city is the **Oval Plaza** (1st century AD) which, with its asymmetrical shape, is a unique monument from the Roman world. The plaza, 80 m by 90 m (262 ft by 295 ft), is enclosed by 160 Ionic columns. Beneath its stone paving runs a complex drainage system. From here, going north, is the **Cardo**, a spectacular paved street about 600 m (660 yards) long, which was lined with the city's major buildings, shops and residences. Chariot tracks are visible in the stones. To the left lies the **Agora**, the city's main food market, which had a central fountain. At the Tetrapylon (crossroads) the Cardo meets a second major street, the **South**

Temple of Zeus (2nd century AD)

**Decumanus**, which runs east–west. Further along on the left side of the Cardo is the 2nd-century **Nymphaeum**, a lavish public fountain. One of its basins has a design of four fish kissing. Nearby is the impressive **Temple of Artemis**, the patron goddess of the city in Greek and Roman times.

Close to the Temple are the remains of several Byzantine churches. The largest is usually referred to as the **Cathedral**. There is also a complex of three churches, dedicated to **SS Cosmas and Damian, St John the Baptist** and **St George**, which dates back to AD 526–33 and has fine mosaic floors. Further along the Cardo, to the right, is the **Propylaeum Church** with the remains of an ornate plaza in front, while next to it are the ruins of an **Omayyad Mosque**. Beyond lie the unexcavated **West Baths**, which preserve a splendid domed ceiling. At the **North Tetrapylon**, once marked by a dome resting on four arches, the road to the left leads to the small **North Theatre**.

Allow at least half a day to see the ruins, and finish off with the **Museum**, displaying sarcophagi, statuary and coins.

Irbid

Modern town

Museum

South Gate

Byzantine city wall

Entrance

Visitors' Centre and restaurant

0 metres 200

0 yards 200

Amman

## KEY TO THE RUINS OF JERASH

The reconstructed South Gate, the 4th-century AD entrance to Jerash

# Amman ❹

Like Jordan itself, Amman is a modern creation, but one whose roots run deep into history. The hills of Downtown hosted the biblical capital of the Ammonites and the Roman city of Philadelphia before the Omayyad Arabs built a palace on the same well-defended hill-top. In the modern age, Amman only began to prosper in the early 1920s when Emir Abdullah made it the capital of Trans-Jordan. Today, it is a bustling, modern and forward-looking Arab city of over two million people.

King Hussein Mosque, built on the site of a 7th-century mosque

## Exploring Central Amman

Amman's most interesting district for the visitor is the recently renovated Downtown, with its bustling markets and fascinating Roman ruins.

More than anything, Amman is a town of hills (*jebels*) and, of these, the most historically important is Jebel el-Qalaa, which rises north of Downtown. This is the site of the Citadel, a Roman temple and the main city museum.

Head of a Semite chief

## Downtown

The backstreet souks (markets) around El-Malek Faisal, El-Hashemi and Quraysh streets form the commercial hub of Amman. Shops here stock everything from marinated olives to gold jewellery, while pastry stalls, falafel stands, and aromatic coffee and spice grinders also compete for the attention of passers-by. There are also several interesting souvenir stalls on El-Hashemi Street.

The central **King Hussein Mosque**, built in 1924 on the site of a mosque erected in AD 640 by the caliph Omar, is the best attended in the city. Also nearby is the **Roman Nymphaeum**, built in AD 191 as a complex of pool and fountain, and dedicated to the nymphs. Jordan's Department of Antiquities is currently excavating the Nymphaeum, and the site should have been restored to something like its original condition by 2010. A new National Museum is also due to open in Downtown in 2008.

### 🏛 Citadel

Jebel el-Qalaa. *Tel* (06) 463 8795.
⬜ winter: 8am–4pm Sat–Thu, 10am–4pm Fri; summer: 8am–7pm Sat–Thu, 10am–4pm Fri. 🏷
For thousands of years Jebel el-Qalaa has served as the fortified heart of Amman. The Ammonite capital of Rabbath Ammon was situated here but most of the remains visible

today are part of what was an Omayyad Palace, completed around AD 750 and destined to last for only 30 years. The large complex includes an impressive audience hall, a colonnaded street, Byzantine basilica, large cistern and the residence of Amman's local governor. The southern Roman Temple of Hercules, with its towering columns and ornately carved stonework, was built at the same time as the city's Roman Theatre (*see p213*) and offers fine views over the city.

**Ruins of the Temple of Hercules at the Citadel**

*For hotels and restaurants in this region see pp262–3 and pp279–80*

## SIGHTS AT A GLANCE

Archaeological Museum ③
Citadel ②
Darat el-Funun ⑥
Downtown ①
Folklore Museum & Museum of Popular Traditions ⑤
King Abdullah Mosque ⑦
Roman Theatre ④
Royal Automobile Museum ⑧
Wild Jordan Centre ⑨

0 metres     300
0 yards      300

**Chequered *keffiyehs* – traditional Jordanian men's headwear**

**Key to Symbols** *see back flap*

### ▦ Roman Theatre
El-Hashemi Street. ○ *summer: 8:30am–7pm daily; winter: 8am–4pm Sat–Thu, 10am–4pm Fri.* 📷
Amman's most obvious remnant from the past is its impressive Roman Theatre, dating from around AD 170 and with a seating capacity of around 6,000. It's a fine place

### 🏛 Archaeological Museum
Jebel el-Qalaa. **Tel** (06) 463 8795. ○ *summer: 8am–7pm Sat–Thu, 10am–4pm Fri; winter: 8am–4pm Sat–Thu, 10am–4pm Fri.* 📷
This small museum at the Citadel records over 8,000 years of Middle Eastern history. Finds include Neolithic skulls and elephant bones from the Jordan Valley, a collection of copper-plated Dead Sea scrolls *(see p137)* and several Nabataean artifacts from Petra *(see pp220–31).* The very modern-looking bug-eyed statues from Ain Gazal are over 8,500 years old. Look out also for the impressive doorway transported here from the Arab castle of Qasr el-Tuba in the Eastern Desert. Local finds include the graceful statue of Athena, from the nearby Roman Theatre, and the head of Tyche, the town god.

### VISITORS' CHECKLIST
**Road Map** C3. 🏘 *2,125,000.*
✈ ℹ *Ministry of Tourism, El-Mutanabbi Street, Jebel Amman (Third Circle), (06) 464 2311.*

to sit, meet the locals and take in the city. The back rows of the theatre were added later and carved out of an existing necropolis. At the foot of the theatre are a Corinthian colonnade and the old Odeon (a small theatre or meeting hall). The nearby Hashemite Square is a popular hangout for local Jordanian families.

### 🏛 Folklore Museum & Museum of Popular Traditions
El-Hashemi Street. **Tel** (06) 465 1742. ○ *summer: 9am–7pm Sat–Thu, 10am–4pm Fri; winter: 9am–5pm Sat–Thu, 10am–4pm Fri.* 📷
The vaults below the Roman Theatre house these two modest but interesting museums. The Folklore Museum has some traditional costumes, a Bedouin tent, fine examples of the rababa (a one-stringed musical instrument) and traditional coffee grinders. The second museum displays Circassian and Armenian silver jewellery, traditionally given to the bride on her wedding day, plus amulets made from Turkish coins and symbols representing the hands of Fatima. There are some fine mosaics from Jerash *(see p210–11)* and the baptism site of Wadi el-Kharrar.

**The Roman Theatre, built during the reign of Emperor Marcus Aurelius**

# Exploring Amman

Although the majority of Amman's places of interest are concentrated in the neighbouring Downtown and Jebel el-Qalaa districts, it is well worth exploring further afield. Just west of the centre, Jebel Amman is the city's main hill, and is home to the Wild Jordan Centre and the landmark King Abdullah Mosque. West again, the upscale districts of Abdoun and, stretching to the north, Shmeisani boast the majority of Amman's shops and restaurants. The city is quite spread out, so taxi is the best way to get around.

The hilly landscape of the modern city of Amman

### Darat el-Funun

Nimer bin Adwan Street, Jebel el-Webdeh. **Tel** (06) 464 3251. ◯ 10am–7pm Sat–Wed, 10am–8pm Thu. www.daratalfunun.org.

This art gallery, pleasant café and small garden dotted with archaeological remains, offer a tranquil escape from the nearby Downtown bustle. The rotating exhibits of contemporary art, regular lectures and occasional music concerts make this the best place to tap into Amman's thriving arts scene. The main gallery is housed in a 1920s villa, next to the charming remains of a 6th-century Byzantine church, itself built on the site of a Roman temple. Above the church is the house in which TE Lawrence is said to have written sections of *The Seven Pillars of Wisdom*.

### ◖ King Abdullah Mosque

Suleyman el-Nabulsi Street, Jebel el-Webdeh. ◯ 8am–11am & 12:30–2pm Sat–Thu, 9am–10am Fri. 🖼

Amman's most impressive Islamic monument is the King (El-Malek) Abdullah Mosque, completed in 1990 and dedicated by King Hussein to his grandfather. The soaring central blue dome covers the largest religious space in the city – the prayer hall can hold up to 7,000 worshippers. The cavernous, octagonal interior is decorated with fine Quranic calligraphy and several huge chandeliers. Remove your shoes when you enter the mosque. Women should wear a headscarf (provided). The attached small **Islamic museum** contains coins and examples of Islamic decorative arts.

### Royal Automobile Museum

King Hussein Park. **Tel** (06) 541 1392. ◯ 10am–7pm Wed, Thu, Sat–Mon, 10am–9pm Fri. 🖼 www.royalautomuseum.jo

The former King Hussein was passionate about automobiles. This museum, 5 km (3 miles) northwest of the city centre, exhibits around 70 classic cars and motorcycles from his own personal collection. These range from a 1916 Cadillac to an array of more modern Lotus, Ferrari and Porsche sporting models, all driven by the King. Also on display is the Mercedes-Benz jeep that carried the casket in the funeral procession of King Hussein in 1999.

### Wild Jordan Centre

Othman bin Aafarn Street, Jebel Amman. **Tel** (06) 463 3589. www.rscn.org.jo

Jordan's innovative Royal Society for the Conservation of Nature (RSCN) runs this cutting-edge centre, which focuses on Jordan's natural heritage. The Wild Nature shop stocks products made in ecotourism initiatives throughout Jordan, including organic soaps and worked silver from Dana, Bedouin-made candles from the Dead Sea and hand-painted ostrich eggs from the Eastern Desert. The excellent café is one of the best places in town for a healthy lunch, and the terrace, in particular, affords fantastic views over Downtown.

This is also the place for information on ecotourism excursions to Jordan's many national parks; possibilities include hiking and canyoning in Wadi Mujib *(see p197)*, and the chance to see Arabian oryx in the wild at the Shaumari Nature Reserve.

The distinctive blue dome that caps the striking King Abdullah Mosque

For hotels and restaurants in this region see pp262–3 and pp279–80

**Detail of a mosaic from the Memorial Church of Moses on Mount Nebo**

## Mount Nebo ❺

**Road map** C3. 10 km (6 miles) NW of Madaba. 🚌 *from Madaba then a 4-km (2.5-mile) walk, or taxi.* ⬜ *7am–7pm daily (Oct–Apr: 5pm).*

This mountain rises at the end of the long chain skirting the Dead Sea, and offers spectacular views of the Jordan River and Dead Sea 1,000 m (3,300 ft) below. It was from here that Moses saw the Promised Land just before he died (Deuteronomy 34: 1–5).

In the early 4th century a sanctuary, mentioned by the pilgrim nun Egeria *(see p32)*, was built on Mount Nebo (Fasaliyyeh in Arabic) to honour Moses, probably over the remains of a more ancient construction. During the Byzantine period, the church was transformed into a fine basilica with a sacristy and new baptistry. Monastic buildings were added later.

Since 1933, reconstruction work has been carried out on the church, now known as the **Memorial Church of Moses**. Mosaics inside include a remarkable example in the Old Baptistry depicting farmers, hunters and an assortment of animals surrounded by geometric decoration. A Greek inscription dates it to AD 531. Next to the New Baptistry, a mosaic cross from the original church stands on a modern altar. Outside, the foundations of the monastery can be seen.

## Madaba ❻

*See pp216–7.*

## Kerak ❼

**Road map** C4. 🏚 *19,000.* 🚌 ℹ️ *El-Mujamma Street, (03) 235 1150.*

The town of Kerak, on top of a hill with a sheer drop on three sides, is dominated by a magnificent Crusader citadel. Kerak was an important city (and for a time the capital) of the Biblical kingdom of Moab. For this reason, the **castle** is also sometimes known as Krak des Moabites.

It was built in 1142 by the Frankish lord of Oultrejourdain, Payen le Bouteiller, to whom the territory had been ceded by King Baldwin II of Jerusalem in 1126. It was the pearl in the chain of fortifications that ran between Jerusalem and Aqaba, and replaced Shobak as the centre of Oultrejourdain. Under Reynald de Châtillon it resisted assaults by Saladin's troops in 1183 and 1184, but finally fell after a siege in 1188.

Arab repairs and additions in white limestone contrast

with the Crusader parts built in dark, volcanic tufa. The upper courtyard, containing a much-damaged Crusader chapel, provides an exceptional viewpoint. Steps lead down to vast, dimly-lit, vaulted rooms and corridors below ground. The lower courtyard gives access to a small **Archaeological Museum** displaying locally excavated artifacts.

♠ **Castle**
El-Mujamma St. ⬜ *daily.*

🏛 **Archaeological Museum**
*Tel* (03) 235 1216. ⬜ *9am–5pm daily.* 🎞

## Shobak ❽

**Road map** C5. 60 km (37 miles) S of Tafila. *Tel* (03) 215 6020. 🚌 *to Shobak village, then taxi.* ⬜ *daily.*

Shobak, isolated on a rocky, conical hill in rough, barren surroundings at 1,300 m (4,265 ft) above sea level, is perhaps the most impressively sited castle in Jordan. It was called Krak de Montréal, or Mons Regalis, and was the first outpost (1115) built beyond the Jordan River by King Baldwin I of Jerusalem to guard the road from Egypt to Damascus. It resisted many sieges until 1189, when it fell to Saladin's troops.

The towers and walls are well preserved and decorated with carved inscriptions dating from 14th-century Mameluke renovations, but the inside is ruinous. Near the gatehouse, a well with over 350 dangerously slippery, spiral, rock-cut steps descends to a spring.

**The impressive and well-preserved Crusader fortress at Kerak**

## Madaba ⑥

**Road map** C4. 🏘 *75,000.*
🚌 *from Amman.* ⓘ *Hussein bin Ali St, (05) 324 3376.*

According to the Old Testament the Moabite city of Madaba was one of those conquered by the tribes of Israel. After changing hands several times it flourished under Roman dominion and by the 4th century AD it had become an important centre of Christianity with its own bishop. The town weathered invasions by the Persians and Muslims but declined under the Mamelukes and was completely abandoned during the 16th century. It was not reoccupied until the late 19th century.

The main attraction is the fabulous mosaic map housed in **St George's Church** in the town centre, but there is also an **Archaeological Park** encompassing the remains of several more 6th-century churches, all with impressive mosaics, including one depicting scenes from the legend of Adonis and Aphrodite. The **Church of the Apostles** on the southern edge of town has a mosaic depicting the sea goddess Thetis surrounded by fish and sea monsters.

🛉 **St George's Church**
◯ *8:30am (10:30am Fri & Sun)–6pm daily.* 🖂

🏛 **Archaeological Park**
◯ *daily.* 🖂

St George's Church, also known as the Church of the Map

# The Madaba Mosaic Map

**Mosaic gazelle from the map**

In the late 19th century clashes with the Muslim community led to a group of Christians from Kerak voluntarily moving to the long-uninhabited site of ancient Madaba. They were permitted to build new churches only on the sites of old ones. In 1884, while clearing such a site, the mosaic map was uncovered. It was incorporated into the new St George's Church but was badly damaged in the process. It wasn't until ten years later that scholars recognized the great historic value of the mosaic, which was probably made during the reign of the Emperor Justinian (AD 527–65).

**The Jordan River** *is shown crossed by a ferry and filled with fish, which stop at the heavily-salted waters of the Dead Sea.*

**Neapolis (modern Nablus)** is badly damaged, but can be identified by its name, spelled out in Greek letters.

**Gethsemane**

**Jerusalem** is depicted in great detail (see above).

**Jericho** *appears on the map as a walled town with towers, agreeing with the evidence found at the site of Tel Jericho.*

**Bethlehem**, famous as the birthplace of Jesus, is shown as a small village dominated by the Church of the Nativity.

The Madaba map, visited by up to a thousand visitors a day

## JERUSALEM AS DEPICTED ON THE MAP

In the 6th century, Jerusalem was still essentially the Roman city of Aelia Capitolina with its walls and gates, and the main streets of the Cardo Maximus and the Decumanus. Identifiable landmarks include Damascus Gate and the Church of the Holy Sepulchre, as well as the long-vanished Nea Basilica *(see p82)* and Damascus Gate column.

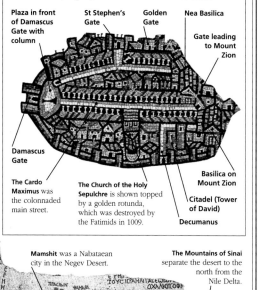

Plaza in front of Damascus Gate with column

St Stephen's Gate

Golden Gate

Nea Basilica

Gate leading to Mount Zion

Damascus Gate

The Cardo Maximus was the colonnaded main street.

The Church of the Holy Sepulchre is shown topped by a golden rotunda, which was destroyed by the Fatimids in 1009.

Basilica on Mount Zion

Citadel (Tower of David)

Decumanus

Kerak sits on top of a high mountain.

Mamshit was a Nabataean city in the Negev Desert.

The Mountains of Sinai separate the desert to the north from the Nile Delta.

The Dead Sea is shown with two boats carrying salt and grain. The sailors have been hacked out, probably by iconoclasts who objected to the representation of living beings in art.

Beersheva, although existing only in part, can be identified by the text – and by its accurate location in the western Negev Desert.

Pelusium was an important Byzantine-era city; it has long since disappeared.

Ashdod, an ancient port on the Mediterranean, remains an important deep-water harbour.

## WHAT THE MAP SHOWS

The map is oriented east–west rather than north–south, with Palestine on the left and Egypt's Nile Delta on the extreme right. The cities and villages are located remarkably accurately for the time, and they are represented in plan form, corresponding to a large degree to modern cartography.

The Nile is depicted as flowing east–west rather than the reality, which is from south to north.

*Gaza was a major port in ancient times with trade links to Egypt and Africa and, by its comparatively large size, the map accords it great importance.*

**The Monastery, one of Petra's most breathtaking monuments** ▷

# Petra ❾

Petra is one of the world's most impressive and atmospheric archaeological sites. Its marvellously preserved rock-hewn tombs and temples once encircled a thriving metropolis. There has been human settlement here since prehistoric times, but before the Nabataeans *(see p227)* came, Petra was just another desert watering hole. Between the 3rd century BC and the 1st century AD, they built a superb city and made it the centre of a vast trading empire. In AD 106 Petra was annexed by Rome. Christianity arrived in the 4th century, the Muslims in the 7th and the Crusaders briefly in the 12th. Thereafter Petra lay forgotten until 1812 when rediscovered by JL Burckhardt *(see p223)*.

**The City of Petra**
*The city's main street leads to the Temenos Gate, entrance to the sacred precinct of Qasr el-Bint, Petra's most important temple (see pp228–9).*

**★ The Monastery**
*The imposing façade of the Monastery, or El-Deir, is 47 m (154 ft) wide and 40 m (131 ft) high. This magnificent Nabataean temple may later have served as a church (see pp230–1).*

### VISITING PETRA

- It is worth spending more than a day here. There are passes for 1–4 days.
- Cars allowed up to ticket gate but not beyond.
- Horses may be hired to take you the 900 m (half a mile) to Siq entrance.
- Two-seater horse-drawn carts go from the ticket office to the Treasury. From there Petra can be covered on foot or camel.
- Basic food and drinking water available in Petra.
- Wear sunhat and high-factor sunscreen.
- Avoid wandering off main walk routes without guide and water supply.
- A new visitors' centre is being built near the Siq.

**Lion Triclinium**
*(see p230)*

**Modern Museum**
*(see p228)*

**Little Petra**
*(see p231)*

JEBEL UMM ZAYTUNA

JEBEL EL-DEIR

WADI ABU 'ULLAYQA

WADI EL-MATAHA

WADI EL-SIYYAGH

WADI MUSA

**Old Museum**
*(see p228)*

**El-Habis Crusader fortress (see p228)**

**Qasr el-Bint**
*(see p228)*

**Outer Siq**

JEBEL EL-QURAY

WADI EL-FARASA

JEBEL ATTUF

WADI EL-THUGHRA

WADI UMM RATTAM

**High Place of Sacrifice**
*(see pp230–1)*

**Aaron's Tomb**
*(see p231)*

**The Theatre**
*Carved into the mountainside by the Nabataeans, probably in the 1st century AD, this theatre follows the standard Roman design of the time. It was large enough to seat up to 7,000 people (see p225).*

★ **The Royal Tombs**
*These monumental façades sculpted into the mountain at
the eastern end of the Petra basin create an awe-inspiring
panorama when viewed from a distance (see pp226–7).*

**VISITORS' CHECKLIST**

**Road map** C5. Wadi Musa,
260 km (160 miles) S of Amman.
to Wadi Musa from Amman,
Aqaba. 6:30am–sunset daily.
passes sold for 1, 2, 3 or 4
days. Ask at the Visitors'
Centre. Petra Visitors' Centre,
(03) 215 6020 (6:30am–5pm
daily). Do not photograph
Bedouin without their
permission. **Museum**
9am–4pm daily.

Mughur el-Nasara
(see p231)

House of
Dorotheos
(see p231)

★ **The Siq**
*Access to Petra is through
this deep ravine, formed when
a split in the mountain was
swept clear by water from the
Wadi Musa (see pp222–3).*

Tomb of Sextius
Florentinus
(see p231)

Petra Forum
Hotel

JEBEL
EL-KHUBTHA

Wadi Musa
Town

Siq entrance

Visitors' Centre

Bab el-Siq

Ticket gate

**KEY**

WADI MUSA

| | |
|---|---|
| – – | Walk to Monastery (see pp230–1) |
| – – | Walk to High Place of Sacrifice (see pp230–1) |
| ☼ | Viewpoint |

Petra Forum
Resthouse

0 metres          500

0 yards            500

**STAR SIGHTS**

★ The Siq

★ The Treasury

★ The Royal Tombs

★ The Monastery

★ **The Treasury**
*The best-known of all Petra's
magnificent temples, deliberately positioned at the end of
the Siq for maximum impact,
the 1st-century BC Treasury
takes its name from Bedouin
folklore. They believed that the
Khasneh el-Faroun (Treasury
of the Pharaoh) was the
magical creation of a great
wizard who had deposited
treasure in its urn (see p224).*

# The Siq: the Ancient Entrance to Petra

To reach the Siq, the narrow Gorge that leads into Petra, you must first walk 900 m (half a mile) along the wide valley known as the Bab el-Siq. This prelude to Petra has many tantalizing examples of the Nabataeans' appetite for sculpting monuments out of mountainsides. The entrance to the Siq is marked by the remains of a monumental arch. It is the start of a gallery of intriguing insights into the Nabataeans' past. These include water channels cut into the rock, Nabataean graffiti, carved niches with worn outlines of ancient deities, Nabataean paving stones, and eerie flights of steps leading nowhere. As the Siq descends, it closes in and at its deepest, darkest point unexpectedly opens out on Petra's most thrilling monument – the Treasury (see pp224–5).

**Djinn Blocks**
*In Arab folklore these carved blocks, of which Petra has 26, house djinn (spirits). They may have been tower tombs.*

**Obelisk Tomb and Bab el-Siq Triclinium**
*Two rock-cut tombs on the way to the Siq stand one above the other. They seem to be one complex but are, in fact, separate. The upper, probably earlier, Obelisk Tomb shows Egyptian inspiration. The lower structure, known as the Bab el-Siq Triclinium (funerary dining chamber), is a superb illustration of the Nabataean Classical style (see p225).*

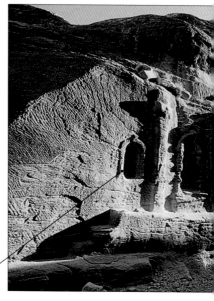

**A votive niche**, to one side of the remains of the monumental arch supports, was reached by steps.

## FROM THE TICKET GATE, THROUGH THE SIQ, TO THE TREASURY

It is about 1.5 km (nearly one mile) from the ticket gate to the end of the Siq. The route follows the course of a wadi which runs through the Siq and into the city. As the Siq descends, almost imperceptibly, it becomes deeper and narrower. At its narrowest point, the walls are only one metre apart.

Visitors' Centre

Treasury

Siq

Niche Monument

Djinn Blocks

Wadi Musa

Ticket gate

City of Petra

Petra Forum Resthouse

**KEY**

**P** Parking

Entrance to the Siq

Obelisk Tomb and Bab el-Siq Triclinium

0 metres    250

0 yards    250

## Nabataean Pavements

*The Siq was probably paved by the Nabataeans in the 1st century AD. Substantial stretches of this paving can still be seen. Next to the most extensive stretch is the Niche Monument (see below).*

### Water Channels

*The water channels were part of a sophisticated system of water conservation and flood prevention devised by the Nabataeans.*

## The Niche Monument

*Carved into a free-standing rock, a quarter of the way along the Siq, is a small Classical shrine. Within the niche are two Djinn blocks, one of which has eyes and a nose.*

**The remains** of the supports of the monumental arch consist of a carved niche flanked by pilasters.

### Entrance to the Siq

*In ancient times, the Siq was entered via a monumental arch. It fell in 1896, leaving only traces of its supporting structures.*

### JOHANN LUDWIG BURCKHARDT

In 1812, after lying hidden for more than 500 years to all except local Arabs, Petra was rediscovered by an explorer called Johann Ludwig Burckhardt. The son of a Swiss colonel in the French army, he was an outstanding student with a thirst for adventure. In 1809 he was contracted by a London-based association to explore the "interior parts of Africa". Three years later, after intense study of Islam and Arabic, he disguised himself as a Muslim scholar, took the name Ibrahim ibn Abdullah and set out for Egypt. On his way through Jordan, however, he was lured by tales of a lost city in the mountains. To get there, he had to persuade a guide to take him. Using the pretence that he wanted to offer a sacrifice to the Prophet Aaron, he became the first modern Westerner to enter Petra.

**Burckhardt in the disguise he assumed to enter Petra**

### View of the Treasury

*The first breathtaking glimpse of the Treasury is when its pink-hued, finely chiselled façade suddenly appears through a chink in the dark, narrow walls of the Siq. It is a moment filled with powerful contrasts.*

# From the Treasury to the Theatre

Set deep in the rock and protected by the valley walls, the magnificent 1st-century BC Treasury creates a formidable first impression of Petra. As its design had no precedent in the city, it is thought that architects from the Hellenistic Near East were brought in to create it. From the Treasury the path leads into the Outer Siq, lined on both sides with tombs of all sizes, some half buried by risen ground levels. At the end of the Outer Siq, in the midst of this great necropolis, is the Classical Theatre. Started by the Nabataeans and possibly added to by the Romans, it was a project requiring advanced engineering skills.

### Treasury Tholos
*The central figure may be the Petran fertility goddess El-Uzza. Bullet marks in the tholos and urn have been made over the years by Bedouin attempting to release hidden treasure.*

### The Outer Siq
*From the Treasury to the Theatre tombs display a range of intermediate design styles. One, freestanding, uniquely combines Classical features with a crowstep used as a battlement.*

**Eagle, Nabataean male deity symbol**

**"Attic" burial chambers** were a device to protect the dead from animals and tomb robbers.

**The vertical footholds** may have been to aid the sculptors.

**Mounted figures** of Castor and Pollux, sons of Zeus, flank the portico.

**The single-divide crowstep** was a design devised by the Nabataeans to complement the Classical cornice.

### THE OUTER SIQ
The artwork above shows some of the major constructions on the left-hand side of the Outer Siq as you walk from the Treasury to the Theatre. In reality, of course, the route bends and twists and on both the left and right sides are a great number of other tombs and features of architectural interest that could not be included.

### Treasury Interior
*A colossal doorway dominates the outer court (left) and leads to an inner chamber of 12 sq m (14 sq yards). At the back of the chamber is a sanctuary with an ablution basin, suggesting that the Treasury was in fact a temple.*

## THE ARCHITECTURE OF PETRA

The Nabataeans were adventurous architects, inspired by other cultures but always creating a distinctive look. The multiple crowstep can be seen as a design of the first settlers, whereas complex Nabataean Classical buildings reflect a later, cosmopolitan Petra. However, the dating of façades is very difficult, as many examples of the simple "early" style appear to have been built during the Classical period or even later.

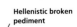

**Multiple crowstep**

**This early design**, *seen in the Streets of Façades, was probably Assyrian-inspired. Fragments of the once brightly painted plaster pediments have been found.*

**Slot for primitive plaster pediment**

**Nabataean concave "horned" capitals, resting on "cushions"**

**Single-divide crowstep, lending height**

**Stacked look, favoured by Nabataeans**

**Hellenistic broken pediment**

**This intermediate style,** *seen frequently in Petra, replaced multiple crowsteps with a huge single-divide crowstep, adding Classical cornices and pillars and Hellenistic doorways. This style continued well into the 1st century AD.*

**Nabataean Classical** *designs, such as the Bab el-Siq Triclinium (above), are complex, possibly experimental fusions of Classical and native styles.*

**Tomb façades** were cut away when the rear wall of the Theatre was being made, leaving just the interiors.

**The stage wall** would have hidden the auditorium from the Outer Siq.

**Stairway to High Place of Sacrifice (see p231)**

**To the Streets of Façades**

**Theatre Vaults**
*For access there were tunnels either side of the stage. Inside (right) these were dressed with painted plaster or marble.*

**Streets of Façades**
*Carved on four levels, these tightly packed tombs may include some of Petra's oldest façades. Most are crowned with multiple crowsteps.*

# The Royal Tombs

Carved into the base of El-Khubtha mountain, a short detour to the right at the point where the Outer Siq opens out on to Petra's central plain, are the Urn, Corinthian and Palace Tombs. They are collectively known as the Royal Tombs, their monumental size suggesting they were built for wealthy or important people, possibly Petran kings or queens. These tombs and their neighbours are also remarkable for the vivid striations of colour rippling through their sandstone walls, an effect heightened in the warm glow of the late afternoon sun. Particularly striking are the Silk Tomb and the ceiling inside the Urn Tomb.

**Panoramic view of the Royal Tombs from the direction of the ruined city**

### Palace Tomb

*The largest of all the Royal Tombs, the Palace Tomb had a grandiose façade on five levels which was taller than the rock into which it was carved. The upper levels, since collapsed, had to be built up using large blocks of stone.*

**Of the four inner chambers**, only the middle two connect.

### Corinthian Tomb

*There is no doubt that this was an important tomb in its day, but its design has baffled archaeologists because of its lack of symmetry. The doorways, each in a different style, are a clear illustration of this.*

## THE ROYAL TOMBS

First in the sequence of Royal Tombs is the towering Urn Tomb *(far right)*, reached by a stairway. Its name refers to a relatively tiny urn on top. Further along is the badly eroded Corinthian Tomb, which seems to be modelled largely on the Treasury, and beyond that the Palace Tomb, thought to be based on Nero's Golden House in Rome.

*For hotels and restaurants in this region see pp262–3 and pp279–80*

## THE NABATAEANS

The Nabataeans were a people whose original homeland lay in north-eastern Arabia and who migrated westward in the 6th century BC, settling eventually in Petra. As merchants and entrepreneurs, they grasped the lucrative potential of Petra's position on the spice and incense trade routes from East Asia and Arabia to the Mediterranean. By the 1st century BC they had made Petra the centre of a rich and powerful kingdom extending from Damascus in the north to Leuke Kome in the south and had built a city large enough to support 20–30,000 people. Key to their success was their ability to control and conserve water. Conduits and the remains of terracotta piping can be seen along the walls of the Outer Siq – part of an elaborate system for channelling water around the city. The Romans felt threatened by their achievements and took over the city in AD 106. Although the Nabataeans ceased to be an identifiable political group, Petra continued to thrive culturally for a time. In the end the transfer of trade from land to sea and two devastating earthquakes in the 4th and 8th centuries AD brought about the city's demise.

**Sculpted head, possibly of a priest**

**Greek (left) and Nabataean pottery vessels found at Petra**

**The Silk Tomb** gets its name from the beautiful streaks of yellow, grey, pink and brown, caused by wind and water erosion, which ripple across the walls and give them the appearance of shot silk.

**The central aperture** contains a badly worn statue of a man wearing a toga.

**Three burial chambers** are carved high in the façade.

## Urn Tomb Interior

*In AD 447 the Urn Tomb was turned into a church and two of the four recesses in the back wall were combined to make an apse. A Greek inscription records the consecration.*

### Urn Tomb Arches

*Two levels of arches support the large terrace in front of the Urn Tomb. Their appearance earned them a place in Bedouin folklore as sinister dungeons underneath a law court.*

# The City of Petra

Just past the theatre, the Outer Siq opens out into a wide plain. The ruins of the city of Petra are in the middle of this vast basin and the path alongside the Wadi Musa leads down to the site. Today, fragmented remains of the main street and a few nearby buildings are almost all that is left of the great city that once filled the valley. The grand Roman-style Cardo would have been Petra's main artery, fringed with markets and leading to the city's most sacred temple, the Qasr el-Bint. This building, like all the important buildings around the Cardo, would have been lavishly decorated. Traces of ornate plasterwork and marble veneer can still be seen on its walls and steps.

**View of the ancient city of Petra from a point just past the Theatre**

**The Monastery**
(see p230)

**Little Petra**
(see p231)

WADI ABU ULLAYQA

## Modern Museum

*Among the exhibits are a marble basin with lioness handles found in Petra Church and a small carved plaque of the Nabataean goddess al-Uzza* (left) *found in the Great Temple.*

**The Old Museum** is in a rock-cut tomb, built, unusually for Petra, with windows. It houses a collection of statuary.

EL-HABIS RISE

**Altar**

**Small temple**

## El-Habis Crusader Fortress

*As its name suggests, this small fortress was built by the Crusaders. While they were here they also used the Qasr el-Bint as a stable.*

**Aaron's Tomb**
(see p231)

## Qasr el-Bint el-Faroun

*The name "Palace of the Pharaoh's Daughter" was a colourful invention of Bedouin mythology. The 1st-century BC building was probably Petra's main temple, the huge slab of stone at the foot of the steps being an altar to the sun god Dushara, chief deity of the Nabataean pantheon.*

## Temenos Gate

*The imposing entrance to the sacred precinct of Qasr el-Bint had freestanding columns in front of its three massive, possibly metal-clad wooden doors. It probably dates from after the Roman annexation. The carvings of animal deities on its capitals are a Nabataean slant on an otherwise Classical design.*

### Temple of the Winged Lions

*The name refers to the winged lions on the column capitals. It is also known as the Temple of al-Uzza as it may have been dedicated to this deity. The temple's monumental entrance was reached by a bridge across the Wadi Musa. Fragments of plaster painted with dolphins and floral garlands suggest rich interior decoration.*

### Petra Church

*Superbly detailed 6th-century AD mosaics adorn the aisles of this once large Byzantine basilica. A cache of 152 scrolls found here revealed details of daily life in Byzantine Petra.*

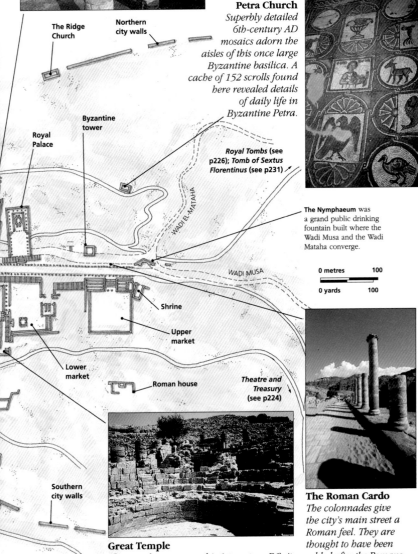

The Ridge Church

Northern city walls

Byzantine tower

Royal Palace

***Royal Tombs** (see p226); **Tomb of Sextus Florentinus** (see p231)*

WADI EL-MATAHA

**The Nymphaeum** was a grand public drinking fountain built where the Wadi Musa and the Wadi Mataha converge.

WADI MUSA

0 metres 100
0 yards 100

Shrine

Upper market

Lower market

Roman house

*Theatre and Treasury (see p224)*

Southern city walls

### The Roman Cardo

*The colonnades give the city's main street a Roman feel. They are thought to have been added after the Romans annexed Petra in AD 106. The street has been partly restored by Jordan's Department of Antiquities.*

*High Place of Sacrifice (see p230)*

### Great Temple

*The grand entrance to this 1st-century BC site led into a colonnaded lower precinct laid with hexagonal paving stones. Under the floor were extensive water ducts. Great stairways swept up to a 600-seat auditorium, of uncertain function. The decor was red and white stucco.*

# Other Sites Around Petra

Many of Petra's most famous sights can be visited in half a day. However, having come so far, it would be a pity not to explore more of this unique capital of a vanished civilization. A full day is enough to do the basic route from the ticket gate to the ancient city (see p228), taking in the Royal Tombs (see p226), and to include a walk to either the Monastery or the High Place of Sacrifice. Two days will enable you to do the basic route, both excursions and leave you with time to explore the area around the Tomb of Sextius Florentinus. Of the more distant sights, Little Petra can be visited in a day, while two days should be allowed for Aaron's Tomb.

**High Place of Sacrifice: the round altar with the main altar behind**

**Façade of the Lion Triclinium**

### Walk to the Monastery

Just beyond the Qasr el-Bint (see p228) a path crosses the Wadi Musa. It leads past the Forum Restaurant to the start of an arduous but thoroughly worthwhile climb to one of Petra's most awe-inspiring and best-preserved monuments – the Monastery. The path, which cuts through the wadi, is paved in parts and features more than 800 rock-cut steps. The afternoon, when the sun is not directly in front, is the best time to do this walk.

A short detour off the main route, indicated by a Department of Antiquities signpost, leads to the **Lion Triclinium**. This monument, with the peculiar keyhole effect in the façade, caused by erosion, has blurred leonine representations of the goddess al-Uzza guarding its entrance. Its largely Classical façade has unusually ornate Nabataean features, such as "horned" capitals with floral scrollwork. After this, the path to the Monastery rises steeply. There are occasional flights of steps through the winding and narrowing gorge,

and several interesting carved monuments along the way. Finally, the path slips between two boulders, and drops on to a wide, once-colonnaded, rock-cut terrace. Immediately to the right is the **Monastery**, Petra's most colossal temple, dedicated to the deified king, Obodas 1, who died in 86 BC. Although it resembles the Treasury (see p224), it was never as ornate, even when statues adorned its niches. Its simple, powerful architecture, thought to date from the 1st century AD, is seen by many as the quintessential Nabataean Classical design (see p225). The interior has one large chamber with an arch-topped niche where the altar stood. It came to be known as the Monastery because of the many Christian crosses carved on its walls.

**The Monastery's massive tholos crowned with an urn resting on Nabataean "horned" capitals**

### Walk to the High Place of Sacrifice

Midway between the Treasury and the Theatre, a rock-cut stairway, marked at the start by several djinn blocks (see p222), leads to the top of Jebel Attuf mountain. It is here, at 1,035 m (3,000 ft), that one of the best preserved of Petra's many places of sacrifice is located. The ascent, while gradual, requires stamina and a good head for heights, and is best attempted in the early morning. The first part of the summit is a large terrace with two 6-m (20-ft) stone obelisks, possibly fertility symbols. The second, reached by a northwards scramble past the ruins of a small Nabataean building, is another plateau. Here, just beyond a rock-cut cistern, is the **High Place of Sacrifice**. In the centre of a large courtyard is a low offering table. Steps at the far end lead up to the main altar, which has a rectangular indentation in the top. The adjacent round altar has a basin with a carved channel, quite possibly for draining the blood of animal and human sacrifices. The nearby cisterns may have been used for ritual ablutions.

The path winding down the other side of Jebel Attuf into the Wadi Farasa valley is a spectacular stepped descent, sometimes with sheer drops. The first thing you see, carved into the rock face, is the **Lion Monument**, representing the goddess al-Uzza. It was originally a fountain, perhaps for pilgrims to the High Place, with water pouring from the lion's mouth. Water channels and the shape of the lion's head and legs can still be seen.

Thereafter, the path becomes a series of steps leading to the delightfully secluded **Garden Triclinium**. The tomb takes its name from the surrounding greenery. On top of the tomb is a large cistern. Further along, to the left, is the **Tomb of the Roman Soldier**, so called because of the remains

**Beautifully carved interior of the Triclinium, unusual for Petra**

in one of the façade niches of a figure wearing the uniform of a high-ranking Roman officer. Although Classical, the façade has Nabataean "horned" capitals on top of the pillars. Opposite is the façadeless **Triclinium**, thought to have been part of the Roman Soldier Tomb complex. It has the only carved interior in Petra and its niches, fluted half columns and cornice are spectacularly enhanced by the amazing bands of colour running through the walls and ceiling.

Further down the track is the relatively plain **Broken Pediment Tomb**, named after its most striking feature. Nearby is the elegant **Renaissance Tomb**, with the three urns above its arched entrance. Similar in style to the Tomb of Sextius Florentinus, it may date from the same period. Past this point the Wadi Farasa widens and the descent ends in the main valley, not far from the Qasr el-Bint (see p228).

## Aaron's Tomb

This site is venerated by Muslims, Christians and Jews as the place where Moses's brother Aaron was buried. The white dome of the shrine can be seen from the High Place of Sacrifice, which may be a close enough viewing for most people. The journey there involves a three-hour ride on horseback and a hard three-hour climb to the top of Petra's highest peak – Jebel Haroun. For those determined to go, a guide and adequate supplies are essential.

## Tomb of Sextius Florentinus

Beyond the Palace Tomb (see p226), along a track skirting the cliff, stands the **Tomb of Sextius Florentinus**. Despite its badly eroded north-facing façade, the beautiful and unusual details of its design are clearly visible. Above its entrance is a Latin inscription listing the positions held by Florentinus up to his last post as Governor of Arabia in AD 127. Further north is the **Carmine Façade** with its vivid striations of red, blue and grey. Continuing alongside the Wadi Mataha brings you to a rock-cut complex known as the **House of Dorotheos** because of two Greek inscriptions found here. On the other side of the wadi is a cluster of homes and tombs known as

**The lonely mountaintop shrine of Aaron's Tomb, Petra's holiest place**

Mughar el-Nasara, including the fine **Tomb with Armour**. Local Christians were probably responsible for the many crosses etched into the walls.

## Little Petra

This northern suburb of Petra, Siq el-Berid, has come to be known as Little Petra because it is like a miniature version of the main city. Situated 8 km (5 miles) north of Wadi Musa town, it is most easily reached by taxi. The journey on foot, north along the Wadi Abu Ullayqa, which starts just past the Qasr el-Bint, is hard, but rewarding. A guide is essential.

**Detail from ceiling of the Painted House**

Little Petra seems to have been a largely residential settlement, as relatively few tombs have been discovered here. It may well have been where Petra's wealthy merchants had their homes. Just outside its Siq-like entrance, which was once controlled by a gate, are a large cistern and a Classical temple. The gorge, shorter than the one leading into Petra, contains a simple temple. As you emerge from the quiet of the gorge into the town, the incredible profusion of façades is overwhelming, with houses, temples and cisterns carved into every exposed rock face. Flights of steps shoot off in all directions, evoking images of a bustling urban centre. One of Little Petra's main attractions is the **Painted House** with its plaster ceiling and walls delightfully decorated with flowers, vines, bunches of grapes, Eros with his bow and Pan playing his pipes.

**Tomb of Sextius Florentinus, Roman governor of the province of Arabia**

# Wadi Rum ⑩

The desert landscape of Wadi Rum is one of the most awe-inspiring sights in the entire Middle East. Huge ochre-coloured rock pinnacles, weathered into bulbous, outlandish shapes, rise up 600 m (2,000 ft) from the flat valley floors, like islands in a sea of red sand. Hundreds of hiking and climbing routes wind their way up and around the many peaks. This area was once on a major trade route, and evidence of settlement here includes ruins of a temple built by the Nabataeans (*see p227*) and carvings and inscriptions left by the later Thamud people. Today the region is still inhabited by semi-nomadic Bedouin tribes.

**Thamudic rock graffiti**

### ★ Lawrence's Spring
*Not far from Rum village, this tranquil spring was described by TE Lawrence as "a paradise just 5 feet square". A Nabataean-built water channel can be seen nearby.*

### Rum Village
*The main settlement is a rapidly growing Bedouin village. The Rest House on the outskirts offers spartan accommodation and simple meals.*

### Khazali Canyon
*This steep defile is dotted with Thamudic inscriptions. It is possible to scramble 200 m into the canyon, starting on a ledge on the right-hand side.*

## STAR SIGHTS

★ Lawrence's Spring

★ Jebel Umm Fruth Rock Bridge

**Map labels:**
Aqaba Petra
JEBEL HUBEIRA
JEBEL LEYYAH
WADI LEYYAH
WADI RUM
JEBEL RUM
JEBEL UMM ISH
Nabataean Temple
Rum
JEBEL UMM EJIL
WADI RUM MAN
WADI U
Abu Aina campsite
JEBEL QATTAR
Aqaba

**Scale:**
0 kilometres   4
0 miles   2

## KEY

═══ Road

– – Walk

– – Hike/scramble

– – Four-wheel-drive/camel track

### Rock Map at Jebel Amud

*In a cave 20 km (12 miles) north-east of Rum is a rock marked with indentations and lines. It is thought by some to be a topographical map of the area, dating from around 3000 BC.*

Diseh
Jebel Amud

Diseh

JEBEL
UMM ANFUS

JEBEL
RASHAASHA

### Seven Pillars of Wisdom

*This spectacular peak, also known as Jebel Makhras, is named after TE Lawrence's famous book, not, as is often suggested, vice versa. Wadi Siq Makhras, just to the south, provides hiking access to Wadi Umm Ishrin and beyond.*

J H R I N

JEBEL
BARRAH

BARRAH CANYON

JEBEL
NFISHIYYEH

JEBEL
ABU
JUDAYDA

KHOR AL AJRAM

JEBEL
UMM
FRUTH

JEBEL
BURDAH

### Jebel Barrah

*This large outcrop, seen here at its northern end, flanks beautiful Barrah Canyon, which is a stunning hike best negotiated from the south.*

**Jebel Burdah rock bridge**
is spectacularly situated and can be reached via a moderately difficult climb.

### ★ Jebel Umm Fruth Rock Bridge

*This dramatic natural phenomenon is one of several rock bridges in the area. It rises straight from the desert floor and can be climbed and crossed without difficulty.*

## TE LAWRENCE (1888–1935)

Lawrence of Arabia, the most famous British hero of World War I, earned his nickname for his exploits fighting alongside the Arab tribes that revolted against Turkish rule in 1915. Sent to Mecca in 1916 to liaise with leaders of the revolt, he then led many Arab guerrilla operations in the desert, including attacks on the Hejaz Railway, some launched from Wadi Rum. He also took part in the capture of Aqaba and the advance on Damascus. *The Seven Pillars of Wisdom*, his account of the Arab Revolt, contains lyrical descriptions of the dramatic scenery around Wadi Rum.

# Exploring Wadi Rum

There are essentially two main ways to explore the desert of Wadi Rum: through a combination of jeep and hiking, or by camel trekking. Jeeps allow you to travel further and faster, but the more traditional means of transport will bring you much closer to the stillness of the desert. Either way, make sure you carry lots of water and avoid travelling during the midday heat, especially in summer. For contact details of companies organising Wadi Rum expeditions, see page 309.

Tourists on a camel-trek through the canyons of the Wadi

Jeeps, the best way to cover large distances quickly in Wadi Rum

## Jeep Tours

A wide range of jeep tour options is posted at the main reception gate, 7 km (4.5 miles) before Rum village. If you have not pre-arranged a trip, you will be allocated a driver here. It is possible to join up with other travellers to share the cost of a jeep. There are two main areas to explore: the main southern section of Wadi Rum and the less-visited northern scenery closer to the village of Diseh.

The most popular destinations include the striking red sand dunes of Jebel Umm Ulaydiyya, the small oasis known as "Lawrence's Spring" and the narrow *siq* (gorge) of Khazali Canyon.

Other noteworthy attractions include the Nabataean inscriptions and petroglyphs of Anfaishiyya, the natural rock bridge of Jebel Umm Fruth and the various "sunset sites", which are all ideal places to witness the changing afternoon colours of the desert rocks.

## Hiking

Many of the best trips offer a combination of jeep travel and hiking. The 5-km (3-mile) stroll through the towering walls of Barrah Canyon is a favourite option. Some hikes require a guide, such as the excellent hour-long scramble up to the Jebel Burdah rock bridge and the exciting half-day hike through labyrinthine Rakhabat Canyon.

Most trips require jeep transport to get you to the start of the hike. The only walk you can really do by yourself is from the visitor centre east to Makharas Canyon and back; take a guide if you are unsure of your route-finding skills.

## Adventure Activities

An excellent alternative to making arrangements on the spot is to arrange a more active itinerary in advance with one of Wadi Rum's excellent Bedouin guides. Most can arrange jeep and overnight trips but you'll need a specialist for climbing or canyoning. Overnight trips that combine a jeep excursion, camel ride and some rock scrambling are very popular.

Camel trekking is fun but the pace is slow and can be highly uncomfortable after a couple of hours. Still, it is undeniably the best way to get a feel for the desert in classic "Lawrence" fashion. The three-day ride from Wadi Rum south to Aqaba (*see p235*) is a challenging adventure.

Horse riding is possible on the periphery of the park, as is mountain biking over the desert flats.

It is well worth fitting in an overnight at a Bedouin camp during your visit. The larger fixed camps can be touristy but are fun nonetheless. The smaller ones shift location regularly and offer a more authentic, but also more basic, experience. The food is generally excellent; you may get to try *mensaf* (a Bedouin dish of lamb and rice) or, if you are lucky, a "Bedouin barbeque" – meat slow-cooked in a desert oven called a *zerb*. Reclining by an open fire, gazing at the stars and sipping a mint tea in the stillness of the desert is perhaps the quintessential Wadi Rum experience.

Hikers taking a break with their Bedouin guides

# Aqaba ⓫

**Road map:** B7. 🏚 62,000. ✈ 🚌
🛈 El-Koornish St (next to the Fort),
(03) 201 3363. www.aqaba.com

The only Jordanian outlet
to the sea, Aqaba is a very
important commercial port
town. The relentless stream
of heavy trucks going to and
coming from Amman along
the Desert Highway is clear
evidence of this.

South of the town however,
away from the busy port, the
crystal clear waters are home
to fabulous coral reefs. These
are the main reason for
Aqaba's popularity with
visitors, as they offer some of
the best scuba diving in the
world. Closer to the shore,
many other types of water
sports also help to provide
escape from the extreme
summer heat. Large sandy
beaches stretch out along the
coast, bounded by modern
hotels, and the steep
mountains behind form a
spectacular natural backdrop.

Aqaba's long and glorious
past also provides it with
some notable archaeological
sites to visit. It is thought to
be close to the site of biblical
Ezion-Geber, the large port
which is said to have been
built by King Solomon. Its
existence has, however, yet
to be proved.

The town's deep freshwater
springs ensured that Aqaba
became a popular caravan
stop for merchants travelling
between Egypt, the Mediterranean coast and Arabia. By the
2nd century BC, the now
prosperous town had fallen

Ruins of the old fortified Islamic town of Ayla, in modern Aqaba

under the control of the
Nabataeans (see p227). Such
prosperity saw it conquered
by the Romans in AD 106,
and later the Muslims in AD
630. Under Muslim control,
Aqaba became an important
stage on the pilgrimage to
Mecca, and the Muslims built
the fortified town of **Ayla**
nearby to the
north. After
suffering a major
earthquake in
748, the town
was rebuilt, and
thrived with an
increasing sea
trade. Following
another earthquake in 1068
however, and then the
Crusader conquests of the
12th century, the city was
finally abandoned. You can
visit the ruins at the Ayla digs,
next to the coastal Corniche
road. Much of the foundations
of walls, towers and a series
of buildings still remain. The
**Archaeological Museum**,

Sign to Aqaba Aquarium

next to the tourist office,
features material from the
digs, as well as illustrating
the history of Aqaba.

The other main archaeo-
logical site in Aqaba is the
**Mameluke Fort**, set between
the palm trees on La Côte
Verte. Built in the 16th century,
its portal now bears the coat-
of-arms of the
Hashemites,
placed there
after Lawrence
of Arabia's troops
conquered the
port during World
War I. The fort
also served as
a caravanserai for hundreds
of years, and some restored
rooms pay testament to this
more peaceful role.

By going west past the
industrial port and just
beyond the ferry passenger
terminal you will come to the
small Aqaba Marine Science
Station **Aquarium**. This
contains a collection of the
most important species of
the varied flora and fauna in
the Gulf of Aqaba, including
moray eels and deadly
stonefish. It also displays
information on the campaign
to protect the Red Sea.

🏛 **Archaeological Museum**
El-Koornish St (next to Fort). **Tel** (03)
201 3731. ◯ 8am–5pm daily. 📷 ♿

⚓ **Mameluke Fort**
La Côte Verte. **Tel** (03) 201 3731.
◯ daily. 📷 ♿

🗡 **Aquarium**
South Coast (near ferry terminal).
**Tel** (03) 201 5145. ◯ 8am–5pm
daily. 📷 ♿

Sailing boats anchored in the Gulf of Aqaba

# THE RED SEA AND SINAI

*O*nce coveted by Egypt's pharaohs for its reserves of turquoise, copper and gold, Sinai is now equally prized by tourists for its white, palm-fringed sands and the limpid waters of the Red Sea, rich with marine life. Its close association with key episodes from the Old Testament also makes the Sinai's mountainous interior an area of deep religious significance for Jews, Muslims and Christians alike.

The Sinai Peninsula forms a triangle between the gulfs of Aqaba and Suez, two finger-like extremities of the Red Sea. Although the whole of Sinai is Egyptian territory, Israel and Jordan also have small stretches of Red Sea coast at Eilat and Aqaba, respectively.

The word "Sinai" probably derives from "Sin", the moon god worshipped in Egypt under the pharaohs. But the region is better known through the Bible as the "great and terrible wilderness" negotiated by Moses and his people in their epic 40-year journey from Egypt to the Promised Land. It's here that God supposedly first spoke to Moses through the medium of a burning bush and here, on Mount Sinai, that Moses received the Ten Commandments. The peninsula has been crossed by countless armies, including most recently that of the Israelis, who held the region from 1967 to 1982 when it was returned to Egypt under the terms of the Camp David peace treaty. In the years since then tourism has boomed as southern Sinai and the peninsula's eastern coast have been developed with all-inclusive resorts, such as Sharm el-Sheikh. But the wilderness is far from tamed. Inland Sinai remains virtually uninhabited with barren mountains sheltering hidden oases such as Feiran, with its thousands of date palms. More dramatic still are the underwater landscapes of the Red Sea, where vast coral reefs provide a home for more than 1,000 species of marine life, making for one of the world's richest dive sites.

**Divers filming at Eilat's Dolphin Reef**

◁ Central Sinai inland of Nuweiba, dramatic but accessible only by four-wheel-drive or camel

# Exploring the Red Sea and Sinai

Most visitors head for where the mountains and desert meet the clear cool waters of the Red Sea; specifically, Eilat, Aqaba and, most picturesque of all, the Sinai peninsula's east coast. Its string of modern resorts, while uninteresting in themselves, are set against a backdrop of extraordinary natural beauty. Nuweiba, Dahab, Naama Bay and Sharm el-Sheikh are the largest and most well-developed tourism centres, but there are many smaller, more private beach retreats. St Catherine's Monastery can be visited as a day trip.

## SIGHTS AT A GLANCE

Dahab ❸
Feiran Oasis ❽
Mount Sinai ❼
Nuweiba ❷
Ras Muhammad
    National Park ❺
*St Catherine's*
    *Monastery*
    *pp246–9* ❻
Sharm el-
    Sheikh ❹
Taba ❶

**Aqaba, with a typical Red Sea scene of beach, palms and looming mountains**

**St Catherine's Monastery, an ancient walled retreat in the Sinai Desert**

**Suez**

Wadi Feiran

Ras
Sharatib

**FEIRAN OASIS** ❽

*Gebel Serbal
2073m*

*Gebel Banat
1511m*

Wadi el Sheikh

*Gebel Umm Ri'
1312m*

Wadi Ghari

66

**ST CATHERINE'S
MONASTERY** ❻

*Blue
Desert*

❼ **MOUNT SINAI**

*Gebel Katarina
2642m*

Wadi Mir

*Gebel Giddat el 'Ila
2207m*

**S I N A I**

Ras Abu
Suweira

**El Tur**

**Gibeil**

Wadi Imlaba

*Gebel el Thabt
2438m*

*Gebel Sabbagh
2266m*

Wadi Thman

*Ras
Garra*

*Gebel Sahara
1459m*

*Ras Kanisa*

66

**RAS MUHAMMAD
NATIONAL PARK** ❺

*Ras Muhammad*

## GETTING AROUND

The coastal roads are good and the main resorts can be reached by car. Travelling in the Sinai interior is trickier, especially as foreigners are not permitted to stray off the main roads. Organized hikes or camel trips are perhaps the best options for those wanting to explore the desert. Buses serve coastal locations, as well as some places in the interior such as St Catherine's Monastery. Israeli and Jordanian visas and Sinai passes can be obtained at the borders *(see p298)*.

Ras el Naqb

*Eilat*

TABA ❶

35

*Coloured Canyon*

*Wadi Watir*

*'i el Biyar*

NUWEIBA ❷

*Ain Khudra Oasis*

*Abu Galum Nature Reserve*

35

*Ras Abu Galum*

*Gebel Feirani 1685m*

❸ DAHAB

*Gulf of Aqaba*

*Nabq National Park*

Nabq

35

Naama Bay

SHARM EL-SHEIKH

The Sinai Desert, where only the hardiest forms of life survive, such as camels and acacia trees

## KEY

— Major road

╌╌ Minor road

– – Four-wheel-drive track

— Scenic route

▬▬ International border

△ Summit

0 kilometres 25

0 miles 10

## SEE ALSO

- *Where to Stay* pp264–5

- *Restaurants, Cafés and Bars* p281

The underwater scenery and marine life of the Red Sea, which is every bit as stunning as the desert and mountain landscapes above

# The Coral Reefs of the Red Sea

The Coral Reef is one of the richest ecosystems on earth. Visitors to the Red Sea cannot but marvel at the contrast between the barren, almost lifeless desert and the explosion of marine life on the coastal reefs. The waters are so clear that even from the surface you can appreciate the huge diversity of species inhabiting the reefs. Scuba divers can use the facilities of the many diving centres along the coast (see pp292–5). Remember that a reef is an extremely fragile and threatened environment and divers should look but not touch.

View of lagoon and the shallow waters covering the reef-top

**The edge of the reef** is the best place for snorkellers to appreciate its wealth of marine life.

**The lagoon** teems with small colourful fish, including the fry of species found on the reef beyond.

**Moray eel,** emerging from its reef-wall lair

**The clown fish** *protects itself from the sea anemone's stinging tentacles with a layer of mucus, using its host as a refuge from predators and for laying its eggs.*

**School of flag basslets,** a very common species in the Red Sea

**Manta rays** *are harmless plankton-eaters. Growing up to 6 m (20 ft) across, they are most common in open water or where there are strong currents.*

**Alcyonarians,** brightly coloured soft corals

## CORALS, THE ARCHITECTS OF THE REEF

Corals are animals, colonies of polyps, which require very precise conditions of water temperature and sunlight to grow. They take many forms – from hard rock-like corals, such as *Acropora* species, to the horny gorgonians which project from the reef into the current to feed on micro-organisms, to various soft corals. Most reefs are built over many thousands of years from the skeletons of hard corals.

**The sea fan** is a horny coral, whose polyps emerge at nights to feed.

**Jacks** are usually seen in large schools in open water, but large solitary individuals will visit the reef.

Gorgonians filtering the water for plankton

An *Acropora* growing in still, shallow water

Feathery red plume of Klunzinger's soft coral

**The reef wall**, *which plunges down to depths of 80 m (260 ft) or more, is home to an immense variety of corals, fish, crustaceans, sponges and many other forms of marine life.*

**Sea turtles** *are quite easy to spot in spring and autumn, especially between the Strait of Tiran and Ras Muhammad. They avoid the noisier, more developed stretches of the coast.*

**Shortnose blacktail shark**

**Coiled-wire coral**

**Despite their huge size**, *bumphead wrasses (or Napoleon fish) feed on snails, crustaceans and small fish. Divers should resist the temptation to give them unsuitable food.*

**Black coral**, so called for the colour of its skeleton

**The jewel grouper**, *in common with the many other species of the family found in the Red Sea, prefers relatively shaded parts of the reef, where it preys on smaller fish.*

**Spotted sweetlips** *are usually found swimming in groups close to the reef wall. The name comes from their large blubbery lips. They make a noise that is clearly audible to divers, hence their other name – grunters.*

**An adult royal angel fish** *searches for sponges and other food on the reef. The young are more yellow with a large eyespot on the dorsal fin.*

Carvings on the Haggar Maktub, in the desert near Nuweiba

## Taba ❶

**Road map** F5.

Since Israel returned ownership of the Sinai peninsula
to Egypt in 1982, the small
coastal town of
Taba has served
as a border post
between the two
countries. A
pleasing stretch
of beach is
overlooked by a
five-star hotel. Just
under 20 km (12
miles) to the south
is the new resort
of **Taba Heights**,
which boasts
some of the most luxurious
hotels in Sinai, as well as an
18-hole golf course and a
marina. There are views from
the resort across the Red Sea
to the Israeli, Jordanian and
Saudi Arabian coastlines.

Between Taba and Taba
Heights, just offshore is
**Pharaoh's Island** (or Coral
Island), which is dominated
by an impressive Crusader
fortress. Tickets for the boat
across to the island are
available from the Salah ed-
Din Hotel on the coastal road.

## Nuweiba ❷

**Road map** F6.
from Aqaba (Jordan).

Nuweiba lies midway along
the Gulf of Aqaba at the
side of a promontory and
consists of two distinct
districts. To the south is the
luxuriant Nuweiba Muzeina
oasis, which for centuries
was a port for pilgrims going
to Mecca. It now has many
hotels and tourist villages.
To the north is Nuweiba
el-Tarabin, named after the
Bedouin tribe
that lives here.
You can visit the
ruins of the large
**Tarabin fortress**,
built in the 16th
century by the
Mameluke sultan
Ashraf el-Ghouri.
The Nuweiba area
is rich in beaches,
and diving and
snorkelling sites.

Bedouin with his camel,
outside Nuweiba

### Environs

Nuweiba makes a convenient
starting point for trips to the
Sinai interior. One of the most
fascinating is to the **Coloured
Canyon**, a narrow sculpted
gorge created by water erosion.
Its sandstone walls have
taken on many hues of
yellow, red and ochre
due to the slow process
of oxidation of the ferrous
minerals in the rocks.
The canyon opening can
be reached by car from
the Ain Furtaga oasis,
about 15 km (9 miles)
from Nuweiba on the
road west, and thence
by following the Wadi
Nekheil track.

Another fascinating trip
uses a jeep track from
Ain Furtaga through the
immense Wadi Ghazala
to **Wadi Khudra**. Midway
along the track you will
come to the Ain Khudra

oasis, a lovely patch of palms
and tamarisks seemingly
wedged between the high,
near vertical, red walls of
the canyon. If you continue
a little further along the trail
you will come to the solitary
Haggar Maktub (Rock of
Inscriptions). Since the
Nabataean period, pilgrims
going to Sinai have left
graffiti carved on the rock.

Heading south from
Nuweiba Muzeina along the
coast leads to the **Abu Galum
Nature Reserve**. A maze of
narrow wadis penetrates the
interior, with an abundance
of plants and wildlife, such
as foxes, ibexes and hyraxes.
The beach at Ras Abu Galum
is usually deserted except for
a few Bedouin fishermen.

## Dahab ❸

**Road map** F6.

In Arabic the word *dahab*
means "gold", and the name
derives from the sand on the
beautiful beaches. The crown
of palm trees, the beaches
and the light blue sea make
this one of the most popular
localities in Sinai. It has grown
up around the old Bedouin
village of Assalah, which still
survives today. The many
camping sites, simple hotels
and beachside restaurants
attract an array of mainly
independent travellers who
lend a raffish air to the town.

Many also visit for the
world-class diving sites
around Dahab. Among the

Raccoon butterflyfish with diver, off the
coast of Dahab in the Gulf of Aqaba

Four Seasons Resort, one of numerous luxury hotels in Sharm el-Sheikh

most famous and dangerous are the "Canyon" and the "Blue Hole". Almost entirely surrounded by reef, the Blue Hole drops to a depth of 80 m (260 ft) only a few metres off the shore. Although many sites are for expert scuba divers only, there are still plenty of others suitable for beginners or snorkellers.

## Sharm el-Sheikh ❹

Road map E7. ✈ 🚌 ℹ Tourist Office, Sharm el-Sheikh, (062) 601 900.

Until relatively recently, the most famous resort in Sinai was only a military airport. Situated on the western side of the Strait of Tiran, Sharm became famous when Egyptian president Nasser decided to block Israeli access to the Red Sea, thus provoking the 1967 war. Under Israeli occupation of Sinai, the first hotels were built and began to attract tourists, especially expert scuba divers. The Sharm el-Sheikh bay is still a military port, but the neighbouring Sharm el-Maiya bay has hotels, shops and small restaurants. Most of the tourist development, however, has focused on **Naama Bay**, a few kilometres to the north. This is the place that most people actually mean when they talk about Sharm el-Sheikh. It has a long beach with a host of luxury hotels and diving centres. Boats take snorkellers

as well as scuba divers out to the open sea. Here, in the Strait of Tiran, you can observe manta rays, sharks, dolphins and, occasionally, sea turtles. For those wanting to stay above water, tourists are taken in glass-bottomed boats to observe the coral reef from above. Other attractions include all manner of water sports, plus camel treks, quad biking and excursions inland.

Another spectacular sight is the long reef under the cliffs to the west of the **Ras Umm Sidd** lighthouse. Reachable from land, here you can admire a forest of gorgonians, huge Napoleon fish and, sometimes, barracuda.

### Environs

A 29-km (18-mile) journey by jeep along the coast road north of Sharm el-Sheikh brings you to the 600-sq km (232-sq mile)

**Nabq National Park**. This coastal park on the edge of the desert boasts crystal-clear lagoons and the most northerly mangrove forest in the world, which extends for 4 km (2.5 miles) along the shoreline. The hardy mangroves are able to live in salt water, making this an extremely important environment, linking land to sea. It is used as a feeding ground by migratory birds, including storks, herons and many species of birds of prey.

## Ras Muhammad National Park ❺

Road map E7. 20 km (12.5 miles) S of Sharm el-Sheikh. ✈ 🚌 to Sharm el-Sheikh, then taxi. ◯ daily. 🅿 ✓

On the southern tip of the Sinai peninsula, where the waters of the Gulf of Suez and the Gulf of Aqaba converge, is a park instituted in 1983 to protect the incredibly varied coastal and marine environment. It includes extensive coral reefs, a lagoon, mangroves and a rugged desert coastline, and there is a series of well-marked trails leading to the most interesting spots. Among the most beautiful of these is the Ras Muhammad headland, the southernmost point in Sinai. Formed from fossilized corals, the headland is surrounded by beautiful reefs. The diving sites are very varied, with both reefs and wrecks to explore. There are also long, sandy beaches and a clifftop "Shark Observatory".

Gazelle at Ras Muhammad National Park

Entrance to Ras Muhammad National Park

Diver exploring coral reef in the Red Sea, surrounded by glittering shoal of sweeper fish ▷

# St Catherine's Monastery ❻

A community of Greek orthodox monks has lived here, in the shadow of Mount Sinai, almost uninterruptedly since the monastery was founded in AD 527 by Byzantine emperor Justinian. It replaced a chapel built in 337 by St Helena, mother of Emperor Constantine, at the place where tradition says that Moses saw the Burning Bush. The monastery was named after St Catherine only in the 9th or 10th century, after monks claimed to have found her body on nearby Mount Catherine.

**Library**
*The collection of priceless early Christian manuscripts is second only to that in the Vatican Library in Rome.*

**★ Icon Collection**
*Most of the monastery's 2,000 icons, such as this one of St Theodosia, are kept here, in the Icon Gallery. A selection is always on public view in the Basilica.*

**The Walls of Justinian,** built in the first half of the 6th century, are part of the complex's original structure.

**The Burning Bush**
*This spiny evergreen is said to be from the same stock as the bush from which Moses heard God's voice, instructing him to lead his people out of Egypt to the Promised Land.*

**Round Tower**

**The Chapel of the Burning Bush** stands where it is claimed the miraculous bush seen by Moses originally grew.

**★ Basilica of the Transfiguration**
*This magnificently decorated church owes its name to the 6th-century Mosaic of the Transfiguration in the apse. It can be glimpsed behind the gilded iconostasis that dates from the early 17th century.*

## STAR SIGHTS

- ★ Basilica of the Transfiguration

- ★ Icon Collection

### Bell Tower

*This was built in 1871. The nine bells were donated by Tsar Alexander II of Russia and are nowadays rung only on major religious festivals.*

**The Mosque** was created in 1106 by converting a chapel originally dedicated to St Basil.

## VISITORS' CHECKLIST

**Road map** E6. *Sinai, 90 km (56 miles) W of Dahab and Nuweiba.* 🛩 *10 km (6 miles) NE of monastery.* 🚌 *from Taba, Nuweiba or Dahab to St Catherine's Village (El-Milga), then taxi 3.5 km (2 miles). Petrol available at monastery.* ◯ *9am–noon Mon–Thu, Sat.* �É *Greek Orthodox hols. Admission free, but offerings welcome.*

**Monks' quarters**

**St Stephen's Well**

**Dispensary**

**Guest house**

### Monastery Gardens

*In the orchard lies the cemetery, from which the monks' bones are periodically exhumed and transferred to the nearby Charnel House.*

**To Charnel House**

**The elevated entrance,** reached by a pulley system, used to be the only access.

**The underground cistern** was dug to store fresh water from the monastery's springs.

**Visitors' entrance**

### Well of Moses

*One of the monastery's main water sources, this is also known as the Well of Jethro, as Moses is said to have met his future wife, Jethro's daughter, here.*

---

## ST CATHERINE OF ALEXANDRIA

St Catherine is one of the most popular of early Christian female saints. Her legend, not recorded before the 10th century, recounts that she was a virgin of noble birth, martyred in Alexandria in the early 4th century. After being tortured on a spiked wheel (hence the Catherine wheel), she was beheaded. Her body was then transported by angels to Sinai, where it was found, uncorrupted, some six centuries later by the local monks.

**Detail from icon showing angels setting down the body of St Catherine in Sinai**

# Exploring St Catherine's Monastery

Fortified by massive curtain walls, the monastery lies at the head of Wadi el-Deir (Valley of the Monastery), surrounded by high, red granite mountains. It is inhabited by about 20 Greek Orthodox monks, who follow the rule of St Basil, and the only buildings normally open to visitors are the Basilica and the Charnel House. Despite this and the constant crowds of pilgrims and tourists, the remote location in the heart of Sinai and spectacular, rugged scenery are awe-inspiring. For the reasonably fit, there are well-marked paths to the top of Mount Sinai and other nearby peaks.

**Coptic Cross in monastery wall**

**Rock steps leading to the Gate of Confession on Mount Sinai near St Catherine's Monastery**

### Inside the monastery

Entry nowadays is through a small postern in the curtain wall, whose impressive thickness varies from 1.8–2.7 m (6–9 ft). Some sections of wall survive from the monastery's origins in the 6th century, but large-scale rebuilding took place in the 14th century, after an earthquake, and in 1800, on Napoleon's orders.

The monastery's Basilica was built in AD 527 with three aisles in typical Byzantine style. Eleventh-century, carved wooden doors open into the narthex (porch), where some of the monastery's splendid icons, all painted on wood, are displayed. The collection is exceptional for its size and quality, and because it contains the only examples of Byzantine painting to have survived the Iconoclast era (726–843). Among them are a *St Peter* (5th–6th century), a *Christ in Majesty* (7th century), both in encaustic painting, and the *Ladder of Paradise* (7th century).

Carved cedar doors, made in the 6th century, lead into the central nave, which contains 12 columns topped by grey granite capitals and hung with icons showing the saints of the months of the year. The marble floor and coffered ceiling are 18th century. The iconostasis, dating from 1612, is by a Cretan monk, Jeremiah the Sinaite. The large figures represent Christ, the Virgin Mary and Saints Michael, Nicholas, Catherine and John the Baptist.

Behind it can be glimpsed the exceptionally beautiful 6th-century Mosaic of the Transfiguration decorating the roof of the apse. It shows Christ surrounded by Elijah, Moses and the Disciples John, Peter and James. In the apse, (often closed), on the right, is a marble coffin containing the remains of St Catherine.

The Chapel of the Burning Bush, behind the apse and also usually closed to the public, is the holiest part of the monastery. It was built on the site where God is thought to have appeared to Moses for the first time (Exodus 3: 2–4). Tradition says that the bush itself (*see p246*) was moved outside when the chapel was built.

The library has over 3,000 manuscripts in Greek, Coptic, Syriac, Arabic, Georgian, Armenian and Old Slavonic. The oldest is the 5th-century *Codex Syriacus*, one of the earliest existing copies of the Gospels.

St Catherine's has, uniquely for a Christian monastery, a mosque within its walls. It was built for the Bedouin who worked in the monastery and also as a way of avoiding attacks by the Muslims.

### Outside the walls

In the gardens (*see p247*) are the monks' cemetery and the Chapel of St Triphonius. The latter's crypt holds the Charnel House containing the bones of deceased monks. The robed skeleton is that of Stephanos, a 6th-century guardian of the path to Mount Sinai.

**Moses receiving the tablets inscribed with the Ten Commandments from God, 6th-century wall painting, St Catherine's Monastery**

Chapel of the Holy Trinity on the summit of Mount Sinai

## Mount Sinai ❼

**Road map** E6. Sinai, 90 km (56 miles) W of Dahab and Nuweiba.

According to tradition, Mount Sinai (Gebel Musa, the Mountain of Moses) is the Biblical Mount Horeb, where Moses spent 40 days and received the Ten Commandments (Exodus 24). Two paths climb to the 2,286-m (7,500-ft) summit from behind the monastery, both requiring three hours' walking. The route said to have been taken by Moses is the most tiring as it consists of 3,700 rock steps called the Steps of Repentance. There are several votive sites along the way.

A cypress-shaded plain, 700 steps below the summit, is the so-called Amphitheatre of the Seventy Elders of Israel, where those who accompanied Moses stopped, leaving him to go to the top alone. It is also called Elijah's Hollow, as Elijah is said to have heard the voice of God here. It contains **St Stephen's Chapel** and is where people spending the night on the mountain are asked to sleep. This is also where the second, longer but easier, path joins the first. Camels can be hired to this point, but the final 700 steps have to be done on foot.

On the summit is the small **Chapel of the Holy Trinity** (often closed). It was built in 1934 on the ruins of a 4th–5th-century church and is said to be where God spoke to Moses from a fiery cloud. Nearby is a small, 12th-century mosque and the cave where Moses spent the 40 days. The summit offers grandiose views, but is often crowded. If you join the many who go up to see the sunrise or sunset, take a flashlight and warm clothes.

The mountain lies at the heart of the St Catherine Protectorate, a conservation area recognised as a Unesco World Heritage site. The area is ideal for trekking. One of the longer hikes is to the top of Mount Catherine (Gebel Katarina), Egypt's highest peak. Angels supposedly transported St Catherine of Alexandria's body here, away from her torturers' wheel. Hikers can pick up informative booklets to trails in the area at the Protectorate Office in the village of El-Milga, 3.5 km from St Catherine's Monastery. All treks must be done with a Bedouin guide, which is also arranged through the office.

## Feiran Oasis ❽

**Road map** E6. Sinai, 60 km (37 miles) W of St Catherine's Monastery.

This is the largest and most fertile oasis in Sinai, verdant with date palms, tamarisks and cereal fields. Just south of the Bedouin village of adobe houses is a small, modern convent built with stone from the Byzantine bishop's palace which formerly stood here.

The oasis was the earliest Christian site in Sinai. Many chapels already existed here when, in 451, it became the seat of a bishopric. This governed St Catherine's Monastery until the 7th century, when Feiran's bishop was deposed for heresy and the city fell into ruin. Excavations have revealed its fortified walls, several churches and many other buildings. Feiran is said to be the place where Joshua defeated the Amalekites (Exodus 17).

Shaded gardens surrounding the convent in the Feiran Oasis

---

### THE BEDOUIN OF THE SINAI PENINSULA

In Arabic the word *bedu* means "desert dwellers" and refers specifically to the nomadic tribes that live in Saudi Arabia, the Negev and Sinai. For centuries the Bedouin have lived in close contact with nature, depending for their livelihood on the breeding of sheep, goats and camels. Those in Sinai descend from the peoples who arrived from the Arabian Peninsula from the 14th to the 17th century. The last 20 years of the 20th century have seen a drastic change in their customs and traditions. Today, about 25,000 Bedouin live in Sinai. Many are still nomadic livestock breeders, while others live in permanent camps in wood and corrugated-iron dwellings, making their living as guides, desert tour operators, or by working in large hotels on the coast.

# TRAVELLERS' NEEDS

# WHERE TO STAY

Jerusalem offers an impressive range of accommodation: from the luxury of the King David and the American Colony hotels, to the plain but welcoming hospices of the various Christian communities, which cater for pilgrims and tourists alike. You will find even more varied accommodation in the rest of the Holy Land. Across Israel, kibbutz hotels offer moderately priced accommodation with good facilities and attractive country settings. Field schools are located near many of the

Doorman at the King David Hotel

country's nature reserves, and have cheaper, more basic rooms. By the Dead Sea there are many hotels and health resorts, while by the Red Sea and along the Sinai coast, large tourist villages offer water sports and diving. Those who want to cater for themselves will also find many options at a range of prices, from rented villas and apartments to the many excellent youth hostels and camp sites. The listings on pages 256–65 give details on a selection of accommodation to suit every budget.

The towering Sheraton Hotel, Tel Aviv

## GRADING AND FACILITIES

At least for the moment, there is no official hotel grading system in Israel, although hotels in Jordan do have their own rating system, with the best (4–5 stars) being comparable to a standard international hotel. Most of the Israeli hotels lie within the medium to high price range, with excellent levels of service and amenities. Rooms are normally equipped with air-conditioning, televisions and minibars, with other facilities often including fitness centres, pools, and business suites. Most hotels also have bars and restaurants, as well as a dining area where a large buffet-style breakfast is served.

For disabled travellers, many hotels have wheel-chair access, and bathrooms and other facilities which have been specially adapted. The largest hotels in the Jewish areas are also equipped to satisfy the needs of practising Jews. These are classed as kosher hotels, and they observe the main Jewish religious laws, especially those concerning the Shabbat and *Kashrut*. Many have synagogues and automatic lifts which can be used during the Shabbat rest.

Larger hotels and tourist villages, such as those by the Red Sea, offer private beaches, scuba diving and a range of water sports; while the Dead Sea hotels, often more akin to health resorts, are ideal for those in need of pampering, with their therapeutic hot spas.

## PRICES

Compared to Western standards, hotel prices in Israel and Jordan are usually rather high, although the same level of accommodation and service will cost you significantly less in Sinai. Hotel rates fluctuate widely, depending on the season and the various Christian, Muslim

and Jewish holidays, so make sure to verify the price before booking. The price of a room almost always includes break-fast, but not other extras. In Israel the room price also includes local taxes, although you can avoid the 17 per cent VAT by paying in foreign currency or on credit card. US dollars, especially, are taken almost everywhere, and all major credit cards are accepted.

In Jordan and Sinai the situation is slightly different. In the large hotels and tourist villages in Sinai all costs over and above the basic room price are subject to double taxation if paid together with the final bill, or on credit card. You can avoid this by paying in cash at the time. Also, listed room rates in Sinai and Jordan exclude tax, which can be as much as 23 per cent, so make sure that you know the final cost. Credit cards are accepted in both Sinai and Jordan, but when using cash, note, that while most major currency is taken in Sinai, you can only use dinars in Jordan.

## BOOKING A HOTEL

During certain periods of the year, such as Christmas and Easter, or during Jewish holidays – Passover, Rosh ha-Shanah, Yom Kippur, Sukkoth and Hannukah *(see pp36–9)* – finding accommodation can be a real problem, especially in Jerusalem. In Israel as a whole, you may also have difficulty finding a room during the hottest months of

◁ Diners at a restaurant overlooking the harbour at Old Jaffa

A reception room at the luxurious American Colony Hotel, Jerusalem

July and August, as this is the busiest time of year, with many Israelis also taking their own holidays.

It is, therefore, always wise to book well in advance, and the **Israel Hotel Association**, the **Kibbutz Hotel Chain**, field schools, youth hostels and some local bed-and-breakfast associations all have centralized booking services, which are often accessible via the internet and e-mail. The same also applies to many independent hotels and guest houses. If you do need to make arrangements yourself over the phone, most hotel staff can speak good English.

## KIBBUTZ HOTELS

These hotels were first established as a source of supplementary income for the largely agricultural kibbutzim, and are completely separate from the very basic type of accommodation offered to those on kibbutz working holidays (see p293). Located mostly in the country, they are ideally placed for visitors wanting a relaxing country break or a base near some of the region's archaeological attractions. Here again there is no grading system: accommodation ranges from very plain lodgings on working kibbutzim, offering bed and breakfast, to more comfortable (albeit

informal) hotel complexes with restaurants, swimming pools and other facilities. Most of the hotels are members of the **Kibbutz Hotel Chain** (KHC), the largest hotel group in Israel. As well as providing accommodation, they also organize package tours, adventure breaks, organized nature tours and fly-drive holidays. These can often be good options, as, owing to their often remote locations, many kibbutz hotels are not served by public transport, and may only be convenient if travelling by car.

Kibbutz hotels are very popular among the Israelis for their own vacations, especially during the Jewish holidays and in July and August. It is consequently difficult to find accommodation during these times, unless you book well in advance. Prices usually range between NIS 300–700 for a double room and breakfast, depending on the type of kibbutz and the season.

## SELF-CATERING

In Jerusalem and throughout the rest of Israel you can find a wide selection of property to rent, from smart city apartments to luxury country homes. The cost can vary considerably, depending on the type of property you require, but if you are a large family or party, then it can often work out very reasonably when compared to the same length of stay in a hotel. One of the biggest agents dealing with rented holiday homes in Israel is **Homtel**.

## CHRISTIAN HOSPICES AND GUEST HOUSES

This type of accommodation, mainly in Jerusalem and near the holy sites, is a popular and inexpensive alternative to hotels. Clean and unashamedly basic, they are often centrally located, and for many are an ideal place to stay for a few nights. You don't have to be a practising Christian to lodge at the Christian hospices, but at times the house rules can be quite strict (you must leave the room early in the morning and the doors are locked at 10–11pm). For unmarried couples it may also be difficult to find a double room. Many guest houses have over the years become bona fide hotels, with their own special charm and character. In this case, prices are slightly higher, although they are still good value when compared to the large hotels.

Enjoying the view of Jerusalem's Old City from the terrace at the King David Hotel

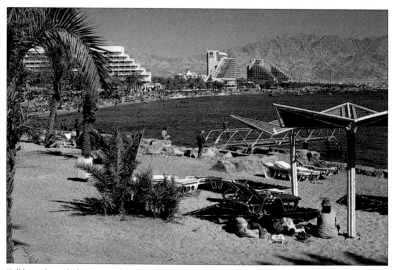

Holiday-makers relaxing on one of the beautiful beaches at Eilat, on the Red Sea coast

## YOUTH HOSTELS

For those on a tight budget youth hostels are ideal, and often the cheapest places to stay in Israel. They have no age limits either, so you will find a mixture of people staying at them, from young backpackers to many older travellers. There are plenty of hostels to choose from, with around 32 **Israel Youth Hostel Association (IYHA)** hostels, affiliated to Hostelling International, as well as a large number of independent ones.

Hostels in Israel are located in the major tourist areas – Jerusalem, Tel Aviv, Eilat and Galilee – and also throughout the rest of the country. Most offer single, double, and family rooms as well as the more usual dormitories, with prices starting between NIS 40 and NIS 120 per person. Israeli hostels are generally modern, with basic facilities and clean, simple accommodation. The price includes linen, and in the Israel Youth Hostel Association hostels it also includes breakfast. In the independent hostels you can pay for the room only, and be entirely self-catering.

If you plan to stay at IYHA hostels for any length of time, you may want to pay for membership. While this is not compulsory, it does entitle you to preferential rates, and may be more cost-effective.

As well as providing basic accommodation, the IYHA also offers package tours. A range of different itineraries includes full dinner, bed-and-breakfast at a choice of hostels, and passes for public transport and national parks. They also organize fly-drive packages, which can be a cheap and easy way of seeing the country if you want to follow your own, more flexible, holiday schedule.

## FIELD SCHOOLS

There are 24 Field Study Centres in Israel, run by the **Society for the Protection of Nature in Israel (SPNI)**. These are located in the vicinity of some of Israel's major natural reserves, and were established as a way of promoting a better understanding of the country's natural environment and history through organized educational holidays, lecture programmes and summer schools. This is still their main focus, and their varied selection of organized holidays revolves around the region's diverse history, archaeology, geology, flora and fauna.

If you would prefer to visit these areas on your own, these centres will also often offer accommodation at a daily rate. The rooms are simple but clean, and all include a private bathroom and air-conditioning. They mostly sleep between four and six people, although some double rooms are also available. If you are paying on a room-only basis, the cost is generally less than NIS 190 per person, although prices for the organized holidays can vary significantly depending on the type of itinerary. Booking in advance is obligatory, and the SPNI's centralized booking office can also reserve rooms at some of the kibbutz hotels located in the natural reserves and parks.

Sunbathing by the Dead Sea

## CAMPING

There are campsites across Israel for those wanting to spend time under canvas and visit more remote places. Details can be obtained from the **Society for the Protection of Nature in Israel (SPNI)** or from tourist information offices. Prices start from NIS 12 per person, increasing at sites with better facilities. These may include launderettes, electricity points, shops, bars and swimming pools. Some places will also hire out tents or trailer homes.

Campsites in Jordan and Sinai are much less common, with fewer facilities. They are found only in some of the more popular national parks and at some Red Sea resorts.

In Israel, camping rough is also quite common, but choose a secluded public area and

leave the site tidy if you want to avoid problems. Places such as the West Bank and Gaza Strip are totally no-go areas, as are all military and border zones. If in doubt, check first. Also be very aware of your possessions and personal safety, especially if in a remote area and alone. Make sure that you have protection against mosquitoes, and check thoroughly for other unwanted guests, such as scorpions.

## JORDAN AND SINAI

Parts of Sinai and Jordan offer the full spectrum of accommodation. Amman, in particular, has a full complement of international five-star chain hotels, including a Four Seasons, Grand Hyatt, Kempinski, Marriott, Le Meridien and Sheraton, plus a healthy budget scene in the Downtown district. The choice is also broad at Wadi Musa (for Petra), although given the large number of visitors, it is wise to book well in advance, especially in March/April and September/October (peak times). Elsewhere in Jordan the choice is greatly diminished, although

**Camping in the woods near the Sea of Galilee**

the country is small enough that most sights can be visited from either Amman or Petra.

Major credit cards are accepted in all mid-range and top-end hotels in Jordan. A sales and service tax of up to 26 % is commonly added to bills.

Sinai resorts such as Dahab, Nuweiba and Sharm el-Sheikh offer many top-class resort hotels, many with prime beach-front locations, some boasting beautiful architecture and all offering a full range of facilities, from multiple bars and restaurants to dive and water sports centres. Such is the abundance of accommodation that a little internet research can sometimes throw up some bargain room rates. Peak seasons are during the Muslim feasts of Eid el-Fitr and Eid el-Adha (see p38), around Christmas and especially New Year, and during July and August; at such times you need to book ahead.

There are no proper hostels in Jordan or Sinai with an official national association, but there are many cheap hotels and dormitories that serve the same purpose. Dahab and other smaller Sinai resorts often have simple bamboo-constructed huts for rent on the beach – these are especially popular with budget travellers.

# DIRECTORY

## BOOKING A HOTEL

### Israel Hotel Association
29 Hamered Street,
PO Box 50066,
Tel Aviv, Israel.
**Tel** (03) 517 0131.
**Fax** (03) 510 0197.
@ infotel@israelhotels.org.il
**www**.Israelhotels.org.il

## KIBBUTZ HOTELS

### Kibbutz Hotel Chain (KHC)
41 Montefurie,
Beit Nesuah,
Tel Aviv, Israel 65201.
**Tel** (03) 560 8118.

**Fax** (03) 560 7710.
@ khc_rsv@kibbutz.co.il
**www**.kibbutz.co.il

## SELF CATERING

### Good Morning Jerusalem
9 Coresh Street,
Jerusalem,
Israel 94144.
**Tel** (02) 623 3459.
**Fax** (02) 625 9330.
@ gmjer@netvision.co.il
**www**.accommodation.co.il

### Homtel
Home Association of Jerusalem,
PO Box 7547,
Jerusalem,
Israel 91074.
**Tel** (02) 645 2198.
**www**.bnb.co.il

## CHRISTIAN HOSPICES AND GUEST HOUSES

### Christian Information Centre
Jaffa Gate
(opposite David Tower).
**Tel** (02) 627 2692.
**Fax** (02) 628 6417.
**www**.cicts.org

## YOUTH HOSTELS

### Israeli Youth Hostel Association (IYHA)
Jerusalem International Convention Centre,
PO Box 6001, Jerusalem,
Israel 91060.
**Tel** (02) 655 8406.
**Fax** (02) 655 8432/8431.
**www**.youth-hostels.org.il

## FIELD SCHOOLS

### Society for the Protection of Nature in Israel (SPNI)
13 Heleni Hamalka St,
Jerusalem,
Israel.
**Tel** (02) 624 4605 (shop),
(03) 638 8688 (rooms).
**www**.teva.org.il

## CAMPING

### Society for the Protection of Nature in Israel (SPNI)
3 Hasfela St,
Tel Aviv,
Israel 66183.
**Tel** (03) 638 8674.
**www**.teva.org.il

# Choosing a Hotel

The hotels in this guide have been selected across a wide price range for the excellence of their facilities, location or character. This section lists hotels in Jerusalem by area, with price ranges given in US dollars. For Jerusalem map references, see the Street Finder on pages 156–9; for further afield see back endpaper map.

**PRICE CATEGORIES**
Prices categories are per night for two people occupying a standard double room, with tax, breakfast and service included:

ⓢ Under $65
ⓢⓢ $65–$100
ⓢⓢⓢ $100–$175
ⓢⓢⓢⓢ $175–$250
ⓢⓢⓢⓢⓢ Over $250

## THE MUSLIM QUARTER

### Ecce Homo Convent                                                                           ⓢ
*41 Via Dolorosa, 97626* **Tel** *(02) 627 7293* **Fax** *(02) 628 2224* **Rooms** *120*                  **Map** *4 D2*

Superbly situated on the Via Dolorosa, this hospice, built in 1856, is just a few minutes' stroll from Jerusalem's holiest sites. There are impressive Roman-era ruins underfoot and just outside the door, and a magnificent view of the Old City from the roof. The rooms are very modest but clean. **www.eccehomoconvent.com**

### Austrian Hospice                                                                           ⓢⓢ
*Via Dolorosa 37* **Tel** *(02) 626 5800* **Fax** *(02) 627 1472* **Rooms** *26*                          **Map** *3 C2*

The historic Austrian Hospice of the Holy Family, inaugurated in 1863, serves as both a guesthouse and a cultural centre. Just off the bustling Via Dolorosa, this island of calm has simple but attractively furnished rooms, a Viennese cafe, a garden and breathtaking views of the old city's roofscape. **www.austrianhospice.com**

## THE CHRISTIAN AND ARMENIAN QUARTER

### Casa Nova                                                                                   ⓢ
*10 Casa Nova St, 97600* **Tel** *(02) 627 1441* **Fax** *(02) 626 4370* **Rooms** *89*                    **Map** *3 B3*

Just two blocks up the slope from the Holy Sepulchre, this simple Franciscan hospice, built in 1866, maintains a high quality of cleanliness and comfort. Its location and the good value it offers make it popular with pilgrimage groups so book well ahead. **www.custodia.org/casanovaj**

### Maronite Monastery Hospice                                                                  ⓢ
*25 Maronite Convent St, 97111* **Tel** *(02) 628 2158* **Fax** *(02) 627 2821* **Rooms** *27*              **Map** *3 B4*

Situated two blocks inside Jaffa Gate, this hospice, also known as Foyer Mar Maroun, is virtually across the street from the Citadel. Ensconced in a centuries-old building that is one of the most beautifully-kept in the Armenian Quarter, its rooms are spotless and well-maintained. **www.maronitejerusalem.org**

### Christ Church Guest House                                                                   ⓢⓢ
*Omar Ibn el-Khattab Square, 97604* **Tel** *(02) 627 7727* **Fax** *(02) 628 2999* **Rooms** *24*          **Map** *3 B4*

Run by an evangelical Anglican organization founded in 1809, this hospice just inside Jaffa Gate was constructed in the 19th century on foundations that go back to Roman times. Rooms are small and plain but comfortable, and there's a good range of services. Very popular, especially during holiday periods. **www.cmj-israel.org**

## THE MOUNT OF OLIVES AND MOUNT ZION

### Mount of Olives                                                                             ⓢⓢ
*53 Mount of Olives Rd* **Tel** *(02) 628 4877* **Fax** *(02) 626 4427* **Rooms** *61*                      **Map** *2 F3*

Set atop Jerusalem's highest hill, this welcoming, family-run hotel is just a short stroll from the Mount of Olives' many Christian, Jewish and Muslim sites, including the Mosque of the Ascension, which is next door. Eleven of the clean, quiet rooms have panoramic views of the Old City. **www.mtolives.com**

### Seven Arches                                                                                ⓢⓢ
*Ruba el-Adawiya St, Mount of Olives Plaza* **Tel** *(02) 626 7777* **Fax** *(02) 627 1319* **Rooms** *196*  **Map** *2 F4*

Offering one of the most spectacular city panoramas in the world, this large, modern hotel, built in classic 1960s style, sits on top of the Mount of Olives. The rooms are comfortable and the service courteous. The Old City is a 15-minute walk down the hill, past half-a-dozen major Christian sites. **www.7arches.com**

**Key to Symbols** *see back cover flap*

# MODERN JERUSALEM

### Agron Guest House
📋 ♿ ⓢ

*6 Agron St, 94265* **Tel** *(02) 621 7555* **Fax** *(02) 622 1124* **Rooms** *55*   **Map** *1 A4*

Sandwiched between the smart Rehavia neighbourhood and West Jerusalem's lively commercial heart, this hostel is a 10-minute walk from the Old City. The Conservative Jewish Movement has a religious and cultural centre next door. Rooms are institutional but comfortable. Reception is closed on the Sabbath. **www.iyha.org.il**

### Azzahra
🍴 📋 🍸 ⓢⓢ

*13 El-Zahra St, 97200* **Tel** *(02) 628 2447* **Fax** *(02) 628 3960* **Rooms** *15*   **Map** *2 D2*

A small, family-run hotel on a quiet alleyway near East Jerusalem's commercial centre. Just a few blocks northeast of Damascus Gate, this place is known for its friendly atmosphere and service. Offers good value for money and has a well-regarded Middle Eastern restaurant. **www.azzahrahotel.com**

### Merkaz Shimshon-Beit Shmuel
🍴 📋 ♿ ⓢⓢ

*6 Shama St, 94108* **Tel** *(02) 620 3455* **Fax** *(02) 620 3467* **Rooms** *51*   **Map** *1 B4*

Part of the Reform Jewish Movement's delightful Jerusalem campus, designed by Moshe Safdie, this place is deluxe by hostel standards. The views of the Old City and the Citadel are superb, King David St is around the corner and the centre of West Jerusalem is just a short stroll away. **www.beitshmuel.com**

### Notre Dame
🍴 📋 ♿ 🍸 ⓢⓢ

*12 Ha-Tsanhanim St, 91204* **Tel** *(02) 627 9111* **Fax** *(02) 627 1995* **Rooms** *140*   **Map** *1 B3*

Built between 1885 and 1904 to house French Catholic pilgrims, this neo-Romanesque complex is now a Vatican-run ecumenical, cultural and pilgrimage centre. The guest rooms are comfortable and offer good value. It is situated across the street from the Old City's New Gate, which leads into the Christian Quarter. **www.notredamecenter.org**

### Palatin
📋 ⓢⓢ

*4 Agripas St, 94301* **Tel** *(02) 623 1141* **Fax** *(02) 625 9323* **Rooms** *28*   **Map** *1 A2*

On a pedestrianized street in the heart of West Jerusalem's commercial centre, around the corner from bustling King George St, this hotel has been run by the same family since it was built in 1936. It is close to Mahaneh Yehuda food market. The rooms are modest but modern, and one has a balcony. **www.hotel-palatin.co.il**

### St Andrew's Scottish Guest House
🍴 ♿ ⓢⓢ

*1 David Remez St, 91086* **Tel** *(02) 673 2401* **Fax** *(02) 673 1711* **Rooms** *20*   **Map** *1 B5*

This delightful hospice has large, simple bedrooms and a somewhat colonial atmosphere, which is not surprising since the all-stone building dates from the late 1920s. Situated a short walk from the cafés and restaurants of Emeq Refaim St. There is disabled access to one room. **www.scotsguesthouse.com**

### Jerusalem
🍴 📋 🕓 🍸 ⓢⓢⓢ

*Nablus Road, 97200* **Tel** *(02) 628 3282* **Fax** *(02) 628 3282* **Rooms** *14*   **Map** *1 C2*

Situated just north of Damascus Gate and housed in a 19th-century Arab house, this place has been run by the same family since 1960. It has spacious rooms with high ceilings, all elaborately furnished in traditional Oriental style. There's a delightful, vine-shaded garden terrace and the service is excellent. **www.jrshotel.com**

### Novotel Jerusalem
🍴 🏊 📺 📋 ♿ 🍸 ⓢⓢⓢ

*9 St George St, 97200* **Tel** *(02) 532 0023* **Fax** *(02) 532 0011* **Rooms** *397*   **Map** *1 C1*

Built in the early 21st century, this large hotel features ultra-modern facilities, an outdoor swimming pool, three restaurants, two bars and spacious, modern rooms. It is situated about 1 km (half a mile) north of the Old City so sites ranging from Mea Shearim to the Church of the Holy Sepulchre are just a short stroll away. **www.accor.com**

### St George
🍴 🏊 📺 📋 🕓 🍸 ⓢⓢⓢ

*8 Salah ed-Din St, 95908* **Tel** *(02) 627 7232* **Fax** *(02) 628 2575* **Rooms** *47*   **Map** *1 C1*

Situated just two blocks north of Herod's Gate and the Muslim Quarter, this hotel is in the heart of East Jerusalem's commercial centre. It was opened by Jordan's late King Hussein in 1965 and still has a 1960s feel, especially in the lobby. Rooms overlooking Salah ed-Din St can be noisy. **www.hotelstgeorge-jer.com**

### YMCA Three Arches
🍴 🏊 📺 📋 🍸 ⓢⓢⓢ

*26 King David St, 94101* **Tel** *(02) 569 2692* **Fax** *(02) 623 5192* **Rooms** *55*   **Map** *1 A4*

Housed in a richly decorated, landmark building dedicated in 1933, the YMCA is just across the street from the King David Hotel. It has a unique Mandate-era ambience and offers superb views of the city, especially from the belltower. Rooms are unexciting but comfortable. Has good sports facilities and offers excellent value. **www.ymca3arch.co.il**

### Mount Zion
🍴 🏊 📺 📋 ♿ 🍸 ⓢⓢⓢⓢ

*17 Hebron Rd, 93546* **Tel** *(02) 568 9555* **Fax** *(02) 673 1425* **Rooms** *134*   **Map** *1 B5*

Built in 1882 as a British-run hospice, this hotel has comfortable, well-furnished rooms with lots of character. Many afford fine views of Mount Zion, the Hinnom Valley, the Judean Desert and, on clear days, the hills of the Hashemite Kingdom of Jordan. Guests can stroll through the delightful gardens at the back of the hotel. **www.mountzion.co.il**

### American Colony
 $$$$$

23 Nablus Rd, 97200 **Tel** (02) 627 9777 **Fax** (02) 627 9779 **Rooms** 84 **Map** 1 C1

This hotel was founded in 1902 by the American family that still own it. Long the preferred hang-out of journalists and diplomats, the fabled American Colony pampers visitors with classic Arabian architecture, a flowery Turkish courtyard, lush gardens and plenty of Oriental charm. **www.americancolony.com**

### King David
$$$$$

23 King David St, 94101 **Tel** (02) 620 8888 **Fax** (02) 620 8880 **Rooms** 237 **Map** 1 B4

A favourite with American Presidents, the historic King David, built of pink sandstone in 1931, is famed for its King Solomon-style lobby, grassy gardens and Mandate-era atmosphere. Rooms have classic styling; the pricier ones afford stunning views of the Old City. Amenities include a tennis court and two kosher restaurants. **www.danhotels.com**

## FURTHER AFIELD

### Yitzhak Rabin Youth Hostel & Guest House
$

1 Nahman Avigad St, Givat Ram, 91390 **Tel** (02) 678 0101 **Fax** (02) 679 6566 **Rooms** 77

A striking and modern establishment whose facilities are positively deluxe by hostel standards, making it an excellent value option for families. Situated near the Israel Museum, the Givat Ram campus of the Hebrew University, the Valley of the Cross and the Knesset, it is served by buses 7 and 19 from the Central Bus Station. **www.iyha.org.il**

### A Little House in Bakah
$$

1 Yehuda St, Bakah, 93627 **Tel** (02) 673 7944 **Fax** (02) 673 7955 **Rooms** 35

About 2 km (1 mile) due south of the King David Hotel, this welcoming place has an arched and colonnaded façade, modest rooms and a garden restaurant. The Sherover Promenade in Talpiyot and the Emeq Refaim St restaurant zone are close by. **www.o-niv.com/bakah**

### Neve Shalom/Wahat al-Salam Hotel
$$

Neve Shalom/Wahat al-Salam, 99761 **Tel** (02) 999 3030 **Fax** (02) 991 7412 **Rooms** 39

Located in a quiet, rural community in which Jews and Palestinians live together and work towards peaceful coexistence, this hotel's name means "oasis of peace". It has modest rooms in single-storey buildings and is situated about 30 km (19 miles) west of Jerusalem, south of Latrun, so guests need to have a car. **www.nswas.com/hotel**

### Notre Dame de Sion Guest House
$$

23 Ha-Oren St, Ein Karem, 95744 **Tel** (02) 641 5738 **Fax** (02) 643 7739 **Rooms** 28

About 8 km (5 miles) west of the Old City in a delightful natural setting, this peaceful, stone-built B&B was built as a French convent in the mid-1800s. Still run by nuns, it has simple, spacious rooms, a cafeteria and a large, peaceful garden that lends itself to contemplation. Rooms have neither phone nor TV. **www.sion-ein-karem.org**

### Ambassador
$$$

Nablus Rd, Sheikh Jarrah, 97200 **Tel** (02) 541 2222 **Fax** (02) 582 8202 **Rooms** 115

Situated in the attractive East Jerusalem neighbourhood of Sheikh Jarrah, with its many consulates, this comfortable hotel is about 2 km (1 mile) north of the Old City and about 1 km (half a mile) west of Mount Scopus. It has a vine-shaded terrace and tasteful rooms. Limited disabled access. **www.jerusalemambassador.com**

### Ramat Rachel
 $$$

Kibbutz Ramat Rachel, 90900 **Tel** (02) 670 2555 **Fax** (02) 673 3155 **Rooms** 164

On the southern outskirts of Jerusalem, this hotel is on the grounds of Kibbutz Ramat Rachel, which was founded in the 1920s. The large, grassy gardens and some of the rooms afford fine views of the Judean Desert. The hotel has a first-rate swimming, fitness and spa complex (additional fee to use fitness and spa facilities). **www.ramatrachel.co.il**

## THE COAST AND GALILEE

### BEIT ALFA (BETH ALFA) Beit Alfa Guest Rooms
 $

Kibbutz Beit Alfa, 10802 **Tel** (04) 653 3026 **Fax** (04) 653 3882 **Rooms** 39 **Map** C2

At the foot of Mount Gilboa, this kibbutz guesthouse is on the grounds of Kibbutz Beit Alfa, known for its ancient synagogue, Japanese garden, mini-zoo and herd of dairy cows. The modest rooms, in low-rise, kibbutz-style buildings, come with a microwave and a fridge. **www.beit-alfa.com**

### BEIT SHEAN Beit Shean Guest House
 $

126 Menahem Begin Ave, 11741 **Tel** (04) 606 0760 **Fax** (04) 606 0766 **Rooms** 62 **Map** C2

Housed in an impressive, ultra-modern stone building and endowed with functional but comfortable facilities, this hostel is an excellent base for visits to the Beit Shean antiquities, the Beit Alfa synagogue and Belvoir Castle. A humorous wall mural with thousands of tiny figures illustrates daily life in ancient Beit Shean. **www.iyha.org.il**

**Key to Price Guide** see p256 **Key to Symbols** see back cover flap

### CAESAREA Dan Caesarea
*Caesarea, 30600* **Tel** *(04) 626 9111* **Fax** *(04) 626 9122* **Rooms** *114* **Map** *B2*

Surrounded by some of the most beautiful coastal scenery in Israel, this quiet hotel is next to Israel's only 18-hole golf course. The superb Roman ruins of Caesarea are a five-minute drive away. The hotel offers a wide variety of sports activities, including scuba diving and sailing. Some rooms have sea views. **www.danhotels.com**

### CARMEL FOREST Carmel Forest Spa Resort
*Near Kibbutz Beit Oren, 31900* **Tel** *(04) 830 7888* **Fax** *(04) 830 7886* **Rooms** *126* **Map** *B2*

Overlooking the Mediterranean and amid the natural beauty of Mount Carmel, this luxury spa-hotel offers a wide variety of spa and health treatments, as well as cooking, wine and yoga courses. Amenities include a genuine Turkish hammam and two swimming pools. Guests must be 16. Cellphones can be used only in rooms. **www.isrotel.co.il**

### GOLAN HEIGHTS Golan Field School
*Katsrin, 12900* **Tel** *(04) 696 1234* **Fax** *(04) 696 5033* **Rooms** *34* **Map** *C2*

On the edge of the Golan's largest town, this hostel is run by the Society for the Protection of Nature in Israel. It has spartan rooms situated in a grassy campus, and is an ideal base for visiting the Golan countryside, including Yehudiya Nature Reserve, and the area's Roman-era Jewish archaeological sites. **www.aspni.org**

### GOLAN HEIGHTS Alaska Inn
*Metulla, 10292* **Tel** *(04) 699 7111* **Fax** *(04) 699 7118* **Rooms** *60* **Map** *C1*

Overlooking Lebanon's Ayun Valley from a spot 20 km (12 miles) west of Banias Spring on the Golan Heights, the village of Metulla is "Israel's Switzerland". The hotel is an ideal base for exploring the northern Golan and the far north of Galilee. Local attractions include the Canada Centre ice-skating rink. **www.alaskainn.co.il**

### HAIFA Dan Panorama
*107 HaNassi Ave, 34632* **Tel** *(04) 835 2222* **Fax** *(04) 835 2235* **Rooms** *266* **Map** *B2*

Occupying two high-rise towers perched high on top of Mount Carmel, this deluxe hotel offers breathtaking Mediterranean panoramas and affords easy access to the charms of Central Carmel. Pricier rooms look out on Haifa Bay. Situated very near the upper station of the Carmelit funicular railway and the zoo. **www.danhotels.co.il**

### KFAR PEKI'IN Peki'in Youth Hostel & Family Guesthouse
*Kfar Peki'in, 24914* **Tel** *(04) 957 4111* **Fax** *(04) 957 4116* **Rooms** *50* **Map** *C2*

This modern, well-appointed hostel is situated in a Druze village in the Galilee hills, 7 km (4 miles) southeast of Maalot-Tarshiha, with views of Mount Meron. Walking tours and hosting by local families help guests get a sense of Druze life and culture. Served by Egged bus 44 from Nahariya and bus 271 from Haifa. **www.iyha.org.il**

### NAHARIYA Carlton Nahariya
*23 HaGaaton Blvd, 22444* **Tel** *(04) 900 5511* **Fax** *(04) 982 3771* **Rooms** *200* **Map** *B2*

Situated 10 km (6 miles) north of Akko on the café-lined main street of the seaside resort of Nahariya, this hotel is just steps from the beach. The comfortable, airy rooms have a modern, Mediterranean ambience. Amenities include spa treatments, a sun terrace with sea views and free bicycles. **www.carlton-hotel.co.il**

### NAHSHOLIM Nahsholim Seaside Resort
*Nahsholim, 30815* **Tel** *(04) 639 9533* **Fax** *(04) 639 7614* **Rooms** *128* **Map** *B2*

Set on a bay along Israel's most gorgeous strip of Mediterranean coastline, this kibbutz-run tourist village is a short walk from the delightful Dor Nature Reserve and a string of fish ponds that attract flocks of migrating birds, making it a great location for bird watchers, if not the local fish farmers. **www.nahsholim.co.il**

### NAZARETH Plaza Hotel
*2 Hermon St, Upper Nazareth, 17502* **Tel** *(04) 602 8200* **Fax** *(04) 602 8222* **Rooms** *184* **Map** *B2*

The Plaza is a modern, 10-storey hotel known for its convenient facilities, efficient service and central Lower Galilee location rather than its character. It makes a good base for car trips to Nazareth, Megiddo, Tsipori, the Jezreel Valley and Beit Alfa. Amenities include a sauna and a jacuzzi. **www.israelhotels.org.il**

### ROSH PINA Auberge Shulamit
*David Shuv St, Rosh Pina, 12000* **Tel** *(04) 693 1494* **Fax** *(04) 693 1495* **Rooms** *4* **Map** *C2*

In one of the oldest and most charming Jewish villages in Galilee, this old basalt house, built in the 1930s, is decorated with exquisite taste and attention to detail. The rooms have jacuzzi baths. The breakfasts are superb and the fine restaurant affords a breathtaking view. Weekends are booked up long in advance. **www.shulamit.co.il**

### ROSH PINA Mizpe Hayamim

*On Hwy 89 between Safed and Rosh Pina, 12000* **Tel** *(04) 699 4555* **Fax** *(04) 699 9555* **Rooms** *99* **Map** *C2*

Midway between Rosh Pina and Safed, on a hillside perch overlooking the Sea of Galilee and Golan, this ultra-luxurious resort is a great place to be pampered. Surrounded by orchards and gardens, its exquisitely designed rooms exude French style. The spa offers some uniquely Galilean treatments. **www.mizpe-hayamim.com**

### SAFED Ruth Rimonim Inn
*Tet-Zayin St, Safed, 13110* **Tel** *(04) 699 4666* **Fax** *(04) 692 0456* **Rooms** *81* **Map** *C2*

In the heart of Safed, the ruins of a 17th-century inn have been transformed into one of Galilee's most attractive hostelries. The atmospheric rooms, built partly of stone, have a very local flavour, and most come with fine views of Mount Meron. There are also spa facilities. **www.rimonim.com**

## SEA OF GALILEE YMCA Peniel-by-Galilee

*On Hwy 90 north of Tiberias, 14101* **Tel** *(04) 672 0685* **Fax** *(04) 672 5943* **Rooms** *13*　　　　　**Map** *C2*

In a superb lakefront location, this guesthouse is ensconsed in a lovely stone building with lots of character and is awash in greenery. The ornate Middle Eastern-style lobby and the lovely chapel are a feast for the eyes. Rooms are simply furnished; the best ones come with great lake views. Lakewater swimming pool. **www.ymca-galilee.co.il**

## SEA OF GALILEE Nof Ginosar

*Kibbutz Ginosar, 14980* **Tel** *(04) 670 0300* **Fax** *(04) 679 2170* **Rooms** *170*　　　　　**Map** *C2*

On the lakeside, 7 km (4 miles) north of Tiberias, this sprawling, grassy place has a fine beach and is a superb choice for a stay by the Sea of Galilee. Rooms are simple, pleasant and comfortable. Kibbutz-style holiday bungalows with kitchenettes are also available. **www.ginosar.co.il**

## SEA OF GALILEE Scots Hotel

*1 Gdud Barak St, Tiberias, 14100* **Tel** *(04) 671 0710* **Fax** *(04) 671 0711* **Rooms** *69*　　　　　**Map** *C2*

Full of character, this former hospital was founded in the late 1800s and is still owned by the Church of Scotland. Sitting on the lakefront and surrounded by a lovely garden, it is an oasis of tranquility in the town centre. The modern and very attractive facilities include a spa and, in summer, a swimming pool. **www.scotshotels.co.il**

## SEA OF GALILEE Vered HaGalil Guest Farm

*On Hwy 90 between Tiberias and Rosh Pina, 12385* **Tel** *(04) 693 5785* **Fax** *(04) 693 4964* **Rooms** *18*　　**Map** *C2*

This quiet, family-run ranch, which doubles as a horseback riding school, offers individual stone-and-wood cottages and cabins, each with lots of woody furnishings and a veranda. The rustic restaurant serves up American fare. The stables supply horses for riding tours of the area. **www.veredhagalil.co.il**

## SEA OF GALILEE Rimonim Galei Kinneret

*1 Eliezer Kaplan St, Tiberias, 14209* **Tel** *(04) 672 8888* **Fax** *(04) 679 0260* **Rooms** *120*　　　　　**Map** *C2*

Right on the shore of the Sea of Galilee, this luxurious spa hotel offers classy, up-to-date facilities and a wide variety of health and beauty treatments. Rooms are decorated in a contemporary style and many come with delightful watery views. Activity options include water-skiing. **www.rimonim.com**

## SHLOMI Shlomi Youth Hostel

*Shlomi, 22832* **Tel** *(04) 980 8975* **Fax** *(04) 980 9163* **Rooms** *100*　　　　　**Map** *B2*

Clean and quiet, if a bit old-fashioned, this unpretentious hostel makes a good budget base for exploring the far northwest of Galilee, including Akko and the coast around Nahariya. Served by Egged buses 22 and 23 from Nahariya. **www.iyha.org.il**

## TEL AVIV HaYarkon 48 Hostel

*48 HaYarkon St, 63305* **Tel** *(03) 516 8989* **Fax** *(03) 510 3113* **Rooms** *18 & dormitories*　　　　**Map** *B3*

Just two blocks from the city's broad, sandy beach and a five-minute walk from the Carmel Market, this bright yellow hostel is welcoming and cheery. Many of the private rooms come with balconies. Dorm beds are cheap. Amenities include bicycle parking and a pool table. **www.hayarkon48.com**

## TEL AVIV Old Jaffa Hostel & Guest House

*13 Amiad St, 68139* **Tel** *(03) 682 2370* **Rooms** *23*　　　　　**Map** *B3*

Just around the corner from Jaffa's famous flea market and Clock Tower, this atmospheric hostel occupies an Ottoman-era residence with sky-high ceilings and a mellow rooftop lounge offering views of the Mediterranean. Dorm beds are cheap. Breakfast is not included but is available in nearby cafés. **www.telaviv-hostel.com**

## TEL AVIV Dizengoff Square Apartments

*89 Dizengoff St & 4 Dizengoff Circle, 64396* **Tel** *(03) 524 1151* **Fax** *(03) 523 5614* **Rooms** *60*　　　　**Map** *B3*

Occupying two Bauhaus-style buildings at Dizengoff Circle, the ever-lively focal point of central Tel Aviv, this place offers tastefully furnished apartments with kitchenettes. Larger suites come with sofas and a kitchen table. Excellent value for money in a great location. **www.hotel-apt.com**

## TEL AVIV Dizengoff Suites Hotel

*39 Gordon St, 63461* **Tel** *(03) 523 4363* **Fax** *(03) 527 3524* **Rooms** *20*　　　　　**Map** *B3*

On the corner of lively Dizengoff St, midway between the beach and Rabin Square, this family-run place has suites with kitchenettes, fridges and, in most cases, balconies. Breakfast can be bought at the stylish, Italian-style café-restaurant on the ground floor. **www.dizengoffsuites.co.il**

## TEL AVIV Alexander

*3 Habakuk St, 63505* **Tel** *(03) 545 2222* **Fax** *(03) 546 9346* **Rooms** *47*　　　　　**Map** *B3*

This all-suites hotel sits at the northern entrance to Metzitzim beach, just two blocks south of the Tel Aviv Port nightlife area and a few minutes on foot from HaYarkon Park and the Yarkon River Estuary. The spacious suites come with a kitchenette and a work area, and can accommodate up to seven people. **www.alexander.co.il**

## TEL AVIV Cinema

*1 Zamenhof St, 64373* **Tel** *(03) 520 7100* **Fax** *(03) 521 7101* **Rooms** *82*　　　　　**Map** *B3*

In a former cinema right on Dizengoff Circle, this stylish hotel has a film-themed lobby that is as evocative of 1930s elegance as its curvaceous, Bauhaus-style façade. Some rooms have balconies and/or kitchenettes. Amenities include a sun roof, sauna and jacuzzi. **www.atlas.co.il**

**Key to Price Guide** *see p256* **Key to Symbols** *see back cover flap*

### TEL AVIV Dan Panorama

*Charles Clore Park, 68012* **Tel** *(03) 519 0190* **Fax** *(03) 517 1777* **Rooms** *500*    **Map** *B3*

Overlooking a grassy, seafront park midway between Dizengoff Circle and Old Jaffa, this 18-storey hotel is across the street from a broad, sandy beach and just three blocks from the chic boutiques and cafés of Neve Tzedek. All rooms have sea views and balconies. Only one room has facilities for wheelchair users. **www.danhotels.com**

### TEL AVIV Sheraton City Tower

*14 Shalom Zissman St, Ramat Gan, 52521* **Tel** *(03) 754 4444* **Fax** *(03) 754 4445* **Rooms** *166*    **Map** *B3*

At the gateway to Ramat Gan's skyscraper Diamond Exchange District, this business-oriented hotel, on floors nine to 17 of a 40-storey tower, is across the Ayalon Expressway from the Central Tel Aviv Train Station, linked by rail with Akko, Haifa, Beersheva and Jerusalem. Amenities include an outdoor jacuzzi and a spa. **www.sheraton.co.il**

### TEL AVIV Sheraton Tel Aviv

*115 HaYarkon St, 63573* **Tel** *(03) 521 1111* **Fax** *(03) 523 3322* **Rooms** *331*    **Map** *B3*

One of the city's most luxurious hotels, this venerable, high-rise hotel overlooks the beachfront and is just steps from several beachside cafés. The public areas are an excellent example of modern Israeli interior design. All rooms are spacious and stylish, and have balconies with Mediterranean panoramas. **www.sheraton-telaviv.co.il**

### TEL AVIV Tel Aviv Hilton

*Independence Park, 63405* **Tel** *(03) 520 2222* **Fax** *(03) 527 2711* **Rooms** *583*    **Map** *B3*

The most luxurious and best equipped of the city's hotels, the Hilton sits on a cliff overlooking the Mediterranean. Rooms are spacious and come with marble bathrooms and wonderful sea views. Activity options include sailing, windsurfing and cycling. The beach is a two-minute walk down the hill. **www.hilton.com**

### YEHIAM Teva be-Yehiam

*Kibbutz Yechiam, 25125* **Tel** *(04) 985 6057 or (050) 444 4362* **Fax** *(04) 952 4567* **Rooms** *60*    **Map** *B2*

In the Galilee hills 23 km (14 miles) northeast of Akko, this kibbutz hotel is built next to the ruins of a Crusader castle. It is a very quiet spot, with lots of greenery and lawns, but the speciality here is arranging challenging outdoor activities for groups, such as kayaking, speedboating, jeep tours and cliff rapelling. **www.rimoney-hagalil.com**

# THE DEAD SEA AND THE NEGEV DESERT

### DEAD SEA Tsell Harim Hotel

*Ein Bokek, 86930* **Tel** *(08) 668 8111* **Fax** *(08) 668 8100* **Rooms** *160*    **Map** *C4*

This low-rise, beachfront complex, centred around an outdoor swimming pool, has modest but serviceable rooms. When it is too hot outside you can take refuge in the indoor pool, filled with Dead Sea water. Amenities include a Finnish sauna and a rooftop solarium; black mud baths are free. **www.tsell-harim.co.il**

### DEAD SEA Magic Nirvana Club

*Neve Zohar, 86910* **Tel** *(08) 668 9444* **Fax** *(08) 668 9400* **Rooms** *388*    **Map** *C4*

On the shores of the Dead Sea, this 10-storey club hotel has indoor and outdoor pools, palm-dotted lawns, plenty of activities and rooms with views across the water to the Mountains of Edom in Jordan. Prices include meals and activities. **www.fattal.co.il**

### EILAT Eilat Field School

*Coral Beach, 88000* **Tel** *(08) 637 2021* **Fax** *(08) 637 1771* **Rooms** *50*    **Map** *B7*

About 3 km (2 miles) south of town, this basic hostel offers bed and breakfast in low-rise buildings surrounded by lawns. It is opposite the Coral Reef Nature Reserve, which has the area's best snorkelling. Experienced guides offer hiking tours of nearby mountain areas. The Coral World Underwater Observatory is a short walk away. **www.aspni.org**

### EILAT Eilat Youth Hostel & Guest House

*7 Arava Road, 88101* **Tel** *(08) 637 0088* **Fax** *(08) 637 5835* **Rooms** *105*    **Map** *B7*

Just a short walk from Eilat's seafront promenade, this hostel's creative architecture incorporates some cleverly shaded public spaces. Rooms are spartan, but clean and serviceable. The rooftop deck affords great views of the city, the deep blue Red Sea and the mountains of Aqaba. **www.iyha.org.il**

### EILAT Ambassador

*Coral Beach, 88103* **Tel** *(08) 638 2222* **Fax** *(08) 638 2220* **Rooms** *251*    **Map** *B7*

Near a quiet strip of sandy coastline about 3 km (2 miles) south of Eilat, next to the Coral Reef Reserve, this hotel is centred around an expansive swimming pool. You are never far from grass and greenery, and shaded areas for relaxing. The diving club offers a wide range of approved scuba courses. **www.isrotel.co.il**

### EILAT Orchid

*Southern Beach, 88000* **Tel** *(08) 636 0360* **Fax** *(08) 637 5323* **Rooms** *180*    **Map** *B7*

Overlooking the Coral World Underwater Observatory from a landscaped hillside about 5 km (3 miles) south of town, this Thai-inspired village has wooden buildings, spacious rooms and a tropical feel. Amenities include free bicycles and snorkelling equipment. The beach is close by and free shuttles give lifts to the town centre. **www.orchidhotel.co.il**

### EILAT Reef
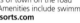 $$$

*Coral Beach, 88103* **Tel** *(08) 636 4444* **Fax** *(08) 636 4488* **Rooms** *79*     **Map** *B7*

Situated on the beach about 3 km (2 miles) south of the city centre, not far from the Coral World Underwater Observatory, this is one of Eilat's smaller, more accessibly-priced hotels. It has an outdoor jacuzzi, balcony-equipped rooms and lots of water sports options, including diving, snorkelling and windsurfing. **www.reefhoteleilat.com**

### EILAT Eilat Princess
 $$$$$

*Taba Beach, 88000* **Tel** *(08) 636 5555* **Fax** *(08) 637 6333* **Rooms** *420*     **Map** *B7*

Situated 5 km (3 miles) south of Eilat near the Taba border crossing to Egypt, this opulent hotel affords fine views across the Red Sea to the mountains of Jordan and Saudi Arabia. Amenities include swimming pools, tennis courts, a spa, a heath centre and cuisine from around the world. **www.eilatprincess.com**

### EIN GEDI Ein Gedi Youth Hostel
 $

*Ein Gedi, 86980* **Tel** *(08) 658 4165* **Fax** *(08) 658 4445* **Rooms** *56*     **Map** *C4*

Set around a quiet courtyard, the location is ideal for guests who want to combine hiking in the nearby oases with relaxing in the Dead Sea. It is situated next to the Nahal David Nature Reserve and served by Egged buses 486 and 486 from Jerusalem. Some rooms have balconies with sea views. **www.iyha.org.il**

### EIN GEDI Ein Gedi Guesthouse
 $$$

*Kibbutz Ein Gedi, 86980* **Tel** *(08) 659 4220* **Fax** *(08) 658 4328* **Rooms** *150*     **Map** *C4*

Overlooking the Dead Sea and the lush Ein Gedi oasis, this kibbutz guesthouse has comfortable, cheerful rooms with creative furnishings inspired by the local desert landscape. Superb hiking, a Dead Sea beach and the Ein Gedi Spa are nearby. **www.ein-gedi.co.il**

### JERICHO Jericho Resort Village
 $$

*Near Hisham Palace* **Tel** *(02) 232 1255* **Fax** *(02) 232 2189* **Rooms** *104*     **Map** *C3*

Set amid spacious, oasis-like grounds, this modern hotel-resort, on the northern outskirts of town on the road leading up the Jordan Valley, has attractive rooms and bungalows for up to six people. Amenities include swimming pools, restaurants and courts for tennis, basketball and sand volleyball. **www.jerichoresorts.com**

### KHAI BAR BIBLICAL WILDLIFE RESERVE Kibbutz Lotan Guesthouse
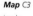 $$

*Kibbutz Lotan, 88855* **Tel** *(08) 635 6935* **Fax** *(08) 635 6827* **Rooms** *20*     **Map** *B6*

Surrounded by the mountains of the southern Arava Desert, this guesthouse is run by the environmentally conscious Kibbutz Lotan, affiliated with the Reform Jewish Movement, and is part of their Centre for Ecotourism and Birdwatching. It is situated 15 km (9 miles) north of the Khai Bar Nature Reserve and 50 km (31 miles) north of Eilat.

### MASSADA Massada Youth Hostel
 $$

*Massada, 86935* **Tel** *(08) 995 3222* **Fax** *(08) 658 4650* **Rooms** *88*     **Map** *C4*

A deluxe option as far as youth hostels go, this appealing place, situated next to the cable car station, has spotless, modern rooms, most with bunk beds, and a lovely swimming pool. The cafeteria offers plentiful, adequate food. The hostel is served by Egged buses 444 and 486 from Jerusalem. **www.iyha.org.il**

### MITZPE RAMON Ramon Inn
 $$$

*1 Ein Akev St, 80600* **Tel** *(08) 658 8822* **Fax** *(08) 658 8151* **Rooms** *96*     **Map** *B5*

A great base for exploring the remote, highland reaches of the southern Negev, including spectacular Makhtesh Ramon, this attractive establishment is architecturally in harmony with the desert. Some apartments have space for up to five people. There is a covered swimming pool and two saunas. **www.isrotel.co.il**

## WESTERN JORDAN

### AJLOUN Al-Jabal Hotel
$

*Al Qala' St* **Tel** *(02) 642 0202* **Fax** *(06) 463 0414* **Rooms** *20*     **Map** *C3*

Set among pine trees on the road up from Ajloun town towards the Crusader-era hilltop castle, this clean, simple hotel offers courteous service, decent rooms (many with superb views) and a sense of isolation. It is quiet out-of-season, but often packed with families in summer so booking is advisable. **www.aljabal-hotel.com**

### AMMAN Shepherd
$

*Zaid bin al-Harith St, Jabal Amman, 11181* **Tel** *(06) 463 9197* **Fax** *(06) 463 9197* **Rooms** *48*     **Map** *C3*

This decent lower-priced hotel is situated in a characterful location between the 1st and 2nd circles, within walking distance of the shops and cafés of Rainbow St and the restaurants and craft outlets around 2nd Circle. Rooms are pleasant – ask for one at the back to avoid street noise. Excellent value for money. **www.shepherd-hotel.com**

### AMMAN Hisham
$$

*Mithqal al-Fayez St, Jabal Amman, 11183* **Tel** *(06) 464 4028/2720* **Fax** *(06) 464 7540* **Rooms** *22*     **Map** *C3*

Peaceful and discreet, this modest, family-run hotel is situated between the 3rd and 4th circles, on a leafy corner in the heart of the diplomatic quarter, just behind the French Embassy. It has a long history and a good deal of character. The rooms are comfortable, and service is outstanding: genial, attentive and accommodating.

**Key to Price Guide** *see p256* **Key to Symbols** *see back cover flap*

### AMMAN San Rock International

$$$

Map C3

*Sa'eed Abu Japer St, Jabal Amman, 11191* **Tel** *(06) 551 3800* **Fax** *(06) 551 3600* **Rooms** *105*

Popular with Western tour groups, this is one of Amman's best mid-range hotels. It is situated near 6th Circle, in a part-residential, part-commercial district on the western edge of the city centre, which cuts down driving time to and from the airport. Decor is a little tired, but service is notably good. **www.sanrock-hotel.com**

### AMMAN InterContinental

$$$$$

Map C3

*Between 2nd and 3rd circles, Jabal Amman, 11180* **Tel** *(06) 464 1361* **Fax** *(06) 464 5217* **Rooms** *475*

One of Amman's, and Jordan's, longest-established hotels has been entirely renovated to international luxury quality. A premier venue for top-level congresses, and a favoured venue for visiting journalists, it offers large, well-appointed rooms, good sports facilities and outstanding restaurants. **www.intercontinental.com**

### AMMAN Marriott

$$$$

Map C3

*Issam al-Ajlouni St, Shmeisani, 11190* **Tel** *(06) 560 7607* **Fax** *(06) 567 0100* **Rooms** *293*

This top-class chain hotel is regularly voted by journalists and business-people as one of the finest hotels in the Middle East. Located in a smart district, it features every luxury, from first-class restaurants and large, elegantly appointed rooms to personal service and a full range of business facilities. **www.marriott.com**

### AQABA Coral Bay

$$$

Map B7

*The Royal Diving Club, South Beach, 77110* **Tel** *(03) 201 7035* **Fax** *(03) 201 7097* **Rooms** *69*

A comfortable hotel attached to the Royal Diving Club, located on its own private, west-facing beach about 18 km (11 miles) south of Aqaba town centre. Rooms are airy and pleasant, and you get access to pools, a restaurant, a beach bar and, of course, the exquisite coral reefs immediately offshore for snorkelling and diving. **www.rdc.jo**

### AQABA InterContinental

 $$$$$

Map B7

*King Hussein St, North Beach, 77110* **Tel** *(03) 209 2222* **Fax** *(03) 209 3318* **Rooms** *255*

This brand new first-class resort hotel faces south over Aqaba's bay and is within easy walking distance of the town centre. The opulent decor includes acres of marble in the public areas and lavish gardens around the hotel's pools and sandy beaches. Rooms are large and modern, many with balconies. The restaurants are outstanding.

### AQABA Mövenpick

 $$$$$

Map B7

*King Hussein St, North Beach, 77110* **Tel** *(03) 203 4020* **Fax** *(03) 203 4040* **Rooms** *235*

A first-class luxury resort hotel, on a prime plot straddling the beach road alongside the town centre: one of the four swimming pools occupies an overbridge linking the main hotel building with its seafront villas and beaches. The hotel design has Arabic influences, and the dining options are lavish. **www.movenpick.com**

### DANA Dana Guest House

$$

Map C5

*Dana Village* **Tel** *(03) 227 0497/0498* **Fax** *(03) 227 0498* **Rooms** *9*

The Dana Guest House sits in idyllic countryside and is run superbly well by Jordan's Royal Society for the Conservation of Nature (RSCN). It looks out over a pristine, silent landscape of mountains and valleys – heaven for birdwatchers. Most rooms have a balcony and one is ensuite (the rest share bathrooms). Book rooms and meals well ahead.

### DEAD SEA Kempinski Ishtar

 $$$$$

Map C4

*Dead Sea Rd, Sweimeh, 11180* **Tel** *(05) 356 8888* **Fax** *(05) 356 8800* **Rooms** *114*

This stylish resort hotel on the Dead Sea has world-class facilities, with chalet-style villa suites dotted around eight pools, including a magical infinity pool, a variety of restaurants, the largest spa in the Middle East and a great beach. Design is cool and contemporary and the service is memorably good. **www.kempinski-deadsea.com**

### DEAD SEA Mövenpick Resort & Spa

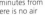 $$$$$

Map C4

*Sweimeh, Dead Sea Rd, 11180* **Tel** *(05) 356 1111* **Fax** *(05) 356 1122* **Rooms** *340*

One of Jordan's flagship Dead Sea resort hotels, boasting unusual taste and character. Design plays a central role, from the Damascene-style hard-carved wooden ceiling in the lobby bar, to the spacious guest rooms, which are housed in low-rise, two-storey villas of local stone and stucco. Pools, beach facilities, restaurants and a spa add to the attraction.

### PETRA Petra Moon

$

Map C5

*Wadi Musa, 71810* **Tel** *(03) 215 6220* **Fax** *(03) 215 6220* **Rooms** *17*

Excellent low-budget hotel located a short walk up the hill behind the Mövenpick Hotel, barely five minutes from the ticket gate into Petra. Rooms are well-kept (all ensuite), and service is pleasant and attentive. There is no air conditioning, but that is rarely an issue outside July and August. **www.petramoonhotel.com**

### PETRA Petra Palace

 $$$

Map C5

*Wadi Musa, 71810* **Tel** *(03) 215 6723* **Fax** *(03) 215 6724* **Rooms** *83*

This comfortable hotel benefits from a location on the "Tourist Road" strip of shops and restaurants, near the Petra ticket gate and is easy to reach after a hard day of walking. Rooms, which are bright and tidy, are therefore priced slightly high, but the atmosphere is pleasant and there is a good bar too. **www.petrapalace.com.jo**

### PETRA Mövenpick

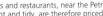 $$$$$

Map C5

*Wadi Musa, 71810* **Tel** *(03) 215 7111* **Fax** *(03) 215 7112* **Rooms** *183*

This is a spectacularly well-designed and well-appointed five-star hotel. The location is unbeatable, directly at the entrance to Petra, a few metres from the visitor centre and ticket gate. The interior is stunning, featuring intricate Arabesque designs and a soaring atrium. Rooms are very comfortable. **www.movenpick.com**

# Choosing a Hotel in the Red Sea and Sinai

This section lists hotels in the Red Sea and Sinai area. The price ranges are given in Egyptian pounds. For key to symbols and map references, see back endpaper.

**PRICE CATEGORIES**

Prices categories are per night for two people occupying a standard double room, with tax, breakfast and service included:

£ Under 150
££ 150–250
£££ 250–650
££££ 650–1,500
£££££ Over 1,500

## THE RED SEA AND SINAI

### DAHAB Bishbishi Camp
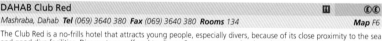
£

*Mashraba, Dahab* **Tel** *(069) 3640 727* **Rooms** *40*                    **Map** *F6*

The camp is ideal for young travellers keen for the experience of living close to nature rather than having luxurious surroundings and lots of modern conveniences. It comprises a series of beachside bamboo-style huts equipped with the essentials. Some have ceiling fans to help ease the heat of the day.

### DAHAB Jasmine Pension
£

*Mashraba, Dahab* **Tel** *(069) 3640 852/ (010) 4498 026* **Fax** *(069) 3640 885* **Rooms** *17*        **Map** *F6*

The Jasmine Pension is an attractive, inexpensive alternative to the many camps that can be found in Dahab. The rooms are basic but comfortable, and are equipped with their own bathrooms and fans. The complex's own restaurant may not be luxurious, but it serves good, hearty food. **www.jasminepension.com**

### DAHAB Club Red
££

*Mashraba, Dahab* **Tel** *(069) 3640 380* **Fax** *(069) 3640 380* **Rooms** *134*                **Map** *F6*

The Club Red is a no-frills hotel that attracts young people, especially divers, because of its close proximity to the sea and good dive facilities. Discounts are offered to divers. Some rooms can be shared to keep costs down, while others come complete with fans and adjoining bathrooms. **www.club-red.com**

### DAHAB Blue Beach club

£££

*Lighthouse, Dahab* **Tel** *(069) 3640 411* **Fax** *(069) 3640 413* **Rooms** *22*            **Map** *F6*

The attractive rooms that form the Blue Beach Club have great views of the surrounding neighbourhood of Asilah, Dahab, in one direction and the beach in the other. Room facilities include a fan and fridge. This quiet hotel is ideal for couples looking for a relaxing base from which to explore the area. **www.bluebeachclub.com**

### DAHAB Nesima Hotel
£££

*Mashraba Asilah, Dahab* **Tel** *(069) 3640 320* **Fax** *(069) 3640 321* **Rooms** *51*            **Map** *F6*

The Nesima Hotel has one of the most popular diving centres in the Asilah area, and is known for its good food served in a traditional-styled restaurant. Its rooms are well-presented, with many featuring domed ceilings and sea views. Its pool overlooks the sea. The hotel welcomes people with disabilities. **www.nesima-resort.com**

### DAHAB Hilton Resort
£££££

*Dahab Bay, Dahab* **Tel** *(069) 3640 310* **Fax** *(069) 3640 424* **Rooms** *163*            **Map** *F6*

The Hilton Resort is a landmark building in Dahab Bay. It is beautifully presented with lush gardens and whitewashed rooms that surround a lagoon-style swimming pool. It is situated on the beachside and offers some superb leisure amenities, including dive and windsurfing centres. **www.hilton.com**

### NUWEIBA Basata
£

*Ras al-Burqa, Nuweiba* **Tel** *(069) 3500 480/481* **Rooms** *26*                    **Map** *F5*

An extremely popular hotel and camp, Basata lies around 23 km (14 miles) north of Nuweiba. Guests live in mud and bamboo huts, a crucial part of the owner's policy on eco-friendliness. Basata has its own kitchen and bakery, and is known for its good snorkelling. Scuba diving, however, is not allowed.

### NUWEIBA Habiba Village

£

*Nuweiba City, South Sinai* **Tel** *(069) 3500 770* **Rooms** *21*                    **Map** *F5*

Situated right on the beachside, this traditionally built hotel village has a beach restaurant to enjoy an evening under the stars, along with its Mataamak eaterie for more formal dining. Rooms are well presented, with most having air conditioning and a private bathroom. Wooden cabins have fans. **www.sinai4you.com**

### NUWEIBA La Sirene

£££

*Beach Road, Nuweiba* **Tel** *(069) 3500 701* **Fax** *(069) 3500 702* **Rooms** *45*            **Map** *F5*

La Sirene Hotel is the centrepiece of a resort set right on the beach at Nuweiba, between the port and the city. It is a compact hotel that is pleasingly presented and well-located for local amenities. As such, it is extremely popular. The hotel's leisure amenities are few, but do include diving.

**Key to Symbols** *see back cover flap*

### NUWEIBA Hilton Nuweiba Coral Resort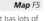

*Nuweiba City, South Sinai* **Tel** *(069) 3520 320* **Rooms** *200*   **Map** *F5*

This large resort is located amidst quiet, beachside gardens and is known for its tranquility and beauty. It has lots of amenities, including diving, windsurfing, tennis and squash courts. Other activities, like kayaking, windsurfing, disco dancing and even swimming with dolphins, are all within walking distance. **www.hilton.com**

### SHARM EL-SHEIKH Shark's Bay UMBI Camp

*Shark's Bay, Sharm el-Sheikh* **Tel** *(069) 3600 942* **Fax** *(069) 3600 944* **Rooms** *96*   **Map** *E7*

One of the most frequently revisited camps in Sharm el-Sheikh and popular with local families, Shark's Bay Camp sits right on the beach in an isolated location, and has its own reef and dive centre. Rooms are either chalets with air conditioning, or bamboo huts without air conditioning. Safari and desert activities available. **www.sharksbay.net**

### SHARM EL-SHEIKH Amar Sina

*Ras Um Sid, Sharm el-Sheikh* **Tel** *(069) 3662 222* **Fax** *(069) 3662 233* **Rooms** *91*   **Map** *E7*

The Amar Sina is designed and built to resemble a traditional whitewashed Egyptian village, with architectural features such as domes and arches. Facilities include a bar, shops, its own fitness centre and restaurants radiating from a central square. Rooms are pleasant and air-conditioned.

### SHARM EL-SHEIKH Camel Hotel

*Naama Bay, Sharm el-Sheikh* **Tel** *(069) 3600 700* **Fax** *(069) 3600 601* **Rooms** *38*   **Map** *E7*

Pretty and compact, the Camel Hotel has gained a reputation for not only providing top-class diving facilities but also offering great cuisine in its award-winning restaurants. The hotel, which is located in Naama Bay and minutes from Sharm el Sheikh, is known for its extensive facilities for disabled guests. **www.cameldive.com**

### SHARM EL-SHEIKH Sanafir Hotel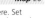

*Naama Bay, Sharm el-Sheikh* **Tel** *(069) 3600 197* **Fax** *(069) 3600 196* **Rooms** *50*   **Map** *E7*

The Sanafir Hotel is best known for being the venue for one of Naama Bay's most popular nightclubs – it comes alive after dark and is ideal for travellers looking for nightly entertainment. It has a good choice of bars and restaurants too. The hotel's air-conditioned rooms are well-presented. **www.sanafirhotel.com**

### SHARM EL-SHEIKH Ritz-Carlton Resort

*Om El Seed Peninsula, Sharm el-Sheikh* **Tel** *(069) 3661 919* **Fax** *(069) 3661 920* **Rooms** *321*   **Map** *E7*

Oozing luxury, this top-class hotel sits in beautifully landscaped gardens where cascading waterfalls combine with subtly lit pools and shrubbery. Its rooms are equally well-presented, while on-site facilities include everything from fine international dining to superb golf, watersports and family fun. **www.ritzcarlton.com**

### SHARM EL-SHEIKH Sofitel Sharm el-Sheikh

*Naama Bay, Sharm el-Sheikh* **Tel** *(069) 3600 081* **Fax** *(069) 3600 085* **Rooms** *298*   **Map** *E7*

Perched high on the coastline next to the beach, this hotel offers a wonderful panoramic view of Naama Bay. Amenities are in abundance and include a Turkish bath complex, archery, ice cream parlour and numerous restaurants, while rooms are attractive and most have sea views. **www.sofitel.com**

### ST CATHERINE St Catherine Guest House

*St Catherine's Monastery, St Catherine* **Tel** *(069) 3470 353* **Fax** *(069) 3470 353* **Rooms** *40*   **Map** *E6*

Although a little lacking in luxuries, the auberge at St Catherine more than makes up for it in atmosphere. Set against a backdrop of countryside at the foot of Mount Sinai and right next to St Catherine's Monastery, it remains a firm favourite with travellers looking for a relaxing, "away from it all" location.

### ST CATHERINE Morgenland Village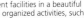

*St Catherine City* **Tel** *(02) 7956 856/ (069) 3470 331* **Fax** *(069) 3470 331* **Rooms** *200*   **Map** *E6*

Newly refurbished and upgraded, the Morgenland Village offers attractive rooms in the main building and a series of chalets in the grounds. Facilities include restaurants and a pool, plus a traditional-style shopping centre where one of the shops sells a selection of medicinal herbs from Sinai.

### TABA Three Corners El Wekala Golf Resort

*Taba Heights, Taba* **Tel** *(069) 3580 150* **Fax** *(069) 3580 156* **Rooms** *215*   **Map** *F5*

This luxury resort hotel occupies a prime location in the Taba Heights Resort, offering excellent facilities in a beautiful setting. The complex includes restaurants, bars and pools, and there's a daily programme of organized activities, such as exercise classes, water games and dancing. A shuttle bus takes guests to a private beach. **www.threecorners.com**

### TABA Tobya Boutique Hotel

*Taba International Road, Taba* **Tel** *(069) 3530 274* **Fax** *(069) 3530 269* **Rooms** *100*   **Map** *F5*

Outstanding architecture, lush greenery and distinctive decor using stone, wood and handwoven rugs, combined with excellent service make the Tobya a relaxing, luxurious retreat. Most rooms have a terrace and many have a view of the Red Sea. **www.tobyaboutiquehotel.com**

### TABA Marriott Taba Heights Beach Resort

*Taba and Nuweiba Highway, Taba* **Tel** *(069) 3580 100* **Fax** *(069) 3580 109* **Rooms** *394*   **Map** *F5*

This is one of many hotels on the extensive Taba Heights development. The luxury hotel's amenities are complemented by the resort's marina, 18-hole golf course, a casino, safari programme and top-class spas, while restaurants offer everything from Japanese sushi and Indian dishes to European meals. **www.marriott.com**

# RESTAURANTS, CAFES AND BARS

Middle Eastern food is often overshadowed by other more glamorous world cuisine, and as such, the Holy Land has been seen by many as a gastronomic desert. Often simple and unpretentious, the food is, however, usually tasty and substantial *(see pp268–9)*. A constantly changing restaurant culture reflects the huge interest in food in the Holy Land, and many restaurants are of a very high standard, offering a wide range of Middle Eastern food sure to excite even the most sceptical palate.

Vendor selling the iced drink *tamahindi*

Aside from the native cuisine, there are many other restaurants offering more international food, reflecting the broad ethnic mix of the Holy Land. You can find South American, Chinese, Indonesian, Italian and French food, along with the ever popular American fast food. There are also many busy and informal cafés, which offer a cheaper, more limited menu. For a quick snack, street food revolves around the *shawarma* and *falafel* stalls, which can be found almost everywhere.

The restaurant in the Arabesque American Colony Hotel *(see p273)*

## PRACTICALITIES

In most Israeli cities, especially Tel Aviv and in Jerusalem's Nakhalat Shiva neighbourhood, you will see people eating at all hours of the day, seated outside at cafés and restaurants or walking along the street with a pitta or *boureka*. In the evening, people tend to eat late, and spend a long time over their meals. Eating is a big social and family event, with children accepted in many restaurants. Dining, when possible, is alfresco, and restaurants often stay open until after midnight, especially during the summer. However, restaurants are not always open all week, especially the Jewish ones. These always close for Shabbat (sundown on Friday until after sundown on Saturday), as well as for Yom Kippur, Shavuot, and the first

and last day of Sukkoth and Passover. In addition, throughout Israel, all Jewish-owned restaurants, whether kosher or not, are closed on Holocaust Day and Remembrance Day *(see p36)*.

Service is not generally included on the bill, a fact often well highlighted, and you should expect to tip around 10–15 %, depending on the type of establishment. Throughout Israel credit cards are widely accepted, and most of the restaurants listed in this guide accept all the major types.

## TYPES OF RESTAURANT

Food is a major part of Middle Eastern life, and there is a huge range of places to eat, from the trendy and expensive city restaurants of Jerusalem and Tel Aviv to the countless cheaper cafés and take-aways. With no fixed

cuisine of its own, Israeli food is a melting pot of flavours, reflecting the cultural mix of the nation and adopting influences from the Middle East, the Mediterranean, and Eastern Europe. The main Israeli food is that of the Jews, largely the Oriental (Middle Eastern) and Ashkenazi (eastern European) communities. Their food is as distinctly different as their origins. Oriental dishes revolve mainly around grilled meats and fish, stuffed vegetables, and a range of *meze*. The Ashkenazi specialities are spicy stews, such as goulash, fish balls and large, stuffed pancakes, known as *blintzes*.

Other major ethnic groups have also brought their own unique and unusual dishes. Armenian favourites include spicy meat stews and sausages, while the Yemenites are famous for their *malawach* –

Dining outside in the spectacular setting of Petra *(see pp220–31)*

large, flaky-pastry pancakes, stuffed with a variety of fillings.

Aside from Israeli fare, you can also find restaurants serving more international food, including French and Italian (which tend to be very expensive), and Chinese, Thai and Korean. There are also the usual fast-food chains. Such a selection of restaurants is far more limited if travelling in Jordan or Sinai, however, as most are found in the hotels. Café culture in Israel is huge, and if you are after something cheaper and less substantial, then cafés offer salads, pizzas, club sandwiches and simple pasta dishes that will provide a tasty light meal. Cafés are also great places to sit and soak up the local atmosphere, and join in with Israeli life.

**Bourj al-Haman Intercontinental restaurant, Jordan (see p280)**

## KOSHER RESTAURANTS

The Jewish dietary laws of *Kashrut* (literally, fitness), determine many of the eating habits in the Holy Land. To the outsider these can prove very confusing, especially as you will find that all types of restaurant can be kosher, not just the Jewish ones. This is especially true in Jerusalem, and the more Orthodox parts of the country. In the rest of Israel, however, more secular Jews do not always adhere to dietary laws, and it poses less of a problem to the visitor.

What these laws mean in practice is that meat considered impure (such as pork, rabbit and horse meat), as well as certain types of seafood (anything without scales and fins), cannot be eaten at all. Animals that are permitted for consumption have to be slaughtered according to Jewish religious practice and cleansed of all traces of blood before cooking. Furthermore, during Passover a kosher restaurant cannot even serve any leavened food, such as bread or pastries.

The major complications of these laws revolve around the fact that meat and dairy produce can never be eaten together in the same meal. Dishes are consequently based on either one or the other, with many of the resulting problems deftly overcome through the use of a range of dairy substitutes.

## VEGETARIAN FOOD

As a vegetarian visiting the Holy Land, your dining options are surprisingly varied. Kosher restaurants serve all types of dairy-only food, such as creamy pasta and yogurt-based dishes, as well as many potato dishes and salads.

Secular restaurants also have a large number of vegetarian options. Much of the cuisine is based around pulses, which are found in anything from houmous to hearty bean stews. Roasted and stuffed vegetables also feature widely, along with a variety of savoury pastries. For a quick vegetarian snack, the *falafel* is hard to beat.

## JORDAN AND SINAI

Jordanian food is a mix of the Lebanese-Syrian-Egyptian fare common throughout the Middle East, mixed in with local Bedouin cuisine. Expect lots of good, fresh *meze*,

**Sidewalk restaurants in Nachlat Shiva, Jerusalem**

salads and grilled meats, plus traditional specialties such as *mansaf*: lamb on a bed of rice sprinkled with pine nuts. You may also be offered *maqlubbeh*, which is steamed rice pressed into a small bowl then turned out and topped with slices of grilled eggplant. Otherwise, places like Amman have plenty of international restaurants, cafés and takeaways.

Food in the Sinai resorts tends to cater to the tastes of package holidaymakers. Most restaurants are attached to hotels and favour Italian and other safe international cuisines. Genuine Egyptian cuisine is rare, although the fish and seafood can be excellent.

**Elvis American Diner (see p274)**

# The Flavours of Jerusalem and the Holy Land

The cuisines of the Holy Land are as varied as its people. Over the centuries, the region has embraced rich culinary traditions from around the Mediterranean, Central and Eastern Europe, the Middle East, North Africa and South Asia. More recently, dishes brought by Jewish immigrants from Ethiopia have appeared, and a growth in travel to East Asia has resulted in the food from this region becoming hugely popular. The local dining scene has come a long way since the spartan communal dining halls of the early *kibbutzim*, and recently an increasingly sophisticated gastronomic culture has transformed the restaurant scene.

**Pomegranates**

**Fish seller's stall at Jerusalem's Mahane Yehuda market**

## STREET FOOD

Stalls and storefront eateries offer a varied array of cheap, nutritious and relatively healthy "fast food". *Falafel* is an excellent option for vegetarians, as are houmous and *bourekas*, a filo pastry from the Balkans filled with salty *kashkaval* cheese, potatoes, spinach or mushrooms. Somewhat less well known

is *sabih*, an Iraqi speciality that consists of potato chunks, fried aubergine (eggplant), a hard-boiled egg, salad, *tahina* (sesame paste), hot sauce and chopped parsley, served in a pitta. A carnivore favourite is *shwarma*, the local, often turkey-based, version of gyros or doner kebab. Griddled meats such as *me'urav yerushalmi* (a mixed grill of chicken livers, hearts and other offal) are served in, or with, a pitta.

## MEZE OR SALATIM

A meal typically begins with a large selection of starters (*meze* in Arabic, *salatim* in Hebrew). Middle Eastern restaurants serve *meze* either as a starter or as a full meal. Dishes you are likely to encounter include houmous (chickpea/garbanzo paste with olive oil, lemon and garlic), tabouleh (cracked wheat with masses of chopped mint and parsley,

**Babaghanoush**

**Pickled vegetables**

**Olives**

**Israeli salad**

**Kibbe**

**Pitta breads**

**Houmous**

**Tabouleh**

**Some of the small dishes that make up a *meze* or *salatim***

---

## DISHES AND SPECIALITIES OF THE HOLY LAND

The edibles you'll run across in the Holy Land range from stuffed grape leaves and *mansaf* (rice and lamb with a sour yoghurt sauce), sometimes called the national dish of Jordan, to gefilte fish and chicken soup with matzo balls, favoured by Jews with roots in Eastern Europe. Popular Palestinian Arab specialities include *meze* salads and sumac-flavoured meat dishes such as *mussakhan*. About half of Israeli Jews have family roots in Asia and Africa, which is why the menus of ethnic restaurants often feature Moroccan couscous, fiery fish dishes from Libya, doughy *malawah* (pan-fried bread) and *jahnoun* (a heavy, slow-baked bread roll) from Yemen, and *kubbe* (or *kibbe*) from Iraq – also a Palestinian speciality.

**Selection of sweets**

**Shashlik and kebab** *are, respectively, pieces of meat and spiced ground meat grilled on a skewer.*

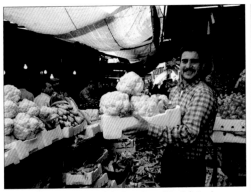

Market trader offers the superb fresh produce of the Holy Land

## LOCAL PRODUCE

Israel has long been known for its excellent selection of cheeses, but in recent years a growing number of so-called "boutique" dairies has been setting ever-higher standards with their goats' and sheep's milk products. These go extremely well with classic Mediterranean specialities such as olives and extra virgin olive oil, produced with great pride by both Jews and Arabs. In both the Galilee and the Negev, travellers will often come across family-run roadside eateries where local farmers sell their own produce, such as delicious honey.

tomato, cucumber oil and lemon), *babaghanoush* (aubergine baked for a smoky flavour and then puréed), along with pickled vegetables and olives. *Kibbe* (cracked wheat and minced meat croquettes with onions and pine nuts) are among the few non-vegetarian dishes.

### FRESH FRUIT

The Bible is filled with references to the produce of the land, and today the Holy Land grows not only ancient favourites such as grapes, pomegranates, figs and dates, but also citrus fruits, which have been exported to Europe under the Jaffa labels, since the 19th century. The largest type of citrus is the pomelo, a thick-skinned fruit that can grow to the size of a volleyball and is a speciality of the Jericho area. The fragrant Galia melon was developed in Israel. Watermelon is often eaten with chunks of salty Bulgarian cheese, similar to féta. Widely available exotic fruits include persimmon, kiwi and passionfruit.

Dried red peppers in the market at Shuk Levinsky, Tel Aviv

### ON THE MENU

**Baklava** Honey-soaked chopped nut and filo pastries.

**Cholent** Sabbath lunch stew of beef, potatoes, carrots, barley, onions and beans.

**Knafeh** Palestinian pastry of cheese, crunchy wheat threads and very sweet syrup.

**Kugel** Egg noodle casserole, either sweet or savoury.

**Labane** Sharp, spreadable white "yoghurt" cheese, often preserved in olive oil

**Za'atar** Seasoning mix of hyssop, sesame seeds and salt.

**Zchug** fiery red or green Yemenite condiment.

**Falafel** *are deep-fried balls of mashed chickpeas (garbanzos) served stuffed into a pitta bread with salad.*

**Tilapia,** *or St Peter's Fish, is popular around the Sea of Galilee, simply grilled and served with lemon slices.*

**Jerusalem salad** *is a meal in itself with olives, féta, and sometimes pomegranate and za'atar sprinkled over.*

# What to Drink in Jerusalem and the Holy Land

**Tea with fresh mint leaves**

Jews and Arabs alike adore coffee but have different ways of making it. It will be offered to you at any hour of the day or night. Teas of many kinds and herbal infusions are also popular. However, the hot, very dry climate makes water of the utmost importance. It is advisable to carry a bottle of it with you at all times and drink some before you feel thirsty to avoid dehydration. Israel now produces a lot of wine of medium to high quality, but it tends to be expensive. Beer is available in all the areas covered in this guide, but neither the Israelis nor the Arabs consume large quantities, preferring to go to cafés or coffeeshops for socializing.

**Enjoying outdoor café life on traffic-free Lunz Street in Jerusalem**

## WATER AND SOFT DRINKS

**Bottled water**

In the entire area described in this guide, bottled mineral water is readily available everywhere. Although tap water throughout Israel is safe to drink, it is more advisable to drink bottled water because it tastes better, especially in the Red Sea area, where tap water is so heavily chlorinated that it is unpalatable. Always make sure that the bottle is sealed when you buy water.

Bottled fruit juice is also popular, but remember that even juices that are sold as "natural" are really long-life juices produced on an industrial scale. Fruit juices freshly squeezed in front of you, especially citrus and pomegranate, are very good. All non-alcoholic beverages except for freshly-squeezed juice are almost always served very cold and with a lot of ice (which may be made of heavily chlorinated water), so if you don't want your drinks this way, remember to say so when ordering.

## BEERS AND SPIRITS

Many restaurants and cafés have draught beer, most of which is locally produced. The main Israeli beers are Maccabee, a slightly bitter, light lager, and Goldstar, which is reminiscent of British ale with a dash of malt. Taybeeh, similar to light, south German beer, is found in the Palestinian regions, East Jerusalem and some Israeli bars. Carlsberg is produced in Israel and Heineken in Jordan, both under licence, while most other major European brands are imported, especially into Israel.

Spirits are less widely available, but are always sold in hotel bars throughout the region. The commonest is arak, the typical Mediterranean distillate of anise.

**Goldstar beer**     **Arak**

## COFFEE AND TEA

In Jewish areas, coffee and tea are drunk in European- or American-style cafés. The most widely available type of coffee is filter coffee, which is always served for breakfast in hotels. Many places also offer espresso coffee, but it is almost always rather weak. For a real espresso, you must ask for a *katzar* (strong coffee). What is called cappuccino almost always has a huge amount of whipped cream added to it. Tea is almost invariably served in tea-bag form, and caffeine-free herbal tea (*zmachim*) is becoming increasingly popular.

Tea and coffee in Arab areas are drunk in coffeehouses (*qahwa*), which serve nothing else – except sometimes traditional water pipes (*nargileh*) to accompany the drink. Arabic coffee (also called *qahwa*) is

**Elaborate Arabic coffee set**

strong and aromatic because of the spices, in particular the cardamom, added to it. It is served in tiny cups holding only a few sips. If you do not specify little or no sugar, it always arrives heavily sweetened. To avoid a gritty texture, allow the sediment to settle in the cup first.

Arabic tea *(shai)* is more aromatic and stronger than Western-style tea and is also drunk without milk and with a lot of sugar. In restaurants it is often served after a meal with fresh mint leaves (*naana*).

In Arab coffeehouses, if you want Western-style tea, ask for *shai-Libton*; in Arab or Jewish establishments, for Western-style coffee ask for *nes* (short for Nescafé).

# WINE

Although the middle east was the home of grape cultivation and wine-making, the first two modern wineries in the Holy Land were founded in the mid-19th century. They belonged to Baron Rothschild (at Zikhron Yaakov, not far from Caesarea) and the Salesian fathers (at Cremisan, near Bethlehem). The Salesian estate is still operating. For years it was the only producer of good, dry white wine, but its standards were later matched by the Latrun Trappist monks' winery, which has French vines and uses French wine-making techniques.

**An Israeli Chardonnay**

The number of vineyards then increased steadily and wine quality has improved dramatically since the early 1980s. The main wine areas are now: Golan and Upper Galilee at around 500 m (1,640 ft) above sea level, with ideal volcanic soil; Lower Galilee, the Jezreel Valley, the Mount Carmel region and Sharon, which are lower and more humid; Samson, the coastal plain south of Tel Aviv; and the hills of Judaea, which have poorer terrain and are very dry. A number of experimental vineyards in the Negev Desert are now in production.

The largest producers are the Carmel Winery, based in Zikhron Yaakov, whose Mizrachi "Private" series is especially good, and the Golan Heights Winery, based in Katsrin, whose main labels are Golan, Yarden, Gamla and Tishbi. Wines from small producers such as Kibbutz Tsora can be excellent.

Jordanian and Egyptian wines are very poor value for their price and, in both countries, imported wine is prohibitively expensive.

**Israeli white wines**, *especially the Chardonnays and Sauvignon Blancs, are generally very enjoyable: often aromatic, sometimes fruity, smooth and full-bodied. Many of the reasonably-priced whites are produced by the Golan Heights Winery.*

## WINE-GROWING REGIONS OF ISRAEL

**KEY**

- Golan, Galilee and the Jezreel Valley
- Mt Carmel and Sharon
- Samson
- Judaean Hills
- Negev Experimental Areas

**Israeli red wines** *are also good, but, with some notable exceptions, tend either to lack body or to be slightly heavy. The grapes most commonly used are Carignan, Cabernet Sauvignon and Merlot, with many wines being a blend of the last two. Among the wines now produced by a growing number of small-scale, specialist wine makers are the fine Cabernets produced by Castel, and the Margalit reds.*

**Yarden white**    **Gamla Chardonnay**    **Tishbi Muscat**

**Carmel Mizrachi**    **Margalit red**    **Kibbutz Tsora**

# Choosing a Restaurant

The restaurants listed here have been selected for their good food, atmosphere and location within the Jerusalem area. The symbols cover some of the factors which may influence your choice (see back cover flap for key). For Jerusalem map references, see the Street Finder on pages 156–9; for restaurants further afield see back endpaper.

**PRICE CATEGORIES**
Prices are based on a three-course meal for one including coffee, tax and service.
Ⓢ Under $15
ⓈⓈ $15–$30
ⓈⓈⓈ $30–$60
ⓈⓈⓈⓈ Over $60

## THE MUSLIM QUARTER

### Abu Shukri  Ⓢ
*63 El-Wad St, cnr Via Dolorosa, 97500* **Tel** *(02) 627 1538*                                        **Map** *4 D2*

This small, simple restaurant, on the main street leading from Damascus Gate into the Muslim Quarter, is renowned for its plates of houmous, topped with whole chickpeas and freshly chopped parsley. It also serves up tahini, freshly baked bread and lots of other dishes. Excellent quality and very reasonable prices.

### Quarter Café  ⓈⓈ
*Tiferet Yisrael St, 97500* **Tel** *(02) 628 7770*                                        **Map** *4 D4*

Known more for its view of the Temple Mount and the Mount of Olives than for its cuisine, this dairy place serves café fare and light snacks. The food is not particularly exciting, but this café is a good stopping-off point in the Jewish Quarter as it is situated just up the hill from the Western Wall.

## MODERN JERUSALEM

### Big Apple  Ⓢ
*13 Dorot Rishonim St, 94625* **Tel** *(02) 625 6252*                                        **Map** *1 A3*

In the pedestrian zone just off Ben Yehuda St, this pizzeria serves New York-style thin-crust pizzas and is especially popular with Orthodox Jewish teenagers from New York who are in Jerusalem to take intensive religious studies courses. The restaurant is open until late and also offers a takeaway service.

### Burgers Bar  Ⓢ
*20 Emeq Refaim St, German Colony, 93105* **Tel** *(02) 561 2333*

Acclaimed by many Jerusalem old-timers as having the city's best hamburgers, this popular place also serves up other types of reasonably priced meat dishes. It is situated about 1 km (half a mile) south of the King David Hotel in the atmospheric German Colony, in the heart of a strip of popular cafés and restaurants.

### Pinati  Ⓢ
*13 King George St, 94229* **Tel** *(02) 625 4540*                                        **Map** *1 A3*

Situated at the spot where Ben Hillel St meets King George St at an oblique angle (hence the name, which means "on the corner"), this popular eatery has long been regarded by many local connoisseurs as the source of the city's most delicious houmous – creamy, delicately seasoned, never too heavy.

### Rahmo  Ⓢ
*5 Eshkol St, Mahane Yehuda, 94322* **Tel** *(02) 623 4595*

A Jerusalem institution, Rahmo serves Israeli and Aleppo-style cuisine as well as authentic Jerusalem houmous prepared according to a secret recipe from the owner's mother. Situated on one of the tiny pedestrianized alleyways in the colourful Mahane Yehuda market, which is a feast for the eyes as well as the stomach.

### Agas ve-Tapuach ba-Kikar  ⓈⓈ
*6 Safra Square, 94141* **Tel** *(02) 623 0280*                                        **Map** *1 B3*

Known in Italian as Pera e Mela in Piazza (The Pear and the Apple on the Square), this venerable Italian restaurant has been serving home-style Italian cuisine, made with recipes from the owner's grandparents, since 1978. Dishes come from both northern and southern Italy and include antipasti, foccacia, bruschetta and, of course, pasta.

### Barood  ⓈⓈ
*31 Jaffa St, 94221* **Tel** *(02) 625 9081*                                        **Map** *1 A3*

Just off Jaffa St on Feingold Courtyard, this laid-back, stone-built place is known for its Spanioli (Sepharadi) cuisine, as well as its juicy steaks and heavenly chocolate soufflé. The bar is decorated with a surprising collection of bottle openers and offers a wide selection of alcoholic beverages. Hosts art exhibits and live concerts of mellow music.

**Key to Symbols** *see back cover flap*

## Focaccia Bar

$$

*4 Rabi Akiva St, 94582* **Tel** *(02) 624 2273*    **Map** *1 A3*

Situated on a quaint courtyard, this romantic place, built entirely of stone, is evocative of the early 1900s. Specialities include meat dishes, pasta, seafood, salads and, naturally, focaccia. Situated in the heart of West Jerusalem, two blocks south of Ben Yehuda St and just off Hillel St.

## HaShipudia
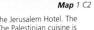
$$

*5 HaArmonim St, Mahane Yehuda, 94322* **Tel** *(02) 625 4036*

In the heart of the Mahane Yehuda market, this good-value eatery serves a range of excellent local dishes, including soups, stuffed vegetables, houmous and grilled meats. Situated just one block west of the main street of Jerusalem's largest fruit and vegetable market. For dessert, try one of the nearby pastry shops.

## Kan Zaman

$$

*Nablus Rd, 97200* **Tel** *(02) 628 3282*    **Map** *1 C2*

Situated in a 19th-century house just north of Damascus Gate, this is the restaurant of the Jerusalem Hotel. The vaulted ceilings, shaded terrace and Oriental decor create a typically Arab atmosphere. The Palestinian cuisine is carefully prepared. There are often live concerts of Arab music on Friday from 8pm.

## Link
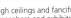
$$

*3 HaMaalot St, 94263* **Tel** *(02) 625 3446*

Housed in a century-old Jerusalem-style building, this café-bistro is known for its superb spicy chicken wings, made with soy sauce and honey, its juicy steaks and, for vegetarians, the soy-and-honey tofu salad. Link has a generously shaded terrace and a congenial atmosphere. It is situated just off King George St, across from Independence Park.

## Mona
$$

*12 Shmuel HaNagid St, 94592* **Tel** *(02) 622 2283*

Housed in the historic, stone-built home of the century-old Bezalel Art School, with its high ceilings and fanciful crenellations, this café-restaurant combines great food with a magical, arty Jerusalem atmosphere and exhibits of contemporary and historic Israeli art. The cuisine is international and includes salads, soups, antipasti and meat dishes.

## Shanti

$$

*4 Nahalat Shiva St, 94240* **Tel** *(02) 624 3434*    **Map** *1 A3*

On a tiny alleyway in the 19th-century Nahalat Yitzhak quarter, this pub-restaurant is popular with young and old alike. Served in a warm and authentic Jerusalem atmosphere, the salads are huge, as are the steaks. The chicken wings prepared with soy sauce, honey and ginger are delicious. Open only in the evening, from 7pm to 3am.

## Shonka

$$

*1 HaSoreg St, 94145* **Tel** *(02) 625 7033*    **Map** *1 A3*

Highlights at this elegant, Italian bar-restaurant include fish, hamburgers and various Mediterranean-style dishes. The lunch specials are particularly good value. The venue becomes a dance bar on weekends. Situated around the corner from where Shlomtzion Hamalka St joins Jaffa Road, just south of the Russian Compound.

## Te'enim
$$

*12 Emile Botta St, 94109* **Tel** *(02) 625 1967*    **Map** *1 B4*

Beautifully situated at the northern edge of Yemin Moshe, in an old stone building known as Beit HaKonfederatzia, this small place is one of Jerusalem's oldest, and best, vegetarian restaurants. The decor is modern, with Armenian ceramic highlights. Diners enjoy a superb panorama of the walls of the Old City and Mount Zion.

## Village Green
$$

*33 Jaffa St, 94221* **Tel** *(02) 625 3065*    **Map** *1 A3*

In the low-rise,19th-century Nahalat Shiva quarter, this veteran vegetarian restaurant serves up everything from miso soup and Greek salad to quiches, ratatouille, lasagna and tofu dishes. Culinary inspiration comes from Europe, Africa, the Middle East and the Mediterranean Basin. Dessert options include fresh, healthy, home-made cakes.

## Adom
$$$

*31 Jaffa St, 94221* **Tel** *(02) 624 6242*    **Map** *1 A3*

On the 19th-century Feingold Courtyard, this restaurant and wine bar serves meat, fish, seafood and vegetable dishes in the traditions of France and Belgium, with light Israeli touches. The daily specials are based on seasonal products fresh from the market. Great selection of wines and beers. Good value business lunch specials.

## Anashim
$$$

*73 Ein Karem St, Ein Karem, 95744* **Tel** *(02) 641 7430*

In the pastoral neighbourhood of Ein Karem, on the far western edge of Jerusalem, this rustic, informal restaurant has a great atmosphere and tasty international cuisine, including focaccia baked in a traditional oven. Specialities include shrimps in a butter, wine and lemon sauce and chicken breast stuffed with goat's cheese.

## Arabesque

$$$

*23 Nablus Rd, 97200* **Tel** *(02) 627 9777*    **Map** *1 C1*

The elegant house restaurant of the legendary American Colony Hotel serves a fine selection of hearty, traditional Arab dishes, some based on lamb, as well as European cuisine and, often, a few off-beat surprises. The wine cellar is excellent and the Saturday lunch buffet is legendary. Turkish-style courtyard and lovely gardens.

### Darna

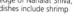

3 Horkanos St, 94235 **Tel** (02) 624 5406 $$$

**Map** 1 A3

Moorish-inspired decor, Moroccan ceramics and lots of cushions adorn this gourmet Moroccan restaurant, whose name means "our home" in Arabic. Specialities include meze, *harira marrakshia* (veal and lentil soup made with fresh coriander) and *mechoui* (roast lamb with almonds). Situated two blocks north of Jaffa St.

### Dolphin Yam

9 Shimon Ben Shetah St, 94147 **Tel** (02) 623 2272 $$$

**Map** 1 A3

For some four decades a Jerusalem favourite for fresh fish and seafood, this place, on the edge of Nahalat Shiva, also serves meat dishes and pasta. The decor is understated and informal. Recommended dishes include shrimp in cream sauce and grilled whole calamari. Has a wide selection of fried or grilled fish.

### Jacksi

1 Shlomtzion HaMalka St, 94146 **Tel** (02) 622 2527 $$$

**Map** 1 A3

This elegant French restaurant, with a French-trained chef and an extensive international wine list, serves creative, artfully presented dishes in a sleek, modern dining room. Favourites include shrimp sautéed with hot chillis and cream, and lamb in pepper sauce. The fixed price menus offer great value. The soundtrack is classic jazz.

### Philadelphia

9 El-Zahra St, 97200 **Tel** (02) 628 9770 $$$

**Map** 2 D2

One of East Jerusalem's best-known Arab restaurants, Philadelphia is much appreciated for its Palestinian-style stuffed vegetables, spit-roasted meats, fish (including St Peter's fish) and seafood. The ambience is welcoming, if a little formal. Live music on Friday from 9pm. Three blocks north of the Old City's Herod's Gate, which leads to the Muslim Quarter.

### Sakura

31 Jaffa St, 94221 **Tel** (02) 623 5464 $$$

**Map** 1 A3

Acclaimed as the city's best sushi bar and Japanese restaurant, this place has authentic Japanese furnishings. Sushi and sashimi, served on little wooden platters, are classic mainstays but you can also order dishes such as tempura with almonds and chicken yakitori. Drinks include sake and Japanese beers. Situated on the edge of Nahalat Shiva.

### Taverna

2 Naomi St, Abu Tor, 93552 **Tel** (02) 671 9796 $$$

A classy, contemporary restaurant that has rave reviews, Taverna is situated in elegant stone pavilion on the Sherover Promenade. It offers a superb panorama over southeast Jerusalem, towards the Dead Sea and the mountains of Jordan. Food is non-meat and Mediterranean in style; desserts are particularly good. Situated off Hebron Road.

### Tmol Shilshom

5 Yoel Moshe Salomon St, 91316 **Tel** (02) 623 2758 $$$

**Map** 1 A3

Hidden at the end of a Nahalat Shiva courtyard in a private house built in the 1870s is this mellow café-restaurant-bookshop. Dining options include superb whole trout, soups, quiches, creative salads, pasta and stuffed mushrooms. Great for a quiet conversation. Has a superb Friday morning buffet (9am to 1pm). Reservations are recommended.

### Arcadia

10 Agripas St, 94301 **Tel** (02) 624 9138 $$$$

One of Israel's most talked-about restaurants, Arcadia is next to Mahane Yehuda market and its super-fresh ingredients. French and Mediterranean traditions are skillfully brought together with dishes from the Jerusalem-Sepharadi tradition and the chef's family's native Iraq to produce cuisine that is uniquely Israeli. Reservations advisable.

### Cavalier

1 Ben Sira St, 94181 **Tel** (02) 624 2945 $$$$

**Map** 1 A3

This up-market French bistro and bar, in Nahalat Shiva, offers classic French cuisine as well as Mediterranean-influenced dishes, all made with only the freshest ingredients and presented with supreme elegance. Dishes include entrecote in pepper and cream sauce and chocolate volcano dessert. Good deals between noon and 3:30pm.

## FURTHER AFIELD

### Abu Shukri

4 Mahmoud Rashid St, Abu Ghosh, 90845 **Tel** (02) 533 4963 $

About 10 km (6 miles) west of Jerusalem (along the highway to Tel Aviv) in Abu Ghosh, near the top of the hill, this lively, informal restaurant is renowned for its houmous. Has splendid views over the valley below and of its great rival, another houmous eatery run by a cousin, and also called Abu Shukri. A second branch is being opened on HaShalom St.

### Elvis American Diner

Neve Ilan, 90850 **Tel** (02) 534 1275 $$

A 1950s-style American diner dedicated to worship of the King of Rock 'n Roll is not what you would expect to find in the Judean Hills, 12 km (7 miles) west of Jerusalem. This proudly kitsch place was founded in the 1970s by a dedicated local Elvis fan and serves both American and Middle Eastern food. The sound track, though, is pure Elvis.

**Key to Price Guide** see p272 **Key to Symbols** see back cover flap

# THE COAST AND GALILEE

### AKKO Humous Sa'eid
*Market, Old City* **Tel** *(04) 991 3945*

Map B2

A perennial contender for the title of "Israel's best houmous restaurant", this small, unpretentious place has fast, efficient service, incredibly reasonable prices and houmous that melts in your mouth. Situated in the heart of the Old City market – just ask anyone for directions. Open only for breakfast and lunch, from 6am to 2:30pm.

### AKKO Uri Buri
*Lighthouse Square, Old City, 24713* **Tel** *(04) 955 2212*

Map B2

Considered to be one of the best places in Israel for fish and seafood, this restaurant has attentive, personal service and some unconventional menu items. The chef loves to serve meals based on lots of different dishes, with everyone at the table sharing them. Regulars say the daily special, whatever it is, is almost always a good bet.

### BETH SHE'AN Herb Farm on Mount Gilboa
*Hwy 667, Mount Gilboa, 19122* **Tel** *(04) 653 1093*

Map C2

The Mediterranean and Israeli dishes at this country-style restaurant receive consistently excellent reviews, as do the fresh mountain air and the panoramic views of Mount Gilboa. Specialities include salads, home-made bread and pumpkin soup with apples and sour cream. Situated 10 km (6 miles) southeast of Afula on Hwy 667.

### CAESAREA Pundak HaTzalbanim
*Old City, 30889* **Tel** *(04) 636 1679*

Map B2

Overlooking the Mediterranean and Caesarea's ancient port, this classy place serves Mediterranean-style fish and seafood, such as crab in white wine and garlic sauce. Also has chicken and meat dishes, and for dessert, *crème brulée*. The service is attentive, the views breathtaking and the seaside atmosphere perfect for a romantic meal.

### GOLAN HEIGHTS Mis'edet HaShalom
*Southern entrance to Mas'adeh, 12435* **Tel** *(04) 687 0359*

Map C1

In one of the four Druze villages on the Golan Heights, this restaurant serves excellent Druze cooking. Options include salads (such as cabbage seasoned with the spice sumac), sour *labaneh* cheese, houmous, sesame-coated *falafel*, soups, grilled meats and fish. Traditional desserts are available here or at the nearby Abu Zayd sweet shop.

### HAIFA Falafel HaZekenim
*18 HaWadi St, Wadi Nisnas, 33044* **Tel** *(04) 851 4959*

Map B2

This veteran establishment, on a lively street in the mainly Arab Wadi Nisnas neighbourhood (four blocks southeast of the German Colony), serves what some say is the best *falafel* in the country. Made according to a secret recipe, the fried green chickpea balls are crispy and always fresh. Guests are greeted with a *falafel* ball dipped in *tahina*.

### HAIFA Shwarma Hazan
*140 Jaffa Rd, 35252* **Tel** *(04) 855 8075*

Map B2

Confirming Haifa's position as a quality leader in the Israeli street food scene, this place is acclaimed by many as serving nothing less than the best *shwarma* in Israel. Situated on the main thoroughfare of the flat, sea-level part of the city, a few blocks south of Rambam Hospital and just a block from the Commonwealth Military Cemetery.

### HAIFA Duzan
*35 Ben Gurion Ave, German Colony, 35021* **Tel** *(04) 852 5444*

Map B2

East meets West in the form of delicious cuisine at this attractive restaurant and bar, ensconced in a German Templar house built in 1870. Menu items come from Lebanon (*kubbe*, *sambusak*, stuffed grape leaves), Italy and France. The interior mixes modern design with antique furnishings and a colourful tiled floor. There's a tree-shaded patio.

### HAIFA Fattoush
*38 Ben Gurion Ave, German Colony, 35023* **Tel** *(04) 852 4930*

Map B2

The specialities at this restaurant, a favourite of Haifa's Jewish and Arab elite, include Lebanese *fatoush* salad (fried pieces of pitta, cucumbers and tomatoes seasoned with olive oil, lemon and sumac) and, for dessert, *knafeh*. Diners can sit outside or on Damascene silk couches along the walls of a barrel-vaulted, Oriental-style chamber.

### KIRYAT SHEMONA Dag Al HaDan
*Just north of Kibbutz HaGoshrim, 11016* **Tel** *(04) 695 0225*

Map C1

Situated 5 km (3 miles) east of Kiryat Shemona at the confluence of two major tributaries of the Jordan, the Dan and the Hatzbani, this non-meat restaurant has specialized in freshwater and saltwater fish since 1986. Other popular options include sandwiches, salads, pasta and cakes. Surrounded by a lush forest of willow, fig and plane trees.

### KIRYAT SHEMONA Dagei Dafna
*Kibbutz Dafna, 12235* **Tel** *(04) 694 1154*

Map C1

Right next to a trout farm so you know what you are eating is fresh, this rural and very informal fish restaurant is situated on the Dan River, a short walk from the Horshat Tal park. It has seating inside a rough-hewn, wooden structure and outside on shaded picnic benches. The menu also includes salads, chicken and steak.

### KIRYAT SHEMONA Focaccia Bar

$$$

*Gan HaTzafon, Hwy 99, near Kibbutz HaGoshrim* **Tel** *(04) 690 4474* **Map** *C1*

Very popular with locals, this eatery also attracts visitors from around the country, especially after they have spent the day exploring the Galilee Panhandle and the Golan. Has a wide selection of tasty, reasonably-priced dishes of generous proportions, including salads, juicy steaks, fish, seafood and pizza. A good choice for families.

### KIRYAT SHEMONA HaTachana

$$$$$

*1 HaRishonim St, Metulla, 10292* **Tel** *(04) 694 4810* **Map** *C1*

Situated 8 km (5 miles) north of Kiryat Shemona in the charming border village of Metulla, this romantic, if somewhat pricey, restaurant is named after a nearby waterfall. It receives excellent reviews for its attentive service and succulent meat dishes, especially the steaks. Reservations are recommended.

### KIRYAT SHEMONA Nechalim

$$$$$

*Gan HaTzafon, Hwy 99, near Kibbutz HaGoshrim* **Tel** *(04) 690 4875* **Map** *C1*

Revered by locals as one of the area's finest restaurants, this romantic, country-style venue delivers a truly first-rate dining experience on the banks of a tributary of the Jordan. The menu is Italian- and French-influenced and the speciality is fresh fish, but seafood and meat dishes are also served. Surrounded by rich vegetation and delightful views.

### NAZARETH Diana

$$$

*51 Paul VI St, 16224* **Tel** *(04) 657 2919* **Map** *B2*

The most famous restaurant in Nazareth, this unpretentious, white-tablecloth place is known for its meat dishes, which range from lamb chops to Arab-style kebab and *shishlik*, and for its *meze* salads, including *tabouleh*, *houmous* and *fatoush*. Also on offer are steaks, fish, seafood and several dozen sorts of wine.

### ROSH PINA Doris Katzavim

$$$

*Main road, Rosh Pina, 12000* **Tel** *(04) 680 1313* **Map** *C2*

After hard a day's Galilee or Golan hiking, this is a good place for a hearty, meaty meal. Specialities, many made with Golan Heights-grown beef, include steaks (New York, Porter House), lamb chops and hamburgers, all of generous proportions. Main courses come with a selection of *meze* salads.

### ROSH PINA Auberge Shulamit

$$$$$

*David Shuv St, 12000* **Tel** *(04) 693 1485* **Map** *C2*

A sophisticated, country-style restaurant in the charming Galilee village of Rosh Pina. Specialities include stuffed vine leaves, seasonal soups, home-smoked goose breast, shrimp in Roquefort sauce, buffalo wings, sautéed trout and *filet mignon*. Outstanding *tarte Tatin* is a good dessert choice. Perfect for a romantic dinner. Reservations recommended.

### ROSH PINA Pina BaRosh

$$$$$

*8 HeChalutzim St, 12000* **Tel** *(04) 693 7028* **Map** *C2*

This rustic, stone-built restaurant, just a short stroll from Rosh Pina's famous art galleries, affords panoramic views of the Hula Valley, the Golan Heights and often-snow-capped Mount Hermon. The French-inspired onion soup, hen-on-rice with lentils, fish dishes, *entrecote* and pasta all get excellent reviews, as does the personalized service.

### SEA OF GALILEE Ein Camonim

$$$

*Hwy 85, 10 km west of Amiad Junction, 20109* **Tel** *(04) 698 9680* **Map** *C2*

Located on a family-run dairy farm in the rugged hills and olive trees northwest of Tabkha is this very rustic, vegetarian eatery. It is known for its fresh, farm-grown products, including goat's cheeses, olive oil and ice cream, and for its all-you-can-eat cheese meals, served with lemonade and red or white wine. Cosy fireplace in winter.

### SEA OF GALILEE Ein Gev Fish Restaurant

$$$

*Kibbutz Ein Gev, 14940* **Tel** *(04) 665 8136* **Map** *C2*

On the eastern shore of the Sea of Galilee, this rather utilitarian restaurant is right on the water, near a swimming beach and a lakefront promenade. It has had a loyal following for decades thanks to the reasonable prices and excellent baked, fried and grilled fish, served with salad, French fries and pickles/gherkins. Also has pasta and quiche.

### SEA OF GALILEE Vered HaGalil

$$$

*Hwy 90, Corazim Junction, 12928* **Tel** *(04) 693 5785* **Map** *C2*

On a family-run horse ranch that rents out rooms, this rustic, vaguely American-style restaurant, built of local boulders and wood beams, garners enthusiastic reviews. Specialities include juicy steaks, hamburgers, chicken dishes, salmon and aubergine lasagna. Children's meals available. Situated 5 km (3 miles) north of Capernaum.

### SEA OF GALILEE Yarden

$$$$$

*Beit Gavriel, Tzemah, 15132* **Tel** *(04) 670 9302* **Map** *C2*

At the far southern tip of the Sea of Galilee, this non-meat restaurant, inside the stunning Beit Gavriel cultural centre, affords unsurpassed views of the sea and the Golan. Specializes in fresh fish and Italian dishes (pizza, pasta, lasagna) but also serves meal-sized salads, stuffed mushrooms, quiche and a good selection of classic desserts.

### TEL AVIV Aboulafia Bakery

$

*7 Yefet St, Jaffa, 68028* **Tel** *(03) 683 4958* **Map** *B3*

A visit to this bakery is a classic Jaffa experience that has been enjoyed for decades – queuing on the pavement at the high glass counters and choosing fresh pittas and sesame rolls topped, or filled, with *za'atar*, olives, a fried egg or cheese. Purchases are best enjoyed as a picnic in nearby Old Jaffa, overlooking the sea or in the hilltop park.

**Key to Price Guide** *see p272* **Key to Symbols** *see back cover flap*

### TEL AVIV Ashkara
⑤

*45 Yermiyahu St, 62594* **Tel** *(03) 546 4547*   **Map** *B3*

Everyone has an opinion on where to find Tel Aviv's best houmous and houmous comparisons often arouse great passions, but Ashkara is certainly a contender. It is situated just a block from Park HaYarkon, Tel Aviv's "Central Park", where lawns, lakes and bike paths stretch along the Yarkon River eastwards from the old Tel Aviv Port.

### TEL AVIV Iceberg
⑤

*108 Ben Yehuda St, 63401* **Tel** *(03) 522 5025*   **Map** *B3*

This ice cream parlour serves the city's best ice cream, sorbet and frozen yogurt. Tel Aviv has some fine gelaterias, but Iceberg's products, made on the premises from all-natural ingredients, are in a class of their own. Photos of huge, natural chunks of ice adorn the walls.

### TEL AVIV Barbunia
⑤⑤

*192 Ben Yehuda St, 63471* **Tel** *(03) 524 0961*   **Map** *B3*

A simple, immaculate restaurant, Barbunia is small but popular and serves excellent fresh fish at reasonable prices. The service is quick and professional. The restaurant is situated two blocks inland from the Hilton Hotel tower and from a cliff that overlooks the beach. Barbunia's bar is just across the street.

### TEL AVIV Boya
⑤⑤

*3 HaTa'arukha St, Tel Aviv Port, 63509* **Tel** *(03) 544 6166*   **Map** *B3*

Situated in the north-western corner of the old Tel Aviv Port, one of the city's major dining and nightlife districts, this chic restaurant has an outside bar so close to the Mediterranean that you could fish while eating your tapas, focaccia, linguini, steak or *Tarte Tatin*. Perfect for a romantic snack or drink, especially as the sun sets.

### TEL AVIV Elimelech
⑤⑤

*35 Wolfson St, Florentine, 66528* **Tel** *(03) 681 4545*   **Map** *B3*

This quaint restaurant, in the rundown but lively Florentine district of south Tel Aviv, serves traditional Eastern European Jewish food, including chopped liver, chicken soup with *kneidelach* (matza balls), steamed cabbage and *schnitzel*. Traditional *cholent* is the big hit on Saturday. Also serves excellent on-tap beer.

### TEL AVIV Frida Hecht
⑤⑤

*20 Ben Yehuda St, 63802* **Tel** *(03) 620 1471*   **Map** *B3*

Once a home delivery service for ethnic Jewish food, this is now an informal, cafeteria-style restaurant with good prices and some excellent home-style cooking. Regulars recommend the lovingly made *gefilte* fish, meatballs, *madjadra* (rice with lentils) and *mafrum* (Libyan-style potatoes stuffed with meat). Open until 7pm, closed Sunday.

### TEL AVIV Lehem Erez
⑤⑤

*53 Ibn Gabirol St, 64361* **Tel** *(03) 696 9381*   **Map** *B3*

A Tel Aviv institution, this popular place is the original venue of what is now a growing chain. It specializes in gourmet sandwiches, some of them with an unexpected fusion of flavours, and excellent, fresh salads. Lehem Erez is also a good place for breakfast. It sits on a main avenue that, in recent years, has become Tel Aviv's hottest café strip.

### TEL AVIV Maganda
⑤⑤

*26 Rabi Meir St, Kerem ha-Teymanim, 65605* **Tel** *(03) 517 9990*   **Map** *B3*

On a narrow street in the old Yemenite quarter, very near the bustling Carmel Market, this Middle Eastern meat restaurant is friendly and down-to-earth. It specializes in carnivorous treats such as grilled steak, *shishlik* and kebabs. Meals begin with a big selection of *meze*, stuffed vegetables and Moroccan-style, meat-filled "cigars".

### TEL AVIV Moon
⑤⑤

*58 Bugrashov St, 63145* **Tel** *(03) 629 1155*   **Map** *B3*

On a street that leads to the sea and is home to a number of relaxed cafés, this sushi bar has sleek, modern decor and a conveyor belt for the transport of raw fish delicacies. Prices are reasonable and quality is high, attracting a loyal following. *Yakitori* and *tempura* are also on offer. Good-value business lunches from noon to 6pm, except Saturday.

### TEL AVIV Orna v'Ela
⑤⑤

*33 Sheinkin St, 65232* **Tel** *(03) 620 4753*   **Map** *B3*

This creative, Israeli-style café and restaurant, long a fixture on Tel Aviv's most Bohemian (and now Bohemian-chic) street, serves both home-style and gourmet dishes. Favourites range from goat kebab and pumpkin *kubbe* to pasta and gnocchi with mozzarella and parmesan. Breads are baked fresh every morning. Delicious desserts.

### TEL AVIV Susannah
⑤⑤

*9 Shabazi St, 65150* **Tel** *(03) 517 7580*   **Map** *B3*

In the increasingly chic 19th-century Neve Tzedek district, this café-restaurant is across the street from the Susan Dallal Cultural Centre, the city's premier dance venue. Mediterranean and home-style Israeli specialities, served on a shaded balcony, include hearty soups, generous salads, *kubbe*, stuffed vegetables and grilled meats. Great breakfasts.

### TEL AVIV Brasserie
⑤⑤⑤

*70 Ibn Gabirol St, 64952* **Tel** *(03) 696 7111*   **Map** *B3*

Dining at this café-bistro, facing Rabin Square, is like a quick trip to Paris. The excellent, traditional French cuisine includes oysters (a rare treat in Israel), *bouillabaisse*, juicy pepper steak, *coq au vin* and *cassoulet* (every Saturday). Reservations are recommended in the evening. Friday brunch is served from 7am to 5pm. Open 24 hours a day.

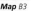

### TEL AVIV Brew House

11 Rothschild Blvd, 66881 **Tel** (03) 516 8666    ⑤⑤⑤

*Map B3*

This micro-brewery, with bulbous copper brewing tanks as the centrepiece, has the sort of warm, beer-infused atmosphere and meaty menu selection that you would expect to find in Düsseldorf or Stuttgart. Main course options include steak, spare ribs, bratwurst, buffalo wings, chicken breast in BBQ sauce, fish and seafood.

### TEL AVIV Dim Sum

120 Allenby St, 65818 **Tel** (03) 560 4341    ⑤⑤⑤

*Map B3*

On the corner of Rothschild Ave in the "City", Tel Aviv's banking and insurance district, this restaurant offers a refined Chinese dining experience. The speciality is steamed and fried dim sum with fillings that range from goose to seafood to vegetables, but rice and egg noodle dishes, soups and sushi are also on offer.

### TEL AVIV Il Pastaio

27 Ibn Gabirol St, 64078 **Tel** (03) 525 1166    ⑤⑤⑤

*Map B3*

Walk into this restaurant and you will feel almost like you are in Italy. The home-made pasta, lasagna and risotto with porcini mushrooms garner rave reviews. The tiramisu, too, is heavenly. Perfect for a long, slow, delicious meal. Open from noon to 3:30pm and 7 to 11pm; closed Sunday evening and Saturday.

### TEL AVIV Kyoto

7 Shenkar St, Herzliya Pituach, 46725 **Tel** (09) 958 7770    ⑤⑤⑤

*Map B3*

On a stylish street lined with trendy restaurants, packed at lunchtime with Israel's high-tech elite, this Japanese restaurant and sushi bar is known for its modern, Japanese-inspired decor, attentive service and professionally prepared cuisine. Tuna blue laguna (tuna braised on the outside, raw on the inside) is highly recommended.

### TEL AVIV Margaret Tayar

HaAliya HaSheniya Quay, Jaffa, 68128 **Tel** (03) 682 4741    ⑤⑤⑤

*Map B3*

Authentic Tunisian, Libyan and Mediterranean cuisine is what keeps bringing people back to this unpretentious, if somewhat pricey, place on the quay below Jaffa's Old City. The service is not quick but the specialities – fish, couscous with mutton and stuffed grape leaves – are very tasty indeed.

### TEL AVIV Nanouchka

28 Lilienblum St, 65133 **Tel** (03) 516 2254    ⑤⑤⑤

*Map B3*

Elegantly and very comfortably furnished, with one corner devoted to low seats with huge cushions, this restaurant is an excellent place to sample the little-known cuisine of the Caucasus nation of Georgia. Favourites include *badridjani* (aubergine stuffed with nuts), *lubio* (thick, sour bean soup) and *khachapuri* (cheese-filled pastries).

### TEL AVIV Orca Kitchen Bar

57 Nahalat Binyamin St, 65163 **Tel** (03) 566 5505    ⑤⑤⑤

*Map B3*

In a 1930s Bauhaus-style building in the historic Nahalat Binyamin area, this very civilized restaurant has elegant table settings, a sleek wooden bar and some surprising artwork on the walls. Fish and seafood, and a few meat dishes, are prepared with a distinct French accent and served with panache.

### TEL AVIV Unami

18 HaArba'a St, 64739 **Tel** (03) 562 1172    ⑤⑤⑤

*Map B3*

Situated on a street lined with trendy, excellent restaurants, this place is considered by local connoisseurs to be one of the city's finest purveyors of Japanese cuisine. Amid elegant surroundings, the outstanding dishes served here include a huge selection of sushi and sashimi. There's also a bar.

### TEL AVIV Yo'ezer Bar Yayin

2 Yo'ezer Ish HaBira St, Jaffa, 68027 **Tel** (03) 683 9115    ⑤⑤⑤

*Map B3*

Situated just outside Jaffa's picturesque Old City, around the corner from the Clock Tower, this very romantic wine bar and restaurant serves outstanding French-style delicacies such as oysters, beef *carpaccio*, salmon fillet and *boeuf bourguignon*. Exceptional selection of wines from Burgundy, Bordeaux, Tuscany and around the world.

### TEL AVIV Mul Yam

Hangar 24, Tel Aviv Port, 63506 **Tel** (03) 546 9920    ⑤⑤⑤⑤

*Map B3*

Israeli restaurants do not get any finer, more exclusive or pricier than this world-class seafood and fish place, in the midst of some of the city's most fashionable pubs, restaurants and nightspots. Specialities include Breton oysters, beef *carpaccio* with Jerusalem artichoke and asparagus, and various shrimp and lobster dishes. Incredible wine list.

## THE DEAD SEA AND THE NEGEV DESERT

### BETHLEHEM Al-Atlal

Manger St, Paradise Hotel **Tel** (02) 274 4542    ⑤⑤

*Map B3*

The sweet smell of *nargila* (water pipe) smoke often wafts through this Arab-style restaurant, decorated with Bedouin-inspired furnishings. Specialities include *gedra* (lamb and rice with yogurt sauce), 10 kinds of salad and grilled meats. Generally open only on weekends; reservations are recommended. Live music Saturday evening.

**Key to Price Guide** *see p272* **Key to Symbols** *see back cover flap*

### EILAT Last Refuge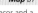
*Coral Beach, 88000* **Tel** *(08) 637 3627* **Map** *B7*

Several kilometres south of the city centre, this restaurant has some of the best fish and seafood in town. Seating is either inside, in a dining room decorated with old nautical equipment reminiscent of New England, or outside (except in winter). The calamari and *coquilles St Jacques* are especially good.

### EILAT Pastory
*7 Tarshish St, 88000* **Tel** *(08) 634 5111* **Map** *B7*

A little north of the main beach, this well-regarded Italian restaurant has slightly overdone rustic Italian decor and a kitchen area that is visible to diners. Specialities include *entrecote*, pasta with shrimp sauce and delicious desserts such as *tiramisu*. The pasta is fresh and home-made, as are the Tuscan-style sauces.

### EILAT Brasserie
*North Beach, 88000* **Tel** *(08) 636 3444* **Map** *B7*

Inside the King Solomon Hotel, this kosher establishment, with sparkling glasses on white tablecloths, is an ideal retreat for lovers of classic French cuisine, although influences from Italy and East Asia are also in evidence. Specialities range from beef Wellington and roasted goose with potato purée to fish and vegetable dishes.

### EILAT Chao-Phya
*Southern Beach, 88000* **Tel** *(08) 636 0360* **Map** *B7*

About 5 km (3 miles) south of town, inside the Orchid Hotel complex, this romantic Thai restaurant occupies a soaring, all-wood building brought over from Thailand, which is where the staff are from too. A great place to dine on delicious, spicy cuisine from another place and time, but with great views of the Gulf of Aqaba.

### JERICHO Al-Rawada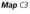
*Ket f'il Wad neighbourhood* **Tel** *(02) 232 2555* **Map** *C3*

This attractive, family-run garden restaurant, is hidden in a grove of citrus and palm trees located off the main road, a little south of the centre of town. The salads and other starters, grilled meat dishes and freshly-squeezed lemon drink are excellent, as is the verdant, tree-shaded setting. Attentive service. Open from 8am until late afternoon.

# WESTERN JORDAN

### AMMAN Hashem
*Opposite Cliff Hotel, Downtown* **Tel** *(06) 463 6440* **Map** *C3*

Founded in the 1920s, this no-nonsense 24-hour budget restaurant is an Amman institution, packed with locals. Only two dishes are served – houmous and *fuul* (hot beans), both with flat bread – although you can pick up a bag of *falafel* balls from the stand next door. Wash it down with a glass of scalding hot, milkless, sweet tea.

### AMMAN Tarweea
*Opposite KFC, Shmeisani* **Tel** *(06) 569 1000* **Map** *C3*

A pleasant, quiet, budget-priced Arabic restaurant tucked away off the main street in this bustling West Amman neighbourhood, with no sign in English (it is attached to the Haya Cultural Centre). The dining area is open, airy and spacious – an unusual setting to try Arabic *meze* and grills, fresh-baked *manaqeesh* bread and stuffed *falafel*.

### AMMAN Blue Fig
*Prince Hashem bin al-Hussein St, Abdoun, 11844* **Tel** *(06) 592 8800* **Map** *C3*

One of Amman's hippest places to hang out, located on the fringes of the city proper. The interior is all subtle lighting and contemporary design, with chic, wealthy Ammanis enjoying the international fare. The wraps, salads and light bites are all done with panache. A fascinating glimpse of Jordan's "beautiful people".

### AMMAN Champions
*At the Marriott Hotel, Issam al-Ajlouni St, Shmeisani* **Tel** *(06) 560 7607* **Map** *C3*

Amman has the full range familiar Western fast-food outlets, but you would do better at Champions. Here, in a brisk and breezy US-style sports bar ambience, with TVs showing live sports events, you can tuck into high-quality burgers with fries, nachos, salads and other fast food offerings, in huge portions. Also at the Marriott on the Dead Sea.

### AMMAN Reem al-Bawadi
*Near Waha Circle, Tlaa al-Ali, West Amman* **Tel** *(06) 551 5419* **Map** *C3*

An excellent choice for top-notch Arabic cuisine in an authentic, informal setting, much favoured by Jordanian families and business-people. Seating is either in the vast interior, or – in warmer months – outside in a gigantic Bedouin-style tent pitched in the gardens. Service is welcoming, accommodating and discreet.

### AMMAN Romero
*Off 3rd Circle, Jabal Amman* **Tel** *(06) 464 4227* **Map** *C3*

Perhaps Amman's finest Italian restaurant, tucked away down a leafy side street opposite the InterContinental Hotel. The ambience is perfect, with bow-tied waiters gliding noiselessly around a cosy, tasteful dining room, and the food is exquisite, using the freshest of ingredients. Upstairs is the informal Living Room, for light bites and lounging.

## AMMAN Wild Jordan
*Othman bin Affan St, off Rainbow St, below 1st Circle, Jabal Amman* **Tel** *(06) 463 3542* **Map** *C3*

A wonderful wholefood café/restaurant attached to the offices of the Royal Society for the Conservation of Nature (RSCN). The building is perched on a hillside overlooking Downtown Amman, with spectacular views from its open terrace. All the food is organically produced and sourced locally – salads, wraps, smoothies and minty iced lemonade.

## AMMAN Fakhr el-Din
*40 Taha Hussein St, between 1st and 2nd circles, Jabal Amman* **Tel** *(06) 465 2399* **Map** *C3*

Quite simply one of Jordan's loveliest restaurants, and one of its best. An elegant 1920s town house, on a quiet residential street, has been beautifully restored and converted into a formal Arabic restaurant of the highest quality. The *meze* and grills are impeccable, as is the service. Reservations are essential: in summer, book a table on the terrace.

## AMMAN Noodasia
*Abdoun Circle* **Tel** *(06) 593 6999* **Map** *C3*

Highly acclaimed Asian restaurant, in the heart of the Abdoun buzz. The building design is smart and contemporary, with exceptionally well-prepared and presented food to match, ranging from Szechuan staples to Thai dishes and sushi, all very authentic. Afterwards, roam the bars and cafés of Abdoun for something sweet or a nightcap.

## AMMAN Tannoureen
*Shatt al-Arab St, Umm Uthaina, West Amman* **Tel** *(06) 551 5987* **Map** *C3*

Vying for the title of Jordan's best restaurant, this is an outstanding place to sample the finest of Lebanese cuisine in an elegant, formal setting. The *meze* are exceptionally good, the mains cover the range of grills and fish and the desserts, if you make it that far, are out of this world. Service is warm, smooth and courteous.

## AQABA Ali Baba
*Princess Haya Circle* **Tel** *(03) 201 3901* **Map** *B7*

Situated in a great location, on a bustling corner overlooking Aqaba's main Princess Haya Circle, Ali Baba is a long-established, informal local restaurant, generally packed with both Aqabawis and tourists sampling Lebanese cuisine, chatting and watching the town go by. The fish and seafood are notably good and the service is genial.

## AQABA Floka
*Al Nahda St, 77110* **Tel** *(03) 203 0860* **Map** *B7*

In the centre of town, the street behind the Aqaba Gulf hotel is lined with interesting cafés and restaurants. Alongside the Alcazar Hotel stands Floka, a great little fish and seafood restaurant. Choose from the catch of the day or pick Arabic specialities from the extensive menu.

## AQABA Bourj al-Hamam
*At the InterContinental Hotel, King Hussein St, North Beach 77110* **Tel** *(03) 209 2222* **Map** *B7*

Aqaba's big hotels all have excellent restaurants, but the InterContinental's Bourj al-Hamam is exceptional, offering exquisite Lebanese specialities alongside the hotel's pool and palms, looking out to the beach and the Red Sea. The *meze* are superb, as are the fish specialities. The restaurant in the InterContinental in Amman is as good.

## AQABA Royal Yacht Club
*Off the main corniche, 77110* **Tel** *(03) 202 2404* **Map** *B7*

Off the main Princess Haya Circle, a side-road (with staffed gates) leads down to the marina, where you will find this wonderful restaurant. Catered by Romero of Amman, it offers a range of Mediterranean cuisine, from fish and wood-fired pizza to salads and Arabic *meze*, in a formal, airy space on the waterfront, with spectacular views.

## DEAD SEA Mövenpick
*Dead Sea Rd, Sweimeh, 11180* **Tel** *(05) 356 1111* **Map** *C4*

Dining at the Dead Sea is a case of picking a hotel. The Marriott and the Kempinski both have excellent restaurants and terrace cafés, but the Mövenpick is perhaps the most atmospheric and offers exceptional quality. Try the lavish Mediterranean buffets at Saraya, in the main building, or Luigi's, a great little Italian on the resort's "village square".

## MADABA Haret Jdoudna
*King Talal St, 11181* **Tel** *(05) 324 8650* **Map** *C4*

On a journey north or south through Jordan, or a trip out of Amman, it is worth the detour to Madaba to try this splendid, traditional Arabic restaurant, occupying a historic building in the town's old quarter. The setting is perfect, with tables dotted around an old courtyard home, and the food – *meze*, grills, fresh-baked bread – is exquisite.

## PETRA Mövenpick
*Wadi Musa, 218101* **Tel** *(03) 215 7111* **Map** *C5*

Dining in Wadi Musa is mostly quite ordinary. For something special, head to the Mövenpick: on one side of their beautiful internal atrium is the Saraya restaurant, offering extensive buffets; on another is the Maqaad bar; and opposite is the formal Liwan restaurant, Wadi Musa's best, with a high-priced menu of Mediterranean specialities.

## UMM QAIS Resthouse
*Umm Qais* **Tel** *(02) 750 0555 or book through Romero in Amman (06) 464 4228* **Map** *C2*

Umm Qais – once the Roman city of Gadara – is located in the northernmost corner of Jordan. Within the ruins, an Ottoman school has been beautifully converted into a splendid restaurant. The menu is simple – salads, *meze*, grills, pasta – but the location is exceptional, on a high plateau overlooking the Sea of Galilee and Golan Heights.

**Key to Price Guide** *see p272* **Key to Symbols** *see back cover flap*

# Choosing a Restaurant in the Red Sea and Sinai

The restaurants listed on this page have been selected for their value, good food, atmosphere and interesting location within the Red Sea and Sinai area. For key to symbols and map references, see back endpaper.

**PRICE CATEGORIES**
Prices are based on a three-course meal for one including coffee, tax and service.

£ Under 30 Egyptian pounds
££ 30–50 Egyptian pounds
£££ 50–100 Egyptian pounds
££££ 100–150 Egyptian pounds
£££££ Over 150 Egyptian pounds

## THE RED SEA AND SINAI

### DAHAB INMO Divers' Home Restaurant
£££    Map F6

*Al-Mashraba, Dahab* **Tel** *(069) 3640 370*

Located right on the beach at Dahab, this restaurant forms part of the INMO Divers' Resort and is built to the same architectural style as the main building, with lots of arches and domes. It serves good Oriental, vegetarian and international cuisine, with its speciality being Egyptian buffets and drinks such as *Sahlab*.

### DAHAB Nesima Restaurant
£££    Map F6

*Mashraba, Dahab* **Tel** *(069) 3640 320*

The Nesima is a cosy and intimate restaurant within the Nesima Hotel, which is renowned for its excellent diving centre. The restaurant serves international cuisine, along with Egyptian dishes such as *koshari* followed by traditional desserts. There is a rooftop bar.

### DAHAB Nirvana Indian Restaurant
£££    Map F6

*Nirvana Dive Center, Lighthouse, Dahab* **Tel** *(061) 046 061*

Open for breakfast, lunch and dinner, the Nirvana offers a mouth-watering selection of fresh Indian dishes, prepared by Indian chefs using only the finest imported spices and ingredients. Food and drinks are served on the beach or the patio. Hotel guests enjoy a discount on their meals and have the option to eat on the first-floor deck with a sea view.

### NAAMA BAY Kokai Grill Room
£££    Map E7

*Ghazala Hotel, Naama Bay, Sharm el-Sheikh* **Tel** *(069) 3600 150*

The Kokai Grill Room at the Ghazala Hotel offers the finest in Polynesian and Chinese cuisine in an elegant setting. Each evening the restaurant's team of chefs theatrically prepares the grilled dishes at table grills. The duck, spring rolls and rice dishes are also recommended.

### NUWEIBA Oasis Restaurant
£££    Map F5

*Nuweiba Resort, Nuweiba City* **Tel** *(069) 3500 402*

The Leserena has a great view over the Nuweiba Resort's beachside gardens and pool area. The cuisine is largely Egyptian and classic international, with dishes like pizzas and pasta, fresh fruits, salads, vegetarian dishes and desserts in abundance.

### SHARM EL-SHEIKH Al-Fanar Restaurant
£££    Map E7

*Ras Un Sid Beach, Sharm el-Sheikh* **Tel** *(069) 3662 218*

Like many of the restaurants in Sharm el-Sheikh, the Al-Fanar serves Italian cuisine, but what makes this one stand out from the rest is that fresh produce from Italy is regularly used and its location right on the beach, below the lighthouse, provides an intimate setting. Good wine list.

### SHARM EL-SHEIKH La Luna Restaurant
£££    Map E7

*Ritz-Carlton Resort, Om El Seed, Sharm el-Sheikh* **Tel** *(069) 3661 919*

With an experienced Italian chef who excels in specialities such as calamari, potato *gnocchi* and homemade pasta, a visit to La Luna will be a memorable experience. A list of fine Italian wines and grappa is served. The restaurant has a luxurious feel and is located within the Ritz-Carlton Resort.

### SHARM-EL-SHEIKH Safsafa
£££    Map F5

*Asia Mall, Sharm-el Sheikh* **Tel** *(069) 3660 474*

The Safsafa restaurant serves well presented fresh fish dishes, along with a good selection of vegetarian meals, such as *Fuul* and *Taamiyya*. It can usually be found full of discerning diners. Located right on the waterside at Naama Bay, in the shopping centre, the restaurant is bright and welcoming.

### TABA Castle Zaman Restaurant
£££    Map F5

*Nuweiba–Taba Road, Taba* **Tel** *(069) 3501 234*

This impressive monument commands a dramatic mountainous view of four countries. Castle Zaman's speciality is slow-cooked food – some dishes are cooked for up to three hours, leaving guests time to enjoy the pool, have a massage, explore the underground treasure room or relax with a fresh cocktail at the bar. Not suitable for children.

**Key to Symbols** *see back cover flap*

# SHOPS AND MARKETS

When it comes to shopping, the main attraction in Jerusalem is undoubtedly the souks, or bazaars, of the Old City. In comparison with the great bazaars of Istanbul or Cairo, Jerusalem's souks can seem small and overly touristy, but they still reward exploration (see pp148–9). The streets of the Old City away from the souks are also dotted with interesting small shops, handicraft centres, workshops and boutiques. Most other towns and cities throughout the Holy Land also have souks, with particularly good ones

**Armenian ceramic tile**

in Akko, Amman, Hebron and Nazareth. Anybody intending shopping in the souks must become acquainted with the art of bargaining. In contrast to the traditional nature of the souk, bigger centres such as Jerusalem, Tel Aviv and Amman, all possess modern shopping districts, as well as large American-style malls, filled with familiar brand names from the West.

In Jordan, the major tourist sites such as Petra and Jerash have small clusters of tourist-oriented shops where, sometimes, you can find local handicrafts and products of interest.

**A typical fruit and vegetable stall**

## OPENING HOURS

Throughout the Holy Land there are often no strictly defined opening hours; it depends on the individual proprietor. In general, however, except for food shops, which open quite early, business activity begins at roughly 9am. Some shops close from 1 to 4pm (this is particularly the case in Jordan), but most remain open all day until around 7pm. In Jerusalem's Old City and elsewhere, the souks don't really get going until perhaps 10am and they close around sunset. Many shops and stalls in the souks are closed all day Sunday, as many of the shopowners are Christian, although others are Muslim and they stay closed on Friday instead. During the holy month of Ramadan, Muslim-owned shops through-

out the Holy Land close 30 minutes to one hour before sunset.

All Jewish-owned businesses in Jerusalem and throughout Israel close from Friday afternoon to sunset on Saturday for Shabbat (Sabbath). These shops are also closed during Jewish holidays (see pp36–9).

## HOW TO PAY

Major credit cards, such as Visa, American Express and Master Card, are accepted in almost all shops throughout Israel; travellers' cheques are not. In Jordan and Sinai, credit cards are less widely accepted. Only in top-end and mid-range hotels and international restaurants are cards usually accepted; in most places, you will have to pay in cash. It is usual to pay in the local currency (in

Jordan and Sinai use of any other currency is illegal), but in Israel, if you are making a large purchase, it is possible to get a discount by paying in US dollars. This is because transactions made in a foreign currency are not subject to Israeli VAT.

## VAT EXEMPTIONS

A wide range of goods in Israel is subject to a Value Added Tax (Mam in Hebrew) of 17 per cent. Tourists are entitled to a refund on this for any purchases amounting to over 400 shekels (about US$100). Make sure the shop you buy from has a VAT (or tax) refund sign displayed. You need to ask the sales assistant for a special invoice showing the VAT paid in both dollars and shekels. This is then presented at the VAT counter at the airport at the time of your

**Examining the wares at an Old City souvenir shop**

Malkha Kanyon Mall in Malkha, Jerusalem

departure. You must have the purchases with you to cross-check against the invoice. Queues at this counter can be very long, so get there with time to spare.

## DEPARTMENT STORES AND SHOPPING MALLS

Israel has a rapidly growing number of large shopping centres and US-style out-of-town malls. Both are filled with standard mall-type outlets that sell everything from greetings cards to electronics items, most of which are imported from Europe and the United States. Jerusalem has several large malls, inlcuding one of the biggest in the country, the **Malkha Kanyon Mall**, out in the Malkha suburb of West Jerusalem. In the centre of the city, **City Tower** is a multi-storey shopping centre at the coner of Jaffa Road and King George V Street. Tel Aviv's newest and biggest mall is the **Azrieli Centre**, in the base of three modern towers on the northeastern edge of town. More centrally located malls in Tel Aviv include the **Dizengoff Centre** on Dizengoff Street and the **Gan ha-Ir Shopping Centre** just north of Rabin Square.

As well as the shopping opportunities, Israel's malls are typically full of good, moderately-priced restaurants, snack bars and cafés. Given that they are air-conditioned, they can be great places for pedestrians to escape from the often stifling heat outside.

Jordan's capital, Amman, has also succumbed to the mall craze. The city's biggest is **Mecca Mall**, out in the north-western suburbs, which also contains a food court, cinema and bowling alley. There's also the smaller but more centrally located **Abdoun Mall**.

## MARKETS

In addition to the souks of Jerusalem's Old City, there are lots of good buys at the **Makhane Yehuda** market in modern West Jerusalem *(see p131)*. Tel Aviv has **Carmel Market** *(see p172)*, which operates every day except Saturday, and, also in the same neighbourhood, the Nakhalat Binyamin **craft market** *(see p172)*, held every Tuesday and Friday. In Jordan, Downtown Amman has several streets filled with colourful market shopping *(see p212)*

## BUYING ANTIQUES

In Jordan and Sinai it is forbidden to export any antique or archaeological find. The border authorities are extremely thorough in their checks in this regard. On the other hand, in Jerusalem and Israel you may buy objects from excavations. For more details and for the addresses of some reputable dealers, see pages 148–9.

## HOW TO BARGAIN

Buying and selling in the Middle East is traditionally a highly ritualized affair, in which bargaining is far more than just haggling for a cheap price. The aim of the exercise is to establish a fair price that both vendor and buyer are happy with. As part of the process, a shopowner may well invite you to have a cup of tea or coffee and may literally turn the place upside down to show you something; you should not feel obliged to buy because of this, it is common sales practice and all part of the ritual.

Bargaining, by the way, is not socially acceptable in city-centre shops, but it is unavoidable in the souks if you don't wish to pay greatly over the odds.

The way to go about it is that once you identify an article that interests you, especially an expensive one, be brave enough to offer half the price quoted by the shopowner. Don't be put off by any feigned indignation on the part of the shopkeeper and only raise your next offer by a small amount. Through offer and counter-offer you should

Haggling over the price – time-consuming but essential to avoid paying over the odds

arrive at a mutually agreeable price. If you don't reach a price you think is fair then simply say thank you and leave. Making to walk away often has the effect of bringing the price plummeting down.

In theory, no one gets cheated because you, the buyer, have set the price yourself; it follows that you are happy with what you have agreed to pay, and the shopkeeper will certainly never sell at a loss.

# Where to Shop in the Holy Land

Jerusalem's souks are the first place to look for many of the items produced in this region (for shopping in Jerusalem, see pages 148–9), but there is also plenty of other good shopping in the Holy Land. Tel Aviv is probably Israel's finest shopping city, with several malls and markets, and lots of great boutique stores on and off Dizengoff Street. Amman, in Jordan, has lots of great arts and crafts items, a lot of which can also be found at stores in the more popular tourist destinations such as Madaba, Petra and Jerash.

Jewish menorahs for sale in the Old City of Jerusalem

### RELIGIOUS ARTICLES

For Christian religious items there are any number of shops in Jerusalem's Old City (see p149). However, prices are generally lower in Bethlehem, which is where many of these items are made. One place worth visiting here is the **Holy Land Arts Museum** on Milk Grotto Street, which specializes in wooden objects with mother-of-pearl inlay, and inlaid metalwork (damascene).

For Judaica, visit the Jewish Quarter in Jerusalem's Old City and along central Ben Yehuda Street in Tel Aviv. Visit **Pninat-ha'kesef** in Tel Aviv for a wide selection of candlesticks and paintings.

### CERAMICS

Jerusalem is the place for beautifully coloured Armenian ceramics, but there are other styles produced elsewhere in the region. **Beit el-Badawi** in Amman sells the designs of local craftspeople who work in both traditional and modern styles. Pieces incorporate Arab calligraphy.

Also in Amman, **Silsal Ceramics** is another good sales studio specializing in modern pottery.

For something really chic, visit **Blue Bandana** in northern Tel Aviv, which stocks a fine array of beautiful tableware, much of which is designed specially for the store.

### TEXTILES AND RUGS

The shops and market in the centre of Ramallah are a good place to look for densely embroidered Palestinian textiles. Cushions and bags made from Bedouin textiles are found in most souvenir shops in Israel. Prices vary little, but for Bedouin rugs, you would do better to buy in Jordan. Madaba (see p216), in particular, is famous for its colourful rugs. These can be bought around town, but one recommended place is **Madaba Oriental Gifts**, which is opposite St George's Church. **Shtihei**

**Carmel** in Rehovot, near Tel Aviv, specializes in Carmel rugs.

### JEWELLERY

Some of the region's most distinctive jewellery is made by the Bedouin. It is sold at the street markets of Nakhalat Binyamin (see p172) in Tel Aviv, in many of the boutiques in Jaffa and at the Thursday market in Beersheva.

For more contemporary pieces **Agas and Tamar** is an upmarket boutique selling exquisite own-designed, one-off pieces. Even if your budget doesn't stretch this far, it's a beautiful shop in one of Tel Aviv's most interesting neighbourhoods.

### HEBRON GLASSWARE

In Jerusalem, the first three shops on the left-hand side of David Street, going from Jaffa Gate, have the best selection of glassware. However, much lower prices are offered in the souk at Hebron. At Madaba in Jordan, **Madaba Oriental Gifts** has a good range of Hebron glassware, often at prices even lower than those in Hebron.

### COSMETICS

The Arab town of Nablus is famed for its olive-oil soap, available at almost any East Jerusalem grocer's and in the Old City souks, especially on Khan el-Zeit Street. In Galilee the soap is sold in many souvenir shops, particularly in Nazareth, but at higher prices.

The reputed health-giving properties of the Dead Sea are exploited in the

Craftsman hand-knotting the fringe of a rug

cosmetic products made by the two companies, Ahava and Mineral. These are sold at all well-stocked pharmacies and at the Duty-Free Shop at Ben Gurion airport. When visiting the Dead Sea, you can buy directly from the **Ahava Factory**, north of Ein Gedi. It is open daily, but closes at 2pm on Fridays. There is also an **Ahava Mineral Lounge** at the Hilton Tel Aviv and a major Ahava outlet at the Ein Bokek spa resort on the Dead Sea shore.

A range of Dead Sea products is also sold at a shop called **Holy Treasures**, opposite St George Church in the town of Madaba, Jordan.

## SOUVENIRS

Sandals, bags and belts are good articles to buy throughout the Holy Land. Copperware is also a good buy, notably coffeepots and trays, often etched with arabesque patterns. A

**Water pipes, or nargilehs**

more exotic souvenir is a nargileh, or Arab water pipe. All of these can be found in Jerusalem and also in Amman, where a particularly good one-stop shopping opportunity is offerd by the **El-Alaydi Jordan Craft Centre**, which has a vast selection of locally produced items, including Hebron glassware, Palestinian embroidery and Bedouin tent accessories.

In Madaba in Jordan, there is a complex of excellent **craft shops** just north of the Madaba Museum, offering everything from textiles to jewellery to mosaics. At Petra, look at for the **Made In Jordan** shop, which is near the entry gate to the site, and which has top-quality locally made items, including camel-hair shawls and olive. Decorative bottles filled with coloured sand are popular Jordanian souvenirs, especially at Wadi Rum and Petra.

**Making sand-filled bottles, Jordan's most prevalent souvenir**

For a very different sort of souvenir, an extensive range of recordings of modern and traditional Jewish music can be found at **Tower Records** in Tel Aviv. Alternatively, the **Bauhaus Centre** in Tel Aviv has a gift shop selling miniature models of some of the city's landmark 1930s architecture (*see p171*), as well as books and prints.

# DIRECTORY

## SHOPPING MALLS

**Abdoun Mall**
El-Hashimi St, Abdoun, Amman, Jordan.
*Tel (06) 5920296.*

**Azrieli Center**
132 Petach-Tikva Hwy, Tel Aviv.
*Tel (03) 6081199.*

**City Tower**
Corner of Jaffa Rd & King George V St, Jerusalem.

**Dizengoff Centre**
Dizengoff St, Tel Aviv.
*Tel (03) 621 2416.*

**Gan ha-Ir Shopping Centre**
71 Ibn Gabirol St, Tel Aviv.
*Tel (03) 527 9111.*

**Malkha Kanyon Mall**
Malkha, West Jerusalem.
*Tel (02) 679 1333.*

**Mecca Mall**
Mekka el-Mukkaramah Rd, Amman, Jordan.
*Tel (06) 552 7945.*

## RELIGIOUS ARTICLES

**Holy Land Arts Museum**
Milk Grotto St, Bethlehem.
*Tel (02) 274 4819.*
www.holylandarts
museum.com

**Pninat-ha'kesef**
1/86 Ha'kishor St, Tel Aviv
*Tel (03) 518 1406.*
www.pninat-
hakesef.ybay.co.il

## CERAMICS

**Beit el-Bawadi**
Fawzi el-Qawoaji St, Amman, Jordan.
*Tel (06) 593 0070.*

**Blue Bandana**
52 Hei Beyar, Kikar ha-Medina, Tel Aviv.
*Tel (03) 602 1686.*

**Silsal Ceramics**
Innabeh St, North Abdoun, Amman, Jordan. *Tel (06) 593 1128.* www.silsal.com

## TEXTILES AND RUGS

**Madaba Oriental Gifts**
Madaba, Jordan.

**Shtihei Carmel**
Bilu Center, Rehovot
*Tel (08) 935 5557.*

## JEWELLERY

**Agas and Tamar**
43 Shabazi St, Neve Tzedek, Tel Aviv.
*Tel (03) 516 8421.*

## COSMETICS

**Ahava Factory**
Kibbutz Mitspe Shalem, Route 90, Dead Sea.
*Tel (02) 994 5100.*

**Ahava Mineral Lounge**
Tel Aviv Hilton, Independence Park, Tel Aviv.
*Tel (03) 520 2222.*

**Holy Treasures**
Talal St, Madaba, Jordan.
*Tel (05) 324 8481.*

## SOUVENIRS

**El-Alaydi Jordan Craft Centre**
El-Kulliyah el-Islamiyah St, Jebel Amman, Amman, Jordan.
*Tel (06) 464 4555.*

**Bauhaus Centre**
99 Dizengoff St, Tel Aviv.
*Tel (05) 522 02459.*
www.bauhaus-center.com

**Craft shops**
Haret Jdoudna Complex, Talal St, Madaba, Jordan.
*Tel (05) 324 8650.*

**Made In Jordan**
Petra, Jordan.
*Tel (03) 215 5700.*
www.madeinjordan.com

**Tower Records**
1 Allenby St, Tel Aviv.
*Tel (03) 517 4044.*

# What to Buy in Jerusalem and the Holy Land

Fish pendants

Visitors on the lookout for unusual souvenirs, or the products of different cultures and ages, will certainly find something to their liking in Jerusalem, either in the souks and alleyways of the Old City, or in particular districts of the modern city. Some artifacts, such as pottery, brass and silver objects, Bedouin textiles and Arab jewellery, are sold throughout the Holy Land. However, in Jerusalem you will find an especially wide range of Jewish religious articles (while other places concentrate on Christian or Muslim items), and Armenian pottery.

Copper goblets

*Firjan* with spirit stove

### Blue Hebron Glass
*Most of this attractive glass, in shades of light blue and turquoise, is made to imitate Roman and Phoenician vessels. Some modern designs and full dinner services are also produced.*

### Copper- and Brassware
*Copper plates, jugs, pots, trays and goblets, all usually engraved, are found everywhere. So, too, are traditional firjan (coffee pots) and large platters made of beaten brass.*

### Armenian Ceramics
*The best-known decorative pottery is produced by the Armenian community, which has had a presence in Jerusalem since the 4th century (see pp106–7) . It is characterized by the abundant use of blue and yellow, and of floral motifs. The designs are usually intricate and painted on a white ground.*

### Silver and Pewter Jewellery
*The Yemenite tradition of silver filigree work has been extensively adopted by religious and secular jewellers in the Holy Land. Look out also for attractive, modern pewter jewellery set with semi-precious stones, as well as traditional blue glass-eye and khamsa (hand-shaped) lucky charms, popular with Arabs and Jews alike.*

### Olive-wood Objects
*Crucifixes, rosaries, Nativity scenes and figures of Christ, the Virgin Mary and the saints carved in hard, light-coloured and attractively-grained olive wood make evocative souvenirs. The best come from the Bethlehem area.*

Blue glass-eye pendants

Modern brooch

Silver *khamsa*

Olive-wood sculpture

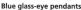

### Jewish Liturgical Articles

*These often beautifully-made objects include the kippah (male skullcap), tallit (pure wool prayer shawl), kiddush (blessing) cup, besamim (spice-holder), mezuzah (prayer container hung at front doors) and shofar (ram's horn blown for Yom Kippur).*

**Kippah and tallit**

**Shofar**

**Silver mezuzah**

**Silver besamim**

### Rugs and Fabrics

*Robust and vividly coloured Bedouin rugs, cushions and bags made from the cloth formerly used as Bedouin saddle covers, and traditional, finely embroidered Palestinian dresses are popular buys.*

**Bedouin cushion covers**

**Bedouin fabrics**

**Palestinian fabrics**

### Ancient Household Articles and Coins

*Reputable dealers in finds from archaeological sites will often have attractive basalt, earthenware and stone kitchen vessels, small terracotta amphorae and Roman and Phoenician glassware. Coins from many historical periods are fairly plentiful, but beware of fakes.*

### Beauty Products from the Dead Sea and Nablus

*A vast range of creams, soap, salts and Dead Sea mud, using the mineral properties of the unique Dead Sea salt, is sold to alleviate skin conditions. Nablus soap, which has olive oil and less than two per cent caustic soda as its only ingredients, is cheap, fragrant and long-lasting, and is good for use in dry climates.*

**Nablus soap**

**Dead Sea lotions**

### Local Delicacies

*Specialist shops stocked with large sacks of nuts, dried fruits, pulses and dried vegetables are fascinating places to explore. They often sell spices, too. All these products make good buys as they are easy to carry, and keep well at home.*

**Dried apricots**

**Chickpeas**

**Mulberries**

**Almonds**

**Pistachio nuts**

**Dried red peppers and aubergines**

# ENTERTAINMENT IN THE HOLY LAND

While Jerusalem has its theatres, concert halls and cinematheque *(see pp150–51)*, Israel's real centre of entertainment lies some 60 km (37 miles) west in Tel Aviv. If Jerusalem is, as Israelis often say, the city where they pray and Haifa is the city where they work, then Tel Aviv is definitely where they play. High culture is catered for by a fine modern

Entrance, Performing
Arts Centre, Tel Aviv

opera house, several theatres, and a busy dance and performing arts centre. Popular culture is supported by myriad bars, clubs and live music venues. Elsewhere, there is far less going on, although Jordan's capital Amman boasts several busy cultural centres and cinema complexes. Down on the Red Sea coast and in Sinai, entertainment is largely limited to bars and nightclubs.

**The Israel Philharmonic Orchestra**

## INFORMATION

The *Jerusalem Post* and the English-language edition of the newspaper *Ha-Aretz*, both of which are available throughout Israel, carry daily entertainment listings. Both also have extensive cultural supplements on Fridays with detailed listings of events for the week to come. There is also an English-language listings magazine *Time Out Tel Aviv* published every two months and available free at certain bars and hotels. Tourist offices *(see p299)* also have abundant events magazines.

In Jordan, look out for the *Jordan Times* and the weekly *The Star*, or, when in Amman, visit **books@cafe**, an internet café-cum-bookshop, whose notice boards provide the best way of finding out what's on in the capital.

In Sinai, look out for the monthly *Egypt Today*, which carries what's on information.

## CLASSICAL MUSIC

The Israel Philharmonic, one of the world's most prestigious orchestras, is based in Tel Aviv at the **Performing Arts Centre**. The neighbouring **Tel Aviv Museum of Art** also hosts regular chamber music concerts and other classical events in its Recanati Hall. Smaller venues include the **Felicia Blumenthal Centre** and **Einav Cultural Centre**, both of which host local and international classical muscians.

In the village of Ein Kerem *(see p138)* near Jerusalem, young musicians give free recitals of chamber music every Friday at noon from October to May at the Fountain of the Virgin in the **Targ Centre**.

In Amman, there's large modern **Royal Cultural Centre**, which presents a varied programme of traditional Arabic music, theatre and dance. The **King Hussein Cultural Centre** also hosts occasional classical and Arab music performances.

## OPERA

Tel Aviv's Performing Arts Centre is home to the **New Israeli Opera**, a world-class company, which puts on four or five new productions a year. The centre also frequently hosts visiting productions from Europe and America.

## ROCK, JAZZ AND BLUES

Even in partying Tel Aviv, the live music scene is surprisingly disppointing. Local rock bands of variable quality perform most nights at **Camelot** and **Ha-Bima Club**, and also at **Mike's Place**, which is a foreigner-friendly bar down on the seafront. **Benchmark** is a relative newcomer featuring live music in the bar-saturated area of Nakhalat Binyamin. For hardcore fans who are prepared to travel, **Barbie** mixes Israeli rock with Russian hard rock.

**Cafe Henrietta, Coffee House** and **Green Racoon**, all

**Classical street musician**

of which are in central Tel Aviv, all feature jazz at least one night a week. Call or see the local press for details.

In Amman, weekly concerts of very varied music are put on by **books@cafe**.

## BARS AND CLUBS

In Tel Aviv, the main cluster of bars is in the Nakhalat Binyamin district, particularly around the southern end of Rothschild Avenue and

Tel Aviv's Suzanne Dellal Centre, renowned for excellence in modern dance

Lillenblum. The venue that has young hipsters queuing outside every night is **Nanuchka**, a rowdy but classy bar-restaurant with surreal decor and a permanent party vibe. Around the corner, the splendidly named **Betty Ford** is a New York-style bar with a SoHo-style buzz. There are also plenty of good late-night spots around the Cinematheque on Ha-Arbaa Street and up in the Old Port *(see p168)* area, which is where you'll find **Hannah'le**, a bar with a wooden deck jutting out over the water.

Also up at the Old Port are a couple of super clubs, including long-time favourite the **Fifth Dimension**. However, perhaps the most fascinating and singular club is **Ha-Hamman**, a strikingly beautiful, converted Turkish bathhouse in Jaffa.

For something more casual and laidback, there's **Mike's Place** down near the seafront

in central Tel Aviv or the **Gordon Inn**, a local pub with a pool table and a reliably friendly crowd.

In Amman, there are plenty of bars and clubs in the uptown neighbourhoods such as Abdoun and Shmeisani. One of the most popular places is the **Big Fellow Irish Pub**, which is run by the Sherton group. Drinks include, of course, Guinness and there's Guinness pie to eat. **Champions** is an American-style sports bar at the Marriott, while the **Living Room** is an attractive lounge bar with a good, American-influenced food menu.

In Petra, do not miss the chance to have a drink at the **Cave Bar**, which occupies a geniune 2,000-year-old Nabataean rock tomb. There's livebedouin music most nights too.

In Sinai, bars and clubs are generally found in the many resort hotels.

## DANCE

The internationally-known Bat Sheva company is the mainstay of modern Israeli dance. There are no classical ballet companies in Israel, but contemporary dance is very much alive here. The focal point of dance activity is the

Spontaneous outdoor dancing on the beach

**Suzanne Dellal Centre**, a superb, old Ottoman building at the heart of the historic, southern Tel Aviv district of Neve Tzedek, which has benefited from extensive architectural renewal. In Jerusalem, dance can be seen at the Centre for Performing Arts in the Jerusalem Sherover Theatre complex, while Jewish and Arabic folk dancing performances take place on Monday, Thursday and Saturday evenings in the **YMCA** auditorium.

In Jordan, there are two well-established national folkloric groups. Both dance at the **Royal Cultural Centre** and, occasionally, at the Roman Theatre, both in Amman *(see p212)*. Folkloric dance also features quite heavily at the **Jerash Festival** *(see p37)*.

Dining, drinking and dancing al fresco in Atarim Square, Tel Aviv

Tel Aviv's Ha-Bima Theatre

## THEATRE

Plays in Israel are almost always performed in Hebrew (or, less commonly, Arabic), although some of the bigger theatres such as Tel Aviv's **Ha-Bima Theatre and New Cameri Theatre** (and Jerusalem's Sherover Theatre, *see p151*) have headphones providing English-language translation for some performances, though there are a lot of performances in English as well. Productions, in all cases, range from revivals of the classics of world drama (both old and modern) to first-run stagings of new Israeli plays.

There are several theatre festivals throughout the year in Israel (*see pp36–9*), the most exciting of which is the **Acre Fringe Theatre Festival**, which stages some performances in the city's subterranean Crusader halls.

In Amman, theatre takes place at the **Royal Cultural Centre** and **King Hussein Cultural Centre**. However, the premier theatrical event is the **Jerash Festival** (*see p37*), which brings together performers from all over the world to present their work amid the ancient ruins.

## CINEMA

Foreign films shown in Israel are not dubbed, but carry Hebrew subtitles. Cinemas are plentiful, especially in Tel Aviv, where complexes such as the **Rav-Chen 1–5** are modern, comfortable and air-conditioned. They tend to screen first-run Hollywood fare. The **Cinematheques**, of which there is one in Jerusalem (*see p150*) and one in Tel Aviv, specialize in art-house and independent films, as well as holding

themed seasons and retrospectives. Israel's biggest movie theatre complex is **Cinema City**, which has 21 auditoriums and three 3D screens.

There are several modern cinemaplexes in Amman offering recent releases, including the **Century Cinemas** in the Zara Centre behind the Grand Hyatt and **Galleria**. Films are shown in their original language with Arabic subtitles.

## SPECTATOR SPORTS

Football is by far the most popular sport throughout the Holy Land. Two teams from Jerusalem play in Israel's premier league, Beitar and Ha-Poel, and matches take place in the new **Teddy Stadium** at Malkha in West Jerusalem.

Basketball is the next most popular sport. The Jerusalem team, Ha-Poel, plays in the Sports Arena near the Teddy Stadium, while the Maccabee Tel Aviv plays at the **Yad Eliahu Arena** just off the Ayalon highway.

A basketball match at the Yad Eliahu Arena

Football is also followed religiously in Jordan. The two main teams in Amman are Wahadat and Faisaly. Games are mostly played at the **Jordan International Stadium**, in the Shmeisani district.

## SWIMMING

Almost all the large hotels have outdoor swimming pools; the YMCA in Jerusalem also has an indoor pool. You can also swim all year round at the **Jerusalem Swimming Pool**, in the German Colony district, south of the centre.

The Red Sea is warm enough for year-round swimming, although most resort hotels also have swimming pools. Swimming in the Mediterranean is fine in summer but it's too cold from around October to April.

## CHILDREN

For information on Jerusalem for children, see page 150. In northern Tel Aviv, the **Ramat Gan Safari Zoo** makes a good outing for children. You can drive through and observe the wildlife in its natural habitat. The **Children's Museum** in Holon, a short drive from Tel Aviv, has lots of fun, interactive exhibits. **Mini Israel**, which is just off the main highway that runs between Jerusalem and Tel Aviv, has over 350 miniature models of the Holy Land's most important landmarks.

On the shores of the Dead Sea, just south of Jericho, **Attraktsion** is a large aquatic amusement park with water slides and splash pools. However, it is only open from April to October.

Tel Aviv's beach, starting to attract swimmers in spring

# DIRECTORY

## INFORMATION

**books@cafe**
Mango St, Jebel Amman,
Amman, Jordan.
*Tel (06) 465 0457.*

## CLASSICAL MUSIC

**Einav Cultural Centre**
71 Ibn Gvirol St, Tel Aviv.
*Tel (03) 521 7763.*

**Felicia Blumenthal Centre**
26 Bialik St, Tel Aviv.
*Tel (03) 620 1185.*
www.fbmc.co.il

**King Hussein Cultural Centre**
Omar Matar St, El-Muhajareen, Amman.
*Tel (06) 473 9953.*

**Performing Arts Centre**
19 Ha-Melekh Shaul Ave,
Tel Aviv.
*Tel (03) 692 7777.*

**Royal Cultural Centre**
Al-Malekah Alia St,
Shmeisani, Amman.
*Tel (06) 566 1026.*

**Targ Centre**
Ein Kerem, near Jerusalem.
*Tel (02) 641 4250.*
www.klassi.net/targ

**Tel Aviv Museum of Art**
27 Ha-Melekh Shaul Ave,
Tel Aviv.
*Tel (03) 696 1297.*
www.tamuseum.com

## OPERA

**New Israeli Opera**
Performing Arts Centre,
19 Ha-Melekh Shaul Ave,
Tel Aviv.
*Tel (03) 692 7777.*
www.israel-opera.co.il

## ROCK, JAZZ AND BLUES

**Barbie**
52 Kibbutz Gayulot St, Tel
Aviv.
*Tel (03) 518 8123.*

**Benchmark**
37 Nakhalat Binyamin St,
Tel Aviv.

**books@cafe**
See Information.

**Cafe Henrietta**
186 Arlozorov St, Tel Aviv.
*Tel (03) 691 1715.*

**Camelot**
16 Shalom Aleichem St,
Tel Aviv.
*Tel (03) 629 8666.*

**Coffee House**
88 Dizengoff St, Tel Aviv.
*Tel (03) 528 0565.*

**Green Racoon**
186 Ben Yehuda St, Tel
Aviv.
*Tel (03) 529 8513.*

**Ha-Bima Club**
Basement, 2 Tarsat St,
Tel Aviv.
*Tel (03) 528 2174.*

**Mike's Place**
86 Herbert Samuel, Tel
Aviv.
*Tel (052) 670 965.*

## BARS AND CLUBS

**Betty Ford**
48 Nakhalat Binyamin St,
Tel Aviv.
*Tel (03) 510 0650.*

**Big Fellow Irish Pub**
Abdoun Circle, Amman.
*Tel (06) 593 4766.*

**Cave Bar**
Behind the Visitors'
Centre, Petra.
*Tel (03) 215 6266.*

**Champions**
Amman Marriott, Isam
el-Ajlouni St, Shmeisani,
Amman.
*Tel (06) 560 7607.*

**Fifth Dimension**
Old Port, Tel Aviv.
*Tel (052) 242 5891.*

**Gordon Inn**
17 Gordon St, Tel Aviv.
*Tel (03) 523 8239.*

**Ha-Hammam**
10 Mifraz Shlomo St, Jaffa.
*Tel (03) 681 3261.*

**Hannah'le**
Old Port, Tel Aviv.
*Tel (03) 488 4884.*

**Living Room**
Mohammed Hussein
Heikal St, Amman.
*Tel (06) 465 5988.*

**Mike's Place**
See Rock, Jazz and Blues.

**Nanuchka**
28 Lilenblum St, Tel Aviv.
*Tel (03) 516 2254.*

## DANCE

**Jerash Festival**
Jerash Festival Office,
Amman, Jordan.
*Tel (06) 567 5199.*
www.jerashfestival.
com.jo

**Royal Cultural Centre**
See Classical Music.

**Suzanne Dellal Centre**
5 Yehieli St, Neve Tzedek,
Tel Aviv.
*Tel (03) 510 5656.*

**YMCA**
King David St, Jerusalem.
*Tel (02) 569 2692.*

## THEATRE

**Acre Fringe Theatre Festival**
*Tel (04) 955 2541.*

**Ha-Bima Theatre**
Habima Square, Tel Aviv.
*Tel (03) 628 5555.*
www.habima.org.il

**Jerash Festival**
See Dance.

**King Hussein Cultural Centre**
See Classical Music.

**New Cameri Theatre**
30 Leonardo Da Vinci St,
Tel Aviv.
*Tel (03) 606 0960.*
www.cameri.co.il

**Royal Cultural Centre**
See Classical Music.

## CINEMA

**Century Cinemas**
3rd Circle, Jebel Amman,
Amman, Jordan.
*Tel (06) 461 3200.*

**Cinema City**
Gilot Junction, Tel Aviv.
*Tel (1-700) 702 25.*

**Galleria**
Abdoun Circle,
Amman, Jordan.
*Tel (06) 593 4793.*

**Rav-Chen 1-5**
Opera Towers, 1 Allenby
St, Tel Aviv.
*Tel (03) 510 2674.*

**Tel Aviv Cinematheque**
2 Sprinzhak St, Tel Aviv.
*Tel (03) 606 0800.*

## SPECTATOR SPORTS

**Jordan International Stadium**
Shmeisani, Amman.

**Teddy Stadium**
Agudat Sport Beitar,
Malkha, West Jerusalem.
*Tel (02) 678 8320.*

**Yad Eliahu Arena**
51 Yigal Allon St, Tel Aviv.
*Tel (03) 537 6376.*

## SWIMMING

**Jerusalem Swimming Pool**
43 Emek Refaim St.
*Tel (02) 563 2092.*

## CHILDREN

**Attraktsion**
Kalia Beach, Dead Sea,
Israel.
*Tel (02) 994 2391.*

**Children's Museum**
1 Mifratz Shlomo St,
Holon, Israel
*Tel (03) 650 3000.*

**Mini Israel**
Kibbutz Nacsho, Latrun,
Israel
*Tel (08) 922 2444.*

**Ramat Gan Safari Zoo**
Ramat Gan, Tel Aviv.
*Tel (03) 631 3531.*

# Sporting and Specialist Holidays in the Holy Land

With terrain that runs from reefs rich in marine life to sometimes snow-capped peaks, and from coniferous forests to stony desert, the region offers a wide assortment of outdoor activities. Added to this, Israel is very much an "outdoors" society. As a consequence, the region is criss-crossed with hiking trails and treks, rivers are busy with rafts and canoes, parks offer opportunities for horse riding, and deserts for exploration by camel. All this is primarily for the locals but visitors can enjoy these facilities too.

**Windsurfing between Eilat and Taba in the Gulf of Aqaba**

**A clown fish swims by brightly coloured soft corals**

## DIVING

Experienced divers claim that the Red Sea offers some of the world's best diving. The various scuba diving centres in Eilat, Aqaba and, especially, Sinai organize courses for beginners, as well as for more experienced divers who wish to qualify for the various international licences. Most centres hire out all the diving equipment you need (the daily rate is about $35–50), including, if desired, underwater photographic equipment.

Although the entire Red Sea teems with marine life, some of the richest dive sites are undoubtedly those within the Ras Muhammad National Park (see p243), which is close to Sharm el-Sheikh at the tip of the Sinai peninsula. Dives in the park must be organized through a dive club.

While it is possible to sort out your own diving arrangements with a local company once you arrive, there are also many international agencies specializing in Red Sea diving holidays.

In Eilat, reputable diving centres include **Aqua Sport**, which organizes daily boat excursions along the Sinai coast to less-dived locations, **Divers' Village** and **Marina Divers**.

In Sinai, some of the better outfits include **Inmo** and the **Nesima Dive Centre** in Dahab, and the **Camel Dive Club**, **Emperor Divers**, **Oonas Dive Centre** and **Sinai Divers** in Sharm el-Sheikh. You can visit their websites (see p297) for more information.

For a different kind of diving experience, **Caesarea Diving** at the Caesarea National Park (see p176) on Israel's Mediterranean coast offers scuba trips that allow you to explore the submerged ruins of Herod's ancient harbour.

## SNORKELLING

Another way of viewing the rich marine life and beauty of the reefs is to snorkel. This has the advantage of being cheap and of not requiring any complicated equipment or specialised training. Dahab and Sharm el-Sheikh in Egypt (see pp242–3) are the best locations, and each has plenty of snorkel-hire shops. It is also possible to snorkel in Israel at Eilat (see p205) and in Jordan at Aqaba (see p235).

## WATER SPORTS

The windsurfing is good in the Gulf of Aqaba, particularly on the coast between Eilat and the border at Taba; there are plenty of places to rent boards, many of them near the small marina by the Club Med hotel. The region's centre for water sports is Eilat (see p205), with everything from snorkels to jetskis for hire, plus a multitude of other activities, including paragliding and glass-bottomed boats. Israel's Mediterranean coast is more exposed, with dangerous currents, but

**A diver enters the Red Sea just off Aqaba in Jordan**

there are water sports activities at Tel Aviv and a few other coastal towns, such as Netanya.

In Egypt, all the larger Sinai resorts, including Taba Heights, Dahab and Sharm el-Sheikh offer extensive water sports facilities.

## RAFTING AND CANOEING

Possibilities exist for rafting and canoeing on the Jordan River in the Golan Heights *(see 181)*; these activities are supervised by **Abu Kayak** in the Jordan River Park, at Tel Bethsaida.

## DESERT HIKING

A large number of specialist organisations lead hikes throughout Israel. A good starting point for finding out about such trips is to visit the **Society for the Protection of Nature in Israel (SPNI)**. Its offices/bookshops in Tel Aviv and Jerusalem carry a wide range of specialized maps and useful publications. The SPNI also runs plenty of hikes itself. Some of the best routes are around Maktesh Ramon *(see p204)* and Ein Gedi *(see p196)*, and up in the Golan Heights *(see p181)*.

The best hiking in Jordan is, without doubt, in and around Wadi Rum *(see p232–4)*. Here you'll find trails that last anything from a couple of hours to several days, all of which are described in the essential *Treks and Climbs in*

**Trekking in one of the canyons of the Judaean Desert**

*Wadi Rum* by Tony Howard. There are numerous guide agencies based in the area; some of the better ones include **Bedouin Roads**, **Rum Trekking**, **Sunset Camp** and **Wadi Rum Adventures**. There is also some excellent hiking around Petra *(see p220–31)* and at Wadi Mujib *(see p197)*. For more information on treks and hikes visit the **Wild Jordan Centre** in Amman.

While not as magnificent as Wadi Rum or Petra, Egypt's Sinai peninsula has an interior that is starkly beautiful and well worth exploring; this can be arranged at most hotels in Nuweiba, Dahab or Sharm el-Sheikh. Some of the most rewarding trekking is around the St Catherine's Monastery region *(see p246–8)*. All treks must be done with a Bedouin guide, and this can be arranged through the services of **Sheikh Musa**, a local Bedouin leader.

## CAMEL TREKKING

One of the best ways to explore the vast sandy expanses of Wadi Rum *(see p232–4)* is on the back of a camel. A wide variety of treks are available, ranging from half-hour explorations to overnight expeditions. It is also possible to arrange longer camel excursions from Wadi Rum – or Petra – down to Aqaba. These take from three to six nights, depending on the route. For more details contact an agency such as **Bait Ali**, **Bedouin Roads**, **Petra Moon Tourism**, **Sunset Camp** or **Wadi Rum Adventures** *(see p297)*.

In Israel, the **Mamshit Camel Ranch**, near Dimona on Route 25 between Beersheva and Sodom, offers desert trips on camels. In Egypt's Sinai, camel trekking can also be arranged by most hotels in Nuweiba, Dahab and Sharm el-Sheikh.

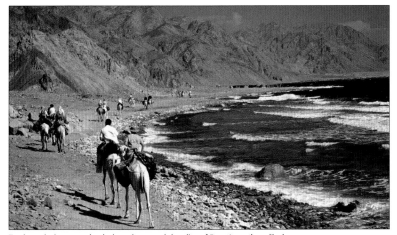
**Tourists enjoying a camel trek along the rugged shoreline of Egypt's southern Sinai**

Horse riders passing the Bab el-Siq Triclinium en route to the entrance at Petra

## CLIMBING

Wadi Rum *(see p232–4)* offers some of the Holy Land's best rock climbing, with the ascent of Jebel Rum high on most climbers' lists. For information on route options see the book *Treks & Climbs in Wadi Rum, Jordan* by Tony Howard and Di Taylor (easily available in Jordan) or try the website www.wadirum.net. Several guides offer instruction in basic climbing techniques, including **Wadi Rum Mountain Guides**, which is run by Attayak Aouda, one of Rum's best climbing guides. Experienced climbers should bring their own equipment.

Jebel Umm Adaami, near the border with Saudi Arabia, is Jordan's highest peak at 1,832 m (or 6,045 ft). It's a fairly easy hike to the summit, plus an hour-long jeep drive each way, and you can stop off at some interesting petroglyphs and lovely scenery en route.

Rope-assisted descents of spectacular gorges in Israel's Judaean Desert are organized by the **Metzoke Dragot Centre**. The same company also offers climbing, hiking, and jeep or truck excursions into the desert.

## HORSE RIDING

Stables and riding schools are located throughout Israel, particularly in Upper Galilee, the Golan region and on the coast between Tel Aviv and Haifa. **Vered ha-Galil**, just north of the Sea of Galilee, is the largest riding school in the country, while the **Haela Ranch** is conveniently close to Jerusalem, up in the hills east of the city.

In Jordan it is possible to explore the desert landscapes of Wadi Rum on horseback. Among the agencies who can organize this are **Bait Ali** and **Rum Horses**. It is also possible to ride at Petra, although this is limited to a one km (half a mile) canter to the site entrance.

In Sinai, several resort hotels offer horse riding by the hour, while in Dahab, Bedouin rent horses on the beach.

## GOLF

Israel has precisely two golf courses and, of these, the **Caesarea Golf Club** is the only one that meets international 18-hole standards. The course, designed in 1961, passes through ancient Roman and Byzantine ruins. In recent years Egypt has sought to market itself as a golfing destination and it has several new courses. Two of these are in Sinai: the **Jolie Ville Golf Resort** at Sharm el-Sheikh, opened in 1998, and, further north, the **Taba Heights Golf Resort** with its views across the Red Sea to Saudia Arabia and Jordan, which opened in 2006.

## BIRDWATCHING

Israel and Sinai lie on one of the principal bird migration routes between Europe and Africa and so are something of a birdwatcher's paradise. In Israel, interested parties should visit the **International Birding and Research Centre**, which is in Eilat, near the Arava border crossing with Jordan, a short distance north-east of the town centre.

In Jordan, the Royal Society for the Conservation of Nature organizes birding trips (visit them at the **Wild Jordan Centre** in Amman), typically out to the Azraq Wetland Reserve, which is about 80 km (50 miles) east of Amman. For information on birding in Sinai, and throughout Egypt, see www.birdingegypt.com.

## WORKING ON A KIBBUTZ

Not as popular as it once was, Israel's pioneering, socialist-style kibbutz movement continues to employ young volunteers (who must be aged between 18 and 32) from abroad to carry out manual work. Typical work involves picking fruit out in the fields, working on a factory production line, or being attached to a dining room, kitchen or laundry. The kibbutz will normally expect a minimum commitment of two months, during which time volunteers work for their accommodation, meals and a small personal allowance, plus one day a week holiday. The kibbutz facilities are

Volunteers working on a kibbutz in northern Israel

available to volunteers; these may include such things as a swimming pool or gym.

Volunteers usually apply through a special kibbutz office in their home country, although there is also a kibbutz office in Tel Aviv, through which online applications can be made (see the directory, below).

## HAMMAMS

Hammams are what are known elsewhere as Turkish baths. At one time, every Arab town would have had several such institutions. They were as much social centres as places to get clean. The advent of domestic plumbing has rendered them largely obsolete but a handful remain. In Amman, Jordan, is the grand **Hammam el-Pasha**, which has separate areas for men and woman. In Aqaba (see p235), the **Aqaba Turkish Baths** are men only – although women may visit by special appointment, in which instance they get the whole place to themselves.

# DIRECTORY

## DIVING AND SNORKELLING

**Aqua Sport**
Coral Beach, Eilat, Israel.
*Tel (08) 633 4404.*
www.aqua-sport.com

**Caesarea Diving**
Caesarea National Park, Israel.
*Tel (04) 626 5898.*
www.caesarea-diving.com/eng

**Camel Dive Club**
Sharm el-Sheikh, Egypt.
*Tel (069) 360 0700.*
www.cameldive.com

**Divers' Village**
Coral Beach, Eilat, Israel.
*Tel (08) 637 2268.*

**Emperor Divers**
Dahab, Nuweiba and Sharm el-Sheikh, Egypt.
*Tel (069) 360 1734.*
www.emperordivers.com

**Inmo**
Dahab, Egypt.
*Tel (069) 364 0370.*
www.inmodivers.de

**Marina Divers**
Coral Beach, Eilat, Israel.
*Tel (08) 637 6787.*
www.marinadivers.co.il

**Nesima Dive Centre**
Dahab, Egypt.
*Tel (069) 364 0320.*
www.nesima-resort.com

**Oonas Dive Centre**
Dahab and Sharm el-Sheikh, Egypt.
*Tel UK (01323) 648 924.*
www.oonasdivers.com

**Sinai Divers**
Dahab, Sharm el-Sheikh and Taba, Egypt.
*Tel (069) 360 0697.*
www.sinaidivers.com

## RAFTING AND CANOEING

**Abu Kayak**
Jordan River Park, Beth Saida, Israel.
*Tel (04) 692 1078.*

## DESERT HIKING

**Bedouin Roads**
Wadi Rum, Jordan.
*Tel (079) 589 9723.*
www.bedouinroads.com

**Rum Trekking**
Wadi Rum, Jordan.
*Tel (079) 512 7148.*
www.rumtrekking.com

**Sheikh Musa**
St Catherine's, Egypt.
*Tel (010) 641 3575.*

**Society for the Protection of Nature in Israel (SPNI)**
13 Heleni ha-Malka Street, West Jerusalem. *Tel (02) 624 4605.* 4 Ha-Shfela Street, Tel Aviv. *Tel (03) 638 8674.* www.teva.org.il

**Sunset Camp**
Wadi Rum, Jordan.
*Tel (077) 731 4688.*
www.mohammedwadirum.8m.com

**Wadi Rum Adventures**
Wadi Rum, Jordan.
*Tel (077) 747 2074.*
www.wadirumadventures.com

**Wild Jordan Centre**
Amman, Jordan.
*Tel (06) 461 6523.*
www.rscn.org.jo

## CAMEL TREKKING

**Bait Ali**
Wadi Rum, Jordan.
*Tel (079) 554 8133.*
www.baitali.com

**Bedouin Roads**
See Desert Hiking.

**Mamshit Camel Ranch**
Mamshit, Western Negev, Israel.
*Tel (08) 655 1054.*

**Petra Moon Tourism**
Petra, Jordan.
*Tel (03) 215 6665.*
www.petramoon.com

**Sunset Camp**
See Desert Hiking.

**Wadi Rum Adventures**
See Desert Hiking.

## CLIMBING

**Metzoke Dragot Centre**
Metzoke Dragot, Dead Sea, Israel.
*Tel (02) 994 4222.*

**Wadi Rum Mountain Guides**
Wadi Rum, Jordan.
*Tel (079) 583 4736.*
*Email attayak@rumguides.com*

## HORSE RIDING

**Bait Ali**
See Camel Trekking.

**Haela Ranch**
Nes Harim, Israel.
*Tel (054) 204 5700.*
www.haelaranch.com

**Rum Horses**
Wadi Rum, Jordan.
*Tel (03) 203 3508.*
www.desertguides.com

**Vered ha-Galil**
Korazim, 20 km north of Tiberias, Galilee, Israel.
*Tel (04) 693 5785.*
www.veredhagalil.co.il

## GOLF

**Caesarea Golf Course**
Caesarea, Israel.
*Tel (04) 610 9600.*
www.caesarea.co.il

**Jolie Ville Golf Resort**
Mövenpick Resort, Sharm el-Sheikh, Egypt.
*Tel (069) 600 635.*
www.jolieville-hotels.com

**Taba Heights Golf Resort**
Taba Heights, Egypt.
*Tel (069) 358 0073.*
www.tabaheights.com

## BIRDWATCHING

**International Birding & Research Centre**
Near Arava Crossing, Eilat, Israel.
*Tel (08) 633 5319.*
www.eilat-birds.org

**Wild Jordan Centre**
See Desert Hiking.

## WORKING ON A KIBBUTZ

**Kibbutz Programme Centre**
18 Frishmann Street, Tel Aviv, Israel.
*Tel (03) 524 6154.*
www.kibbutz.org.il

## HAMMAMS

**Aqaba Turkish Baths**
King Hussein Street, Aqaba, Jordan.
*Tel (03) 203 1605.*

**Hammam el-Pasha**
El-Mahmoud Taha Street, Jebel Amman, Amman, Jordan.
www.pashaturkishbath.com

# SURVIVAL
# GUIDE

# PRACTICAL INFORMATION

The area covered by this guide is not very large, but because it includes the territory of three nations (Israel, Jordan and Egypt), as well as the Autonomous Palestinian Territories, getting about from one place to another may not always be straightforward. The political situation in this part of the world changes frequently, and before

Israeli tourist board logo

embarking on a trip that involves any crossing of borders, you should make sure that there have been no significant changes to the international agreements between these countries. Israel, Jordan and Egypt all have their own tourist organizations, which have offices abroad (see p301 for a directory of contact details for these).

## CROSSING BORDERS

Peace agreements of recent years have made it possible to travel overland between Israel and Egypt, and between Israel and Jordan. There are two commonly used crossings between Jordan and Israel (plus a third, less convenient crossing near Beth Shean).

The King Hussein Bridge (also known as the Allenby Bridge) is 16 km (10 miles) east of Jericho. From East Jerusalem (opposite Damascus Gate) you can take a taxi or minibus to the border then, once across, pick up transportation on to Amman. There are hefty Israeli exit and Jordanian entry taxes to pay. The crossing is open 8am–noon Sunday–Thursday and 8am–3pm Friday and Saturday. A second border crossing point exists at Wadi Arava 4 km (2 miles) from Eilat and 10 km (6 miles) from Aqaba. Its opening hours are the same as the King Hussein Bridge. Again, the most convenient way to cross is to use public transport.

To enter Sinai you can take the ferry or catamaran from Aqaba in Jordan to Nuweiba. Both depart once a day, and you can get your Sinai Permit on board. You can also cross overland using public transport from Eilat in Israel to Taba. Allow plenty of time if crossing any of these borders, as there are strict security measures in place and crossing often takes one or two hours.

## VISAS FOR ISRAEL

You must have a passport that is valid for at least six months to enter Israel. Citizens of European nations, as well as those from North America, Australia and New Zealand, do not, however, need a visa. Citizens of most Arab, Asian, African and South American countries do need visas, and must obtain them in advance from an Israeli consulate in their home country. The visa is usually valid for up to a three-month stay, but can be extended. You can also obtain a "volunteer visa" (valid for 6–12 months) that allows you to work temporarily in a kibbutz (see pp294–5).

An Israeli visa in your passport will bar you from entering some Arab countries, notably Syria and Lebanon, but not Egypt or Jordan. You can avoid this by asking at the airport that the visa be stamped on a separate piece of paper. Other than at the Allenby Bridge crossing, this cannot be done at the land borders.

At present there are checkpoints for visitors crossing the borders between Israel and the Palestinian territories. Here Israeli or Palestinian police will ask to see your passport and may carry out security checks.

Entry card for Israel, and visa required to enter Jordan

## VISAS FOR JORDAN

Tourists arriving in Jordan must have a passport valid for at least six months, and also a visa. If you are arriving at Queen Alia international airport you can obtain a one-month tourist visa upon arrival. The price of this can vary dramatically depending on your nationality.

If you are entering Jordan by land then you must have already obtained your visa in advance, as the border posts do not issue them (the only exception to this being the Wadi Arava border crossing). Visas can otherwise be issued either by the Jordanian consulate or embassy in your home country, or by those in Tel Aviv or Cairo.

Israeli soldiers checking cars coming from the Palestinian Autonomous Territories

◁ Bedouin tents in the mountainous wilderness of Wadi Rum

## VISAS FOR EGYPT

If you are entering Sinai from Israel, you can obtain a special Sinai Permit that allows you to stay for up to 14 days; this is obtained at the border and is free. Bear in mind, however, that the Sinai Permit cannot be changed into a full visa. Neither can a full visa for Egypt be obtained at the border. If you plan to visit other parts of Egypt beyond Sinai, you

**Israeli road signs**

must obtain a visa in advance from an Egyptian consulate or embassy in your home country, or else in Amman, Aqaba, Tel Aviv or Eilat.

## DUTY-FREE ARTICLES AND CUSTOMS

The duty-free allowance in all three countries is 200 cigarettes or 200 grams of tobacco, a litre of spirits and two bottles of wine. Valuable electrical objects such as computers and video cameras will be entered in passports by customs officers to prevent their resale in the country.

## LANGUAGE

English is very much a second language in Israel, where many immigrants do not speak Hebrew. All signs are bilingual and it is rare to meet someone who doesn't understand any English at all. The story is very different in

Palestinian areas and in Jordan, however, where Arabs will make every effort to communicate with foreigners, even if it means resorting to sign language. In areas frequented by tourists it is easier to find English speakers, although attempts to speak Arabic will always be welcomed. Away from the main tourist circuit it can be much harder to get your message across without some rudimentary grasp of the language.

## ETIQUETTE

Israeli society, on the whole, is not that different from the West. There are exceptions; in ultra-Orthodox areas such as Jerusalem's Mea Shearim and parts of the Galilee town of Safed, behaviour and dress should definitely err on the side of conservatism. This is also the case in Arab areas, both in the Palestinian Autono-mous Territories and in Jordan. Arab women usually cover their arms, legs and sometimes their heads in public, and men do not wear shorts. Visitors are not always expected to cover up in the same way, but you must be suitably clothed when visiting certain public places and any of the holy sites *(see p300)*.

Intimate physical contact with a person of the opposite sex in public is also taboo in Arab society; Arabic couples are rarely seen kissing, embrac-ing or even holding hands.

# DIRECTORY

## EMBASSIES AND CONSULATES

**In Israel**
**UK Embassy**
192 Ha-Yarkon Street, Tel Aviv.
*Tel (03) 725 1222.*
www.britemb.org.il
**UK Consulates**
19 Nashashibi Street,
Sheikh Jarah, East Jerusalem.
*Tel (02) 541 4100.*
**US Embassy**
71 Ha-Yarkon Street, Tel Aviv.
*Tel (03) 519 7575.*
http://telaviv.usembassy.gov
**US Consulates**
18 Agron Street, West Jerusalem.
*Tel (02) 625 3288.*
17 Nablus Road, East Jerusalem.
*Tel (02) 625 3288.*

**In Jordan**
**UK Embassy**
Damascus Street, Abdoun,
Amman.
*Tel (06) 590 9200.*
**US Embassy**
Damascus St, Abdoun, Amman.
*Tel (06) 590 6950.*

**In Egypt**
**UK Embassy**
7 Ahmed Ragheb Street,
Garden City, Cairo.
*Tel (02) 794 0852.*
**US Embassy**
5 Latin America Street,
Garden City, Cairo.
*Tel (02) 795 7371.*

**In the UK**
**Egyptian Consulate**
2 Lowndes Street, London SW1.
*Tel (020) 7235 9777.*
**Israeli Embassy**
2 Palace Green, London W8.
*Tel (020) 7957 9500.*
**Jordanian Embassy**
6 Upper Phillimore Gardens,
London W8.
*Tel (020) 7937 3685.*

**In the US**
**Egyptian Consulate**
1110 2nd Avenue, New York.
*Tel (212) 759 7120.*
**Israeli Embassy**
3514 International Drive NW,
Washington DC.
*Tel (202) 364 5500.*
**Jordanian Embassy**
3504 International Drive NW,
Washington DC.
*Tel (202) 966 2664.*

**Arab women in customary dress, outside the Dome of the Rock, Jerusalem**

# Tips for Tourists

Israeli tourist
office sign

Tourism in Jerusalem and the Holy Land is considerable, given the region's major historical and religious importance, as well as its great natural beauty. As such, most towns are well adapted for visitors, with good public facilities and helpful tourist offices. Major sites are open long hours for much of the week, and also have good facilities as well as useful educational material. Some sites, however, are well off the beaten track, and difficult to reach using public transport. If visiting desert areas, make sure you arrive early, to avoid the extreme afternoon heat.

Free brochures
available from tourist sites

Free tourist office brochure

## TOURIST INFORMATION

As well as providing useful information in the form of free brochures and maps, Israeli tourist offices are usually able to help with other matters, such as finding accommodation and arranging transport. In smaller towns, or at archaeological sites, the tourist offices are of more limited use, and information is usually confined to the immediate area. The Autonomous Palestinian Territories are also in the process of organizing a network of information bureaus, but for the present, their sole office is in Bethlehem.

In Jordan the only tourist information offices are in the main tourist destinations such as Amman, Petra and Jerash, while in Sinai there are no tourist information offices at all. All three countries have international tourist bureaux, however, which you can use before you leave. The national airline offices can also often help with travel information.

## ENTRANCE FEES

Most of the historic and archaeological sites in Jerusalem and the Holy Land have some kind of admission charge, although some smaller churches and mosques have no fixed fee at all. In these cases a small donation is customary. Prices are generally very reasonable, with most minor sites in Israel charging only a few shekels. Larger places may charge slightly more, with the most expensive site to visit by far being Petra.

In Israel you can purchase a 14–day Green Card for around NIS 120, that gives free access to all sites under the control of the Nature and National Parks Protection Authority. These are mainly natural and more minor archaeological sites, but if you are planning to spend some time sightseeing in Israel, this may be a good investment.

## OPENING HOURS

Because of the many religious holidays *(see pp36–9)* celebrated in the region (Jewish, Muslim and Christian), opening hours for the many tourist sites and historic monuments can vary greatly. As a general rule, however, sites in Israel are usually open daily, except for Friday, when they keep more restricted hours, and Saturday, when they are closed altogether. Christian

sites, other than the churches, are open on Saturdays but closed on Sundays.

In Jordan the main sites (including Petra and Jerash) are open daily, but other, smaller sites, including many of the museums, are closed on Tuesdays. From around October to March (considered the winter season), most sites in the Holy Land close an hour earlier than usual.

## WHAT TO WEAR AT SACRED SITES

When visiting holy sites such as churches, synagogues and mosques, it is essential that you dress appropriately. This means that your arms and legs must be fully covered; shorts or short skirts and sleeveless tops are not acceptable. At certain

Visitors removing footwear before entering
The Dome of the Rock, Jerusalem

places cloaks are provided to cover up visitors who are deemed to be immodestly dressed. Shoes must be removed before entering a mosque, and at some Jewish holy sites, such as the Western Wall, heads must also be covered. In such cases a *kippah* (skullcap) is provided free of charge.

## TIME

The time in Israel, Jordan and Egypt is two hours ahead of Greenwich Mean Time (GMT), and seven hours ahead of Eastern Standard Time (EST). All three countries have daylight saving time which lasts from approximately March to September.

## DISABLED VISITORS

Israel is very aware of the needs of disabled visitors, and many hotels and modern museums are adapted for disabled use. **MILBAT** is a useful advisory centre on such matters, while **JDC-Israel** is also able to advise on suitable hotel accommodation and site accessibility. The **Yad Sarah Organization** lends out wheelchairs and other useful aids free of charge.

Jordan and Sinai make no real provision for the disabled, and as most sites are surrounded by rough terrain, visiting these areas can be very problematic.

Student ISIC identity card

## STUDENT INFORMATION

In Israel, the presentation of a recognized student card, such as an International Student Identity Card (ISIC), will get the holder a ten per cent discount on bus fares, as well as discounts on most museum and site admissions. The **Israel Student Tourist Association (ISSTA)** can arrange cheap flights and accommodation, and provide information on student discounts, as well as arranging its own package holidays. There are no student discounts offered in Jordan, but Egypt offers a 50 per cent concession on most site admissions.

## WCS

Public toilets are easily found throughout Israel, and are of the standard type found in the West. In Jordan they are much less common and a lot more rudimentary, but still usually clean, as they are tended by caretakers. In Sinai public toilets do not exist at all. It is always wise to have a supply of paper with you, as

**Sign for public toilets**

this is often not provided. All paper should be disposed of using the bins provided, and not put down the toilet, as the local plumbing cannot cope.

## ELECTRICAL ADAPTORS

The electric current in Israel, Jordan and Sinai is 220V. Plugs in Israel are round-pronged and three-pinned, whereas in Jordan and Sinai they are round-pronged and two-pinned. Adaptors should be bought prior to departure.

**Two-pin plug adaptor for use in Jordan and Sinai**

## CONVERSION CHART

**Imperial to Metric**
1 inch = 2.54 centimetres
1 foot = 30 centimetres
1 mile = 1.6 kilometres
1 ounce = 28 grams
1 pound = 454 grams
1 pint = 0.6 litres
1 gallon = 4.6 litres

**Metric to Imperial**
1 centimetre = 0.4 inches
1 metre = 3 feet, 3 inches
1 kilometre = 0.6 miles
1 gram = 0.04 ounces
1 kilogram = 2.2 pounds
1 litre = 1.8 pints

# DIRECTORY

## TOURIST INFORMATION

### Israel Ministry of Tourism
www.goisrael.com

**In the UK:**
180 Oxford Street,
London W1N 0EL.
*Tel (020) 7299 1111.*

**In the US:**
800 Second Avenue,
New York 10017.
*Tel (212) 499 5660.*

### Jordan Tourist Board
PO Box 830688,

Amman 11183, Jordan.
www.seejordan.org

**In the UK:**
32 Brook St, London W1.
*Tel (020) 7878 6333.*

**In the US:**
535 Fifth Ave, New York.
*Tel (212) 949 0060.*

### Egyptian Tourist Authority
Misr Travel Tower,
Abbassia Sq, Cairo, Egypt.
*Tel (02) 285 4509.*
http://touregypt.net/
tourism/

**In the UK:**
170 Piccadilly, London W1.
*Tel (020) 7493 5282.*

**In the US:**
Suite 1706, 630 Fifth
Avenue, New York.
*Tel (212) 332 2570.*

### Palestinian Authority
*Tel (02) 274 8484.*
www.pna.gov.ps

## DISABLED VISITORS

### MILBAT
Sheba Medical Centre,

Tel ha-Shomer,
Ramat Gan, Tel Aviv, Israel.
*Tel (03) 530 3739.*
www.milbat.org.il

### JDC-Israel
www.jdc.org

### Yad Sarah Organization
124 Herzl Blvd, Jerusalem.
*Tel *6444.*

## STUDENT INFORMATION

### ISSTA
31 Ha-Neviim St, Jerusalem.
*Tel (02) 621 3600.*

# Security and Health

Israel and the Middle East suffer from a bad press when it comes to security. However, despite the occasional alarming headline, Israel and its neighbouring territories of Jordan and Sinai are perfectly safe for tourists. Visitors rarely encounter crime, and there are next to no hazards in the form of dangerous animals, or endemic diseases. Political unrest does from time to time result in acts of terrorism or rioting, but this hardly ever affects visitors. With the present ongoing attempts to reach peace between Israel and the Palestinians, even these infrequent incidents of violence may, hopefully, soon be a thing of the past.

Israeli Defence Force soldiers at Damascus Gate

perform military service in the Israeli Defence Force (IDF) as soon as they reach the age of 18. The term of service is three years for men and two years for women. Men serve for an additional 30 days a year until the age of 35. Consequently, you will see armed soldiers around all the time, particularly at bus stations, as they are usually on the way to or from their bases.

## LAW AND ORDER

Israel, Jordan and Sinai all have special tourist police to deal with any complaints or problems visitors may encounter. These police mostly speak English, and are posted at most major sites and at tourist resorts. They wear identifying armbands. The Jordanians have a special form of tourist police, active in the Wadi Rum area, known as the Desert Patrol. These officials are easily identified by their smart khaki uniforms, their distinctive red-and-white checked headdress and by the fact that they often ride camels.

Normal Israeli police wear navy blue uniforms and peaked caps. Also part of the police force are the border guards, who wear a military style uniform and a green beret. They operate mainly in the Israeli-controlled areas of the West Bank. The Palestinians also have their own security forces, who come in a multitude of guises.

Visitors will notice a preponderance of military personnel on the streets in Jerusalem and Israel. Every citizen must

## PERSONAL SAFETY

On arrival at Ben Gurion Airport, you will almost immediately experience just how tight security is in Israel. During your stay, you may be subject to security checks on

A member of the Desert Patrol, Wadi Rum, Jordan

entering hotels, restaurants, bars, cinemas and shopping complexes, so it is wise always to carry some identification, preferably your passport. But as far as the visitor is concerned, terrorism is not a major worry. Tourists have never been the target of terrorists and most attacks have occurred well away from all tourist sites. Naturally, you have to be alert when in the streets, and also keep an eye on the local news. Among the "sensitive" areas are East Jerusalem and West Bank towns such as Hebron and Ramallah. In times of unrest you should definitely give such places a wide berth. Should you be unlucky enough to encounter a disturbance in the streets, move away from the scene quickly, and make it completely clear that you are a foreign tourist.

Israeli policeman

Stories of theft, mugging and other similar opportunistic crimes are rare in the Holy Land. Crime is not the problem here that it is in many other parts of the world. As a rule, all areas are considered safe for visitors, unless the visitor is an unaccompanied woman. Lone females are frequently subjected to unwanted verbal pestering and harrassment from local males, both Israeli and Arab. This problem is particularly acute in Jerusalem's Old City and its surrounding areas, such as the Mount of Olives and Mount Zion. Incidences of rape have even been reported, and so our advice to women must be that they should not walk alone in unpeopled areas or in the Old City after dark.

## PERSONAL PROPERTY

On the whole Israelis and Arabs are very honest people. Arabs, especially, will go to great lengths to return lost property. If you lose anything it is always worth going to the last place the item was seen, or going to the tourist police. On occasion, unpleasant experiences do happen. To minimize the risk of this, do not leave valuable objects inside a car or in full view in your hotel room. Leave your valuables in the hotel safe or at the reception desk. The fact that credit cards are accepted almost everywhere is a good reason not to carry a lot of cash with you. In case of theft, remember to make a report to the police and to ask for a copy of the report, which you will then have to present to your insurance company when you make your claim.

Security considerations mean that you should not leave luggage or packages unattended (especially in airports and bus stations), as they might cause alarm or trigger a reaction on the part of the security forces.

## HEALTH PRECAUTIONS

Medical care in Jerusalem and the Holy Land is costly, making it inadvisable to travel without some form of medical insurance. The policy should at least cover the cost of a flight home.

No specific vaccinations are legally required before entering Israel, Jordan or Sinai, but doctors may advise inoculation against hepatitis A (spread through contaminated food or water), hepatitis B, tetanus and also typhoid.

There are no particular endemic diseases in the Middle East, but the hot climate necessitates that you take certain precautions, at least until you are used to the change in diet. It is advisable to drink mineral water (which is sold everywhere) and not use ice in your drinks. Avoid raw vegetables or food that has obviously been left standing for some time since it was cooked, and peel fruit. Continually

**A small pharmacy in Jerusalem**

drinking large quantities of liquids is essential: the lack of humidity in the air causes rapid dehydration, even though you may not be aware of it. Other than this, the most frequent problems are intestinal. A change of diet often upsets the stomach. It is recommended that you should always carry diarrhoea pills. If the upset continues then consult a doctor or pharmacist for more powerful medication.

Mosquitoes can sometimes be a nuisance, but there is no threat of malaria. Bring repellent lotion or spray from your own country – although, if you forget, it is easy to find in any pharmacy. If you go diving in the Red **Pharmacy** Sea, you need to be **sign in Israel** careful of sharp corals and be aware of which species of fish are poisonous and are to be avoided.

## PHARMACIES

Good pharmacies are easy to find throughout both Israel and Jordan. However, if you need a particular medicine, it is

**Magen David Adom ambulance**

still advisable to travel with your own supplies and keep a note of the product and its composition so that, if worst comes to worst, a pharmacist will be able to find a local equivalent. In Israel, the *Jerusalem Post* lists the names and addresses of pharmacies that stay open late and during Shabbat and holidays.

## MEDICAL TREATMENT

In an emergency in Israel, you can call 101 to request an ambulance or to ask about the nearest casualty department. Alternatively, contact the local branch of the **Magen David Adom** (Israel's equivalent of the Red Cross), or call its countrywide toll-free number.

In Jordan, if you need a doctor, call into a pharmacy and ask for a recommendation or call your embassy. In Sinai, most large hotels have a resident doctor. For divers, there is a special **Hyperbaric Medical Centre** in Sharm el-Sheikh equipped with a recompression chamber.

## DIRECTORY

### EMERGENCY NUMBERS

**In Israel**
**Ambulance**
*Tel 101.*
Private Ambulances (Natali):
*Tel 1-700-700-180.*
**Police and General Enquiries**
*Tel 100.*
**Directory Assistance**
*Tel 144.*

**In Jordan**
**Ambulance**
*Tel 193.*
**Police**
*Tel 191.*
**Local Directory Assistance**
*Tel 131.*

**In Sinai**
**Ambulance**
*Tel 123.*
**Hyperbaric Medical Centre**
*Tel (069) 366 0922/3 (24 hr).*

**Police**
*Tel 122.*
**Tourist Police**
*Tel 126.*

# Banking and Currency

**Mizrahi bank logo**

Exchanging and obtaining money pose no problems in Israel and the Holy Land. Cash and traveller's cheques can be exchanged at banks, exchange offices and in many hotels. Credit cards are widely accepted and can be used to obtain funds. The only issues to be aware of are the greatly varying levels of commission charged on transactions, and the limited opening hours of banks.

**Official money exchange office**

## BANKS

Banks in Israel, Jordan and Sinai will exchange all major European currencies, but the most welcome currency of all is the US dollar. ATMs (automatic cash dispensers) linked into international banking networks, such as Cirrus or Plus, are widespread in Israel. You will find them in the foyers of most banks. These machines are less common in Jordan and Sinai, and found only in Amman, Petra and Sharm el-Sheikh. Some banks in Israel also have automatic currency exchange machines, which are accessible 24 hours a day. The drawback is that these machines usually charge a high transaction fee combined with a very poor rate of exchange.

Jerusalem's banking district is centred on Zion Square, at the bottom of Ben Yehuda Street in the New City. Banks are generally open from 8:30am to 12:30pm, reopening for another hour or two from around 4pm (but not on Wednesdays). They are shut on Fridays and Saturdays. In

**Automatic currency exchange machine**

Jordan and Sinai banking hours are similar to Israel, except that they are closed only on Fridays.

## EXCHANGE OFFICES

The banks often charge a considerable commission on currency exchanges; one way to avoid this is to use an official exchange office such as **Change Spot**. These places charge no commission. They also tend to be open much longer hours than the banks (from 9am to 9pm in some cases). Such exchange offices in Jerusalem can be found mainly on Jaffa Road and Ben Yehuda Street. There are also several small Arab exchange offices just inside Jaffa and Damascus gates in the Old City.

In Jordan, central Amman is full of small exchange offices, but there are not so many outside the capital. You can use one of the big hotels, but beware of the commission they may charge.

## TRAVELLER'S CHEQUES AND CREDIT CARDS

Traveller's cheques can be exchanged at banks but commission is charged per cheque. Better to cash them at exchange offices, where no commission is charged at all.

Major credit cards, such as VISA, Master Card, Diners Club and American Express are widely accepted throughout Israel, Jordan and Sinai in shops, restaurants and hotels. If you have your PIN number you can draw cash from ATMs.

**ATM machine at an Israeli bank**

## CURRENCY

Israel's national currency is the new Israeli shekel (NIS), referred to simply as the shekel. It is also the currency in the Palestinian Autonomous Territories, although there are plans to introduce a Palestinian national currency in the near future. Jordan has dinars (JD), while the currency in Sinai is the Egyptian pound (LE). These currencies are only valid in their home countries so, for example, you cannot spend excess Israeli shekels in Jordan. Exchange rates between the three tend to be very bad. This means, for example, that it is wise to use up all your shekels before leaving Israel and then to exchange dollars for dinars or pounds on arriving in Jordan or Egypt.

## DIRECTORY

### EXCHANGE OFFICES

**Change Spot**
5 Nordau Street, Haifa
*Tel* (04) 864 4111.
2 Ben Yehuda St, Jerusalem.
*Tel* (02) 624 0011.
4 Salomon St, Jerusalem.
*Tel* (02) 624 2166.
32 Jerusalem St, Safed.
*Tel* (04) 682 2777.
13 Ben Yehuda St, Tel Aviv.
*Tel* (03) 510 0573.
140 Dizengoff St, Tel Aviv.
*Tel* (03) 524 3393.
**www**.changespot.co.il

**Money Net**
84 Paulus VI St,
Nazareth.
*Tel* (06) 655 2540.

## Israeli Banknotes

*Israeli banknotes come in four different denominations: 200, 100, 50 and 20 NIS. The most recent series of notes is in the style of the 20- and 100-shekel notes shown here.*

**Two hundred shekels (200 NIS)**
**(This is the old style 200-shekel note.)**

**One hundred shekels (100 NIS)**

**Twenty shekels (20 NIS)**

## Israeli Coins

*The shekel is divided into 100 agorot. There are coins to the value of 10, 5 and 1 shekels, as well as 50 and 10 agorot.*

**Ten shekels**  **Five shekels**  **One shekel**  **Fifty agorot**  **Ten agorot**

## Jordanian Currency

*The Jordanian dinar is divided into 1,000 fils and, confusingly, also 100 piastres (100 fils therefore equals 10 piastres). Notes come in denominations of 20, 10, 5, 1 and ½ dinars. Coins exist to the value of 500, 250, 100, 50, 25, 10 and 5 fils, and 10, 5 and 2½ piastres.*

**20 dinars**

**10 dinars**

**5 dinars**

**½ dinar**  **100 fils**  **5 piastres**

## Egyptian Currency

*The currency in Egypt is the Egyptian pound (abbreviated to LE). The pound is divided into 100 piastres. Notes come in denominations of LE 200, 100, 50, 20, 10, 5, 1 and 50 and 25 piastres. Coins exist to the value of 50, 20, 10 and 5 piastres.*

**Twenty Egyptian pounds (LE 20)**

**Five Egyptian pounds (LE 5)**

# Communications

**Israeli post office logo**

Israel's postal service is generally efficient, but letters to Europe and North America can still take a week or more to arrive. This, however, is quicker than the Jordanian or Egyptian postal systems, which are highly unpredictable. Calling overseas is very straightforward from Israel, and it is similarly easy to call overseas in Sinai, but telephone communications from Jordan are considerably more complicated, and expensive.

## PUBLIC TELEPHONES IN ISRAEL

Israel's public telephones are almost all operated by the national phone company, Bezek. They take prepaid phonecards, which are sold at post offices, shops and lottery kiosks. They are available in denominations of 20 units (13 NIS), 50 units (29 NIS) or 120 units (60 NIS). Calls made from 10pm to 1am and all day Saturday and Sunday are 25 per cent cheaper than the standard rate. Calls made between 1am and 8am are 50 per cent cheaper. To dial abroad using Bezek, the international access code is 014.

Bezek competes for custom with other telephone companies, including Golden Lines (012 to dial abroad) and Barak (013 to dial abroad). These rival services are often cheaper than Bezek, although it does depend on the country you are calling. You can also make discounted calls from Solan Telecom, whose offices are found throughout Israel.

**Israeli telephone and phonecards**

Visitors can rent mobile phones on arrival at Ben Gurion Airport. Rental rates start at about US$1 per day. Israel's mobile network does not have reciprocal roaming arrangements with many countries. Anyone who plans to take their mobile with them should check with their home service whether it can be used in Israel.

## PUBLIC TELEPHONES IN THE PALESTINIAN TERRITORIES

In the west bank and Gaza Strip, the Palestinians have their own telephone network with their own phonecards. These Palestinian phonecards can be purchased in Arab post offices and some shops. They cannot, at present, be used in Israeli phones.

**An Israeli lottery kiosk, where phonecards can also be bought**

## PUBLIC TELEPHONES IN JORDAN AND SINAI

Jordan's telephone network is creaky, but it is in the process of being upgraded. International calls can be made from public cardphones, for which the cards are purchased from nearby shops. However, phonecards for international calls only come in the denomination of JD 15. A better option is to use one of the many unofficial telephone bureaus, where you write the number you want on a piece of paper and the desk clerk makes the call. These calls are charged by the minute and, with a great many offices competing for custom, rates are reasonable.

The Egyptian telephone network in Sinai also uses phonecards. These come in denominations of LE 15, 20 or 30 and they can be bought at post offices.

## POSTAL SERVICES

Using Israeli post offices is a very straightforward procedure. The exception is if you are sending parcels or bulky items; this entails a series of security inspections. When it comes to posting letters, the yellow post boxes are for local correspondence and the red are for the rest of country and abroad. Post offices are open in the mornings and evenings, and are shut in the middle of the day, the afternoons and Tuesday. Postal rates vary according to the type of post and its weight, but a standard airmail letter to Europe or the US costs the equivalent of half a USdollar.

The Palestinian Authority also has its own postal service, and issues its own stamps, but it is not as efficient as the Israeli service.

A letter posted in Jordan can take anything up to two weeks to reach Europe and a month to the US. It can help to speed things up if you post

**Red Israeli post box**

**Jordanian stamps**

**Israeli stamps**

**Egyptian stamps**

your letters at a five-star hotel or a main post office, rather than a post box on the street. Post offices are closed Friday.

### NEWSPAPERS, RADIO AND TV

English-language readers are well catered for in Israel. The leading English-language publication is the daily *Jerusalem Post* (no Saturday edition). This is worth picking up on Fridays for its extensive cultural supplements and entertainment listings. The weekly *Jerusalem Times* is a Palestinian publication, which is usually available only in East Jerusalem and Arab areas of the Old City. In Jordan, look out for the *Jordan Times*, published daily except for Fridays. Foreign newpapers

**Local English-language press**

and magazines, such as *The Times, The Washington Post and Newsweek*, are widely available, and are usually just one or two days old.

Israeli TV has two state channels, both of which show a large number of subtitled English-language programmes. Most hotels also offer satellite channels such as BBC, Sky News and CNN. In Jordan, Channel 2 devotes a lot of screen time to US programmes, and has English-language news nightly at 10pm. Most hotels have satellite TV.

Israel Radio broadcasts news in English each week-day evening at 6:16pm.

### INTERNET CAFES

Despite being an extremely computer literate society, there are few internet cafés in Israel. This is possibly because most Israeli families have internet access of their own at home. There are only a few internet cafés in Jerusalem, and a handful dotted around the country. Jordan has an excellent internet venue, **books@cafe**, located in central Amman. There are further internet cafés in Jordan at Wadi Musa (Petra), Madaba and Aqaba. In Sinai the internet is available at many hotels and there is an internet cafe near the Fayrouz Hilton in Sharm el-Sheikh. Internet services are also offered at various shops in Dahab. Online time is usually charged by the half hour.

**Newspaper seller in Tiberias, Israel**

# TRAVEL INFORMATION

The easiest way to get to Jerusalem and the Holy Land is to fly direct. Jerusalem is served by Ben Gurion Airport, and there are also international airports at Eilat, Amman in Jordan and Sharm el-Sheikh in Sinai. There are frequent flights to Ben Gurion and, being a busy tourist destination, it is possible to get cheap

The logo of leading Israeli airline El Al

deals, especially if you are prepared to travel with a smaller, lesser-known airline, or take advantage of a charter package. There are no direct sailings to Israel from mainland Europe; the only sea route is from Athens via Cyprus. Travelling overland is an arduous business as all European trains terminate at Istanbul.

Arrival hall of Terminal 3 at Ben Gurion, Israel's main international airport

## FLYING TO ISRAEL

The Israeli national airline is **El Al**. It has direct flights to Ben Gurion Airport from most major European cities, as well as from New York, Los Angeles, Chicago, Miami, Baltimore and Orlando in the United States. Ben Gurion is also served by a great many foreign airlines, including Air France, Alitalia, British Airways, Lufthansa and Swissair; and American Airlines, Delta, Tower Air and TWA.

Fares are seasonal. The high season is during the Jewish and Christian holiday periods, in particular Passover, Easter and Rosh ha-Shanah *(see pp36–9)*. At such times fares are at a premium and it can often be hard to find seats.

It is always worth looking into flights to Eilat's Ovda airport. This largely caters for charter traffic, and it is on these flights that the cheapest fares are to be found. The drawbacks are that there are often restrictions on the dates you may travel and you have

to make your own way up to Jerusalem and back, a bus journey of between four and five hours each way.

## BEN GURION AIRPORT

Named after the first prime minister of Israel, Ben Gurion Airport lies southeast of Tel Aviv, just off the road to Jerusalem. All international flights arrive at and depart from the ultra-modern Terminal 3, which opened in 2004. Services at the airport include duty-free shops, a telecommunications office, foreign currency exchange offices, car-hire outlets and tourist information and hotel

El Al aeroplane on the runway at Ben Gurion airport

reservation desks. There is a domestic terminal for flights to Eilat; Jerusalem and Tel Aviv both have small city airports for internal flights.

Ben Gurion reputedly has the tightest security of any airport in the world. The time taken to inspect every item of baggage means that passengers must check in three hours before departure. However, anyone flying with El Al can check in luggage the day before at special offices in Jerusalem, Tel Aviv and Haifa. Those who do this need only turn up at the airport an hour and a quarter before departure.

## GETTING TO AND FROM BEN GURION AIRPORT

Ben Gurion Airport is at Lod, about 22 km (14 miles) from Tel Aviv and some 45 km (28 miles) from Jerusalem. Private taxis take about 45 minutes to Jerusalem, or you can take a shared taxi, or *sherut (see p310)*, which is much cheaper. These leave from just outside the arrivals hall. They do not set off until they are full, but it is rare to have to wait more than 10 or 15 minutes. The *sheruts* run through the night and will drop passengers anywhere in the city.

Egged buses Nos. 945 and 947 depart every half hour from around 5:30am until 9pm for Jerusalem's Central Bus Station on Jaffa Road. While this is the cheapest method of getting from the airport into the city, the bus station is more than a kilometre from the centre of the New City, and most people will then have to catch a further bus or taxi on to their hotel. The buses do not run on Shabbat – sundown Friday to sundown Saturday.

To get to the airport from Jerusalem, book a taxi the day before departure. Most hotels can usually organize this or call the number for licensed taxis at Ben Gurion Airport.

## FLYING TO JORDAN AND SINAI

Jordan's principal airport, and the home base for the national carrier **Royal Jordanian Airlines**, is Queen Alia International. Royal Jordanian has direct services between Amman and most major European capitals. It also flies, via Amsterdam, to New York and Chicago.

Other major carriers flying into Amman include Air France, Alitalia, British Airways and KLM. There are no non-stop flights from the US – instead you have to fly via a European hub. There is a second airport, known as Marka, about 5 km (3 miles) east of central Amman, but this handles only short-hop flights to Israel and Egypt.

**Compact Queen Alia International Airport, Jordan's main air transport hub**

There is also a further airport about 10 km (6 miles) north of Aqaba, but it receives few international flights.

Flights to Amman are not cheap. In general, it is much more economical to fly into Ben Gurion or Eilat in Israel and take a bus across the border. The airport at Sharm el-Sheikh in Sinai lies about 17 km (11 miles) north of town. It is served by Air Sinai and Egypt Air, but these are not direct flights; they involve a change of plane in Cairo.

## GETTING TO AND FROM QUEEN ALIA AIRPORT

Queen Alia Airport is about 30 km (19 miles) south of Amman. Comfortable Airport Express buses depart hourly between 7:15am and 9:15pm

for Downtown from just outside the arrivals terminal. Other buses head for the northern parts of town. Be sure to check the destination before boarding. Baggage is charged extra. Alternatively, you can catch a private taxi, but bear in mind that the official going rate is some 15 times the fare on the bus.

## FLIGHTS WITHIN THE HOLY LAND

Within Israel domestic flights are operated by **Arkia**. In Jerusalem these flights use Atarot Airport, 7 km (4 miles) north of the city centre. They connect to Tel Aviv (Sde Dov Airport), Eilat and Haifa. With distances in Israel being so short, it only makes sense to fly internally to or from Eilat.

El Al and Royal Jordanian both fly between Ben Gurion and Amman, while El Al and Air Sinai connect Ben Gurion with Sharm el-Sheikh and Cairo. Fares are not cheap, but you can, of course, save a lot of time by flying.

# DIRECTORY

## AIRPORTS

**Ben Gurion**
*Tel* (03) 975 5555.
www.iaa.gov.il

**Eilat (Ovda)**
*Tel* (08) 638 4848.

**Queen Alia International**
*Tel* (06) 445 2000.
www.jcaa.gov.jo/Airports/queen_alia.htm

## NATIONAL AIRLINES

**Arkia**
42 Agripas St, Jerusalem.
*Tel* (02) 621 8444.

11 Frishman St, Tel Aviv.
*Tel* (03) 690 2222.
www.arkia.co.il

**El Al**
12 Hillel St, Jerusalem.
*Tel* (02) 677 0200.

32 Ben Yehuda St, Tel Aviv.
*Tel* (03) 526 1222.
Eilat.
*Tel* (08) 632 6504.
Amman.
*Tel* (06) 562 2526.
Cairo.
*Tel* (20-2) 736 1795.
www.elal.co.il

**Royal Jordanian Airlines**
Seventh Circle, Amman.
*Tel* (06) 560 7300.
www.rja.com.jo

## OTHER AIRLINES

**Air France**
Tel Aviv.
*Tel* (03) 755 5050.
Amman.
*Tel* (06) 566 6055.
www.airfrance.com

**Alitalia**
Tel Aviv.
*Tel* (03) 796 0700.

Amman.
*Tel* (06) 463 6038.
www.alitalia.com

**American Airlines**
Tel Aviv.
*Tel* (03) 795 2122.
www.aa.com

**British Airways**
Jerusalem.
*Tel* (02) 828 8654.
Tel Aviv.
*Tel* (03) 510 1581.
Amman.
*Tel* (06) 582 8801.
www.britishairways.com

**Delta Air Lines**
Tel Aviv.
*Tel* (03) 681 4000.
www.delta.com

**KLM**
Amman.
*Tel* (06) 465 5267.

Tel Aviv.
*Tel* (03) 611 2727.
www.klm.com

**Lufthansa**
Tel Aviv.
*Tel* (03) 513 5353.
www.lufthansa.com

**Swissair**
Tel Aviv.
*Tel* (03) 714 8666.
www.swiss.com

## AIRPORT TAXIS

**Ben Gurion Airport**
*Tel* (02) 971 1103.

# Getting Around Jerusalem

Street sign

Most of Jerusalem's major historical and religious sites are concentrated in the Old City, which has to be explored on foot, as it is almost a completely vehicle-free zone. Elsewhere, the city bus network functions efficiently and will get visitors to more or less everywhere they might want to go. This is just as well, as taxis tend to be prohibitively expensive for frequent use. The one time when visitors might have to resort to taxis is on Shabbat, when public transport stops running from sundown on Friday to sundown on Saturday.

## JERUSALEM ON FOOT

The old city is very much a pedestrian zone. Its narrow streets and alleys do not allow for vehicles. This makes it a wonderful area to explore. Flat-soled footwear is essential, as many of the ancient streets are either cobbled or unevenly paved. There are some areas of the New City that are also easy and rewarding to get around on foot, notably Yemin Moshe and Nakhalat Shiva, but elsewhere wide roads and aggressive traffic can make walking very unpleasant.

Finding your way around poses little problem as street signs are in at least two languages (either Hebrew and English, or Arabic and English). In the Old City, they are in the scripts of all three.

White Israeli taxi

## TAXIS

It is easy to find a taxi in Jerusalem. You can either book one by phone, hail one on the street, or find one at an official rank. Restaurant and hotel staff will always phone a cab for you.

Taxis are white if they are Israeli and yellow if they are Arab. There is little difference between them. Occasionally an Israeli driver may refuse to drive to an address in Arab East Jerusalem, while an Arab driver may balk at venturing into parts of West Jerusalem. Arab or Israeli, Jerusalem taxi drivers have a bad, but very well-deserved, reputation for over-charging. Although the taxis have modern meters (which can print out a receipt on request), drivers are not in the habit of using them. They will often claim that the meter is not working. You should insist that it is used. If it is not, you will pay a variable fare, which will be dependent on your haggling skills, but which will almost certainly be substantially more than the meter would have indicated. Note also that taxi fares are officially higher between 9:30pm and 5:30am.

Israeli shared taxi, or *sherut*

Yellow Palestinian taxi

## SHARED TAXIS

One slightly unusual means of transport in Jerusalem (and throughout the Holy Land region) is the shared taxi. Known to the Israelis as a *sherut* and to the Arabs as a "service" (pronounced "servees"), shared taxis are a cross between a bus and a taxi. They operate fixed routes like a bus, but they run far more frequently and, like a taxi, they can be hailed on the street. At the start of the route drivers wait until every seat is taken before setting off. Points of origin and final destinations are displayed in the front window (although in the case of "services", this will be in Arabic only). There are no set stops; passengers indicate to the driver when they wish to be let off. Fares are a little more expensive than the equivalent bus ride but much cheaper than a taxi.

Israeli shared taxis are often white vans, while the Arabs favour large sedans, usually Mercedes or Peugeots.

## BUSES

Jerusalem's city bus system is run by Egged, the national carrier, which claims to be the world's largest bus company after Greyhound in the United States. Tickets are bought from the driver on boarding. The fare is the same for all destinations – the equivalent of just over one US dollar.

Buses are identified only by a number displayed in the front window, and destinations are not usually written. Major bus routes include: bus No. 1 from **Egged Central Bus Station** to Jaffa Gate and on to Mount Zion and the Western Wall bus station in the Old

Taxi rank on Omar ibn al-Khattab Square inside Jaffa Gate, the Old City

**Jerusalem's Central Bus Station**

City's Jewish Quarter; bus No. 20, which runs between Jaffa Gate and Yad Vashem, passing along Jaffa Road; and bus No. 27, which runs between the Hadassah Hospital, along Jaffa Road past the central bus station, terminating at Nablus Road Bus Station in East Jerusalem near Damascus Gate.

Most buses run between about 5:30am and midnight. There are no night buses and no services on Shabbat.

East Jerusalem is served by Arab-run buses, which are not nearly so efficient as their Israeli counterparts. It is unlikely that many visitors to the city will find it necessary to use these buses.

### THE NO. 99 BUS

One of the best things the first-time visitor to Jerusalem can do is to take a ride on the No. 99 bus. This bus follows a circular route that in just under two hours takes in most of the important sites outside the Old City. It departs four times per day from Egged Central Bus Station on Jaffa Road: 9am, 11am, 1:30pm and 3:45pm (the last bus does not run on Friday, and there are no buses on Saturday). Tickets can be bought on the bus, but it is wise to book in advance as it is often full. Bookings can be made at Central Bus Station, or at the city tourist information office.

A ticket is valid for a whole day and you can hop on and off wherever you like. It is also possible to get a two-day ticket. A guided tour is available on a personal listening device available in eight languages.

## USEFUL INFORMATION

**Egged Central Bus Station**
224 Jaffa Rd.
*Tel* *2800 (information on all public bus routes, including No. 99).

**El-Ittihad Taxis**
East Jerusalem.
*Tel* (02) 628 4641.

**Ha-Palmakh Taxis**
20 Shay Agnon Ave.
*Tel* (02) 679 2333.

**Rehavia Taxis**
3 Agron St.
*Tel* (02) 625 4444.

---

### THE NO. 99 BUS ROUTE

The clockwise circuit made by this bus passes many important Jerusalem landmarks. The bus makes 28 stops in total, but key points along the route include:

**Central Bus Station** ①
**Mahane Yehuda Market** ②
**Mount Scopus** ③
**Lion's Gate** ④
**Dung Gate** (see p84) ⑤
**Jaffa Gate** (see p100) ⑥
**King David Hotel/YMCA** (see p122) ⑦

**Haas Promenade** ⑧
**Biblical Zoo** (see p138) ⑨
**Herzl Cemetery and Museum** (see p138) ⑩
**Yad Vashem** (see p138) ⑪
**Israel Museum** (see pp132–7) ⑫
**Knesset** (see p131) ⑬

**KEY**

— Old City walls

— No. 99 bus route

# Public Transport in the Holy Land

By far the best and most popular way of getting around Israel and the Holy Land is by bus. Every town and city has a bus station, and inter-urban services tend to be frequent and very affordable. In comparison, rail networks in this part of the world are extremely limited: Israel has just two lines, and Jordan one, which is of little use, running, as it does, north to Damascus. There are no railways at all in Sinai. Sea transport is limited to just one route, across the Red Sea between Jordan and Sinai.

**Long-distance Egged buses parked at Jerusalem central station**

## LONG-DISTANCE BUSES

Nearly all long-distance bus routes in Israel are operated by the Egged company. This virtual monopoly at least has the advantage of making bus travel straightforward and simple. Except to the Dead Sea region, services are frequent. For example buses depart from Jerusalem to Tel Aviv every 15 minutes, to Haifa every 45 minutes, and to Tiberias every hour. There is rarely any need to book in advance; you can simply turn up at the city bus station and get a ticket for the next service out. The only time that you might need to book in advance is if you are travelling to Ein Gedi, Masada or Eilat, as there are only about four buses a day that head in this direction.

Given the small size of the country, journeys are never very long (the longest one is from Jerusalem to Eilat, which lasts around five hours). Egged buses are comfortable and air-conditioned, with plenty of space in the baggage holds.

There are passes for an unlimited number of journeys, which are valid for one or more weeks. These are called Israbus cards. For information on these passes and reduced

fares for students, contact the bus stations or **Egged Tours**, which has sales offices in all major towns and cities.

The one drawback to Israeli buses is that there are no services on Shabbat (Sabbath). This means that you should not plan to travel any time from late Friday afternoon to early evening Saturday. There are no buses either on Jewish holidays *(see pp36–9)*. This can prove highly disruptive for any visitors caught unawares.

## TRANSPORT IN THE PALESTINIAN TERRITORIES

With the constant new developments in the administrative situation, public transport in the Palestinian territories is forever changing. In general, there are two options: Arab buses or shared taxis *(see p310)*. Arab buses depart from two stations in East Jerusalem, one on Nablus Road (mainly for city services), the other on Suleyman Street, opposite the Old City walls. From one of these two, visitors can catch

services for West Bank Palestinian towns such as Bethlehem, Hebron, Jericho and Ramallah.

Arab shared taxis depart from a parking lot just outside the walls opposite Damascus Gate. They serve all the same destinations as the buses, but they are faster and depart far more frequently.

In general Arab buses do not go to Israeli towns, and vice versa. It is possible to catch an Israeli Egged bus to Bethlehem, but it drops you off on the highway outside town necessitating a 20-minute walk into the centre.

**A modern, long-distance Egged bus**

## TRAVELLING BY TRAIN

Israel's very limited railway system comprises just two lines: one from Tel Aviv to Jerusalem and a second from Tel Aviv to Nahariya. The latter runs up the northern Mediterranean coast to near the border with Lebanon. Although the line serves several important destinations, including Haifa and Acre, the drawback is that there are few services each day and on Jewish holidays trains are very crowded.

**The line up the north coast of Israel, slow but scenic**

Bright yellow taxis amid the busy traffic of central Amman

Stations also tend to be some distance from the town centre, often requiring a taxi ride to reach them.

The other line, between Jerusalem and Tel Aviv (following on to Haifa), was upgraded in 2005 and it passes through some particularly lovely scenery. However, the train is much slower than the bus – allow an extra 40 minutes. There are 6–10 trains per day.

### TRANSPORT IN JORDAN

There are several national bus companies in Jordan. The main one is **JETT**, which runs blue-and-white air-conditioned buses between Amman and Aqaba, the King Hussein (Allenby) Bridge and Petra. Booking your seat in advance is advisable. The JETT bus station in Amman is on King Hussein Road. Ten minutes' walk downhill on King Hussein is the Abdali bus station, which is where all the other Jordanian bus companies depart from for routes north and west, including services to Ajlun, Jerash and the King Hussein Bridge. All non-JETT buses to the south (including services to Kerak, Petra and Aqaba) leave from the Wahdat station, some 5 km (3 miles) south of the city centre.

The one destination that is hard to reach from Amman is the Dead Sea. There are no scheduled bus services. The only way to get here is by minibus or shared taxi.

Shared taxis are common in Jordan and far more frequent and convenient than buses. A shared taxi ride from Amman to Aqaba takes about five hours and one from Amman to Petra about three.

The only regular rail service in Jordan is the three times a week train up to Damascus. It runs on the Hejaz Railway, built at the turn of the 20th century by the Turks but more famous for being repeatedly blown up by Lawrence of Arabia and his Arab fighters *(see p233)*. The trip takes about nine hours but you must have a visa in advance to enter Syria.

To get about in Amman there are city buses, but the destination is indicated only in Arabic. Taxi drivers tend to be honest and use the meter, making this an acceptable way of getting around. Only late in the evening or for longer journeys (such as to and from the airport) will you have to agree upon the price beforehand.

### TRANSPORT IN SINAI

The resorts of the east coast of the Sinai peninsula are served by the buses of Egypt's East Delta Bus Company. Services are not particularly frequent with no more than about half a dozen buses a day. All of these buses are either coming from or heading to Cairo (which is between seven and nine hours away). Only one or two of these buses pass by St Catherine's Monastery, so you need to check timetables carefully.

A very informal shared taxi service also operates in Sinai, but it can take time for the cars to fill up and the drivers can be alarmingly reckless.

### RED SEA FERRIES

Aqaba in Jordan and Nuweiba in Sinai are linked by a ferry and a catamaran. Both of these make one sailing each way, once a day. The ferry, which also carries cars, takes three hours, while the catamaran completes the trip in around one hour. Booking in advance is not necessary unless you are travelling with a car. It is possible for passengers to obtain a Sinai Permit *(see p299)* on board both vessels – this allows you to stay in the region for up to 14 days.

## DIRECTORY

### BUS INFORMATION IN ISRAEL

**Eilat Bus Station**
Ha-Temarim St.
*Tel (08) 636 5120.*

**Haifa Bus Station**
Ha-Mifratz and Hof Ha-Karmel Stations
*Tel (04) 847 3555.*

**Jerusalem Bus Station**
224 Jaffa Rd.
*Tel (02) 530 4704.*

**Tel Aviv Bus Station**
Levinsky St.
*Tel (03) 694 8888.*

**Egged Tours**
Central Bus Station, Eilat.
*Tel (08) 636 5123.*
4 Nordau St, Haifa.
*Tel (04) 862 3131.*
59 Benhuda St, Tel Aviv.
*Tel (03) 527 1222.*
*Egged Information*
*Tel *2800*
**www**.egged.co.il

### BUS INFORMATION IN AMMAN

**JETT Bus Station**
King Hussein Rd.
*Tel (06) 566 4146.*

### TRAIN STATION

**Tel Aviv Central Train Station**
Arlosoroff St.
*Tel (03) 577 4000.*

# Travelling Around by Car

**Road sign in three languages**

With well-maintained roads, light traffic away from the big cities and Israel's coastal highway, short distances between towns and some enchanting scenery, the Holy Land should be a pleasure to drive around. The one black spot is other road users. Both Israelis and Arabs can be reckless behind the wheel, and road fatalities are high. While this should not put you off driving, you do need to be cautious. On the positive side again, Israel is full of small places of beauty and interest, located well off any bus route, and having a car at your disposal can really open up the country.

## CAR HIRE

Most major international car hire companies are represented in Israel. Most have offices (or counters) at Ben Gurion Airport, in Tel Aviv and in Jerusalem. For the sake of convenience, it is better to use one that has a representative at the airport.

**Sign for a car rental company**

To rent a car, you must have a full, clean driving licence (an international driving licence is not necessary). Cars are rented only to those over 21 years old, although some companies require that you be 23. Prices vary dramatically and it is recommended that you shop around before settling on a deal. Local companies, such as **Eldan**, frequently offer the best rates. Be aware that rental charges are usually quoted exclusive of insurance and collision waivers.

Note that it is not allowed to take cars hired in Israel over into Jordan or Sinai.

Car hire is not very popular in Jordan and Sinai because there are so few roads to explore. It also works out as very expensive when compared with getting around by other forms of transport, such as the bus or hiring a taxi for a day or two.

Petrol stations in Jordan, Sinai and even certain parts of Israel, particularly the Negev and Dead Sea areas, are few and far between. You are strongly advised to fill up your tank before setting off on any long journeys.

## THE RULES OF THE ROAD

Driving in Israel is on the right-hand side of the road. At unmarked junctions drivers give way to traffic on the right, and overtaking is done on the left. The speed limit in towns is 50 km/h (30 mph) and 90 km/h (55 mph) on out-of-town roads. On some motorways the speed limit is 100 km/h (60 mph). Seat belts must be worn. Children under 15 must sit in the back and children under four must be restrained in a suitable child's seat.

## ROAD SIGNS IN ISRAEL

Although there is a lack of cautionary and warning signs on Israel's roads, all places of interest are well indicated. Signs are in both Hebrew and English (and sometimes in Arabic too). A problem arises, however, with the lack of consistency in the

**Petrol station in Israel**

transliteration of place names from Hebrew and Arabic into English. You could be following directions for Beersheba one minute and for Be'er Sheva the next. These are, of course, the same place. In this book we have tried to present place names as you will see them spelled on Israeli road signs but local inconsistencies mean that this is not always the case.

**No entry sign**

**School sign**

**Two-way sign**

**Right-hand bend**

**Tourist site sign**

**Parking sign**

## DRIVING IN THE PALESTINIAN TERRITORIES

Cars in Israel and the Palestinian Autonomous Territories have licence plates of different colours. Israeli cars have yellow plates, while Palestinian cars' plates are blue or green. It is inadvisable to drive a car with yellow, Israeli plates into Palestinian areas, particularly frequent troublespots such as Hebron and Ramallah. Cars hired in Israel are usually not insured for the Palestinian Territories. Conversely, driving a car with Palestinian plates in Israel will make you the object of a great deal of unwelcome attention from the security forces.

## DRIVING IN JORDAN

While driving is on the right, Jordanians seem to consider most other road rules open to interpretation. Overtaking takes place on both sides of the road and right of way goes to he or she

Typically heavy traffic on the seafront promenade in Tel Aviv

who hesitates least. Roads are often in a poor state of repair. Many are badly surfaced, and road markings are often absent.

Speed limits are generally 100 km/h (60 mph) on open roads and 40 km/h (25 mph) in built-up areas. Care is needed on desert roads, where drifting sand can put the car into a spin if hit at speed.

Direction signs are frequently positioned right at the junction, offering no advance warning and making it all too easy to drive past your turn-off.

## DRIVING IN SINAI

There are very few roads in Sinai, so routes to drive are limited. They do, however, pass through some stunning scenery. Traffic is light but what traffic there is, is mainly composed of buses and large shared taxis; these generally travel at high speed, paying little heed to other road users. Car drivers must constantly be on the lookout and be prepared to take evasive action.

Other than on recognized trails, off-road driving is not encouraged as it can damage the fragile desert environment. Several such trails begin in the region of Nuweiba (see p242).

## DRIVING IN CITIES

Traffic in and around Tel Aviv and, to a lesser extent, Jerusalem is nightmarish. You should aim to avoid rush hour, which is roughly 7–9am and 4–6pm. That said, it is not unknown to encounter traffic jams in Tel Aviv at 1am.

## HITCH-HIKING

Known in Israel as *tremping*, hitch-hiking used to be a common way of getting about the country. It was particularly popular with soldiers heading home or returning from leave. But recently hitch-hiking has become increasingly unsafe. Women soldiers are now banned from hitching and we recommend visitors do not hitch-hike either.

## CYCLING

Parts of Israel are excellent places for cycle touring. The best regions are Galilee and the Golan Heights, where the scenery is at its most varied and the altitude serves to moderate the extreme summer temperatures. Even so, from June to August it is best to plan to cycle only in the mornings, to avoid the afternoon heat.

In Tiberias, it is possible to hire bicycles by the day to explore the shores of the Sea of Galilee (see pp182–4). In Jerusalem you can rent bicycles by the day from **Walk Ways**, who will deliver to your hotel. For general cycling advice and to enquire about joining organized rides, enthusiasts could also try contacting the **Jerusalem Cycle Club**.

Cycling in Jaffa

# DIRECTORY

### CAR HIRE IN ISRAEL

**Autoeurope**
Tel Aviv.
*Tel (03) 524 4244.*
www.autoeurope.co.il

**Avanti**
www.avanti.co.il

**Avis**
*Tel *2722 or
1-700-700-222.*
www.avis.co.il

**Budget**
*Tel *2200 or
1-700-70-41-41.*
www.budget.co.il

**Eldan**
*Tel 1-700-700-740.*
www.eldan.co.il

**Europcar**
www.europcar.com

**Hertz**
Ben Gurion Airport.
*Tel (03) 975 4505.*
Jerusalem.
*Tel (02) 623 1351.*
www.hertz.co.il

**Pery**
Tel Aviv.
*Tel (03) 688 1111*
www.pery.net

### CAR HIRE IN JORDAN & SINAI

**Avis**
Amman.
*Tel (06) 569 9420/30.*
www.avis.com.jo

**EuroDollar**
Amman.
*Tel (06) 569 3399.*
www.eurodollar-jo.com

**Europcar**
Amman.
*Tel (06) 445 2012.*
www.europcar.jo

**Hertz**
Sharm el-Sheikh/Cairo.

www.hertzegypt.com.
Amman.
www.hertz.com.jo

**Oscar Car Rental**
Amman.
*Tel (06) 553 5635.*
www.1stjordan.net/oscar

**Rent a Reliable Car**
Amman.
*Tel (06) 592 9676.*
www.reliable.com.jo

### CYCLING

**Tzubike**
*Tel (02) 534 7667.*
www.tzubike.co.il

# General Index

# Acknowledgments

Dorling Kindersley would like to thank the
following people whose invaluable
contributions and assistance have made the
preparation of this book possible.

**Senior Managing Editor**
Louise Bostock Lang.

**Managing Art Editor**
Jane Ewart.

**Editorial Director**
Vivian Crump.

**Publishing Manager**
Scarlett O'Hara.

**Revisions Coordinator/Editor**
Rose Hudson.

**Art Director**
Gillian Allan.

**Publisher**
Douglas Amrine.

**Main Consultants**
Felicity Cobbing, Andrew Humphreys,
Jonathan Tubb.

**Translator**
Richard Pierce.

**Maps**
Rob Clynes, James Macdonald (Colourmap
Scanning Ltd).

**Production**
Imogen Boase, Marie Ingledew.

**Additional Contributors
and Consultants**
Jonathan Elphick, Professor Jonathan
Magonet, Peter Parr, Amir Reuveni,
Wolfgang Tins.

**Visualizer**
Joy FitzSimmons.

**Additional Illustrations**
Richard Bonson.

**Additional Photography**
Steve Gorton, Noam Knoller, Ian O'Leary.

**Design and Editorial Assistance**
Gillian Andrews, Sam Borland,
Esther Labi, Pollyanna Poulter, Lee
Redmond, Marisa Renzullo.

**Editor**
Jude Ledger.

**Factchecker**
Noam Knoller.

**Proof Reader**
Stewart J Wild.

**Indexer**
Hilary Bird.

**Special Assistance**
Sheila Brull, Egyptian Tourist Authority,
Giovanni Francesio and Mattia Goffetti at
Fabio Ratti Editoria, Efrat Goller at Keter
Publishing, Tony Howard and Di Taylor at
N.O.M.A.D.S. (New Opportunities for
Mountaineering and Desert Sports), Israel
Ministry of Tourism, Jordan Tourism Board,
Amalyah Keshet and Tal Sher at the Israel
Museum, Deborah Lipson at the Tower of
David Museum of the History of Jerusalem,
Hila Reuveni, Shelly Shemer at the Israel
Wine and Gourmet Magazine. Special
thanks to Massimo Acanfora Torrefranca.

**Additional Picture Research**
Julia Harris-Voss.

**Photographic and
Artwork Reference**
Dale Harris, Ben Johnson, Albatros,
Jerusalem.

**Photography Permissions**
The publisher would like to thank
all the churches, museums, hotels,
restaurants, shops, galleries and sights too
numerous to thank individually, for their
co-operation and contribution to this
publication.

**Picture Credits**
t = top; tl = top left; tlc = top left centre; tc =
top centre; tr = top right;
cla = centre left above; ca = centre above;
cra = centre right above;
cl = centre left; c = centre; cr = centre right;
clb = centre left below;
cb = centre below; crb = centre right below;
bl = bottom left; b = bottom;
bc = bottom centre; bcl = bottom centre left;
br = bottom right; (d) = detail.

Works of art have been reproduced
with the permission of the following
copyright holders: *Reclining Figure*
(1969–70) Henry Moore, Gift of Maurice
and Bella Wingrave, London. Through the
British Friends of the Art Museums in Israel
170bc.

The publisher would like to thank the following individuals, companies and picture libraries for permission to reproduce their photographs:

ALAMY IMAGES: Tibor Bognar 214cla; Charles Bowman 204tr; Paul Doyle 214br; Eddie Gerald 192; Nick Hanna 243tl; 295br; ImageState/David South 11tr; Israel images/Hanan Isachar 138tr; Shein Audio Visual 288cl; Jochen Tack 212bl; Danny Yanai 269c; AMERICAN COLONY HOTEL: 266cl; ANCIENT ART & ARCHITECTURE COLLECTION: 28cb, 29ca, 30cr, 41c, 41br, 42t, 44cl, 47ca; R Sheridan 24t, 41bl, 44tl, 46b, 50cb, 107cla, 107cl; G Tortoli 27cra; ANDES PRESS: Carlos Reyes-Manzo 23cr; AKG, LONDON: 42crb, 46t, 50t, 54bl, 233br; Erich Lessing 20cl, 21ca, 22br, 29b, 30b, 45cb, 45b, 46cb, 92ca, 189c, 216t, 216ca, 216br; Jean Louis Mou 59t; FABRIZIO ARDITO 20b, 26t, 35cra, 78tl, 103b, 110tl, 179t, 217b, 222t, 224t, 232t, 233t, 233cb, 235t, 235c, 298t, 299t, 300tl, 300tcr, 300tr, 300c, 304c, 304b, 306c, 306c, 306br, 307c, 310tbr, 310c, 314cl, 314cb; ASAP, JERUSALEM: 120ca; Eyal Bartov 34tl, 34cl, 35t, 35ca, 33bl; Lev Borodulin 255tr; Bridgeman Art Library 24cl, 27cr, 51bl, 71c; C.Z.A. 52ca; Shai Ginott 34clb, 58bl; Avi Hirschfield 79c, 79cb; Hanan Isachar 132tr, 137cra, 312b; Itsik Marom 34bl, 35cl, 35clb, 35cb; Garo Nalbandian 3 (inset), 24bl, 24br, 107cr, 110ca, 110cb, 246b, 247b; Richard Nowitz 110tr; Nitsan Shorer 308bc; Vivian Silver 53t; Israel Talby 34cr.

BRIDGEMAN ART LIBRARY: *Christ Carrying the Cross* Eustache Le Sueur (1651) 31b, 32b, *Jerusalem from the Mount of the Olives* Edward Lear (1859) 33t, *The Finding of the Saviour in the Temple* William Holman Hunt (1854–60) 33b, 40, 248b; Archeological Museum, Amman, Jordan 212c; Bibliothèque Municipale de Lyon 48clb; British Library 20cr, 21t; Galleria Borghese *St Jerome Writing* Caravaggio (1604) 195b; Giraudon 26cl; Musée Condé, Chantilly 28b; BRITISH LIBRARY: 22t.

CAMERA PRESS: Fred Adler 309t; CORBIS: Aaron Horowitz 268cl; Hanan Isachar 296br; Reuters/Ali Jarekji 213tc; Peter Turnley 55br.

JO DORAN: 90c.

EGGED: 312cr; EL AL ISRAEL AIRLINES: 308tc; E.T.ARCHIVE: 49t, 49br; MARY EVANS PICTURE LIBRARY: 9 (inset), 32t, 32c, 33c, 48bl, 48br,

57 (inset), 87tc, 251c.
ffOTOGRAFF: Patricia Aithie 17t, 50b, 60, 67t, 98b, 99t, 104ca, 115b, 122t, 122c, 125br, 129t, 138c, 138b, 143c, 197c, 253c, 284t, 287cra, 288b, 306bl, 310tl, 314t; Charles Aithie 22–23c, 31clb, 59tr, 114b, 121ca; GINO FRONGIA 16, 24–25c, 34cla, 68c, 70tr, 102tr, 104tr, 105ca, 174tl, 187b, 190b, 254c, 300b, 302tl.

CRISTINA GAMBARO: 5ca, 62ca, 62cb, 65t, 67c, 93b, 99b, 109t, 179c, 182b, 197t, 202t, 302tr, 304l; EDDIE GERALD: 11br, 30cl, 62b, 68tl, 78cla, 78c, 79ca, 83t, 106b, 107t, 107bl, 111cb, 120cb, 124t, 125bl, 164, 174tr, 174ca, 174bl, 182tl, 183t, 183c, 195cra, 207, 228b, 238b, 242c, 246cb, 247ca, 285c, 289t, 289c, 289b, 290b, 303t, 303c, 303b, 306t, 310tr, 312c, all 314cra, all 314cr, 314crb, 314b. GETTY IMAGES: AFP/Andre Brutmann 55crb.

SONIA HALLIDAY:Laura Lushington 137bl; ROBERT HARDING PICTURE LIBRARY: 25cr; ASAP/Nalbandian 58t, 100br; Gascoigne 28c; HEMISPHERES IMAGES: Franck Guiziou 269tl; HOLMES PHOTOGRAPHY: 249, Jean Holmes 49crb, Reed Holmes 232b, TONY HOWARD:232ca.

IMAGES COLOUR LIBRARY: 244–245; INTERCONTINENTAL HOTEL, AQUABA: 267cl; HANAN ISACHAR: 1c, 4b, 5t, 5clb, 11clb, 19b, 25t, 25cra, 25crb, 31t, 35crb, 36t, 36c, 36b, 37ca, 37br, 38cra, 38b, 39c, 39b, 61t, 88, 91t, 92cb, 93t, 93cra, 94ca, 94cb, 100bc, 110b, 162ca, 166c, 167b, 175ca, 175cb, 175b, 176t, 176b, 178t, 182cb, 189t, 194ca, 194cb, 197clb, 200t, 205bl, 207, 216cl, 218–219, 221b, 226c, 249t, 282b, 284b, 311tl, 315b; WWW.ISRAELIMAGES.COM: Raffi Rondel 290tl; Israel Talby 267br, 267tr, 308cl; ISRAEL MUSEUM: 44cbl, *Destruction and Sack of the Temple of Jerusalem* Nicolas Poussin (1625–6) 45t, 45cr, 49cra, 53b, *Apple Core* Claes Oldenburg (1929), 132tl, 132cla, 132cra, *Red-Blue Chair* GT Rietveld (1918) © DACS, London 2006, 133t, *The Rabbi* Marc Chagall (1912–13) ©ADAGP, Paris and DACS, London 2006, 133ca, 134tl, *Jeanne Hebuterne seated* Modigliani (1918) 134tr, 134b, 135t, 135c, 135b, 136c, 137t, 137cl, 137c, 137cr, 201c; *Woman Combing Her Hair* Alexander Archipenko (1914) © ARS, NY and DACS, London 2006, 132bl, 136b; David Harris 133cb, 133bl, 134c, 137br; Ann Levin 136t.

PAUL JACKSON: 174b, 175t, 225bl, 227br; JORDAN TOURIST BOARD: 197crb, 234bl. 234cla, 234tr, 294bl, 294cla, 296tl.

MAGNUM PHOTOS:54t.

NHPA: Henry Ausloos 35br; RICHARD NOWITZ: 2–3, 18t, 74–75, 92b, 93c, 95c, 162b, 163t, 163cb, 165b, 178c, 178b, 186, 188ca, 189b, 193tl, 196b, 197b, 200br, 201bl, 203br, 206, 217t, 223b, 225br, 230b, 236, 239t, 242t, 247t, 247bl, 249b, 250–251, 252t, 285t, 287ca, 299b, 307b; Air Photos, Israel 186.

CRISTINE OSBORNE PICTURES: 163b, 229c, 248t, 248c.

PA PHOTOS: Ariel Schalit 290c; PLANET EARTH PICTURES: Kurt Amsler 239b; POPPERFOTO: 51br, 52c, 52bl, 52br, 53c, 54br.
ZEV RADOVAN: 4–5t, 20tr, 21cb, 22cl, 22bl, 23t, 23tr, 28t, 29cb, 42bl, 42br, 43cb, 43b, 51t, 67b, 71b, 76, 77t, 130c; FABIO RATTI: 72c, 103ca, 117b, 212t, 212b, 213t, 213b, 301b; RETROGRAPH ARCHIVE: 54c; REUTERS: Ronen Zvulun 55tl; REX FEATURES: 19c.

PETER SANDERS PHOTOGRAPHY: 26bl, 26br, 27t, 70tl, 70c; SCIENCE PHOTO LIBRARY: CNES, 1990 Distribution Spot Image 12ca; THE ORIGINAL SHAKESPEARE COMPANY 37bl; EITAN SIMANOR: 39cra, 44b, 56–57, 182tr, 254bl, 290t; JON SPAULL: 163ca, 208t, 208b, 209t, 209b, 296–297, 313c.

VISIONS OF THE LAND: American Colony Hotel 51cb; Tony Malmqvist 237b, 240t, 240c, 240cb, 240bl, 240bc, 240br, 241tl, 241tr, 241cra, 241cb, 241bl, 241br, 243c, 243b, 292t; Beni Mor 29t, 63t, 64b, 90tl, 90tr, 91b, 101c, 114c, 115t, 116t, 116b, 177b, 180t, 180b, 181t, 181b, 184t, 184b, 190t, 191t, 191b, 192t, 203b, 222cl, 233ca; Garo Nalbandian 26–27c, 35cla, 59crb, 63cb, 68b, 69cr, 69b, 72b, 73cr, 100t, 100clb, 106t, 106c, 107cb, 107br, 112tl, 112tr, 113t, 113b, 124b, 125t, 185t, 193t, 198–199, 211b, 223tl, 223tr, 223c, 224c, 224b, 226t, 226b, 227tr, 227tl, 227cla,

228t, 229cb, 229b, 230t, 230c, 231t, 231cl, 231cr, 231b, 235b, 205t, 246t, 246cla, 246b, 255t, 266t, 266c; Basilio Rodella 43ca, 62t, 63ca, 64t, 64c, 66t, 66c, 66b, 69t, 72tr, 73tr, 73b, 78b, 79b, 82t, 82c, 82b, 84t, 84c, 84b, 85t, 85c, 85b, 90ca, 92t, 104tl, 114t, 117t, 121cb, 122b, 123b, 126t, 126bl, 126br, 127c, 127b, 130t, 130b, 131c, 131b, 138t, 177c, 184cr, 185b, 190c, 192b, 196t, 200c, 200bl, 201t, 201ca, 202b, 203t, 210t, 210b, 253t, 288t, 293t; SPNI Collection/Yossi Eshbol 203c, 243t; Studium Biblicum Franciscanum Archive 216–217c, 217cr; Ilan Sztulman 5crb, 252c, 268tr, 268tl, 268tc, 268cla, 268ca, 268cra, 268cl, 268cr, 268clb, 268bl, 268bc, 268br, 269t, 269tl, 269tr, 269cla, 269cra, 269c, 269cb, 269bl, 269bra, 269br, 270tl, 270cl, 270cr, 270cr, 270b, 271bl, 271clb, 271bc, 271cbc, 271brc, 271br, 283t, all 286cla, 286crc, 286clb, 286cb, 286bcl, 286bc, 287tl, 287tc, 287tr, 287trr, 287cla, 287c, all 287crb, 298b, 312t.

WERNER FORMAN ARCHIVE: British Museum 21b; PETER WILSON: 17b, 34tr, 34br, 160–161, 167t, 183b, 188t, 211t, 222–223, 227b, 228cb, 229t, 232cb, 233bl, 238t, 302b, 315t.

Front Endpaper: All commissioned photography except ffotoGRAFF: Patricia Aithie tr; EDDIE GERALD tcl; HANAN ISACHAR c; RICHARD NOWITZ tl, bcl, bl; ZEV RADOVAN brc.

COVER:
FRONT COVER: CORBIS: JAI/Jon Arnold; main image; DK IMAGES: Eddie Gerald clb.
BACK COVER: Kurt Amsler: cla; DK IMAGES: Alistair Cuncan clb, tl; Richard T Nowitz: bl.
SPINE: CORBIS: JAI/Jon Arnold t; DK IMAGES: Magnus Rew b.

## SPECIAL EDITIONS OF DK TRAVEL GUIDES

DK Travel Guides can be purchased in bulk quantities at discounted prices for use in promotions or as premiums. We are also able to offer special editions and personalized jackets, corporate imprints, and excerpts from all of our books, tailored specifically to meet your own needs.

To find out more, please contact:
(in the United States) **SpecialSales@dk.com**
(in the UK) **Sarah.Burgess@dk.com**
(in Canada) DK Special Sales at **general@tourmaline.ca**
(in Australia) **business.development@pearson.com.au**

# Hebrew Phrase Book

Hebrew has an alphabet of 22 letters. As in Arabic, the vowels do not appear in the written language and there are several systems of transliteration. In this phrasebook we have given a simple phonetic transcription only. Bold type indicates the syllable on which the stress falls. An apostrophe between two letters means that there is a break in the pronunciation. The letters "kh" represent the sound "ch" as in Scottish "loch", and "g" is hard as in "gate". Where necessary, the masculine form is given first, followed by the feminine.

## In Emergency

| | |
|---|---|
| Help! | Hatzilu! |
| Stop! | Atzor! |
| Call a doctor! | Azminu rofe! |
| Call an ambulance! | Azminu ambulans! |
| Call the police! | Tzaltzelu lamishtara! |
| Call the fire brigade! | Tzaltzelu lemekhabei esh! |
| Where is the nearest telephone? | Efo hatelefon hatziburi hakhi karov? |
| Where is the nearest hospital? | Efo bet hakholim hakhi karov? |

## Communication Essentials

| | |
|---|---|
| Yes | Ken |
| No | Lo |
| Please | Bevakasha |
| Thank you | Toda |
| Many thanks | Toda raba |
| Excuse me | Slikha |
| Hello | Shalom |
| Good day | Boker tov |
| Good evening | Erev tov |
| Good night | Laila tov |
| Greetings (on the Sabbath) | Shabat Shalom |
| Have a good week (after the Sabbath) | Shavu'a tov |
| morning | boker |
| afternoon | akhar hatzohoryim |
| evening | erev |
| night | lyla |
| today | hayom |
| tomorrow | makhar |
| here | po |
| there | sham |
| what? | ma? |
| which? | eizeh? |
| when? | matai? |
| who? | mi? |
| where? | efo? |

## Useful Phrases

| | |
|---|---|
| How are you? | Ma shlomkha/shlomekh? |
| Very well, thank you | Beseder, toda |
| Pleased to meet you | Na'immeod |
| Goodbye | Lehitraot |
| (I'm) fine! | Beseder gamur |
| Where is/Where are? | Efo…? |
| How many kilometres is it to…? | Kama kilometrim mipo le…? |
| What is the way to…? | Ekh megi'im le…? |
| Do you speak English? | Ata/at medaber/medaberet anglit? |
| I don't understand | Ani lo mevin/mevina |
| Could you speak more slowly, please? | Tukhal/tukhli ledaber yoter le'at, bevakasha? |

## Useful Words

| | |
|---|---|
| large | gadol |
| small | katan |
| hot | kham |
| cold | kar |
| bad | lo tov |
| enough | maspik |
| well | beseder |
| open | patuakh |
| closed | sagur |
| left | smol |
| right | yamin |
| straight | yashar |
| near | karov |
| far | rakhok |
| up | lemala |
| down | lemata |
| soon | mukdam |
| late | meukhar |
| entrance | knisa |
| exit | yetzia |
| toilet | sherutim |
| free, unoccupied | panui |
| free, no charge | khinam |

## Making a Telephone Call

| | |
|---|---|
| I'd like to make a long-distance call | Haiti rotze/rotza lehitkasher lekhutz lair |
| I'd like to make a reversed-charge call | Haiti rotze/rotza lehitkasher govaina |
| I'll call back later | Etkasher meukhar yoter |
| Can I leave a message? | Efshar lehashir hoda'a? |
| Hold on | Hamtin/hamtini (Tamtin/tamtini) |
| Could you speak up a little, please? | Tukhal/tukhli ledaber bekol ram yoter? |
| local call | sikha ironit |
| international call | sikha benleumit |

## Shopping

| | |
|---|---|
| How much does it cost? | Kama zeh oleh? |
| I would like… | Haiti rotzeh/rotza… |
| Do you have…? | Yesh lakhem…? |
| I'm just looking. | Ani rak mistakel/mistakelet. |
| Do you take credit cards? | Atem mekablim kartisei ashrai? |
| Do you take traveller's cheques? | Atem mekablim traveller's cheques? |
| What time do you open? | Matai potkhim? |
| What time do you close? | Matai sogrim? |
| this one | zeh |
| that one | hahu |
| expensive | Yakar |
| inexpensive/cheap | lo yakar/zol |
| size | mida |
| shoe size | mida (midat na'alyim) |
| white | lavan |
| black | shakhor |
| red | adom |
| yellow | tzahov |
| green | yarok |
| blue | kakhol |

## Types of Shop

| | |
|---|---|
| antiques shop | khanut atikot |
| bakery | ma'afia |
| bank | bank |
| barber's | maspera |
| bookshop/newsagent | khanut sfarim/ve'itonim |
| butcher's | itliz |
| cake shop | ma'adania |
| chemist's | bet merkakhat |
| clothes shop | khanut b'gadim |
| greengrocer's | yarkan |
| grocer's | makolet |
| hairdresser's | maspera |
| jeweller's | khanut takhshitim |
| market | shuk |
| post office | snif hadoar |
| shoe shop | khanut na'alyim |
| supermarket | supermarket |
| travel agency | sokhnut nesiyot |

## Sightseeing

| | |
|---|---|
| bus station | takhana merkazit |
| bus stop | takhanat otobus |
| church | knesia |
| closed | sagur |
| library | sifria |
| mosque | misgad |
| park | park |
| synagogue | bet haknesset |
| taxi | monit |
| tourist information office | merkaz hameida letayar |
| town hall | bet ha'iria |
| train station | takhanat rakevet |

## Staying in a Hotel

| | |
|---|---|
| I have a reservation | Yesh li azmana |
| Do you have a free room? | Yesh lakhem kheder panui? |
| double room | kheder zugi |
| room with two beds | kheder im shtei mitot |
| room with a bath or a shower | kheder im sherutim ve ambatia o miklakhat |
| single room | kheder yakhid |

| | |
|---|---|
| key | mafteakh |
| lift | ma'alit |
| Can someone help me with my luggage? | Mishehu yakhol la'azor li im hamisvadot? |

## Eating Out

| | |
|---|---|
| Have you got a table free? | Yesh lakhem shulkhan panui? |
| I would like to book a table | Haiti rotze/rotza lehazmin shulkhan |
| The bill please | Kheshbon, bevakasha |
| I am vegetarian | Ani tzimkhoni/ tzimkhonit |
| menu | tafrit |
| fixed-price menu | tafrit iskit |
| wine list | tafrit hayeinot |
| glass | kos |
| bottle | bakbuk |
| knife | sakin |
| spoon | kaf |
| fork | masleg |
| breakfast | arukhat boker |
| lunch | arukhat tzohoryim |
| dinner | arukhat erev |
| starter | mana rishona |
| main course | mana ikarit |
| portion | mana |
| rare | mevushal me'at |
| well done | mevushal hetev |

## Food and Drink

| | |
|---|---|
| almonds | shkedim |
| apples | tapuakhei etz |
| apricot | mish mish |
| aubergine/eggplant | khatzilim |
| beans | shu'it |
| beef | bakar |
| beer | bira |
| bread | lekhem |
| broad beans | ful |
| broccoli | brokoli |
| butter | khem'a |
| cabbage | kruv |
| cake | ugha |
| carrot | gezer |
| cauliflower | kruvit |
| cheese | gvina |
| cherries | dudvanim |
| chicken | off |
| chickpeas | khumus |
| chips/fries | chips |
| chocolate | shokolat |
| coffee | kafe |
| cold cuts | pastrama |
| coriander | kuzbera |
| courgettes/zucchini | kishuim |
| crabs | sartanim |
| cucumbers | melafefonim |
| dessert | kinuakh |
| draught beer | bira mihakhavit |
| dry | yavesh |
| eggs | betza |
| figs | te'enim |
| fish | dag |
| French beans | shu'it yerokha |
| fried | metugan |
| fruit | peirot |
| garlic | shum |
| grapes | anavim |
| grey mullet | buri |
| grilled | al haesh |
| grouper | lokus |
| hard-boiled eggs | betza kasha |
| herbal tea | tei tzmakhim |
| hot (spicy) | kharif |
| ice | kerakh |
| icecream | glida |
| kebab | shipud |
| lamb, mutton | keves |
| lemon | limon |
| liver | kaved |
| meat | basar |
| milk | khalav |
| mineral water | myim mineralim |
| nuts | egozim |
| olive oil | shemen zyit |
| omelette | khavita |
| onion | batzal |
| orange juice (freshly squeezed) | mitz tapuzim (tiv'i sakhut) |

| | |
|---|---|
| oranges | tapuzim |
| peaches | afarsekim |
| pepper (condiment) | pilpel |
| peppers (capsicums) | pilpelim |
| pickles | khamutzim |
| plums | shezifim |
| potatoes | tapukhei adama |
| prawns/shrimps | shrimps |
| red snapper | denis |
| red wine | yain adom |
| rice | orez |
| roast | betanur |
| salad | salat yerakot |
| salmon | salmon |
| salt | melakh |
| sandwich/filled roll | lakhmania |
| sauce | rotev |
| seafood | peirot yam |
| smoked | me'ushan |
| soup | marak |
| spinach | tered |
| spinach beet (Swiss chard) | alei selek |
| squid | kalamari |
| steak | steik |
| strawberries | tut sade (tutim) |
| stuffed vegetables | memulaim |
| sugar | sukar |
| tea | tei |
| tomatoes | agvaniot |
| trout | forel |
| turkey | hodu |
| vegetables | yerakot |
| vinegar | khometz yain |
| water | myim |
| white wine | yain lavan |

## Numbers

| | |
|---|---|
| 0 | efes |
| 1 | akhad |
| 2 | shtaim |
| 3 | shalosh |
| 4 | arba |
| 5 | khamesh |
| 6 | shesh |
| 7 | sheva |
| 8 | shmone |
| 9 | teisha |
| 10 | eser |
| 11 | ahadesreh |
| 12 | shtemesreh |
| 13 | shloshesreh |
| 14 | arbaesre |
| 15 | khameshesreh |
| 16 | sheshesreh |
| 17 | shvaesreh |
| 18 | shmona'esreh |
| 19 | tshaesreh |
| 20 | esrim |
| 21 | esrim veakhad |
| 30 | shloshim |
| 40 | arba'im |
| 50 | khamishim |
| 60 | shishim |
| 70 | shiv'im |
| 80 | shmonim |
| 90 | tish'im |
| 100 | mea |
| 200 | matyim |
| 300 | shlosh meot |
| 1,000 | elef |
| 2,000 | alpyim |
| 3,000 | shlosha elef |
| 4,000 | arba elef |
| 10,000 | asara elef |

## Time

| | |
|---|---|
| one minute | daka |
| one hour | sha'a |
| half an hour | khetzi sha'a |
| Sunday | yom rishon |
| Monday | yom sheni |
| Tuesday | yom shlishi |
| Wednesday | yom revi'i |
| Thursday | yom khamishi |
| Friday | yom shishi |
| Saturday | shabat |
| week | shavu'a |
| month | khodesh |
| year | shana |

# Road Map of the Holy Land

0 kilometres   30
0 miles   30

**KEY**

✈ International airport
☒ Domestic airport
⚓ Major port
— Railway
— Motorway
— Major road
— Minor road
····· Wadi
—··— International border
x x Disputed border/Cease-fire line

MEDITERRANEAN SEA

SYRIA

El-Juweif

DAMASCUS
Daramanah
Zebdani
Manaa
Dimas
Raghaiya
Qatana
W. Sakhr
Jezzine
Beit el-Dine
Sidon
Tyre
Qana
Bint Jbeil
Nabatiye
Banias
Kiryat Shmona
Ein Rosh
Safed
Rosh Pina
Golan Heights
Kuneitra
Sheikh Miskin
Suweida
Salkhad
El-Hamitka
Deraa
Sea of Galilee
Ein Gev
Tiberias
Umm Qais
Irbid
Mkad
Erash
El-Hashiniyya
Jerash
El-Zarqa
El-Mafraq
El-Azraq el-Janubi
El-Umari
El-Hadithah

Shlomi
Nahariya
Acre
HAIFA
Tirat Karmel
Kiryat Tivon
Yoknaamilt
Zikhron Yaakov
Caesarea
Pardes Khana-Karkur
Khadera
Netanya
Herzliya
TEL AVIV
Jaffa
Rishon le-Zion
Rekhovot
Yavne
Ashdod
Ashkelon
GAZA
Netivot
Kiryat Gat
Beth Shemesh

Afula
Meddo
Beth Alpha
Nazareth
Belvoi
Megiddo
Tulk Karm
Taibe
Kfar Saba
Rosh ha-Ayin
Lod
Ramla
Jenin
Nablus
Tubas
Fatsael
Ramallah
El-Bira
Beth
Jordan
El-Makhrug
Beth Shean
Ajlun
AMMAN
Mount Nebo
El-Salt
Sweimeh
Madaba
Dhaba
Khan el-Zabib
Dhiban

JERUSALEM
Jericho
Qumran
Herodion
Bethlehem
Dead Sea
Hebron
Karmel
Ein
Netivot

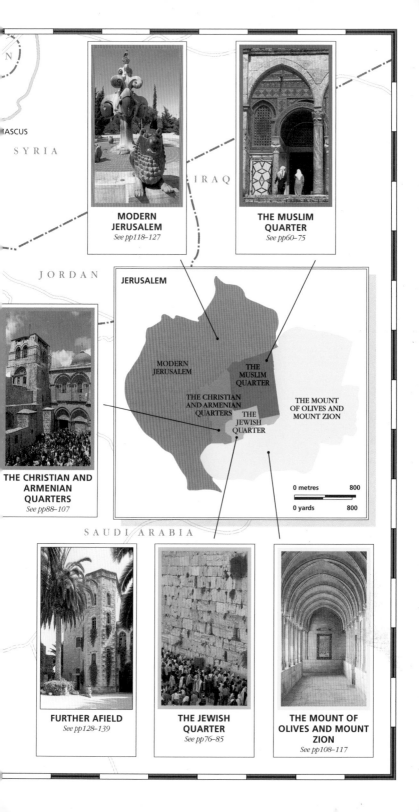

**MODERN JERUSALEM**
*See pp118–127*

**THE MUSLIM QUARTER**
*See pp60–75*

SYRIA

ASCUS

IRAQ

JORDAN

JERUSALEM

N

MODERN JERUSALEM

THE MUSLIM QUARTER

THE CHRISTIAN AND ARMENIAN QUARTERS

THE JEWISH QUARTER

THE MOUNT OF OLIVES AND MOUNT ZION

| 0 metres | 800 |
| 0 yards | 800 |

**THE CHRISTIAN AND ARMENIAN QUARTERS**
*See pp88–107*

SAUDI ARABIA

**FURTHER AFIELD**
*See pp128–139*

**THE JEWISH QUARTER**
*See pp76–85*

**THE MOUNT OF OLIVES AND MOUNT ZION**
*See pp108–117*